THE MOST DANGEROUS MAN IN AMERICA

ALSO BY JOHN K. WILSON

President Barack Obama: A More Perfect Union

Patriotic Correctness: Academic Freedom and Its Enemies

Barack Obama: This Improbable Quest

How the Left Can Win Arguments and Influence People: A Tactical Manual for Pragmatic Progressives

Newt Gingrich: Capitol Crimes and Misdemeanors

The Myth of Political Correctness: The Conservative Attack on Higher Education

THE MOST
DANGEROUS
MAN IN
AMERICA

RUSH LIMBAUGH'S ASSAULT ON REASON

JOHN K. WILSON

THOMAS DUNNE BOOKS

St. Martin's Press

New York

THOMAS DUNNE BOOKS.
An imprint of St. Martin's Press.

THE MOST DANGEROUS MAN IN AMERICA. Copyright © 2011 by John K. Wilson.
All rights reserved. Printed in the United States of America. For information, address
St. Martin's Press, 175 Fifth Avenue, New York, N.Y. 10010.

www.thomasdunnebooks.com
www.stmartins.com

Library of Congress Cataloging-in-Publication Data

Wilson, John K., 1969–
   The most dangerous man in America : Rush Limbaugh's assault on
reason / John K. Wilson.—1st ed.
       p. cm.
   Includes bibliographical references and index.
   ISBN 978-0-312-61214-6 (alk. paper)
   1. Limbaugh, Rush H.—Political and social views.   2. Right-wing
extremists—United States.   3. Radio in politics—United States.   4. United
States—Politics and government—2001–2009.   5. Conservatism—United
States.   I. Title.
   PN1991.4.L48 W55
   791.4402'8092—dc22
                                                              2010040190

First Edition: March 2011

10 9 8 7 6 5 4 3 2 1

To Lynn

CONTENTS

INTRODUCTION

I T'S SEVEN MINUTES AFTER noon, and the familiar bass strains of the Pretenders' "My City Was Gone" are wordlessly looping in the heavily fortified Southern Command of the Excellence in Broadcasting (EIB) network in sunny south Florida, echoing in millions of car radios, offices, computers, and homes across the fruited plain. Over five million Dittoheads are waiting to receive their ideological marching orders for the day from the most powerful voice in the world, the all-knowing, all-caring, all-sensing, all-feeling Maha Rushie.

He has proclaimed himself the most dangerous man in America, serving humanity simply by opening his mouth, destined for his own wing in the Museum of Broadcasting, executing everything he does flawlessly, doing the show with half his brain tied behind his back just to make it fair, with talent on loan from God.

At the cutting edge of societal evolution, this benevolent dictator, in a great act of magnanimity, is greeting conversationalists across the country. The doctor of democracy, coming from high atop the EIB building, firmly ensconced behind the Golden EIB Microphone in the prestigious Attila the Hun chair at the Limbaugh Institute for Advanced Conservative Studies, sometimes deigning to explain what he means for all you people in Rio Linda: this is America's truth detector, America's real anchorman, the doctor of democracy, all combined as one harmless, lovable little fuzz ball. As he holds in his formerly nicotine-stained fingers the Stack of Stuff, the most dangerous man in America opens his mouth.

His audience listens intently—from the mind-numbed robots to the glittering jewels of colossal ignorance and even the long-haired, dope-smoking, maggot-infested, good-time rock 'n' roll plastic banana FM types.

But it's the Dittoheads, the devoted followers of Chief Waga-Waga El Rushbo of the El Conservo Tribe, who dominate the audience, who want to hear every word from America's Truth-Detector and the Titular Head of the Republican Party.

His voice resonates from Cuber to Club Gitmo to the Oval Orifice. A command to call Congress jams the phones of the capitol. A URL that slips from his lips can overload servers instantly. A denunciation can send Republican politicians trembling in fear about the repercussions. A product endorsement can mean millions of dollars.

Rush Limbaugh is the biggest star of the conservative movement and he knows it like he knows every glorious inch of his naked body. A November 2009 poll by CBS/*Vanity Fair* found that Rush Limbaugh was identified as the "the most influential conservative voice in America." Limbaugh was named by 26 percent of respondents, beating Glenn Beck (11 percent) and Sarah Palin (10 percent) by a wide margin.[1]

Rush is revered by an audience of millions of adoring fans and Republican politicians afraid to disobey him. But fewer people know about the real Limbaugh: a pompous right-wing conspiracy nut who spews hatred toward women and minorities and routinely distorts the facts.

A SHORT HISTORY OF RUSH LIMBAUGH

Rush Limbaugh is the most influential and successful radio show host in history. To understand how he thinks, it's necessary to examine how he got to where he is.

Born in the small Mississippi river town of Cape Girardeau, Missouri, in 1951, Limbaugh grew up in a deeply conservative family of well-educated lawyers. He was devoted to his father but unable to please him; he was a terrible student, and his father admired education. Nevertheless, Limbaugh never once doubted his father's conservative ideas: "The only time my dad was wrong that I could ever remember was when he told me I would not amount to anything if I didn't go to college."[2] Limbaugh sought to prove himself to his father and, unable to succeed in school, he tried to be dutiful in his ideology. Limbaugh has never questioned his conservative views at any time in his life; to do so would be a betrayal of his father and his family. He believed without doubt what his father taught him: "I had a very fortunate thing happen to me: I was born a Limbaugh. And I learned starting at nine what liberals are, who Democrats are."[3] Limbaugh even claimed that he inherited an understanding of the law from his father: "My dad was a lawyer, I know this stuff."[4]

Rush had the worst of both worlds: an ideologically inflexible father who demanded obedience, and an intellectually lazy resistance to the type of formal education that might have offered him an opportunity to question those beliefs. In fact, Limbaugh's refusal to question his father's teachings might explain why he hated school so much. Limbaugh believes he learned everything he ever needed to know from his father, and what he was taught in school may have challenged some of those ideas. It was easier for him to slack off and ignore his teachers, even at the risk of disappointing his father, than to risk challenging those beliefs.

That's one reason why Limbaugh regularly discourages his listeners from getting an education. He always says "screwls" instead of "schools" to imply that educators are screwing up children. He sees himself as a father figure for his listeners, instructing them in ideology and protecting them from hearing any corrupting ideas.

Despite his hatred of education, Limbaugh attended Southeast Missouri State University, a small public college near home, for two semesters and one summer. Pushed into a speech class by his father, Rush did miserably. His communications teacher gave him a D and told him, "You need to make an outline. You need some data to support your assertions" but says that "Frankly, he wouldn't do those things."[5] Many decades later, Limbaugh hasn't changed his approach at all: He's still riffing off the top off his head like a DJ introducing a song, not caring about having the data to support his position. But the methods of that intellectually lazy failed student have brought Limbaugh to the forefront of the conservative movement.

In college Limbaugh was so indifferent to education that he regularly skipped class. He noted, "In my first year of college at Southeast Missouri State I had to take a phys ed course: ballroom dance, taught by a former drill sergeant in the Women's Army Corps. Ballroom dance. I didn't go." His parents had to make sure their son went to his class by driving him there in his own car: "They drove me to ballroom dance just so I couldn't skip class."[6]

Radio was the only thing Rush cared about.

A LOVE OF RADIO

For Limbaugh, radio was liberation from his failures as a student. As he once said, "I started being interested in radio when I was eight years old because I hated school. Second grade, whatever it was, I despised it. It was prison. I wanted to be like that guy. I wanted to be the guy on the radio having fun."[7]

But pursuing an interest in radio wasn't an act of rebellion; his parents supported his hobby. When Limbaugh was nine, his family gave him a treasured Christmas present he still has as a keepsake: a Remco Caravelle, which allowed him to pretend to be a DJ broadcasting to his parents at home.[8] And Rush even got started in radio thanks to his family connections. He noted that his father "owned a little bit of a radio station when we were growing up and sold it to some guy. Obviously, he knew who the guy was. And I got a chance to go in and intern. And that's all it took. And I was hooked."[9] With the assistance of his father, Limbaugh had a radio job while he was going to high school. For a shy guy and a lousy student, radio became his outlet for success. He wrote, "One of the early reasons radio interested me was that I thought it would make me popular. I wanted to be noticed and liked."[10]

After dropping out of college, Limbaugh got a job in 1972 at WIXZ, a small AM radio station near Pittsburgh. He made $150 a week as a DJ using the name Jeff Christie. He was fired after eighteen months, he claimed, because he played "Under My Thumb" by the Rolling Stones too often.[11]

As a DJ, Rush did a lot of silly radio pranks. He called a department store and claimed to be on one of the new "picture phones."[12] Hilarity ensued, no doubt. By 1973, as a DJ on Pittsburgh's KQV, Limbaugh was already using some of his famous catchphrases such as "across the fruited plain" and "excellence in broadcasting," even though there was nothing political about his show.[13] But Limbaugh was fired again in 1974 after the station was sold to a new owner, and he moved back home to Cape Girardeau.

Rush moved on to KUDL-AM in Kansas City, where he turned a little meaner to imitate the early shock jocks that were trendy then: "I'd hang up and insult people." But the AM station shifted to all syndicated news, and the radio host moved to FM. At KFIX, personality conflicts ultimately cost Rush his job.[14] By 1979 he was a failure in radio, without any immediate job prospects. He took a part-time job in the group sales office of the Kansas City Royals, where he earned eighteen thousand dollars a year by the age of thirty-two,[15] and he even collected government welfare for a time, although he predictably blamed someone else for it: "My wife made me go and file for unemployment."[16]

After years of languishing as a low-level office staffer, Limbaugh used his Royals connections to get a job at KMBZ in Kansas City in 1983. Though he was hired as a news reader, he kept inserting his conservative opinions into the news, and eventually he got his own show.[17] His controversial views annoyed managers, but the final straw was when Limbaugh criticized the Kansas City Chiefs and the team's president, Jack Steadman, when KMBZ was bidding for the broadcast of the Chiefs football games. Steadman demanded the firing of Limbaugh during the negotiations, and he was let go (an act that revealed a lot about corporate radio).[18]

Despite his cries about liberal bias, Rush was never fired from any radio show for his conservative views. To the contrary, his right-wing attitudes probably saved him. Limbaugh most often lost his shows due to technological changes (the rise of syndicated news and automated music stations) or personality conflicts; in the only case where Limbaugh's views cost him a job, it was because he did something he rarely ever did: criticize a corporation. When he began his radio career, Limbaugh wanted to be a DJ, not a conservative icon. As he says, "At that point I had no earthly desire to do politics on the radio."[19]

In 1984 Rush Limbaugh was lucky enough to have a friend recommend him to replace Morton Downey Jr., an apolitical shock jock at KFBK in Sacramento.[20] Downey had been fired for telling a joke about "chinks" and refusing to apologize. Ironically enough, Rush got his big break in talk radio because of another host's racism. As Limbaugh put it, "My most common experience in radio had been failure. Sacramento was the only place I'd succeeded."[21]

With his success in Sacramento, Limbaugh was ready for the big time: his move to New York City, where he began his nationally syndicated program on August 1, 1988. Despite his rapid success, the radio host was annoyed that he wasn't welcomed into the club of leading journalists. He complained, "I thought my success would launch me into a circle of accomplished people. Look, I admired these people. Peter Jennings, Tom Brokaw, Dan Rather—people watched these guys. I thought they would welcome me as one of them. I was wrong."[22] Angry that he was not greeted as a personal friend by the nation's top news anchors, Limbaugh turned to the adulation of his fans. During his early years of syndication, he flew almost every weekend to hold paid events at his local stations, which earned him almost a million dollars a year by 1990 and helped to boost his audience.[23] By 1991 he had 350 stations, 1.8 million listeners each quarter hour, and 7.1 million listeners a week.[24]

The technological changes in radio did more to change Limbaugh than he did to change radio. Until the mid-1980s, syndicated radio shows required phone lines, making them expensive, especially in rural areas.[25] Satellite technology helped make Rush Limbaugh's success possible by reducing the price of distributing syndicated radio at a time when AM stations were desperate to cut costs due to declining ratings.[26]

Limbaugh quickly became the most influential conservative in America. In a 1996 poll, 18 percent of Americans listened to call-in political talk radio at least twice a week, and Limbaugh dominated the airwaves. Seven percent of Americans listened exclusively to Rush, while 4 percent listened to him *and* other talk show hosts.[27]

Though Limbaugh's audience has never been accurately measured, Michael Harrison, editor of *Talkers Magazine,* estimated the radio host's audience at 14.25 million weekly in 2008, though he suggested that it may have spiked to 25 million in 2009 as publicity about Limbaugh peaked.[28] Limbaugh's recent fight with the Obama administration certainly added to his listeners; in the first few months of 2009, his ratings jumped from 4.6 to 6.7 in New York, 5.2 to 6.9 in Chicago, and 6.0 to 9.8 in Houston.[29] The August

2009 Arbitron ratings had *The Rush Limbaugh Show* as the number-one show in its time slot in Los Angeles, Houston, Phoenix, Seattle, Detroit, and San Diego; second in Chicago and San Francisco; and fourth in New York City.[30]

For Rush, a Democrat in the White House is good for business. When Republicans are in charge, he's the sheepdog of the party, herding his listeners to follow the leadership. When Democrats are in charge, he's the pit bull of the party, loudly and derisively denouncing the enemy and leading the attack. Of course, Limbaugh is always on the offensive, targeting liberals no matter which party is in charge. That's when the radio host is at his best (or worst), and it's what his listeners want to hear.

In 2001 Limbaugh signed a $250 million eight-year contract with a $38 million signing bonus.[31] In 2008 he signed an eight-year contract worth $484 million with Clear Channel's Premiere Radio Networks—a $100 million signing bonus and $38 million per year[32]—after which he declared: "I'm not retiring until every American agrees with me." Limbaugh's contract also included millions for selling advertising and endorsing companies.[33] He makes over $2,000,000 per show. In the time it takes to replay one parody song, Rush has earned more than the average American worker's monthly wage.

LIMBAUGH AND THE AGE OF HATE

Rush Limbaugh has built a radio empire based on hate. His cousin Julie Limbaugh once noted: "Rush once told me, 'The only way to make millions is for half the nation to hate you.'"[34] He has succeeded at both. He makes a million dollars a week, and more than half of Americans have an unfavorable view of him. The radio host once said, "Nobody hated me, until I started on the radio. Then statistically, I'm told, half the country hates me—and I had to learn how to take 'hate' as a measure of success."[35] Limbaugh sees the hatred directed against him as proof that he's right: "People who don't like the truth consider the truth to be hate. They consider the truth to be hate speech, people who don't like the truth, people who are enmeshed in political correctness and don't like the truth. When you utter the truth, that's when they hate you. They consider the truth to be hate."[36] One study of Limbaugh's program found that he averaged 5.43 percent of the total radio audience when he was being positive, but 5.71 percent when he was being negative.[37] Hatred brings him ratings and makes him rich.

He enjoys hating his enemies almost much as he likes being hated. He said about Bill Clinton, "I literally hated him. I hated what was happening to the country, I hated what was happening to the culture . . . I thought it was one of the worst periods of my life, and I have never been happier."[38] Hatred is Limbaugh's invigorating force.

Rush Limbaugh has done much more than make his own show popular; he has also pioneered a new way of doing media, in which expressing his own views matters far more than any traditional reporting. This shift in media has had many benefits for society, but a downside as well: Accurate news reporting has often been replaced with pure opinionizing.

By merging entertainment and opinionated politics, he has also set the stage for a wide range of new voices, from Bill O'Reilly and Sean Hannity to Jon Stewart and Stephen Colbert. Before this, openly liberal or conservative hosts with strongly expressed views were largely unknown in American mass media culture, and political commentary was largely limited to humorless newspaper columns.

Those who blame Rush for dumbing down the realm of radio, though, should remember that there was never any golden age of intellectual debate on radio. Rush's show and its imitators didn't replace important discussions of politics; they took over AM radio slots that had been devoted to bad Top 40 music. The opinion shows that existed when he started were largely local talk shows focused on mindless chatter and overnight shows that emphasized discussions of UFOs and conspiracy theories.

Limbaugh has played a critical role in making political argument a hugely popular radio and TV format. And in doing so, he performed a great service to society while making himself fantastically rich. But like any innovation, political talk radio also has a destructive side. Misinformation and hateful speech are common, and talk radio has been used by the right as a highly effective political lobbying tool.

Limbaugh's influence extends far beyond his millions of listeners. He helps to create a tidal-wave effect. The words he speaks into a microphone in Florida are repeated by his listeners on other talk shows, as well as other hosts. These words are then often incorporated into Republican talking points, and form the basis of mainstream media stories. What starts as a loud but small wave grows into a powerful political force.

No one doubts the radio host's power. Microsoft's search engine, Bing, reported that Limbaugh was the most searched-for political figure of 2009, beating out President Barack Obama,[39] and AdweekMedia named Limbaugh the radio personality of the decade in 2009.[40]

In the pages that follow, I rely almost entirely on Limbaugh's own words, as reported on his Web site, so that there can be no doubt about what he has said. I do not rely on confidential sources or questionable rumors. This is a critique of Limbaugh's ideas. It delineates his prejudices (with chapters on racism as well as sexism and homophobia), his fears (in chapters about Obama and his long history of conspiracy theories), his policy errors (including chapters on his weak understanding of economics, environmentalism, and health care), and his hatreds (including chapters about liberalism and the media). The book concludes with an analysis of how the radio host is transforming conservatism and destroying the Republican Party, and why we should all be concerned about his detrimental impact on American culture.

On December 11, 1992, Ronald Reagan sent Rush a handwritten letter signed "Ron" that praised Limbaugh as the "the Number One" voice for conservatism in our country. Reagan wrote, "I know the liberals call you 'the most dangerous man in America,' but don't worry about it, they used to say the same thing about me."[41] But the danger posed by Limbaugh extends far beyond his conservative policies.

As a progressive, I disagree with most of his policy views. However, this is not a book about why I think conservative ideas are wrong. Even conservatives who agree ideologically with almost everything Limbaugh says should be deeply troubled by his influence. His impact on the conservative movement has been destructive rather than constructive. Rush ridicules science and mocks intellectual arguments. He makes bigotry more publicly acceptable with his use of racial insults and sexist comments. He destroys the moderate wing of the Republican Party by imposing rigid adherence to his particular brand of conservatism. Rush Limbaugh is dumbing down America and coarsening our culture.

1

RUSH LIMBAUGH'S RACISM

W HEN RUSH LIMBAUGH TRIED to buy a share of the St. Louis Rams in 2009, it sparked a national debate about race that went far beyond the football field. Several NFL players, including Mathias Kiwanuka, Bart Scott, and Donovan McNabb, announced publicly that they would not play for a team owned by Limbaugh.[1]

But the discussion of Limbaugh's racism was quickly diverted by two fake quotes that had been attributed to the radio host around the Internet. In one, Limbaugh was falsely accused of saying, "I mean, let's face it, we didn't have slavery in this country for over one hundred years because it was a bad thing. Quite the opposite: slavery built the South. I'm not saying we should bring it back; I'm just saying it had its merits. For one thing, the streets were safer after dark." The other fake quote declared: "You know who deserves a posthumous Medal of Honor? James Earl Ray. We miss you, James. Godspeed." These quotes were apparently put up on Wikiquote in 2005 and then spread around the Internet by someone using the nickname Cobra.[2] The fake quotes about Limbaugh were repeated by Rachel Maddow, Jesse Jackson, James Carville, Tamron Hall, CNN's Rick Sanchez, MSNBC's David Shuster, *St. Louis Post-Dispatch* columnist Bryan Burwell, AlterNet's Rory O'Connor, *The Nation*'s Dave Zirin, and many others.[3]

Rush rightly denounced "these slanderous, made-up, fabricated quotes found in a sewer on the Internet."[4] But Limbaugh wasn't upset by these fake quotes; he was thrilled to draw attention away from all of his real racist quotes that he can't deny. And the critics of Limbaugh had no sure way of knowing that the quotes had been faked, since he had never denied them. Limbaugh said, "Whatever happened to journalists calling people and saying, 'Did you actually say this? I'm doing a story on blah, blah, blah. Did you actually say this?'"[5] But when I sent the radio host an email asking if the quotes were real, he never responded to me.[6]

Bill O'Reilly declared: "The reason that Limbaugh is not going to be able to buy into the NFL is because a bunch of made-up stuff became legend. And he got hammered. . . . So what we have here are accusations without merit. But in our hypermedia age, that's enough to paint someone as a racist."[7] However, the fake quotes had nothing to do with Rush being dropped from the bid; to the contrary, the quotes undermined the critics of Limbaugh by discrediting those who used them.

Limbaugh, like anyone else, should be free to buy a football team. But it is the NFL owners who restrict team ownership. It wasn't liberal bias that caused his friends to drop him from their bid; he claimed the organizer of the bid, Dave Checketts, told him he "cleared [his] involvement with people at the highest levels of the National Football League."[8] As Dave Zirin noted, "This has nothing to do with Limbaugh's conservative politics. Most NFL owners are to the right of Dick Cheney. Over twenty years, officials on twenty-three of the thirty-two NFL clubs have donated more money to Republicans than Democrats."[9] It was the corporate bias of the NFL, which feared the consequences of having a controversial figure owning a team, that led to him being dumped.

RACE AND THE BLACK QUARTERBACK

The statement that caused the most controversy for Limbaugh's NFL bid came during his short-lived stint as a commentator on ESPN in 2003 when he said about Philadelphia Eagles quarterback Donovan McNabb: "The media has been very desirous that a black quarterback can do well."[10] Plenty of people have criticized prominent athletes or alleged that they're overrated. But Rush did something very different by claiming that a black athlete was overrated because all of these white sports journalists love black people so much.

The radio host claimed, "All this has become the tempest that it is because I must have been right about something. If I wasn't right, there wouldn't be the cacophony of outrage that has sprung up in the sportswriter community."[11] This is a standard technique Limbaugh offers against all criticism. Whenever he says something outrageous, he then claims that there wouldn't be any outrage if it were untrue.

But it wasn't true. As Thomas George reported in *The New York Times,* "Among the black quarterbacks and the three black head coaches on the thirty-two NFL teams, there is a definitive feeling that they are on shorter leashes than their white counterparts."[12] FOX Sports cohost James Brown said: "In my eighteen years covering the NFL, I have not seen any of my media colleagues coddling McNabb or any other black quarterback. Just ask Kordell Stewart. That's the way it's supposed to be."[13] A scientific study of more than ten thousand sports articles found "no support to Limbaugh's position" that black quarterbacks were treated better by the media.[14] Yet Limbaugh never apologized and never retracted his claims. He said about McNabb in 2009, "I said exactly what I meant, and if you want me to, I'll say it again."[15]

Rush Limbaugh's harsh attacks on a black quarterback and accusations of media bias stand in sharp contrast to how he dealt with a white quarterback. Limbaugh came to the defense of white Chicago Bears quarterback Rex Grossman after media commentators criticized his performance in the 2007 Super Bowl: "They're just all over this guy. They can't wait for this guy to fail. They are hoping he fails."[16] While he may be an expert at hoping for failure, Limbaugh certainly isn't one at media analysis: "The media, the sports media, has got social concerns that they are first and foremost interested in, and they're dumping on this guy, Rex Grossman, for one reason, folks, and that's because he is a white quarterback."[17] (Obviously, the media hate white quarterbacks, such as Brett Favre, Tom Brady, and Eli Manning.)

Grossman wasn't criticized because he was white. He was criticized because he wasn't very good. Grossman was replaced by Kyle Orton, a white quarterback who was less talented but made fewer mistakes, who in turn was replaced in 2009 by Jay Cutler, a white quarterback praised as the savior of the team by all of the media Limbaugh claimed to be prejudiced for blacks and against whites. Grossman had a career passer rating of 70.2.[18] McNabb had a career passer rating of 85.9.[19] Except for his rookie year, McNabb had nine consecutive years with a passer rating higher than Rex Grossman had ever achieved in any year. McNabb was voted to the Pro Bowl five times, and Grossman zero times. Coaches, players, and fans select the Pro Bowl players, and the media have no role. According to every statistical category, McNabb is a superior quarterback to Grossman.[20]

After being criticized for his racial remarks about Grossman, the radio host claimed: "Later in the program, I let the audience in on the gag, which was to tweak the media."[21] But that's not true. He never made any comment during the program indicating that his comments about Grossman were some kind of joke.

LIMBAUGH'S DEFENDERS IN CONGRESS

Representative Steve King (R-IA) diverted a 2009 House committee hearing on severe football head injuries to focus on the person he thought was most victimized by the NFL: Rush Limbaugh. King read Limbaugh's quote about Donovan McNabb and the media, and declared: "I've scoured this quote to try to find something that can be implied as racism on the part of Rush Limbaugh, and I can't find it. There is an implication of racism on the part of the media."[22] Actually, the racism in Limbaugh's comment is clear to see: If McNabb is an excellent quarterback, then diminishing his accomplishments and falsely claiming that race was the only reason why he was praised would indeed be racist.

It's certainly possible to argue that McNabb is overrated—many quarterbacks on successful teams with good defensive squads are overrated—but it was Rush, not the media, who made race the overriding issue. In 2009 Limbaugh said once again that "the MEDIA was obsessed with the color of his skin" and claimed that his assertion was "undeniable."[23] If the media was really obsessed with McNabb's race, then you'd imagine that Limbaugh would be able to come up with at least one solitary example of someone in the press expressing this racial preference for McNabb because he is a black quarterback. But Limbaugh has never offered any evidence.

Rush Limbaugh wasn't racist for criticizing a black quarterback. But claiming without any evidence that everyone in the sports media is racially biased in favor of black people certainly falls into the category of what racists think. If someone declared that the only reason a successful black musician got positive reviews was because music critics want black artists to succeed, we would all wonder why such an individual was bringing up race when it should be irrelevant.

Representative King claimed, "I don't think anything Rush Limbaugh said was offensive."[24] Perhaps that's because King didn't think Limbaugh had actually made the offensive comments he was quoted as saying. King said about the McNabb comment, "That's the only quote that seems to survive the scrutiny of chase-checking back original sources in at least nine quotes that were alleged to the radio host. And, by the way, of those, eight are complete fabrications. They're not based on anything. They're not a misquote. They're not a distortion. They're complete fabrication."[25]

I asked Representative King's communications director what these eight "fabrications" are. I never got a response. That's probably because there are not eight fabricated quotes. There were two apparently fabricated quotes that Limbaugh has denied making, and King's claim of eight quotes that are "complete fabrications" is itself a complete fabrication. Yet Limbaugh had no problem promoting King's statement without bothering to correct or question his error. Rush said: "Steve King, I was stunned when I saw that. It was a fabulous job. I was very moved by it."[26] For Limbaugh, spreading one more fabrication was just another day at work.

The radio host didn't complain in 2005 when Republican congresspeople spoke out against the possibility that George Soros might help buy the Washington Nationals and threatened to overturn the antitrust exemption for baseball. Soros, unlike Limbaugh, was attacked as a potential sports owner solely for his political views and political activities. (Ironically, Rush even imagined that Soros was secretly made the primary owner in his bid to buy the St. Louis Rams: "I was told who it was, but now I'm wondering if it was Soros and I wasn't told."[27]) Perhaps most important of all, Soros, unlike Limbaugh, had never been accused of racist comments.

LIMBAUGH'S BLACK FRIENDS

After he was accused of racism in denouncing McNabb, Limbaugh was quick to note that he couldn't be racist because some of his best friends are black: "Charles Barkley is a friend of mine, for crying out loud."[28] In his 1993 book, Limbaugh wrote: "Another person from whom we can all learn, despite his controversial nature, is Phoenix Suns star Charles Barkley."[29] So what did Barkley say about his friend Limbaugh in 2009? "But the Republican Party went right wing whack nut job on America and screwed up the country. I'm so disappointed in this partisan politics. And I want to call out Rush Limbaugh because he talks about how he wants President Obama to fail and things like that. . . . First of all I just think that's unpatriotic for somebody who's successful. We should want him to succeed. I mean, you look at this country now, we've got all these foreclosures, we've got all these people laid off. We should be behind him 110 percent, hoping he's successful. And I just thought it was unpatriotic and basically B.S. for Rush Limbaugh and that idiot Sean Hannity and Glenn Beck and all those idiots to not root for this guy."[30]

How does Rush Limbaugh generally describe black athletes? He said once, "Look, let me put it to you this way: the NFL all too often looks like a game between the Bloods and the Crips without any weapons. There, I said it."[31] He was oddly fond of describing predominantly black athletes with the Crips and the Bloods analogy, as when he said, "I think it's time to get rid of this whole National Basketball Association. Call it the TBA, the Thug Basketball Association, and stop calling them teams. Call 'em gangs. . . . They're going in to watch the Crips and the Bloods out there wherever the neighborhood is where the arena happens to be, and be who you are."[32] Limbaugh also revealed his deep understanding of gangs and fashion: "You look at NBA players and the uniforms, you don't have to go back very far. The uniforms have changed totally. They're now in gang colors."[33] To him, a black athlete is just another gang member.

MISSING THE MARK: FALSE ACCUSATIONS AGAINST LIMBAUGH

Some of the accusations of racism against Limbaugh have backfired. At the 1993 White House Correspondents' Dinner, Bill Clinton declared that Limbaugh had defended Janet Reno against criticism from Representative John Conyers "because she was attacked by a black guy." Rush responded: "It's not funny . . . I'm the absolute furthest thing from a racist."[34] Well, he was half right. Clinton's remark wasn't funny or clever, and it brought the radio host enormous sympathy. He recounted how Chris Matthews urged him to hold a press conference and demand an apology.[35]

In 1993 *Washington Post* columnist William Raspberry wrote an op-ed criticizing Limbaugh for his "demagoguery . . . his gay bashing, his racial putdowns." Raspberry compared him to Mississippi segregationists and declared, "Limbaugh is a bigot."[36] Eleven days later, Raspberry wrote another column retracting his charge: "Rush, I'm sorry." Raspberry wrote: "When a caller asked me, quite reasonably, to give him an instance or two of a bigoted opinion from Limbaugh, all he got was my embarrassed silence. Sure he's taken digs at poor people and rioters and feminists and the NAACP [National Association for the Advancement of Colored People], but why should any of these be immune?"[37] Unfortunately, Raspberry wrote a column criticizing Limbaugh without examining his evidence of bigotry, and then compounded his error by writing another column exonerating Rush, again without examining the evidence.

While some of the attacks on Limbaugh's racism are made with shaky evidence, his defenders are equally guilty of ignoring the evidence when they claim he has never said anything racist. When journalist Carl Rowan accused Limbaugh of making "wicked, often bigoted, jokes," Howard Kurtz in *The Washington Post* came to his defense: "Not a single example is offered, most likely because there are none."[38]

It's true that no one should be immune from critique. But when Limbaugh repeatedly attacks people based on race and makes explicitly racial putdowns, it's hard to find an innocuous explanation for it. What is it about Rush's racial obsession? Why does he constantly inject race into so many discussions where it is irrelevant? Limbaugh is hypersensitive to every possible instance of reverse racism against whites, real or imagined, and completely incapable of seeing racism against black people.

The radio host frequently makes bizarre racial comments like "Stop blaming me for slavery. I wasn't alive."[39] No one has ever blamed Rush Limbaugh for slavery. The fact that he imagines it reveals how obsessively he sees race in everything. The evidence of Mr. Limbaugh's racism is simply too overwhelming to deny. I do not make the accusation of racism against Limbaugh lightly, nor do I make it as part of some ridiculous "all white people are racist" charge. I do not make similar charges of racism against other high-profile conservatives; for instance, I do not have any evidence that Michael Medved, Bill O'Reilly, or Sean Hannity are racists, and without that evidence I do not accuse them of being racists. We should never accept unsupported accusations of racism. But we should likewise never refuse to criticize racism.

It's not that any singular comment definitively proves that Rush Limbaugh is a racist. Rather, racism is a kind of lifetime achievement award one must give to a man with such a lengthy track record of bizarre and offensive racial comments. As Timothy Egan of *The New York Times* observed, "Race is an obsession with Limbaugh."[40]

Racism does not require some personal animus toward black people. It's quite possible that Rush is perfectly nice to every African American he meets face-to-face, and feels no hatred toward them. However, that doesn't stop him from using race to attack those he opposes.

What probably turned Rush into a racist was his hatred of liberalism. He despises all things liberal, and what he regards as liberal institutions, such as schools and the media. Because African Americans vote overwhelmingly for Democrats, he regards them with the same contempt that he applies to all liberals. Limbaugh once said about black voters, "They are 12 percent of the population. Who the hell cares?"[41] What he really meant was, African Americans always vote for Democrats, so why should conservatives care about them? The radio host has the same approach to his show: When his audience is almost exclusively white, why should he care about the views of minorities? He has no economic motive for racial sensitivity, and no fear that anything racial he says will alienate his white, conservative listeners.

LIMBAUGH'S LONG HISTORY OF RACISM

As a young broadcaster in the 1970s, Rush Limbaugh once told a black caller: "Take that bone out of your nose and call me back."[42] But this comment wasn't some youthful mistake; it reflects a racial obsession that has permeated his career. After he got his syndicated talk show, Limbaugh asked: "Have you ever noticed how all composite pictures of wanted criminals resemble Jesse Jackson?"[43] In 2004, when Reverend Jackson joined John Kerry's campaign, Limbaugh declared, "The Kerry campaign has finally gotten a chocolate chip."[44]

He routinely associates African Americans with criminal behavior. In 1992 Limbaugh criticized Spike Lee for suggesting that black students skip school to see the film *Malcolm X*: "Spike, if you're going to do that, let's complete the education experience. You should tell them that they should loot the theater, and then blow it up on their way out."[45] He also accused Spike Lee of using "looter lingo."[46]

Rush sees all black people as associated with riots. He once said, "The NAACP should have riot rehearsal. They should get a liquor store and practice robberies."[47] Limbaugh claimed about Obama, "You organized riots and communities and stuff in Chicago."[48] Of course, Obama never "organized riots." The NAACP has never been involved in any riots (in fact, the organization formed in response to the riots of white mobs).[49]

The radio host accused Obama of "inciting riots" in a speech because he used the phrase "quiet riot": "He's talking about there's a quiet riot brewing in America today because Bush doesn't care, because Bush isn't doing enough. This guy was inciting, he was inciting riots. . . . And to talk about a quiet riot that is brewing out there it is dangerous, it is reckless."[50] The fact that Limbaugh falsely associates all black people with riots, including the nation's leading civil rights organization and the president of the United States, says a great deal about his bigotry.

Limbaugh even declared in 2008 that whites are rational to fear black men: "I wonder how white college students at the University of North Carolina, Chapel Hill, are feeling these days. I wonder if they are nervous walking down the street, and they see a couple of black boys dressed in baggy clothes with their hats on backwards swaggering toward them. I wonder how they feel. I wonder if it makes them fear that they're going to be shot in the face for their ATM cards and their PIN numbers. Obama, do you think there might be reasons here rather than this being inbred?"[51]

To mock Carol Moseley Braun, the first African American woman elected to the U.S. Senate, Limbaugh played the "Movin' On Up" theme song from the TV show *The Jeffersons*.[52] He also played an announcer saying, "I don't know nothin' about runnin' for the president" to ridicule her.[53]

Rush embraces the most primitive racial stereotypes. On his TV show, he promised to display the everyday life of "welfare recipients" and then showed a video of apes in zoos.[54] In 1994 he praised a Chicago teacher for making a math question that began: "Rufus is pimping three girls" because the teacher was "understanding the culture these kids come from."[55] In 2006, when the CBS reality TV show *Survivor* divided contestants into racial groups, Limbaugh declared the contest was "not going to be fair if there's a lot of water competition" and added, "looking at the Olympics, you'd have to say the white tribe would be the best swimmers."[56]

In response to a University of Chicago study finding that "a majority of young blacks feel alienated from today's government," Rush said in 2007: "Why would that be? The government's been taking care of them their whole lives."[57] It's hard to imagine how anyone would think that the government has "taken care of" all young black people their entire lives.

Attacks on the civil rights movement are a routine part of the radio host's show. He complained that leaders of civil rights groups "do not have normal jobs" because the leader "raises money and keeps a percentage of it for himself as head of the organization."[58] But Limbaugh promotes nonprofit conservative groups such as the Heritage Foundation, which gets its money in donations in the same way as civil rights groups do. When nonprofit groups address civil rights, Rush says their leaders don't have "normal jobs"; when a nonprofit group is a charity or engages in conservative advocacy, he praises it. But among all nonprofit advocacy groups, liberal and conservative, he especially singles out the black leaders of civil rights groups.

CONSERVATIVE COLOR BLINDNESS

Sounding like Stephen Colbert parodying conservatives, Rush Limbaugh has claimed that he doesn't see race: "When I look out at you in this audience, I don't see a Walmart voter. And I don't see a black, and I don't see a woman, and I don't see a Hispanic."[59] He said on the *Today* show, "I don't look at people with the color of their skin. Notice that it's my critics who are always noticing the color of somebody's skin or their gender or their sexual orientation. I don't see—I see people as people, see them as Americans."[60] He has also claimed, "I am truly color blind and I wish everyone else was."[61] For someone who claims not to see race, he certainly talks about it obsessively.

Limbaugh sees race in the strangest of circumstances. When Senator Ted Kennedy died, Rush declared: "I'm gonna take a drink for every black person I see on the parade route. And I was sober at the end of the parade. They forgot to stack the deck with any black people, but there were a lot of union thugs out there."[62] He merged the bizarre idea that no black people mourned the death of Kennedy with the equally bizarre idea that "union thugs" were hired to "stack" the route for Kennedy's body. Why would Limbaugh turn the death of a notable Democrat into a racial issue? Yet Limbaugh was so proud of his strange comment that he repeated it the next day.[63]

When John Kerry claimed to be "fascinated by rap and by hip-hop," Limbaugh accused him of "pathetically pandering" to blacks: "Don't stand up for white music, associate yourself with rap."[64] But why does Limbaugh think that anyone needs to "stand up for white music"? As the defender of white males, the radio host sees race everywhere: "The dirty little secret is that people that win elections win it with white males."[65] That's quite a secret to President Barack Obama, who won the 2008 election with 41 percent of the white male vote. Before that, no Democrat since Jimmy Carter had won more than 38 percent of the white male vote, even though Al Gore (2000) and Bill Clinton (1992 and 1996) prevailed in the popular vote.[66] Democrats have won four out of the last five presidential elections without even coming close to winning a majority of white male voters. Yet Limbaugh has referred at least five different times in the past few years to this "dirty little secret" that white men determine elections.[67] Why would he believe that white males, a group composing only 35.5 percent of voters (fewer than white women), decide every election?[68] Why is Limbaugh so obsessed with race that he has these delusional fantasies of white men controlling every election?

Limbaugh sees the white male conservative as the true victimized minority in America today. He has said, "It's really uncool to be [a] white male to-day."[69] He's happy to ignore the fact that white males dominate every impor-tant part of America today, from corporations to politics to talk radio; his imagined feelings of oppression as a white male matter more than the facts.

Indeed, Rush has no aversion to using the word "racist" himself; he even complained that "we can't use the word 'racist' when it actually applies."[70] When a black Republican is being criticized by a white liberal, even in the mildest of terms, Limbaugh is quick to call it a "lynching." When Senator Barbara Boxer observed that then-secretary of state Condoleezza Rice didn't have any family members serving in Iraq, he declared: "Here you have a rich white chick with a huge, big mouth, trying to lynch this—an African American woman—right before Martin Luther King Day, hitting below the ovaries here."[71] He used that racially charged word to describe himself after his NFL bid failed: "I, too, have had my high-tech lynching."[72] But Limbaugh regularly calls blacks and Latinos racist if they disagree with his conserva-tive views.

LIMBAUGH'S AFRICA OBSESSION

Race dominates policy decisions in Rush's mind. He denounced Democrats for opposing genocide, accusing them of favoring Africa to gain black votes: "They want to get us out of Iraq, but they can't wait to get us into Darfur. . . . What color is the skin of the people in Darfur? It's black."[73] But his com-ments made no sense. Democrats have solid control of the black vote, and there's not the slightest evidence that anyone expressing concern about genocide in Darfur did so because of race. A distinction between Iraq and Darfur is that there was an ongoing genocide in Darfur and not in Iraq. The other difference is that America invaded Iraq and not Darfur, and few if any Democrats endorsed an invasion of Darfur.

Yet Limbaugh complained, "So you go into Darfur and you go into

South Africa, you get rid of the white government there. You put sanctions on them. You stand behind Nelson Mandela—who was bankrolled by communists for a time, had the support of certain communist leaders."[74] The United States never went "into" South Africa, and never did anything to "get rid of the white government there." Mandela is one of the most celebrated men in the world and a Nobel Peace Prize winner for his courageous stand against apartheid, but to Limbaugh he's just a communist.

Rush Limbaugh has an odd obsession with Africa. In his first book, he claimed, "In schools we're teaching kids about tribal Africa instead of Aristotle."[75] It's unlikely that Limbaugh learned much about Aristotle in his schooling, since few students ever do, and the amount of teaching about tribal Africa in American schools is insignificant. But his fear of "tribal Africa" and the idea that anything might be taught about it speaks volumes about his racial attitudes.

LIMBAUGH, THE VICTIM OF RACISM

Rush loves to play the race card by complaining that he is a victim of unfair criticism. "There is nothing worse than being branded a racist," he has said. Actually, being branded a racist appears to have no discernible effect on Limbaugh's very fat wallet. To the contrary, it's one more way that he appeals to his conservative listeners. He claimed, "Prior to doing this show no one hated me. No one thought I was a racist, sexist or homophobic bigot. No one thought I was a hate-monger. I was not raised to be hated. I was raised to be loved."[76] It's probably true that until the "Maha Rushie" began loudly and publicly speaking about race, he wasn't called a racist. But that has nothing to do with all of the evidence that he is a racist. He complained in 1992, "All you have to do is criticize black people and they call you a racist."[77] But it was never the criticism of blacks that caused Limbaugh to be called a racist; it was his racist language.

And when racial issues don't exist, he simply invents them and then blames the mainstream press for his mistakes. In 2006 he declared about the U.S. Senate race in Ohio, "And don't forget Sherrod Brown is black. There's a racial component here, too." The radio host added, "The newspaper that I'm reading all this from is *The New York Times,* and they, of course, don't mention that."[78] Unfortunately for Limbaugh, Sherrod Brown is white. Predictably, Limbaugh used his error as proof that he's always right: "What it said to me was that even the mainstream media knows I get it right all the time, and it is such an odd thing when I am wrong that it is news."[79] Of course, even if Brown had been black, what would have been the "racial component" Limbaugh claimed to see? For a man who claims not to see race, he certainly discusses the racial component a lot. Only he could see a racial issue that didn't exist, blame the liberal *New York Times* for ignoring this imaginary "racial component," and then declare that his dumb mistake proved that he's "right all the time."

Rush is actually proud of his racism. It's his way of signaling to his audience how much he resists liberal orthodoxy. If he is willing to violate the "politically correct" barriers of race, then it proves that he is beholden to nothing about liberalism. As with everything else about Mr. Limbaugh, his racism is really all about his hatred of liberalism, not some deep-seated hatred of black people.

Being accused of racism is a badge of honor for Limbaugh: "I'm called a racist twenty thousand times a day by my opponents—and they're lying."[80] Of course he would be offended by any suggestion he is racist, because he judges racism purely in terms of his emotional state toward black people: If he doesn't feel racist, then he can't be racist, no matter what he says. After all, some of his best employees are black.

Limbaugh is a racist because he hates liberalism. That doesn't mean that anyone who hates liberalism is a racist. It means that Rush Limbaugh expresses racist ideas because he despises everything associated with liberalism. Since fighting racism is a core principle of liberalism, he is constantly skeptical of it. And he expresses that skepticism using racist language.

Racism only exists in Limbaugh's eyes with the proviso that whites are just as victimized by it as any other race: "I admit that racism continues to exist in every imaginable direction among all races."[81] Racism appears to be the only thing that he believes is shared equally among all people. Although Limbaugh usually denies that there's any racism or sexism in America, he makes an exception when contemplating the political benefits for conservatives that might result from it: "Let's say it is Obama and Hillary. . . . Let's put Hillary at the top—That's a position she's familiar with. Therefore, you've got a woman and a black for the first time ever on the Democrat ticket. Ahem. They don't have a prayer."[82] If there's no bigotry in America, exactly why would having a black man and woman on a ticket destroy the Democratic Party's chances of victory?

UNDERSTANDING LIMBAUGH'S RACISM

Despite this lengthy record of bigotry, Limbaugh's racism has been a matter of hot debate. Steve Rendall of Fairness and Accuracy in Reporting (FAIR), a progressive media criticism group, wrote, "No one who's listened to Limbaugh can honestly say that he doesn't say racist, hateful or stupid things."[83] Rendall certainly underestimated the capability of Limbaugh's fans to deny any racism in anything he's ever said.

Conservative writer Andrew Klavan claims he has never heard Limbaugh "utter a single racist, hateful or stupid word," and expresses "the certainty" about his critics that they've "never listened to Rush Limbaugh."[84] It takes a lot of chutzpah to declare that those who denounce Limbaugh, and quote the exact words from his mouth, have never listened to him.

Limbaugh has claimed, "You don't have the number-one most-listened-to radio show in America, the most respected, the most feared, the most loved, the most whatever, if it's filled with hate and racism and bigotry and all this—it's just not the case."[85] His assumption is deeply flawed: Just because something is popular doesn't prove that it's not hateful or racist. Someone who openly confesses his or her racism might have some difficulty attracting a mass audience, but what Limbaugh offers is bigotry with a laugh, the lighter side of the far right. If Archie Bunker listened to a talk show, *The Rush Limbaugh Show* would be it. Limbaugh even bears some physical resemblance to Carroll O'Connor, but the true similarity is their anger at liberalism. However, where Archie Bunker was a caricature at times, an object of ridicule, Limbaugh is the full flowering of the character. He is Archie Bunker with a microphone, and with 20 million listeners instead of just his wife.

The Rush Limbaugh Show is a complex phenomenon, combining humor with hard-core conservatism and a side of racism. Not everyone who listens to it approves of all of the radio host's comments, nor do they necessarily hear the racist comments scattered in his broadcasts. Like Klavan, they pretend never to have heard a racist remark from his mouth; they forget every racist invocation; they imagine that any racist comment is simply a joke and therefore immune from critique. When Tucker Carlson was reminded of Rush's racist "bone out of your nose" remark, he advised, "Lighten up. It's not a kook radio show. Look, you know the guy's telling jokes. . . . If there's one issue that divides the parties, it's humor. You have on the one side this kind of relentless, harsh, grim, dour humorlessness, and on the other side, you know, I don't know Rush Limbaugh, whatever you think of him, he's pretty amusing."[86] To Carlson, telling a black person to take that bone out of his nose is just great humor.

The proof of racism, ultimately, is found in the evidence of what Limbaugh has said. His claims to have good intentions, and the desire of his listeners to deny any racism, cannot overcome the facts. Limbaugh's long history of racism has only intensified with the election of a black president, and those who deny the reality of his racism must ignore a mountain of evidence to claim that he does not see race.

LIMBAUGH'S RACIAL HATRED OF OBAMA

During Obama's inauguration week, Limbaugh claimed: "Racism in this country is the exclusive problem of the left. We're witnessing racism all this week that led up to the inauguration. We are being told that we have to hope he succeeds; that we have to bend over, grab the ankles, bend over forward, backward, whichever; because his father was black, because this is the first black president. We've got to accept this. The racism that everybody thinks exists on our side of the aisle has been on full display throughout their primary campaign."[87] There was racism during the Democratic primary, but nothing in comparison to the racism displayed by Limbaugh on his program. It's perfectly normal for all Americans to hope the president succeeds, and it has nothing to do with race. But Limbaugh's opposition to Obama, his belief that everyone was being told to "grab the ankles" because he's black, reflected racial paranoia.

The radio host has claimed, "So I think the fact that he's African American—his father was black—to me, it's irrelevant."[88] Despite this statement, the race of Barack Obama was a source of endless discussion and scrutiny for him. A month after Obama joined the U.S. Senate, Limbaugh was attacking him on racial grounds, telling one caller: "I kind of like that analogy that he's the Donovan McNabb of the U.S. Senate . . . in the sense that he is being propped up . . . because they want to see him do well."[89]

Even before Obama decided to run for president, Limbaugh was attacking him on racial grounds, declaring in 2006, "You are not African American, Mr. Obama. You do not share the heritage of this country that African American implies."[90] In January 2007 he continued the racial attack, calling Obama a "Halfrican."[91] Rush proclaimed that Obama could choose to be white: "So are we to conclude here that he didn't define himself as black, that the way he looks does? Well, if you didn't decide it, then how did it happen? . . . Well, renounce it, then! If it's not something you want to be, if you didn't decide it, renounce it, become white! . . . If you don't like it, you can switch. Well, that's the way I see it. He's got 50-50 in there. Say, 'No, I'm white.' "[92] Rush even suggested that Obama, and all blacks, are not real Americans: "Obama is telling us he is a black American first and an American second."[93]

Limbaugh was fond of using racial insults against Obama, calling him "a Chicago street thug," "a half-minority," and even "the little black man-child."[94] It is difficult to conceive of any situation where a nonracist would call the most admired black man in America, a forty-seven-year-old man serving in the U.S. Senate, "the little black man-child." This was Limbaugh's variation of the ancient insult "boy" (which Limbaugh has also invoked to describe Obama), used by racists to demean black men. Limbaugh grew up in Missouri in the 1950s during the era of Jim Crow, so he must have understood the implications of his "man-child" language. And he often uses racially demeaning language, declaring that "Obama is essentially a primitive indigenous guy."[95] When Limbaugh describes the man who ran the most technologically sophisticated political campaign in history as "primitive," race is the only possible explanation. And there can be no doubt that Rush would never describe a white person born in America as "indigenous."

Obama, the Arab

One example of Rush Limbaugh's racial obsession and his ability to sway public opinion on race came during the 2008 election, when he claimed that

Obama was an Arab. On September 22, 2008, he said: "He's not black. Do you know he has not one shred of African American blood? He doesn't have any African—that's why when they asked whether he was authentic, whether he's down for the struggle. He's Arab. You know, he's from Africa. He's from Arab parts of Africa. He's not—his father was—he's not African American. The last thing that he is is African American."[96]

Arabs make up less than 1 percent of the Kenyan population, and there's no evidence at all that Obama's family had any Arab background. In fact, no one other than Rush and a few crackpots ever made this accusation. But it reveals the power of Limbaugh's voice, that he can promote a racist lie about Obama and almost without any effort convince a substantial part of the public to believe in it.

The Arab accusation against Obama also reveals Limbaugh's peculiar ideas about race. Why would anyone care if Obama's father was an African of Arab background? How would that change Obama's African heritage or his blackness? But to Limbaugh, claiming that Obama was an Arab was a continuation of the "anti-American" attacks he was making against him. Unlike other conspiracy claims made by Limbaugh, this one wasn't widely repeated in the right-wing media or in the crazy e-mails about Obama being a Muslim born in Kenya, bigoted and false allegations that have been widely spread in the conservative media and via e-mail rumor mongering. Yet thanks to Limbaugh's influence it had a remarkable power across the country. John McCain famously informed one woman at a town hall meeting that Obama wasn't an Arab: "He's a decent family man."[97] More amazing, an Annenberg Public Policy Center poll of three thousand people after the 2008 elections found that 22 percent believed that Obama is half Arab—a number even higher than the 19 percent who believed Obama is a Muslim.[98] The number of Americans who thought Obama is an Arab is surprising, since it was a far less common rumor. In fact, there was only one major media figure who promoted the idea that Obama was an Arab: Rush Limbaugh.[99]

Rush's "Arab" smear was just one example of how powerful (and racist) his voice is, especially when it goes unnoticed and unchallenged by the mainstream media. Limbaugh continued to repeat the smear even after Obama became president. Limbaugh said that a photo of Obama wearing traditional Somali clothing "looks like Ayman Zawahiri."[100] Comparing a presidential candidate to Osama bin Laden's chief associate probably wouldn't have occurred to Limbaugh if the candidate had been white.

Limbaugh has particularly odd views of Arabs. During the Abu Ghraib scandal, Limbaugh read from an Associated Press article: "'One detainee wrapped in an Israeli flag, some were shackled hand and foot in fetal position for eighteen to twenty-four hours, forcing them to soil themselves.'"[101] He declared, "Ugh! I thought they did that anyway over there. But this is news to me that this is news."[102] Limbaugh defended torture by smearing everyone in the Middle East as people who "soil themselves" and therefore deserve abusive treatment.

The Racial Authenticity of Barack Obama

Although Limbaugh regularly complains about media bias in favor of every Democratic politician, he claims that Obama was the beneficiary of racial bias for blacks: "Normally a mainstream media would have vetted this guy and we would know this. We don't know what he is. That's the whole point. People don't care what he is. They don't care who he is. They care that he's black."[103] And he has said, "If Barack Obama were Caucasian, they would have taken this guy out on the basis of pure ignorance long ago."[104]

Yet Limbaugh has persisted in claiming that conservatives like him pay no attention to race: "We didn't ask if he was authentically black."[105] However, he has specifically challenged Obama's blackness. After Obama became president, Limbaugh called him "the greatest living example of a reverse racist" and accused him of "fooling white people."[106] He also claimed that only Obama's supporters paid attention to race: "People don't care what he is. They don't care who he is. They care that he's black."[107] That Obama was supported only because he's black was one of the most racist assertions about the 2008 campaign. Limbaugh claimed, "The only reason Obama's anywhere is because whites are willing to support him because they feel so guilty over slavery."[108] He also accused Obama of "inciting racism" and "inflaming racial hatred."[109] But it's Limbaugh, not Obama, who focuses on race. It's Limbaugh, not Obama, who said Obama "wants to be the black FDR."[110]

African Americans are regularly mocked on Limbaugh's show for saying "ax" instead of "ask."[111] Limbaugh even accused Obama of pronouncing "ask" as "ax" and declared, "Obama can turn on that black dialect when he wants to and turn it off." He went on to claim that Obama was not "psychologically grounded in reality" and said, "I've been 'axing' people about this on the break, if I should go further on this. Some people think I should explore it, and I'll keep 'axing.' "[112] In reality, Obama said "ask," not "ax," but Limbaugh's overactive racial imagination led him to obsessively accuse Obama of sounding too black.

In 2008 Limbaugh said of one of his employees, "Bo Snerdley got a promotion. He's now officially the Obama criticizer—certified black enough to criticize—limiting the racial aspect."[113] Only in Limbaugh's twisted world could he assign one of his black employees to be the "official" Obama criticizer because of his race and claim to be "limiting the racial aspect."

Throughout the campaign, Limbaugh made numerous racist attacks on Obama. He called Obama "stupid" and asserted that Obama "probably didn't get outta Harvard without affirmative action."[114] The notion that Barack Obama could not have graduated from Harvard Law School without preferential grading is amazing. No one can possibly believe that Obama's success—including his selection to the *Harvard Law Review,* election as its president, graduation as magna cum laude in the top 10 percent of his class, passing of the bar, and becoming a top teacher at the University of Chicago Law School—was all somehow granted to him through a conspiracy of Harvard Law professors to raise his grades because he's black, especially since many law school professors use blind grading.

In 2010, Limbaugh made up another smear about Barack Obama: "I think this is the first time in his life that there's not a professor around to turn his C into an A, or to write the law review article for him he can't write. He is totally exposed. There is nobody to make it better. I think he's been covered for, all his life."[115]

I asked some Harvard law professors about this charge. Laurence Tribe responded to me, "The allegation's absurd. Obama earned every one of his enormously high grades. 'Affirmative action' had nothing to do with his success there. He was the most impressive student and research assistant I have taught in my forty years at Harvard." Charles Fried, a Harvard Law professor who served as solicitor general during the Reagan administration, wrote to me, "It's paranoid nonsense. Grading is anonymous by a randomly generated exam number and it takes a vote of the faculty to change a grade."[116]

Limbaugh claimed there was a similar conspiracy at Columbia University to raise Obama's grades: "I think Obama's the kind of guy that had people turning C's into A's for him if he needed to for whatever reason."[117] He never had any evidence for his position. But to a racist like Rush who never finished college, such nonsense becomes believable if it's a black person who is succeeding: "It is striking how unqualified Obama is, and how this whole thing came about within the Democrat [sic] Party. I think it really goes back to the fact that nobody had the guts to stand up and say no to the black guy." Limbaugh went on to say: "I think this is a classic illustration here where affirmative action has reared its ugly head against them. It's the reverse of it. They've, they've ended up nominating and placing at the top of their ticket somebody who's not qualified, who has not earned it." He added: "It's perfect affirmative action. And because of all this guilt and the historic nature of things, nobody had the guts to say, well, wait a minute, do we really want to do this?"[118] Rush never questioned the credentials of George W. Bush, a man who was far less qualified for the presidency than Obama and who achieved his success almost entirely due to his family name. Yet Obama's success was deemed by Limbaugh undeserved and unearned because of his race.

Limbaugh's Magic Negro

Limbaugh repeatedly played a parody song called "Barack the Magic Negro" (to the tune of "Puff the Magic Dragon"), featuring Limbaugh's parody song maker Paul Shanklin badly imitating Al Sharpton, singing about Obama as a "magic Negro" (a term used by a *Los Angeles Times* op-ed writer) and declaring, "He's black, but not authentically."[119]

The song uses these words:

Barack the Magic Negro lives in D.C.
The *LA Times,* they called him that
'cause he's not authentic like me.[120]

The term "magic Negro" was used by a left-wing columnist in the *Los Angeles Times* as a way to talk in complex ways about race and how whites love to have a "magic Negro" in movies who quietly saves them. For Limbaugh, it was an excuse to use an archaic, derogatory term toward a black politician and get away with it. It was the equivalent of whites who think they are entitled to call blacks "niggers" because some black rapper used the word. After being criticized for the song, he decided to expand it with Sharpton singing about "da hood" and calling Obama "ar-ti-coo-late."[121]

Obama said about the song, "I have not heard it, but I've heard of it. I confess I don't listen to Rush on a daily basis. On the other hand, I'm not one of these people who takes myself so seriously I get offended by every comment made about me. What Rush does is entertainment."[122] But as a black politician, Obama can't make accusations of racism without alienating white voters and members of the press.

The song "Barack the Magic Negro" was played over and over on Limbaugh's show during the 2008 election, but it received critical scrutiny from Republicans only after Chip Saltsman, a candidate for the chairmanship of the Republican National Committee, sent members a CD including the "Barack the Magic Negro" song. It finally sparked outrage from some Republicans. RNC chair Mike Duncan declared, "I am shocked and appalled that anyone would think this is appropriate as it clearly does not move us in the right direction."[123]

LIMBAUGH'S RACIAL RHETORIC

Limbaugh takes advantage of any opportunity to use racist and sexist insults. In 2008, when Hillary Clinton innocuously said Obama "hasn't done the spadework necessary to be president," Limbaugh seized upon the moment to repeatedly call Obama a "spade" and Clinton a "hoe": "Obama is holding his own against both of them, doing more than his share of the 'spadework,' maybe even gaining ground at the moment, using not only the spade, ladies and gentlemen. But when he finishes with the spade in the garden of corruption planted by the Clintons, he turns to the hoe. So the spadework and his expertise, using a hoe."[124] In 2009 he noted that food safety advocates were "going to go after Oreos" but would wait until Obama was out of office, which was Limbaugh's way of calling Obama an "oreo" (black on the outside, white on the inside).[125]

When a racist caller declared that Obama was fighting "against white America," Rush agreed with him wholeheartedly—"You're right down the line"—and supported the idea that "Obama hates white people."[126] Limbaugh routinely viewed President Obama's actions through the prism of race. When Somali pirates who kidnapped an American were shot, he declared, "President Obama turns on Somali counterparts."[127] Limbaugh made a point of emphasizing the race of the Somalis who were killed, to draw a comparison between the blackness of the pirates and the blackness of Obama.

Even Obama's policies were guided purely by race in Limbaugh's eyes. He repeatedly attacked Obama's economic policies as "reparations" for slavery. Limbaugh said, "Obama's entire economic program is reparations!"[128] Playing excerpts from a fourteen-year-old speech by Obama, he claimed, "Obama believes that white Americans should be made to pay extra taxes for the wrongs done to blacks throughout the history of this country. Only through 'collective salvation' can all of us be saved. He's talking reparations here."[129] No, he wasn't. Obama mentioned nothing about reparations in this 1995 speech. Not a word about extra taxes for whites. Obama talked about "responsibility" and the fact that his "individual salvation is not going to come about without a collective salvation for the country." Collective salvation referred to equal rights, not reparations.

Limbaugh applied the racially charged term "reparations" to every Obama policy: "The objective is to take the nation's wealth and return to it to the nation's quote, rightful owners. Think reparations. Think forced reparations here if you want to understand what actually is going on."[130] Why does Limbaugh constantly bring up "reparations" for slavery when discussing Obama's economic policies? Has he ever used the word to discuss the economic plans of a white politician? The idea that reparations for slavery fueled Obama's "entire" economic plan, and the assumption that only black people would benefit from it, has no basis in reality. That Limbaugh said this, however, confirms how he sees the world through race-colored glasses. Comedy Central star Stephen Colbert noted about Limbaugh's comments, "Those guys aren't racist. They're just saying that a program that helps the poor is actually a secret plot by African Americans to steal white people's money."[131]

Rush claimed Obama was pushing racial conflict in order to promote liberalism: "The left, from Barack Obama on down, are committed to a divided country. They are committed to people in this country at war with each other over race, over gender, over sexual orientation, over whatever they can promote. The more chaos, the better, because the more chaos, the less gets done—and the ever greater cry, the ever greater apparent need for more government to solve these insoluble problems."[132]

Rush often falsely accuses others of something he's done, as when he said, "The anti-Jew rhetoric in this country today comes from the American left and from the circle of people that are close to Barack Obama."[133] But Rush cited no evidence of any such "anti-Jew" rhetoric. He condemned Obama because, he claimed, "I've never had a friend like Khalidi who hates Jews."[134] Columbia University professor Rashid Khalidi is a distinguished professor, and there is no proof that he is anti-Semitic. By contrast, Limbaugh not only has anti-Semitic friends, he actually endorsed Pat Buchanan for president at the very moment when conservative icon William F. Buckley Jr. concluded that Buchanan was an anti-Semite.[135]

Limbaugh has personally promoted anti-Semitic stereotypes: "For some people, 'banker' is code word for 'Jewish,' and guess who Obama's assaulting? He's assaulting bankers. He's assaulting money people, and a lot of those people on Wall Street are Jewish. So I wonder if there's starting to be some buyer's remorse there."[136] Abraham Foxman, national director of the Anti-Defamation League, declared: "Rush Limbaugh reached a new low with his borderline anti-Semitic comments about Jews as bankers, their supposed influence on Wall Street, and how they vote."[137]

This enraged Limbaugh, who demanded an apology from Foxman and said, "I was referring to the Jew haters, the bigots."[138] He was indeed referring to the view of the bigots—immediately before agreeing with them. Rush was so eager to attack Obama as anti-Semitic for criticizing bankers that he failed to notice that he himself was embracing the stereotype of Jews as "money people."

As the defender of white men, Limbaugh sees their oppression everywhere: "How do you get promoted in a Barack Obama administration? By hating white people—or even saying you do, or that they're not good or put 'em down, whatever. Make white people the new oppressed minority, and they're going right along about it 'cause they're shutting up. They're moving to the back of the bus. They're saying, 'I can't use that drinking fountain?

Okay! I can't use that restroom? Okay!' That's the modern-day Republican Party, the equivalent of the Old South: the new oppressed minority."[139] Only a racist or a lunatic believes that white people in America are the "new oppressed minority" equivalent to the era of segregated restrooms during Jim Crow.

COLIN POWELL AND RACE

When Republican Colin Powell endorsed Barack Obama for president, Rush claimed it was all about race. Powell said: "I think what Rush does as an entertainer diminishes the party and intrudes or inserts into our public life a kind of nastiness that we would be better to do without."[140] Rush responded: "I just think he's just mad at me because I'm the one person in the country that had the guts to explain his endorsement of Obama. It was purely and solely based on race. There can be no other explanation for it."[141]

He also declared, "Secretary Powell says his endorsement is not about race. OK, fine. I am now researching his past endorsements to see if I can find all the inexperienced, very liberal, white candidates he has endorsed. I'll let you know what I come up with."[142] Of course, Powell did endorse an inexperienced white candidate whom he had some disagreements with, a man named George W. Bush. But Limbaugh could see only race.

Powell retorted on CNN, "And when you have non-elected officials such as we have in our party who immediately shout racism or somebody who is quite prominent in the media says the only basis upon which I could possibly have supported Obama was because he was black and I was black even though I laid out my judgment on the candidates, then we still have a problem."[143]

When Powell was a loyal Republican, Limbaugh had nothing but praise for him. In 1997 he said about Powell, "Look at him. He is dignity. He is honor. He's a four-star general. He is a man who is perceived to be the epitome of honor and integrity, and he's a leader."[144] How did Powell go from being the "epitome of honor and integrity" to being a racist? The answer is purely political: Powell endorsed a Democrat, and therefore Limbaugh used the accusation of racism he makes against every nonwhite liberal.

THE ANGRY BLACK MAN

One of most common racial stereotypes in America is that of the angry black man. Even Barack Obama, one of the most even-tempered politicians in recent memory, who has the nickname "No Drama Obama," fell into this racial stereotype in Limbaugh's eyes: "This is an angry man."[145] He called Obama "an angry black guy,"[146] and added, "Let's face it, President Obama is black, and I think he's got a chip on his shoulder,"[147] and, "I think Obama is angry, he's not this cool, calm, collected guy. He's very cold, he's very angry, he's angry at the British over the colonization of Africa, he's angry at Churchill, he's angry at this country for its discrimination and slavery past and so forth, and he doesn't think that the proper price has been paid for it."[148] The idea that Obama is boiling with anger at Winston Churchill and the British over colonizing Africa generations ago is bizarre. What made this accusation so strange was Obama's unusually calm persona. Unlike Bill Clinton, Hillary Clinton, John McCain, and many other politicians who have a legendary angry temper behind closed doors, every insider account of Obama's candidacy noted how calm he always was.[149] As Michael Eric Dyson noted, "To call Barack Obama an angry black man is as ridiculous as calling Rush Limbaugh a first-class intellectual."[150] Yet Limbaugh projected that it was Obama who was angrily obsessed with race: "Almost all of his beliefs are founded in race and anger and racial division."[151]

When Obama criticized police for arresting Harvard professor Henry Louis Gates Jr. in his home, Limbaugh said, "Here you have a black president trying to destroy a white policeman."[152] Invoking another disturbing racial stereotype about black men, Limbaugh said about Obama: "He's like a lot of other dictators. He's got the private sector, and he thinks it's always going to be there to be raped."[153] Limbaugh's vision of Obama as a "dictator" who has "raped" the private sector evokes not only the paranoid imagination of the far right, but also the ancient racist smear that black men are out to rape white women, the property of their men.

LIMBAUGH'S LATINO PROBLEM

Rush's racism goes beyond black people: It is also directed at Latinos. In 2008 the Obama campaign ran Spanish-language commercials declaring that "John McCain and his Republican friends have two faces" based on quotes from "El Rushbo" about Mexicans. Obama was widely attacked for running a false ad because Limbaugh and McCain had a long-running hatred. But Rush was particularly offended by the accusations that he was anti-Mexican and accused Obama of "prejudice" and using "the tactics of the old segregationists."[154] Limbaugh asserted that his words were taken out of context. That may have been true for a "Shut up, or get out!" quote from 2006, where he was pointing out the restrictions of Mexican immigration law (albeit while arguing for similar restrictions in American law).[155] But it was the other quote, about "stupid and unskilled Mexicans," that drew Limbaugh's ire and his assertion that it was "a 1993 humorous monologue poking fun at the arguments against the North American Free Trade Agreement."[156] According to the radio host, "A caller called here and was giving me grief for not wanting to do what it took to protect American jobs, and so I said to him, 'If you are unskilled and uneducated, your job is going south. Skilled workers, educated people are going to do fine 'cause those are the kinds of jobs NAFTA is going to create. If we are going to start rewarding no skills and stupid people, I'm serious, let the unskilled jobs that take absolutely no knowledge whatsoever to do—let stupid and unskilled Mexicans do that work.' "[157]

Limbaugh argued, "My point, which is obvious, was that the people who were criticizing NAFTA were demeaning workers, particularly low-skilled workers. I was criticizing the mind-set of the protectionists who opposed the treaty."[158] But not very many humorous monologues include the reassurance, "I'm serious." And he himself declared ABC News reporter Jake Tapper "dead right" in his summary of Limbaugh's argument: "His larger point was that NAFTA would mean that unskilled stupid Mexicans would be doing the jobs of unskilled stupid Americans."[159] If Tapper was "dead right," then Limbaugh wasn't mocking those who demeaned unskilled workers, he was agreeing with them. Rush's implication was that Mexico was filled with these stupid, unskilled workers, and therefore

NAFTA would pose no threat to all the skilled, intelligent workers in America. He may not have been calling every single Mexican "stupid and unskilled," but he certainly was indicating that a lot of them were.

In other comments, Limbaugh has expressed contempt for Mexicans and Latinos. Early in his radio career, he explained why a Mexican won the New York marathon: "An immigration agent chased him for the last 10 miles."[160] Rush referred to a former boyfriend of Madonna as "some gang-member type guy" because he was Latino, even though he had no connections to gangs.[161] In 2004 Limbaugh declared, "there's some little strife going on in Venezuela with that wacko, César Chávez, down there. Hugo. Hugo, César—whatever. A Chávez is a Chávez. We've always had problems with them."[162]

In 2005 Limbaugh compared Mexican illegal immigrants to an "invasive species."[163] In 2006 he described them as "a renegade, potential criminal element that was poor and unwilling to work."[164] He admitted in 2008 that when Bill Clinton introduced him to Los Angeles mayor Antonio Villaraigosa at a high-priced New York restaurant, he thought at first he was "maybe a shoeshine guy."[165] It's difficult to believe that if Limbaugh had been introduced by a former president to a white man in a suit at a place that serves $295 steaks, he would have thought he was a shoeshine guy.

However, when a Republican Latino is involved, Limbaugh is quick to play the race card. He declared in 2007: "So you have the first Hispanic American attorney general—a minority—under fire by white liberal racists in the Senate. I guarantee you that—and he's not the first, by the way. We'll never forget what happened to Miguel Estrada. And that was just—wife ended up committing suicide over what they did to him. It was horrible."[166] Bush's attorney general, Alberto Gonzales, was criticized for his incompetence, not his race. Estrada (whose appointment as an appellate judge was never approved by the Democrats) was a victim of politics, not racism—unless Limbaugh believes that opposing any minority's appointment is racist. And Estrada's wife apparently died of an accidental overdose, but Limbaugh's sudden sensitivity to suicide victims is remarkable considering his jokes about Vince Foster's death.

SOTOMAYOR, THE SUPREME COURT "RACIST"

Rush Limbaugh declared about Supreme Court Justice Sonia Sotomayor immediately after her nomination in 2009, "She's a bigot. She's a racist."[167] He reiterated his point repeatedly: "She is a racist, and she would bring racism and bigotry to the court."[168] Sotomayor is not the first Supreme Court justice denounced as a racist by Limbaugh. He called Sandra Day O'Connor a "racist" for upholding affirmative action programs.[169] Rush asserted that Obama "chose her because she is a reflection, she reflects his racial attitudes."[170]

But it's Limbaugh who had the odd racial attitudes about the Sotomayor nomination. When Obama urged the approval of Sotomayor to the Supreme Court so she could "start providing justice," Limbaugh called this "street talk. This is the talk of somebody angry."[171] Since when is speaking of "justice" considered "street talk" and "angry"? After all, the Founding Fathers made the title of the position Supreme Court *justice,* and the Founding Fathers were not usually accused of "street talk." If this had been a white president appointing a white nominee, would anyone equate "justice" with "street talk"?

Limbaugh claimed, "She ruled on the basis of just a racist belief that minorities should always be found in favor of simply because they're minorities, pure and simple, regardless the merits of any particular case."[172] In reality, Sotomayor often ruled against minorities making discrimination claims.

But as Limbaugh put it, "A racist is a racist!" and he claimed he was correct because "nobody has said, 'No, she's not a racist.'"[173] This only proves how little attention Limbaugh pays to anyone but himself. His claim was dismissed as ridiculous, and not one Republican official was willing to follow Limbaugh in his bizarre assertions.

Limbaugh even compared Sotomayor to David Duke, the famous Ku Klux Klan leader and Republican political candidate.[174] And Limbaugh cited Sotomayor's Wikipedia page as evidence of her racial obsession: "Her Wikipedia entry mentions 'Latino' 30 times, 'Hispanic' 17 times, 'Puerto Rican' 24 times. She's fixated on being Latino or Hispanic, she's fixated on it."[175] Perhaps Limbaugh was unaware that people do not write their own Wikipedia pages. He certainly is unaware that talking about race and racism in America is not the same as a fixation.

Limbaugh claimed about Sotomayor, "She was taught that white males destroyed this country, this continent. That's what she was taught. That's what all people are taught today, multicultural curriculum."[176] This makes no sense. Sotomayor was then fifty-five, only a few years younger than Limbaugh himself. She went to Catholic school in the 1960s, and then to Princeton in the early 1970s, when it admitted few women or Latinos. Limbaugh has probably never stepped foot on Princeton's campus, let alone studied the history of its curriculum. And his accusation, while laughable historically, is equally nonsensical when it comes to today's schools. There's probably not one school in America where children are taught that "white males destroyed this country, this continent." What does that even mean?

After a caller who was a classmate of Sotomayor's confirmed that they read the classics in high school, Limbaugh complained about his own education: "I'm seventeen and eighteen and we were reading *Beowulf*. I hated it. But we had to read this stuff. The idea that a New York high school was not teaching that stuff, and a little high school in Cape Girardeau, Missouri, had it on its curriculum is just a little hard to believe. But we have the answer now, Anastasia has confirmed they didn't teach Marx and Hegel."[177] It's unclear what Beowulf has to do with Marx, or why Limbaugh imagines (incorrectly) that students across the country are being assigned Hegelian philosophical tracts.

Limbaugh claimed about Sotomayor, "She has been overturned 80 percent by the Supreme Court."[178] In reality, three of her opinions (60 percent) were overruled by the Supreme Court, and this is nothing unusual. In 2005–2006, the Supreme Court overturned 73.6 percent of the cases it ruled on, and it's not surprising that an activist conservative court overruling liberal precedents would overturn a liberal judge who is following those precedents.[179] Yet Limbaugh declared, "The only people overturned more than Sotomayor is the Ninth Circus [*sic*] Court of Appeals in San Francisco."[180] There's not the slightest evidence that Sotomayor is the second-most overturned judge in the country. Even if this false statement were true, it wouldn't mean anything. The current activist conservative Supreme Court is most likely to reverse liberal judges when it overturns precedent. But when a judge who is reversed less frequently than the average is condemned as the second-worst in the country, it shows Limbaugh's indifference to the facts.

Not content with distorting Judge Sotomayor's record, Limbaugh even condemned her because "there's not a whole lot of humility here."[181] Humility is not usually a qualification for the Supreme Court. And Rush Limbaugh criticizing someone for a lack of humility is like Charles Manson calling somebody crazy.

In his introduction to Mark Levin's book *Men in Black,* "El Rushbo" wrote: "Increasingly, liberals are also denying the president his judicial appointment power by blocking his well-qualified appointments purely for political reasons."[182] Yet he did not hesitate to oppose an Obama Supreme Court nominee for political reasons, even though she had better qualifications than any of Bush's Supreme Court nominees. Instead, Limbaugh said about Sotomayor, "She is an affirmative action case extraordinaire."[183]

When Rush condemned Sonia Sotomayor as a "racist," he declared, "None of us get a do-over."[184] Limbaugh doesn't deserve a "do-over" for his past racist comments. He also deserves no apologists because he refuses to retract any of his bigoted statements.

DEFENDING THE CAUCASIANS

Limbaugh believes whites are a dispossessed minority fighting against oppression. Responding to a caller in 2009 who wondered "when will Caucasians become the minority," he didn't challenge her racism but instead shared her concerns about the declining power of the white race: "The problem is that you've got people running the show now from Obama all the way down through his administration through the House of Representatives who, regardless of their race, are racists." In that same show, Limbaugh asserted that blacks are already controlling America: "When I say does it really matter when Caucasians become a minority, what I mean by this is we already have a governing majority. He's gonna treat them that way. It's reverse racism."[185] The facts are contrary to Limbaugh's belief that we have a nonwhite, reverse-racist governing majority in America. In Congress, 95 out of 100 senators are white, and 362 out of 435 representatives (83.2 percent) are white.[186] Only the worst of the white supremacists imagine that America is controlled by nonwhites. Sadly, Limbaugh seems to be one of them.

When the leading conservative commentator in the country makes openly racist (and obviously false) attacks on a black candidate, without any protests or serious media coverage, it shows how far America still has to go in achieving racial equality. Yet Limbaugh imagined himself as the opponent of viewing everything through a racial prism: "I have had it with race baiters. In twenty-one years I have had my fill of it, and I rarely have my fill of anything, but I have had my fill of this, this race crap."[187]

After seeing a video of two black kids on a school bus beating up a white student in a case that police said had nothing to do with race, Limbaugh said: "It's Obama's America, is it not? Obama's America—white kids getting beat up on school buses now. I mean, you put your kids on a school bus, you expect safety, but in Obama's America, the white kids now get beat up, with the black kids cheering."[188] Limbaugh mockingly proposed segregated buses to protect blacks from racist white kids. As Stephen Colbert observed, "Sadly, anytime a racist criticizes the president, someone cries 'racist.' "[189]

Suddenly the country's whitest talk show host proclaimed himself the arbiter of blackness: "Obama is not black to me." Yet the very same day, he wondered: "Can this nation really have an African American president? . . . Or does having an African American president paralyze the process by which people with that kind of power in our representative republic are kept, quote, unquote, honest?"[190]

Only Limbaugh could question whether America would be destroyed by having a black president. And while he denounced Obama's race, he complained: "Every bit of criticism of Obama is now labeled racism."[191] In Rush's eyes, his regular invocation of racist views is entirely rational, and any criticism of it is race baiting. By crying racism against his critics, he was desperately trying to hide his own troubling racial views. Limbaugh is increasingly willing to spout openly racist views due to his hatred for an African American president.

2

BITCHES, BUTT BOYS, AND FEMINAZIS: LIMBAUGH'S SEXISM AND HOMOPHOBIA

Rush Limbaugh is a sexist pig, and he's proud of his misogyny. One of his most famous statements is "Feminism was established so that unattractive women could have easier access to the mainstream of society."[1] Limbaugh said that feminism was represented by a "frumpy-looking woman who has been discriminated against because she is unattractive and hasn't found a decent guy to marry."[2]

Limbaugh believes that feminism is a vast liberal conspiracy to spread conflict between men and women and therefore create liberal policies: "Feminism is a way to get men and women arguing with one another about things and get them distracted . . . Sponsoring hate, promoting hate, is an exclusive of the left. They own it. They thrive on the promotion of hate and angst and contempt and unrest and chaos. It is the only way to distract people sufficiently so that the left can accomplish its statist objectives."[3] It's typical of Limbaugh that not only are his conspiracy theories wrong, but they don't make any sense. The idea that feminists promote equality for all as part of a conspiracy with liberals to distract people from their secret policies requires complete ignorance of history.

Limbaugh sometimes does defend women, if they are conservative. He complained about the media treatment of Sarah Palin and declared, "Nobody should be attacked because they're a woman."[4] Nobody, that is, unless it's a liberal woman. Limbaugh has joked that to keep the birth rate down, "simply put pictures of Nancy Pelosi . . . in every cheap motel room."[5] He said that late Texas governor Ann Richards "was born needing her face ironed" and compared Hillary Clinton to a Pontiac hood ornament.[6]

HATING HILLARY

Limbaugh despises no woman more than Hillary Clinton. When she laughs, he invariably describes it as a "cackle."[7] He even bragged about his insults: "You know that cackle that she has, we named that cackle."[8] He declared that Hillary Clinton "sounds like a screeching ex-wife,"[9] and said about her voice: "Oh, gosh, that hurts, my friends. It reminds me of my first wife. Ah! Gee! It is just painful to hear this, and then she starts yelling everywhere."[10] To Limbaugh, Hillary is "like everybody's third and fourth ex-wife,"[11] and he referred to her as "the B-I-itch."[12]

Apparently obsessed with Hillary Clinton's physical appearance, he wondered, "Will this country want to actually watch a woman get older before their eyes on a daily basis?"[13] Limbaugh said that she would lose in a general election because she's too ugly: "Let me give you a picture, just to think about . . . the campaign is Mitt Romney vs. Hillary Clinton in our quest in this country for visual perfection, hmm?"[14]

When Limbaugh wanted to insult Hillary Clinton, he accused her of being mannish. Limbaugh said about her in 2005, "She puts her pants on one leg at a time like every other guy,"[15] and earlier wondered, "I mean, where are the real men in the Democratic Party? Where are the real men? Hillary Clinton's one of them, but where are the others?"[16]

Rush also tried to insult Obama's manliness by comparing him to Clinton: "He's just a man, puts his pants on one leg at a time like Hillary does."[17] Limbaugh declared about Clinton: "The scary thing is she's twice the man Obama is."[18]

Sleazy rumors peddled by Limbaugh pushed the lie that Clinton is a lesbian: "I've got some interesting, juicy details on this book on Hillary by Ed Klein, but I'm not going to be the first to mention them. I'm not going there. It will come out eventually. It has to do with sexual orientation."[19] Then, after spreading these malicious rumors from the book, Limbaugh tried to claim that it was all a conspiracy from the left to discredit critics of Clinton: "If you want to talk about conspiracies, I wouldn't be a bit surprised if this whole thing is a left-wing idea—put the book out there, label it a right-wing hatchet job, and use that to inoculate any information in the book or to inoculate her against any criticism down the road."[20]

When Hillary Clinton got emotional before the New Hampshire primary, Limbaugh saw it as yet another conspiracy: "Emotional blackmail. This is calculated. Make no mistake about it, folks. This is not spontaneous. Because nothing with the Clintons is coincidence."[21]

Limbaugh thinks Hillary Clinton embodies the worst: "I see Nurse Ratched. I—when I see Hillary, I feel like I'm in the insane asylum of a hospital, and she's the nurse."[22] He has said, "She reminds men of the worst characteristics of women they've encountered over their life: totally controlling, not soft and cuddly. Not sympathetic. Not patient. Not understanding. Demanding, domineering, Nurse Ratched kind of thing. Everything you do, you have to do behind her back, that kind of—and then, after all of that, with Mrs. Clinton with this—the characteristics I just described—with the flick of a light switch, all of a sudden, she's a victim of evil men and bad Republicans and she starts crying and she wants sympathy. She's a classic manipulator."[23] Limbaugh can't deal with women in a professional role. Women, in his mind, are supposed to be "soft and cuddly" while running for president. And if they're not, they're a "domineering Nurse Ratched" from *One Flew Over the Cuckoo's Nest.*[24]

PELOSI, THE AIRHEAD

Limbaugh's sexist obsessions have also focused on Nancy Pelosi. The day after Pelosi became Speaker of the House, he declared about a Democratic congressman, "Heath Shuler, not the sharpest knife in the drawer to begin with, I have a story in which he says his two-year-old daughter, who he named Island, his two-year-old daughter is inspired by Nancy Pelosi's ascension to the speakership. . . . But a two-year-old being inspired, 'Daddy!' Do two-year-olds talk? Tell me. Do they know the word 'inspire'? They don't know the word 'inspire,' do they? 'Daddy, daddy, Mrs. Pelosi, she inspires me. I want to be just like Miss Pelosi, Dad.' "[25]

This entire story appears to be invented by Rush. The eight stories linked on his Web site for this segment don't include anything about Shuler, and according to one book account of the event, "Heath Shuler, the new congressman from North Carolina, was pleased that his daughter Island, two, was sitting in his lap. She was too young to understand the significance of Pelosi's ascent, he knew, but later she might take pleasure from knowing she had been there."[26] So Limbaugh's tale of the inspired talking two-year-old seems to be completely imaginary.

But the bigger issue is what he said about Pelosi during his little fantasy: "Maybe Pelosi breast-fed him, I don't know, when the kid was pregnant. Who knows? She's capable of doing everything else." His official transcript "corrects" what he actually said to say instead, "Maybe Pelosi breast-fed her when the kid was—who knows," fixing Limbaugh's gender error about the child and his bizarre use of the word "pregnant."[27]

Limbaugh was particularly obsessed about his imagined breast-feeding by the sixty-six-year-old grandmother: "Look at Ms. Pelosi. Why, she can multitask. She can breast-feed, she can clip her toenails, she can direct the House, all while the kids are sitting on her lap at the same time."[28] Limbaugh uses standard sexist terms in his attacks on Pelosi: "I wonder when she loses next if she'll go back to the kitchen. What do you wanna bet she hasn't been in the kitchen for a long time anyway?"[29] It's a bit strange for a man with a personal chef to attack the Speaker of the House for not spending enough time in the kitchen. He also criticizes Pelosi's appearance: "She wears Armani clothes—fashionable. Botox shots—fashionable."[30]

Limbaugh denounces Pelosi as a "ditz" and a "complete airhead."[31] Of course, he routinely insults the intelligence of Democrats. But it is certainly no coincidence when Limbaugh uses a sexist term like "ditz" to describe the highest-ranking woman in American political history. He also described former Kansas governor Kathleen Sebelius, the secretary of Health and Human Services, as a "ditz."[32] Every woman is just one ideological disagreement with Limbaugh away from being condemned as "ugly," "ditz," "bitch," or "feminazi." It's how he views all women, except those who prove their devotion to him by being docile, conservative housewives admired as subservient sex objects. Does he oppose Pelosi solely because she is a woman? No, he opposes her because she's a Democrat. But the manner in which he opposes her is sexist.

THE CHICKIFICATION OF THE MEDIA

Although Limbaugh's most vicious comments about women's looks are directed at liberals, his sexism affects how he sees every woman. Female journalists on TV are invariably described as "anchorettes" or "info babes."[33] In 1994 he warned the House Republican majority to be wary of the siren call of the dangerous "female reporter" with her sexual wiles: "Some female reporter will come up to one of you and start batting her eyes and ask you to go to lunch. And you'll think: 'Wow! I'm only a freshman. Cokie Roberts wants to take me to lunch!' Don't fall for this."[34]

In 2007 Limbaugh lamented "the fact that newsrooms—local and national newsrooms in television—have been overrun with women" and denounced the "'chickification' of the news."[35] He has complained that "the chickification of the news in this country from local to national newsrooms and networks has been accomplished. They're all over the place. . . . We've got anchorettes. We've got info babes. They're all over cable news. In fact, most of them are blonde. Where does this supply come from? There's an endless supply of them out there. One blonde goes, another blonde comes in."[36]

Limbaugh blames "the chickification of news" on "the chicks in high positions in the media."[37] He even saw this "chickification" in the coverage of South Carolina governor Mark Sanford and his love letters to his mistress in Argentina. Rush bizarrely claimed (without any evidence to support him) that "news chicks across this country are now swooning."[38]

Limbaugh is particularly insulting toward female journalists, saying at one point, "I'm making a supreme effort to ingratiate myself to the babes, but I'm sorry, ladies. The female reporters I've seen so far that are getting a chance to ask Obama a question are embarrassing. 'Thank you, Mr. President, for calling on me. Thank you, Mr. President. You're wonderful. Thank you so much for calling on me.' "[39] Rush offered no evidence, and he even blamed "the feminization of the country" for reporters of all genders not asking Obama enough critical questions.[40] It's true that reporters do not ask enough tough questions of presidents, whether it's Obama or Bush. But it has absolutely nothing to do with gender. Limbaugh sees feminist conspiracies everywhere, even complaining that "advertising agencies are polluted with little feminists" who funnel advertising revenue to CNN.[41] Limbaugh even insults entire networks as too feminine; he always refers to MSNBC as "PMSNBC," believing that comparing anything to a woman's ailment is the worst possible insult.

CONSERVATIVE SEXISM

Limbaugh's sexism extends to conservative women, too. He initially dismissed Sarah Palin as "some babe McCain met at a convention."[42] Rush quickly began to admire her, but never without first mentioning her physical appearance: "We're the ones that have the babe on the ticket."[43] He noted Palin's positive values: "She can wear skirts, she's got nice-looking ankles, and I'm not trying to be funny. This irritates the American left; it irritates the media."[44] No one was irritated by Palin's skirts, although Rush may have been the only one turned on by her ankles. Limbaugh's first comment about Palin came when she was a long-shot vice-presidential possibility promoted by a caller: "Plus she's a housewife, before that, she's a babe. I saw a picture."[45] Palin wasn't a housewife. She had worked as a sports reporter, mayor, and was governor of Alaska when Limbaugh made his comment. But to him, a traditional subservient woman is so desirable that he imagined Palin fit that stereotype.

He also carries his sexist attitude toward women into his personal life. One associate said about Limbaugh's second wife, Michelle Sixta, "She totally subordinated her interests to his. Her role in life was to say, 'Yes, Rush.' "[46] In Limbaugh's eyes, women just need a man to cure them of their liberal delusions: "I don't even know that I accept the premise that all women are miserable. I think liberal women probably are miserable. The ones that have men are not miserable."[47]

Limbaugh's view of women is perhaps best expressed by this anecdote he told about his cat: "My cat comes to me when she wants to be fed. I have learned this. I accept it for what it is. Many people in my position would think my cat's coming to me because she loves me. Well, she likes me, and she is attached, but she comes to me when she wants to be fed. And after I feed her—guess what—she's off to wherever she wants to be in the house, until the next time she gets hungry. She's smart enough to know she can't feed herself. She's actually a very smart cat. She gets loved. She gets adoration. She gets petted. She gets fed. And she doesn't have to do anything for it, which is why I say this cat's taught me more about women, than anything my whole life. But we put voices in their mouths."[48] It's no surprise that Limbaugh loves his cat, and has been divorced three times. He wants a pet, not a wife; he wants adoration, not someone with a voice.

Limbaugh believes that he loves women, so long as they are beautiful and subservient. When women display any independent thinking, or the slightest signs of liberalism, he turns his sexist rhetoric against them with great passion.

FEARING WOMEN

Rush Limbaugh is particularly fearful of women controlling men. He wrote, "Militant feminists are pro-choice because it's their ultimate avenue of power over men. . . . It is their attempt to impose their will on the rest of society, particularly on men."[49] Only Limbaugh could imagine that supporting the right of women to control their own bodies is intended solely to exert power over men. That's because he doesn't regard women as independent human beings; he treats them as helpers to men, and attacks them whenever they create a different role for themselves. Women, to Limbaugh, are purely irrational and emotional: "I read a story the other day that a lot of women in the country, they're just feeling, and they're not—They don't even know what they're feeling, they're just feeling. . . ."[50] The irony is that Limbaugh's sexism is itself an irrational and emotional hatred rather than anything based in evidence or logic.

His ineptitude at dating may help explain why Limbaugh harbors a long-standing resentment toward women, such as his complaint that "nice guys never get laid."[51] His mother has famously recounted how Rush never dated in high school. But Limbaugh's hatred toward women reflects much more than simply a shy, bitter man who had trouble getting dates.

Rush Limbaugh sees sexual harassment as just a joke. He once declared that he had a sign on his office door that read, SEXUAL HARASSMENT AT THIS WORK STATION WILL NOT BE REPORTED. HOWEVER . . . IT WILL BE GRADED!!![52] Limbaugh even claimed that women desire sexual harassment:

"Some of these babes, I'm telling you, like the sexual harassment crowd. They're out there protesting what they actually wish would happen to them sometimes."[53] He said that some women "would love to be hired as eye candy."[54] Limbaugh declared about Anita Hill, "My guess is she's had plenty of spankings, if you catch my meaning."[55] Everyone got his meaning. Accusing women of being whores is the ancient response of men when they are caught mistreating women.

Rush even compared criticism of him from feminists to the genocidal murders in Bosnia, accusing feminists of "political cleansing": "It's just like this ethnic cleansing in Bosnia. They're trying to wipe out and shut up all the opposition."[56] As with his comparison of feminists to Nazis, Limbaugh's belief that critiques of his sexism are the equivalent of genocide reveals a sickening dismissal of mass murder.

To Limbaugh, women are a mix of sexual mystery and erotic danger; they are fundamentally irrational and unfathomable: "I'm a normal, red-blooded American guy. I love women; I'm intrigued by all of them. I try to figure them out, even though it's not possible. They'll never even figure themselves out."[57] He claimed, "I love women,"[58] or, as he also put it, "I love the women's movement. Especially when I am walking behind it."[59] But Limbaugh views women as power-hungry bitches, defined by their physical measurements, who want to control men by having abortions and stealing their money.

Limbaugh's sexism includes joking about rape. He once played video from a rape trial, laughing and saying, "I'm trying not to laugh" as a traumatized woman detailed anal rape.[60] He uses "rape" as a political term. When Maryland passed a law requiring large employers to provide health insurance, he called it "government-sanctioned rape of an American business."[61] He also complained, "I'm tired of colleges that turn out female graduates that are prepared to be raped or beat up or discriminated against somehow, and are just waiting for some man to discriminate, take advantage, or be cruel, unkind, or whatever."[62] It's sickening for someone to imagine that women are "prepared to be raped" by getting a higher education. But he routinely trivializes rape. When violence was threatened against Democratic women, Limbaugh sympathized with the criminals. Discussing a man who made death threats to Nancy Pelosi, he declared: "Do you people in the White House, do you people in the media, do you ever stop to consider that you have an intelligent, informed electorate who simply doesn't like being raped, and being raped is what is happening to people in this country by their government. No other way to put this."[63] To call America's moderate levels of taxation and regulation the equivalent of rape is an insult both to common sense and to women victimized by rape. To use it to defend death threats against female Democratic leaders is nothing but disgusting.

SMEARING CHELSEA CLINTON

Limbaugh is fond of denouncing others for the very same offenses he commits. He attacked David Letterman for making a joke about Alex Rodriguez getting Sarah Palin's daughter pregnant, declaring, "The joke's inappropriate whether the age of the woman is fourteen, eighteen, or forty. . . . A joke like that about any woman is just in bad taste and it's not funny." He claimed, "Shows like that are beneath me."[64]

Limbaugh declared about Letterman's joke, "It was not decent. It was not something that very many people would say in public, period. But the double standard clearly exists, and it always will." According to Limbaugh, unlike Palin's daughter, "Chelsea Clinton was off-limits all during the Clinton presidency and the Drive-Bys bent over forward, grabbed the ankles, said, 'Okay Clinton, whatever you want.'"[65] He contended that the media "left Chelsea Clinton alone."[66] Rush was wrong; there was media attention to Chelsea's boyfriends during the Clinton administration, but since Chelsea never got pregnant, it never became a major story.[67] But there was one member of the media who never left Chelsea alone: Limbaugh.

On November 6, 1992, Rush said on his television show: "In: A cute kid in the White House. Out: Cute dog in the White House. Could—could we see the cute kid? Let's take a look at—see who is the cute kid in the White House. [A picture is shown of Millie the dog] No, no, no. That's not the kid. [Picture shown of Chelsea Clinton] That's—that's the kid. We're trying to . . . [Applause] No, just kidding."[68]

According to one defense of Limbaugh, "The real version has Rush talking about a 'cute dog' as well as a 'cute kid,' obviously not a set-up for calling the kid a dog. It is not an assault on Chelsea, as her picture only comes up in the context of correcting the error. . . . Rush has always maintained the incident was an accident."[69]

The "cute kid" reference was nothing but an excuse to compare Chelsea to a dog. If Limbaugh had not intended to show Chelsea's picture, he would never have said, "Just kidding." There was no mistake, and his fake apology was just another excuse to show the picture over and over again: "There I go. My friends, I apologize again. I—that's the third time the crew makes a mistake by showing you Millie the dog when I intended to show you Chelsea Clinton."[70]

This wasn't the first time Limbaugh tried to hide behind a technician to excuse his hateful comments toward women. A *USA Today* reporter at Limbaugh's radio studio two weeks earlier noted that while playing the song "Men" for his Feminist Update, "Limbaugh's technicians, at his command, punctuate the song with a sounds of cows mooing. Every time the cows moo, Limbaugh orders 'Men' stopped. 'Don't do that!' Stop. The music starts again. More moos. Stop! Music. ('Throw another one in there!' he says off mike, chuckling)."[71] So Limbaugh had a documented record of ordering his staff to compare women to animals and then pretending that the technicians were violating his commands.

Nor was this the first daughter of a president that Limbaugh had insulted, since he had also called Amy Carter ugly.[72] Continuing his tradition of insulting the daughters of Democratic presidents, in 2010 Limbaugh referred to Malia and Sasha Obama as the president's "two fat daughters" and falsely claimed that the First Lady had called them fat.[73]

Limbaugh is indifferent to his own hypocrisy; he is happy to denounce a comedian for joking about the daughter of a conservative politician while ignoring his far more hateful comments about the daughter of a liberal politician. He said about Sarah Palin's daughter, "It is just despicable, what we have become in this country, to destroy a seventeen-year-old girl in the hopes of destroying her mother and her father."[74] Apparently that same logic didn't apply to the thirteen-year-old daughter of a Democratic president.

Limbaugh continued to smear Chelsea Clinton after she became an adult. In 2009 he claimed: "Chelsea Clinton said it was Bush's tax cuts that led to 9/11. She did."[75] No, she didn't. Chelsea Clinton wrote an article for *Talk Magazine* explaining what she was doing in lower Manhattan when 9/11 happened: "I was expounding on the detriments of Bush's tax cut as we approached Grand Central Terminal and were met with hordes of people running out of the station. . . . Once we stopped running, I started praying. I prayed for my country and my city. I stopped berating the tax cut and started praying that the president would rise to lead us."[76]

So Chelsea Clinton never blamed 9/11 on the Bush tax cuts; she happened to be criticizing the Bush tax cuts when 9/11 happened, and then promptly stopped doing it to unify with the rest of the country behind Bush. Yet Limbaugh, the man who compared Chelsea at thirteen to a dog and then lied about what she wrote in 2001, had the audacity to claim, "Chelsea has had a charmed life in terms of not having to deal with any kind of press that is especially critical or probing."[77]

HATING WOMEN

Although Mr. Limbaugh has claimed, "I revere women. I respect women,"[78] his idea of reverence and respect is rather unusual, considering such statements as "We're in bad shape in this country when you can't look at a couple of huge knockers and notice it."[79] He reveres women's "huge knockers" rather than their brains. Early in his talk show career, Limbaugh called the National Organization for Women (NOW) "a terrorist organization" and described two members of the group on the air as "ugly dogs."[80] Rush often judges women by their appearance; his nickname for Senator Mary Landrieu (D-LA) is "Cute Little Baby Fat."[81]

Limbaugh would play the 1966 song "Born a Woman": "A woman's place in this old world / Is under some man's thumb / And if you're born a woman / You're born to be hurt" and then yell, "She said hurt, not heard."[82] His idea of a joke is shouting that women should be "hurt, not heard," and he has justified his sexism by claiming women like his style of abuse: "We're not sexists, we're chauvinists—we're male chauvinist pigs, and we're happy to be because we think that's what men were destined to be. We think that's what women want."[83] It's more accurate to say that Limbaugh is doing what men want. According to a Pew Research Center study, 72 percent of his listeners are men.[84]

Pandering to his demographics, Limbaugh regularly calls the National Organization for Women (NOW) the National Association of Gals (NAGs).

He has complained about "a core of angry, bitter, anti-male women hell-bent on 'Get-even-ism' "[85] and claimed that "militant women" are "upset with their God-given role in human nature."[86]

Yet Rush defends himself against charges of sexism with tokenism: "This notion that people like me and you have some fear or bias against women—I would have voted for Margaret Thatcher every chance I had, had I been a Brit. I would have voted for Jeane Kirkpatrick for president had she sought the office. We all have tremendous respect for Golda Meir, who ran Israel for awhile."[87] This is Limbaugh's tired old excuse, that some of his best political friends are women. The fact that he would support a handful of right-wing women for election doesn't mitigate his sexism; the point is that he invokes sexist attacks against liberal women, even if he admires a few conservative women. Limbaugh is suspicious of women until they prove their conservative credentials.

He also fears women taking power in any field: "What I mean by the feminization of America is that feminist doctrine of the modern era, which has its roots in the late sixties and early seventies, has cowed men. Men now have linguine spines, and women and the way they think and do things, pretty much taking over, or is making inroads in a lot places, particularly in education, all the way up to higher education." Limbaugh uses the term "slaveowner and husband" to describe "wife and husband."[88] In 2006 he called Friends of the Earth international climate campaigner Catherine Pearce a "B-I-itch" after watching her criticize President Bush's State of the Union proposals on CNN.[89]

THE RISE OF FEMINAZIS

Nothing irritates Rush Limbaugh more than being called a sexist: "Name-calling becomes a substitute for meaningful debate of the issues and it works quite well in the political arena. That is unfortunate, because the name-calling, while it may have a chilling effect on the genuine discussion of issues, does nothing to satisfy the millions of people who share the views of those who are the targets of those insults."[90]

This opposition to name calling is strange for a man who may be most famous for popularizing the word "feminazi." For decades Limbaugh has been using the term, without apology, to smear the feminist movement. He wrote in his first book, "A feminazi is a feminist to whom the most important thing in life is ensuring that as many abortions as possible occur. There are fewer than twenty-five known feminazis in the United States."[91] The comparison of feminists fighting for gender equality to the most brutal and murderous regime in human history should shock everyone. But he delights in repeating the word over and over again. Media Matters for America found that during a six-week period in 2005, Limbaugh used the term eight times.[92]

Limbaugh has repeatedly asserted that he has been misquoted and was only describing a "few" feminists as feminazis. He told *Playboy*, "I have been misstated, misrepresented, misreported on this. A feminazi is not a feminist."[93] He told Barbara Walters, "No, I never did call feminists feminazis. There are a select few feminists who I call feminazis, and you have to really work hard to earn your way into the feminazi status. You know what a feminazi really is is a woman who is so consumed with the advancement of the feminist agenda that she gets mad when a woman who's pregnant, who was going to have an abortion, is talked out of it; and women who think that, for example, all sex is rape, even the sex in marriage."[94]

In reality, Limbaugh used that definition of feminazis to define all feminists: "Do you think looking at someone is sexual harassment? Do you think all men are rapists? Do you think all sex is rape? If your answer to any or all of these questions is no, you are simply not, by definition, a feminist."[95] Considering that it would be almost impossible to find anyone who agrees with any of these statements, he is trying to define an entire movement by a grotesque exaggeration of its most extreme advocates.

He claimed in 1992, "A feminazi is a woman who gets mad when a woman decides to have a baby, is talked out of having an abortion."[96] There are no feminists who get mad when a woman decides to have a baby; Limbaugh's entire definition of feminazi is a complete fabrication about the feminist movement.

The claim that Rush is only insulting twenty-five feminists is absurd, since he argues that "they drive the movement."[97] Rush must believe that the leaders of the feminist movement are secret radicals who have fooled the millions of feminists who agree with them. When he complains that he's been misquoted about feminazis, he is being disingenuous. In fact, Limbaugh has said exactly what he's been accused of. When asked in 1995 about the term "feminazi," he declared: "It's the way I look at the feminist movement."[98] Limbaugh referred to the National Center for Women and Policing and the Feminist Majority Foundation as "feminazis."[99] So it's not just twenty-five individuals, but every single feminist organization, its leaders, and millions upon millions of Americans with the same views whom Limbaugh compares to Nazis.

In 2004 Limbaugh named "Gloria Steinem, Susan Sarandon, Christine Lahti, and Camryn Manheim" as "famous feminazis."[100] He never explained why he thinks these activists and actresses are opposed to women having babies. Limbaugh has never, in his twenty-five-year career on talk radio, offered any evidence of a single person who fits his definition of a "feminazi": "The definition and real agenda of the feminazi: radical feminists whose objective is to see that there are as many abortions as possible."[101] By this definition, there are literally no feminazis.

And Limbaugh's claim that he's always used a very narrow definition of feminazi is belied by his proposal for "feminazi trading cards": "On the front, an action shot of a leading feminist burning a bra, dominating a TV show, picketing an all-men's club. On the back, all the vital statistics: waist, hips, the documented age, the number of abortions and, where applicable, the alimony payments and divorce settlements."[102] His imagined feminazi trading cards would feature Anita Hill, Gloria Steinem, Molly Yard, Eleanor Smeal, Bella Abzug, Judge Susan Hoerchner, and Betty Friedan.[103] None of these feminists fit Limbaugh's claim that "feminazis" are only people who want as many abortions as possible. The inclusion of Anita Hill on Limbaugh's feminazi list is notable, since Hill's accusation of sexual harassment against U.S. Supreme Court Justice Clarence Thomas never raised the issue of abortion.

Perhaps the clearest evidence of the radio host's extraordinarily broad definition of "feminazi" came in 2007. When Debra Dickerson wrote a Salon .com article about Michelle Obama quitting her job to campaign full-time for her husband, he declared, "That's truly bitter. These are angry women. I'm telling you, these militant feminazis are angry."[104] But Dickerson's article never mentioned abortion at all.[105] Dickerson merely expressed a common feminist concern that a politician's wife was expected to give up her professional career. Worrying about gender equality, Limbaugh claimed, makes you one of the "militant feminazis."

In 2010 Limbaugh turned his incisive analysis to a march by topless women in Portland, Oregon: "I've been wondering, you know, how long are the feminazis going to take to get to this?"[106] So now women without shirts are "feminazis"—because nothing embodies the genocide and terror of Hitler's Germany more than bare breasts.

Responding to a caller who called him a Nazi for endorsing torture, Limbaugh declared: "You call me a Nazi, you call me somebody who supports torture, and you want credibility on this program? You know, you're just plain embarrassing and ludicrous."[107] He's got a point. People who foolishly toss around the term "Nazi" over policy disagreements are embarrassing, ludicrous, and lacking in credibility—as he is when he calls feminists feminazis.

THE CALLER ABORTION

One of Rush's earliest DJ ploys to gain attention by offending listeners was the "caller abortion," using the sound effects of a vacuum cleaner and a scream. He explained, "The shit that hit the fan over that feature was unlike anything I've ever done."[108] He has stopped doing caller abortions, but abortion remains an obsession of his. However, Limbaugh never expresses a concern about fetuses; instead, he worries that abortion is used to make feminism powerful.

Limbaugh thinks that liberals love abortion: "The last place you want to be is between a—a liberal woman and her morning-after pill."[109] According to Limbaugh, "You put up an adoption center next to an abortion clinic and what will happen is the Planned Parenthood people come out and try to keep every pregnant woman possible from going into the adoption center."[110] There are no lines of pro-abortion activists surrounding adoption clinics to try to force women to get abortions. It's another Rush fantasy.

For him, it's a common delusion. Limbaugh has said, "If the Democrats and their ideology reigned supreme in biblical days, since Mary's was an unwanted pregnancy, they would probably be demanding that she have an abortion."[111] It's obscene to imagine that pro-choice advocates have ever "demanded" that anyone have an abortion. Abortion, to Limbaugh, is part of a grand feminist plot to get rid of men: "Abortion is the single greatest avenue for militant women to exercise their quest for power and advance their belief that men aren't necessary. . . . Feminazis have adopted abortion as a kind of sacrament for their religion/politics of alienation and bitterness."[112] He argues that abortion gives feminists "their ultimate avenue to power over men."[113]

It may seem ridiculous to imagine that giving women control over their own bodies is a secret plot to control men. But Limbaugh sees it in even more ominous terms: "Margaret Sanger's Planned Parenthood is no different than any of the people that use concentration camps, mass gassings, so-called ethnic cleansings."[114] "Feminazi" to Rush is not an exaggerated comparison; he literally believes that feminists who support the right to choose are the equivalent of Nazis engaging in mass murder at concentration camps.

BUTT BOYS AND ANAL POISONING: LIMBAUGH'S HOMOPHOBIA

There's no doubt about it: Rush Limbaugh is an ass man. No other leading talk show host is quite so obsessed with rear ends, especially those of powerful men. While recording an episode of *The Family Guy* in 2009, Limbaugh reported: "I said, 'Hey, why don't you take a picture of my butt?' so I bent over and grabbed the ankles and said, 'Take a picture of my butt.' "[115] Limbaugh's strange fetishes about "anal poisoning" and being "bent over" for sexual domination reflect the depth of his homophobia.

Early in his career, he was particularly outspoken in his hatred of gays and lesbians. He referred to gay men as "faggots" and "perverts." He created a "Gerbil Update" segment to promote the legend that gay men use animals for sexual pleasure.[116] In his 1993 book Limbaugh wrote about homosexuality, "Surely no one can argue that it is healthy to encourage such a lifestyle."[117] He called AIDS Rock Hudson's disease until his station managers objected.[118] In 1995 Limbaugh complained that AIDS "is the only federally protected virus. It does have civil rights."[119] For his "AIDS Update," he played Dionne Warwick's "I'll Never Love This Way Again" or "Back in the Saddle Again" by Gene Autry.

Later Limbaugh said, "It's the single most regretful thing I've ever done."[120] But though Rush may have regretted mocking people dying of AIDS, he continues to denounce homosexuals and mock liberals in homophobic terms.

One of Limbaugh's most disturbing ideas is his belief that homosexuals recruit children. He told *Playboy*, "I do think that if you get hold of people young enough and attempt to sway them, that homosexuality can be steered into them."[121]

Limbaugh mocked the use of condoms by having "safe talk" with a condom over his microphone.[122] To a caller who merely said that condoms help stop the spread of AIDS, Limbaugh flatly declared, "You're wrong. There is no other side. There is no disagreement."[123] He even claimed, "Mass condom distribution is a disservice and borders on being lethal."[124]

Many of his "jokes" are full of homophobic fears of gay men, such as "When a gay person turns his back on you, it is anything but an insult; it's an invitation." He has also joked, "I seldom bend over forward in public, for obvious reasons."[125] The obvious reason would be that Limbaugh is a homophobe.

He has a particular obsession with what he calls "anal poisoning," which is Rush's peculiar verbal invention. Denouncing British Prime Minister Gordon Brown's "slobbering" over Obama, Limbaugh declared Brown would "come down with anal poisoning and may die from it." Democratic honcho Terry McAuliffe, Limbaugh warned, "will die of anal poisoning because he is so close to drilling Hillary." He also said that Senator Lindsey Graham "is certainly close enough to [McCain] to die of anal poisoning."[126]

A variation of this anal attack is Rush's frequent use of the term "butt boy." He said about NBC reporter Andrea Mitchell "she does come off like a 'butt boy,'" and also referred to Ed Henry of CNN as a "butt boy."[127] But Limbaugh's favorite butt reference is the classic "bend over, grab the ankles" to describe the experience of being screwed over by a dominant force. In 2008 he declared about the Democratic leaders in Congress, "Dingy Harry and Pelosi [are] bending over and grabbing the ankles at every MoveOn.org meeting or at every Daily Kos convention."[128]

Limbaugh particularly loves to "grab the ankles" for any gay-related topic. In the 1990s, when New York City mayor David Dinkins was caught up in a dispute between gay activists and the black mayor of Denver, Limbaugh declared: "And the question is should he bend over forward and grab the ankles for this narrow special interest group or should he remain in solidarity with his black bro?" When Republican National Committee chairman Ken Mehlman sought African American votes, Limbaugh announced, "Republicans are going to go bend over and grab the ankles." He accused Democrats of submitting to black and gay voters: "Democrats will bend over, grab the ankles, and say, 'Have your way with me,' for 10 percent and 2 percent of the population?"[129]

THE TESTICLE LOCKBOX

In addition to his anal obsession, Rush Limbaugh gives tremendous attention to testicles. Reading a story about prosthetic testicles for dogs, he suggested that feminists and their "male companions" might want to get them.[130] He repeatedly talks about the "testicle lockbox," especially when discussing Hillary Clinton.[131] Limbaugh declared, "Mrs. Clinton's testicle lockbox is big enough for the entire Democrat hierarchy, not just some people in the media. And whether they have been taking steroids and the testicles are smaller than usual doesn't matter. Her lockbox, her testicle lockbox can handle everybody in the Democrat hierarchy."[132]

Limbaugh thinks women (especially liberal women) are castrating bitches. The "testicle lockbox" is his favored metaphor for describing women politicians who cut off men's balls and capture them. Limbaugh's castration fantasy is meant to insult both women (genital-chopping Amazons) and men (castrated eunuchs) who commit the crime of being liberal.

Even when defending himself against accusations of sexism, Limbaugh unintentionally reveals how much he hates women: "I have no fear of women. In Hillary's case, I have huge fear of her policies, and her utter, total demand to control as much of American life as possible based on those policies. . . . To the extent that I believe that the testicle lockbox exists in a figurative sense, look at whose testicles get snared in that box. Not mine. And nobody on my side. Well, there might be some elected Republicans afraid of her. But it's lib testicles that get ensnared in the testicle lockbox. . . . It's you libs that have checked your testicles at the door, and put them in the lockbox."[133] Limbaugh is proud to wave his testicles around.

He, of course, is a man, and so he would never fear women and their testicle-locking wiles.

On the other side of Limbaugh's "testicle lockbox" being held by controlling bitches is the emasculated, castrated liberal man, the "new castrati." While women get uniformly dismissed as "ugly" or treated as sex objects by Limbaugh, liberal men are attacked for lacking masculinity. When discussing liberal ideas, Rush often puts a gay lisp in his voice to represent "the voice of the New Castrati, by the way, guys who have lost their guts."[134] He has said, "What's happening in our culture is that men are being neutered."[135]

Limbaugh regularly depicts liberal straight men as gay. For instance, he declared: "Rahm Emanuel is the power behind the throne—and don't let his effeminate nature and his ballerina past mislead you on this. He may look effeminate (he was a ballerina at one time) but he has the feral instincts of a female rat defending its young. Well, take a look. When Emanuel and Carville and Begala are together (and I've seen pictures) it looks like a reunion of the Village People."[136]

In 2004 Limbaugh mocked Democratic presidential nominee John Kerry and John Edwards and claimed that they were gay lovers: "OK, Johns, why don't you finish. Just, you know, stop play-acting, stop pretending, stop the little rump pats, stop with the tousled hair. Let's see the kiss. Let's see the smooch. You're putting your hands on his face. He's putting his hands on your face. You're cupping each other. Well, let—let's just—let's just—let's cement this."[137]

Limbaugh likes to taunt liberal men and insult their masculinity. In 2004 he again insulted John Kerry by saying, "He's basically a skirt-chaser, folks. He's a gigolo. He has not been somebody that a lot of people have taken seriously."[138] Several days later he said, "John Kerry's daddy is his wives, I mean, he's a gigolo. Everybody knows this."[139]

Rush regularly called John Edwards "the Breck Girl" (mocking his supposed obsession with his hair) and played a parody of Helen Reddy's song "I Am Woman" as a tribute to Edwards. Limbaugh claimed, "John Edwards was going to be the first female president," and declared, "Well, now Mrs. Edwards has confirmed it today. Elizabeth Edwards has said Hillary is just—she's—well, let me get it up here. I don't want to paraphrase this because it's too important. Hillary is behaving like a man, unlike her husband.

So vindication, ladies and gentlemen."[140] What Elizabeth Edwards said was too important to paraphrase, so instead the "Maha Rushie" made it up completely. Edwards actually said about Clinton, "I'm not convinced she'd be as good an advocate for women" as her husband.[141]

Limbaugh played the song "Sisters are Doin' It For Themselves" during updates on John Edwards, and he speculated on who would design his "inaugural gown."[142] To Rush, the best way to insult a liberal man is to compare him to a woman. The best way to insult a liberal woman is to compare her to a man. And the best way to insult all Democrats is to question their sexuality, such as when Limbaugh joked that the delegates to the Democratic National Convention were all "lesbian, gay, bisexual, transgender."[143]

Surprisingly, Limbaugh's misogyny is one of the few areas where he's bipartisan. When Edwards cheated on his wife, Rush defended his adultery because Elizabeth Edwards talks too much: "Edwards might be attracted to a woman whose mouth did something other than talk."[144] Limbaugh thinks women exist to give men blow jobs, not to speak their minds.

As much as Limbaugh hates women, he is equally derisive toward men he thinks are too feminine (that is, liberal). He attacked a Supreme Court justice with this insult: "David Souter's a girl. Everybody knows that."[145] Limbaugh accused Obama of "basically having no gonads"[146] and declared, "It's time to take the skirt off Obama and time to put a pair of slacks on him."[147] Limbaugh even said that Obama's first pitch before the 2009 All-Star game was "a girly toss" and added, "That's how girls throw." He also said, "He golfs like a girl," and then called him "a big athletic klutz."[148] Obama is the most athletic president in history, but to Rush, every liberal must be denounced as effeminate.

Limbaugh smeared Jack Carter, son of former president Jimmy Carter, by calling him a "classic example of the castrati, the new castrati. Jack Carter is—has been castrated by the feminization of this culture since he grew up."[149] Limbaugh's castration anxiety is so severe that he warned, "If we need to save our penises from anybody, it's Obama," because the Centers for Disease Control might encourage circumcision of baby boys as a way to reduce the transmission of HIV.[150] In 2009 Limbaugh claimed, "The administration said that they were going to have mandatory circumcision in this country as one of the tools to fight HIV."[151] Of course, he was wrong.

While Limbaugh worries that Obama will cut off his penis, he regards every male conservative as a manly man. When conservative Democrat Zell Miller spoke at the Republican National Convention in 2004, he was instantly raised to "manly" status by Limbaugh: "I tell you who else going to be on fire last night—American women. Because American women did not see a girly man, did not see some guy out there trying to finesse things. They saw a guy. They saw a man be a man, talking about manly things, defending the country, defending family."[152]

By contrast, the self-proclaimed "Doctor of Democracy" has said that liberal pundits Michael Kinsley and Al Hunt were not "real men."[153] He likes to refer to the "long-haired, maggot-infested, dope-smoking peace pansies."[154] Limbaugh has argued that women taking birth control pills has caused men to become less masculine: "Look at the Hollywood stars today, they're a bunch of girlie wusses, and it's the pill that makes women like girlie men."[155]

Limbaugh claimed about liberals and the Mark Foley scandal: "In their hearts and minds and their crotches, they don't have any problem with what Foley did. They've defended it over the—over the years."[156] Rush doesn't give any examples of liberals defending anyone who abused his position as Foley did, but by referring to their "crotches," he is trying to imply that liberals are secretly gay and that all gay men are pedophiles.

When a liberal is also gay, Limbaugh becomes particularly crude. He denounced Representative Barney Frank as "the banking queen" because he's gay, complete with a parody song of that title.[157] Limbaugh has also played the song "My Boy Lollipop" for his Barney Frank update. According to Limbaugh, "Isn't it an established fact that Barney Frank himself spends most of his time living around Uranus?" Later he added, "He occupies Uranus."[158] He has described his line "Barney freely cavorts around Uranus" as "a great and funny line!"[159] Rush's intellectual and comedic level would be dismissed as too juvenile by a third-grader, yet his crude homophobic jokes appeal to his conservative, homophobic, predominantly male audience. For Limbaugh, homophobia isn't just a lot of fun; it's also good business to appeal to the baser instincts of his conservative audience.

While Limbaugh hates gay men and the "castrati" with a passion, he shows remarkable support for certain kinds of homosexuality. Limbaugh compared the photos from Abu Ghraib to "pictures of homoeroticism that looks like standard, good old American pornography." He must like watching some weird porn. He claimed, "I thought we were supposed to love homo-erotic things. I thought we were supposed to be open-minded and tolerant to homoerotic things."[160] Yes, we are, Rush. And if a bunch of Muslim men wanted to get together in a sweaty, naked pile of flesh, I'd fully support their right to do that, albeit perhaps not with Limbaugh's remarkable enthusiasm for the assembly. Apparently he doesn't understand the concept of sexual consent. After all, photos of rape probably look like some kinds of pornography to him, but that doesn't change the fact that a crime has been committed. In Rush's mind, the fact that these were prisoners forced to commit sexual acts for the sadistic pleasure of guards makes absolutely no difference. If anything, he objects to homoeroticism far more than he opposes the sexual abuse of prisoners.

"You can see these pictures on American Web sites, where they win awards," he claimed. "These kinds of pictures with these kinds of acts depicted. They win awards. They are considered progressive." Nothing about the Abu Ghraib photos would be considered progressive or award-winning. But Limbaugh called the Abu Ghraib photos "a brilliant maneuver, no different than what happens at the Skull and Bones initiation at Yale." He later defended himself by saying about his critics, "They don't get the joke."[161] What's so funny about torture? For him, anything liberals object to is a good reason for a joke. Conservative Republicans such as George W. Bush were appalled by the Abu Ghraib photos and recognized the serious damage done to American foreign policy. But Limbaugh stood so far on the right wing of his party that he remained oblivious to the harm caused by Abu Ghraib, and celebrated it instead.

Limbaugh has an obsession with homosexuality. He wrote in 1992, "The *New York Times* estimated that 30 percent to 40 percent of NOW's membership is lesbian or bisexual."[162] The *New York Times* rarely goes around estimating the gay percentage of national organizations. But even if this bizarre "fact" were true, what exactly is its relevance? Why does Limbaugh condemn an organization for having gay members?

In an attack on Kevin Jennings, who works in the Office of Safe and Drug-Free Schools in Obama's U.S. Department of Education, Limbaugh falsely claimed that Jennings "was actually in charge of a curriculum that taught various techniques of homosexual sex, including fisting."[163] Jennings ran an organization that held a conference at which, during one session, Massachusetts state officials openly answered questions about sexuality from teen activists. But in Limbaugh's twisted world, Jennings is "a raging pervert who taught fisting."[164]

Meanwhile, Limbaugh defended harassment of gay students, claiming that they are "trumpeting" their sexuality and "inviting dissent."[165] In response to a conservative teacher who called in worried about her gay students who face vilification, he declared, "How do we know who's gay and who's straight unless somebody's out there making a big case about it . . . I think some of the militants in the gay community are actually asking for this fight, because they want to be confrontational."[166] In the perverse world of Rush Limbaugh, gay students flaunt their homosexuality because they're militants who *want* to get beat up and harassed by homophobes.

Limbaugh no longer calls gay men faggots on the air as he once did.[167] But he remains an unrepentant homophobe, deliberately mocking gay men and lesbians for their sexual orientation and attacking all liberals as gay and feminine. His hatred of gays and lesbians, and his vile language about women, are all part of his fears that liberals are gaining power.

3

BASHING OBAMA: WHY LIMBAUGH
HATES THE PRESIDENT

THE MAN RUSH LIMBAUGH hates more than anybody else in the world is
Barack Obama. He even made the astonishing claim that "Barack Obama
has the inside track on becoming the worst president in the nation's history."[1] Limbaugh hates all liberals, but he hates Obama with a particular
passion. The reason is simple: Obama is a successful liberal, someone widely
admired by the American people and capable of speaking in eloquent words
about the importance of liberal values. Limbaugh hates Obama so much that
he even recorded two public service announcements for the Humane Society
of the United States after the organization criticized Obama's selection of a
purebred dog.[2]

The radio host's initial reaction to Obama's presidential candidacy was
to give him the nickname "Barack Hussein Odumbo" (in reference to Obama's
"big ears").[3] As he put it, "I make fun of his ears, I make fun of his speech
pattern."[4] He also routinely referred to him as "Osama Obama," based on a
slip of the tongue by Senator Edward Kennedy.[5]

But Limbaugh paid little attention to Obama during the primaries, preferring to attack front-runner Hillary Clinton and to search for a viable conservative in the Republican primary. However, once John McCain became the
Republican nominee and Obama took a surprising lead on the Democratic
side, Limbaugh quickly began his campaign against Obama.

OPERATION CHAOS

As it became clear in the spring of 2008 that Barack Obama would win the Democratic nomination, Limbaugh hit upon what he thought was a brilliant innovation: Convince Republicans to cross over and vote in the Democratic primary for Hillary Clinton in order to extend the Democratic race and divide the party. He called it Operation Chaos. Ultimately, Operation Chaos was an act of egotism: Limbaugh wanted to prove that he has the power to control his listeners and influence an election.

Limbaugh decided in an interview with Laura Ingraham, "We need Barack Obama bloodied up politically." In that same interview he was explicitly partisan about Operation Chaos: "I want our party to win. I want the Democrats to lose. They're in the midst of tearing themselves apart right now. It is fascinating to watch. And it's all going to stop if Hillary loses. So, yeah, I'm asking people to cross over and—if they can stomach it. I know it's a difficult thing to do, to vote for a Clinton. But it will sustain this soap opera, and it's something I think we need."[6]

Operation Chaos never had a large impact on the voting, but even swaying the results by a few percentage points affected the Democratic primary. Obama campaign manager David Plouffe later noted, "If Rush Limbaugh had not encouraged Republicans to vote in the Indiana primary for Hillary as a way of extending our race, we would have won outright. . . . Over 12 percent of the Indiana primary vote was Republican and Hillary carried it, despite her through-the-roof unfavorable numbers with these voters. Limbaugh's project worked in Indiana—it cost us that victory."[7] Approximately 5 percent of the Indiana electorate in the Democratic primary consisted of Republicans who supported Clinton as part of Operation Chaos, which easily accounted for her twenty-three-thousand-vote margin.[8] But in Pennsylvania, where Operation Chaos operatives had to change parties for the closed primary, the Limbaugh effect probably amounted to only 1 percent of voters.[9]

Still, Limbaugh proved that he has the power to influence elections. In the early voting during January and February 2008, an average of 3.8 percent of the voters in the Democratic primary were Republicans, and they strongly supported Obama. But for the March primaries after Rush launched Operation Chaos, in Texas, Ohio, and Mississippi, Republicans were 8 percent of the voters in the Democratic primary, and they heavily favored Hillary Clinton.[10]

Limbaugh said, "Folks, can we agree, just between us . . . has it not been brilliant how I have strategically inserted myself into this campaign . . . ?"[11] In reality, his intervention in the 2008 campaign was a disaster for Republicans from start to finish. By pressing McCain to shift to the right, the Republicans lost what little hope they had of swaying moderates and winning the election.

Operation Chaos was a tactical success and a strategic failure. Limbaugh succeeded at getting Republicans to vote for Hillary Clinton, succeeded in making the Democratic race slightly closer, and perhaps even succeeded in convincing Clinton to stay in the race until after the last primary. The strategic problem for Rush was that the lengthy primary season didn't hurt Obama, it helped him. The media attention was inevitably focused on Obama, and it allowed the American people to become more familiar with a relatively unknown political figure.

Limbaugh actually dreamed of having riots at the 2008 Democratic National Convention: "It's called Operation Chaos. The dream end, I mean, if people say what is your exit strate . . . strategery, the dream end of this is that if this keeps up to the convention, and we have a replay of Chicago 1968, with burning cars, protests, fires, literal riots, and all of that, that's the objective here." That same day he called for "riots in Denver, the Democrat Convention would see to it that we don't elect Democrats."[12] This prompted Denver councilman Charles Brown, a Republican, to say: "For any radio announcer to wish a riot on a city so his party could win, that's disgraceful and it's absurd."[13] Limbaugh's fantasies about his attempts to divide Democrats leading to people being beaten on the streets of Denver never came to fruition despite his best efforts. He also claimed, "Phase three of Operation Chaos makes it quite possible that my operatives will determine your nominee. It's quite possible I will be choosing the Democrat nominee with operatives inside the Democrat National Convention, covert operatives."[14] No such operatives ever appeared.

OPERATION REPUBLICAN CHAOS

For Limbaugh, Operation Chaos was a distraction from the real chaos go-
ing on within the Republican Party. He could not bring himself to praise
John McCain, and, rather than face the internal divisions of the Republican
Party, he chose to try to create some within the Democratic Party.

Rush later explained, "I came up with Operation Chaos because we
were facing a Republican primary that was over, with most of my audience
dissatisfied with the choice. My audience wasn't up. Excited. Jazzed. I figured
we had many more months of the liberal media salivating over the Democratic primaries on the cable networks and that that could be divisive. I don't
want Obama to be President, he would be a disaster, but I do want him to be
bloodied up politically, be forced to acquit himself to a political audience
that isn't sycophantic. Someone had to do it."[15]

Operation Chaos wasn't the radio host's first effort to intervene in the
2008 primaries. He earlier made an all-out effort to spread chaos in the Republican primary, to mobilize his supporters behind Mitt Romney in hopes
of stopping John McCain's easy victory over the other Republicans. But
Limbaugh was too slow, and McCain's unstoppable Straight Talk Express
caught him by surprise.

In the lead up to the primary, Limbaugh denounced not only McCain
but, oddly enough, the conservative Mike Huckabee, a favorite of the religious right in Limbaugh's audience: "I'm here to tell you, if either of these
two guys get the nomination, it's going to destroy the Republican Party. It's
going to change it forever, be the end of it."[16] There was no real ideological
reason for Limbaugh to attack Huckabee. Instead, his opposition was tactical. He understood that the conservative bloc had to unify in order to defeat
McCain, and Mitt Romney was the candidate best positioned, thanks to his
personal wealth, to compete against McCain.

One unintended effect of Operation Chaos was that it handed Democrats a sixty-seat majority in the Senate. In Pennsylvania the primaries are
closed to independents and members of the other party, so Limbaugh encouraged his listeners to change parties: "They've registered as Democrats.
So this is all good. This is all good."[17] A year later, Republican senator Arlen
Specter was facing a tough primary. When he decided to become a Democrat,

he noted that it was because he was struggling in the polls (which included Limbaugh's Republicans, because that's how they still identify themselves), and added: "Last year, more than 200,000 Republicans in Pennsylvania changed their registration to become Democrats."[18] Operation Chaos helped fool Specter into thinking that all of the moderate Republicans were converting to the Democratic Party, when some of those numbers reflected Limbaugh listeners. And because Specter changed parties, the Democrats were able to pass health care reform.

Beyond generating chaos within the Democratic Party, Rush had another motive for his operation. By showing a serious flaw in the open primary system, he was hoping to push for closed primaries in the Republican Party. He believed that open primaries had resulted in McCain's selection as the presidential nominee, and he was right: Independents voting in the Republican primary were crucial to McCain's victory in New Hampshire, which revived his candidacy.

Operation Chaos was a failure in every political sense, but a victory for Limbaugh's ratings and the media attention he received. In the end, Democrats united behind Obama, despite all of Limbaugh's efforts to drive them apart.

THE LIMBAUGH SMEAR CAMPAIGN

With Operation Chaos failing, Rush took direct aim at Obama in a classic smear campaign. Limbaugh repeatedly claimed that Obama "voted three times to allow doctors to kill a baby after it's born because the mother wanted an abortion."[19] But there was never any vote to allow "infanticide" as Limbaugh imagined, and it was always illegal in Illinois.[20]

Other attacks were equally fictional. Limbaugh said, "We have uncovered—we have dug deep and we have found something Obama has done. It is called Senate Bill 2433, the Global Poverty Act of 2007. . . . The legislation would commit the United States to spending 0.7 percent of GDP on foreign aid, which amounts to a phenomenal thirteen-year total of $845 billion above what we already spend on foreign aid."[21] Limbaugh not only didn't dig deep, he didn't even bother reading the bill he was talking about.

If he had, he would have discovered that the bill said absolutely nothing about spending 0.7 percent of the GDP, and does not require the United States to spend anything on foreign aid.

Much of what the radio host predicted about Obama's presidency was immediately disproved. For example, Limbaugh declared before the 2008 election, "Obama intends no tax relief for anybody."[22] In reality, Obama quickly fulfilled his campaign promise for tax relief and included a tax cut for most Americans in the stimulus bill passed a month after he took office.

Limbaugh also asserted that Obama "has never held a real job in this country," defining "real job" as "one that requires you to get up every morning, go to work, make a profit for yourself or for your employer." He then added: "He has been paid by foundations and the taxpayer most of his life to promote a socialist agenda that'll destroy everything that you have worked for."[23] In fact, Obama worked for a company after college, and at the law firm of Davis, Miner, Barnhill, and Galland from 1993 to 2002. Obama also worked at the University of Chicago Law School. But Limbaugh's bigger lie is that anyone who works for government or a charity doesn't have a "real" job; he declared that people who work at "nonprofit" groups are "bloodsuckers"[24] and asked, "How much did community organizing pay him? It's whatever you could steal, right?"[25]

As the polls consistently predicted an Obama victory in November 2008, Limbaugh grew more desperate, straining to find every possible attack on Obama, no matter how ridiculous or implausible. Limbaugh claimed that Obama did not have the intellectual capacity to write his own books, and that Bill Ayers wrote them.[26] (Perhaps because Limbaugh didn't write either of his two books, he imagined that Obama must not have done so, either.) There is not even the slightest evidence to support this attack, but Limbaugh contended that Obama's use of the word "ballast" in his books was proof that he didn't write them: "He doesn't talk this way. You know, there are stories out there he may not have written this book." He claimed, "Jack Cashill has compared some of these passages in Obama's book to Bill Ayers, who does write very well. There's no evidence that Obama has ever written anything prior to this except a poem. . . . There's no evidence that he has any kind of—we haven't seen anything that he wrote at Harvard Law, when he was at Columbia, any of the tests that he's written. But if you listen to the—if you read his books, you listen to his audio reading of the book here, you don't hear this when Obama goes out and speaks. I would like for him to be given a test on his own book."[27]

Ayers was a favorite target of Limbaugh's lies about Obama. Long after Obama was president, Rush was continuing to make up stories about Obama and Ayers: "A domestic terrorist, Bill Ayers, is one of his best buddies."[28] Limbaugh is the only major figure in the media who ever described Obama and Ayers's distant relationship as being "best buddies." He claimed, "[This] guy now runs education in Chicago, Bill Ayers."[29] Ayers doesn't run anything in Chicago, except the classes he teaches. He has no control over schools in Chicago or anywhere else. Limbaugh falsely declared, "We all know that Bill Ayers will provide primary advice on education."[30]

In Limbaugh's imagination, Obama didn't write anything in high school, college, or law school, nor did he write his books. Rush has repeatedly said "Obama did not write the book Obama boasts he has written with his own hand. Bill Ayers wasn't just a guy in the neighborhood. This was a significant and easily proven lie—apparently! So this is a fraud, it's a telling and it's an important fraud, and it goes back to the heart of the Obama myth."[31]

This is an "important fraud," but it's Limbaugh's fraud. There is literally no evidence that Ayers wrote Obama's books, and there are numerous essays and speeches that Obama himself has written, in addition to the books Limbaugh calls "alleged autobiographies."[32]

The Tale of the Teleprompter

As columnist Richard Roeper noted, "In a few short months, we've gone from hearing 'Barack Obama is one of the great extemporaneous speakers,' to, 'Obama can't speak without a teleprompter.' "[33] Limbaugh was almost solely responsible for pushing the bizarre idea that Obama is incapable of speaking without a teleprompter.

Little mention was made about Obama's "teleprompter" during the 2008 campaign, when John McCain was notably bad at reading from them, and President George W. Bush used them in every speech. But when Obama became president, Limbaugh instantly seized upon this common piece of technology as if it were a new device Obama had invented on inauguration day. Conservatives began referring to Obama as "TOTUS" (Teleprompter of the United States).[34]

"He's lost without the teleprompter," Rush said,[35] and later, "It's clear he doesn't know what he's doing when he's off that teleprompter."[36] In reality, Obama has spoken without a script to a national audience far more than George W. Bush did. George W. Bush held fifteen press conferences in his first term, about one every hundred days.[37] By contrast, Obama held three prime-time press conferences in his first hundred days in office, exposing his unscripted answers to a vast audience. In addition to his numerous press conferences, Obama did nearly ninety-three interviews in his first six months in office, more than George W. Bush and Bill Clinton combined, and all without a tele-prompter.[38] And Obama held a series of town hall meetings about health care in 2009, speaking without a teleprompter to the American people.

In one of the rare examples in which Limbaugh brought up the issue during the 2008 campaign, he was wrong: "When he—when his tele-prompter breaks down, or when he doesn't have a teleprompter, all this flowery, vapid speech filled with hope—it vanishes. And he reverts into the typical liberal: angry, full of rage, ripping Bush, ripping Rove, ripping Exxon Mobil—every, every standard Democrat talking point."[39] In reality, Obama said the same things in the speech Limbaugh cited that he'd always been saying in his prepared stump speeches.

When Irish prime minister Brian Cowen accidentally read part of Obama's speech off a teleprompter at the White House, Obama was attacked by Lim-baugh for it: "When Obama got there, the teleprompter had then switched back to the Cowen speech. The teleprompter switched back to the Cowen speech while Obama of [sic] his laughing and heading to the podium. So when Obama then reached the podium to try to 'coolly, calmly' save the day, he ended up thanking himself for throwing a huge party because he ended up reading the speech the teleprompter wrote for the Irish prime minister."[40]

Obama did say, "First, I'd like to say thank you to President Obama," but it was a joke. The pool report about the incident noted that, as Toby Harn-den, U.S. editor for the U.K.'s *Telegraph*, observed, Obama was making "a good-natured and well-received joke" at the expense of Cowen. Fox News anchor Bret Baier reported that Obama had "jokingly" made the comment.[41]

But Limbaugh preferred to see Obama's impromptu joke as more evidence that Obama was incapable of thinking without a teleprompter. Rather than admit his error, he simply returned to a common motif: that the mainstream media were concealing the evidence of Obama's "gaffe." Limbaugh declared at the Conservative Political Action Conference (CPAC), "For those of you in the drive-by media watching, I have not needed a teleprompter for anything I've said. . . . Nor do any of us need a teleprompter, because our beliefs are not the result of calculations and contrivances."[42] Yet George W. Bush and Ronald Reagan relied on their teleprompters and speechwriters as much as Barack Obama does.

"I Hope He Fails"

The inauguration of Barack Obama drove Limbaugh further into a fit of anger against him. On January 16, 2009, he told listeners he had been asked by a major publication for a four-hundred-word statement about his hopes for the new administration: "I'm thinking of replying to the guy, 'OK, I'll send you a response, but I don't need four hundred words. I need four: I hope he fails.' "[43] With those four words, Rush summarized his political philosophy and launched an unending assault on Obama that made him the most controversial Republican in the country.

Limbaugh was explicit in declaring that he not only wanted Obama's agenda defeated, he also wanted the country to suffer when Obama's proposals were enacted: "I hope it prolongs the failure. I hope it prolongs the recession. Because people are going to have to figure out here that this is not how economies recover. Government is not the central planner."[44] Yet Limbaugh's declaration "I hope it prolongs the recession" as the definition of failure was ignored by a pileup of apologists trying to defend his comments.

Representative David Vitter (R-LA) said, "I hope Obama fails in advancing leftist policy that I strongly disagree with. I think what Limbaugh was saying was largely what I am saying."[45] Even Senator John McCain, once a nemesis of Limbaugh's, said: "I'm sure when he's saying he wants the president to fail that he's talking about his policies; he made that clear."[46]

In fact, Limbaugh had made it clear that he meant much more. He said: "Of course I want Obama to fail. And after this stimulus bill package passes, I want it to fail."[47] So he defined "fail" not to mean that Obama would fail to get his policies passed, but that once these policies were enacted into law, Limbaugh wanted the economy to become worse. He stated, "Not only do I want Obama to fail, I want this package to fail. I want this to blow up in their face. I want this to be seen by the American people for what it is, nothing to do with getting them jobs, nothing to do with reviving the gross domestic product of this country."[48] The only way the stimulus could "blow up in their face" and prove to everyone that it had nothing to do with reviving the economy was if the recession got much, much worse. Limbaugh was explicit about wanting economic disaster to occur in America: "I want the stimulus package to fail. 'Cause if this thing for the first time ever does what it never has done before, we're in even worse trouble. If it becomes established that the federal government and the federal government alone can manage the economy and take over the private sector, then forget it, folks. I'm looking for property in New Zealand, and I'm going to put my money in Singapore."[49] In Limbaugh's view, if the stimulus package succeeded in ending the recession, the result would be a long-term disaster for America by encouraging more liberal policies.

Yet the radio host turned his misstep into evidence of a vast conspiracy to destroy him. When Harry Reid declared, "Congress will not be sidetracked by those who devise strategies only to trip up progress rather than contribute in good faith. This country has no place for those who hope for failure," Limbaugh responded: "I think he's threatening me, again."[50] Limbaugh publicly announced, over and over again, that he wanted Americans to suffer economic misery to advance his political ideology, and then whined about how victimized he was whenever someone dared to criticize him for it.

A man making $50 million a year who wants his fellow Americans to suffer in poverty isn't exactly a poster child for the oppressed, but in Limbaugh's mind anything is possible. Leading Republicans understood how politically stupid his comment was. Limbaugh said, "Mark Sanford, I mean I've met him, I met him at a wedding in South Carolina and he was very nice. He did say, by the way, he thought it was crazy for me to say I hope Obama fails."[51] When a politician who flies to Argentina to meet his mistress thinks Limbaugh is crazy, it shows how far out of the mainstream his "hope he fails" comment was.

Even televangelist Pat Robertson, the man so crazy he blamed 9/11 on

God's punishment of America for gays and feminists and said the Haiti earthquake was caused by a pact with the devil two centuries ago, denounced Limbaugh as irrational: "That was a terrible thing to say. I mean, he's the president of all the country. If he succeeds, the country succeeds. And if he doesn't, it hurts us all. Anybody who would pull against our president is not exactly thinking rationally."[52]

As the attacks on Limbaugh grew for wishing pain and misery on America for political reasons, he toned down his explicit definitions of "fail" because he recognized how unpopular it was and claimed, "Everybody who heard me say it knew exactly what I meant."[53] But Rush never repudiated what he said. Every time he reiterated his hope that Obama would fail, his most devoted listeners understood that he was dreaming of economic disaster for America.

By October 2009, Limbaugh was desperately trying to rewrite history. He told the *Today* show, "Every one of these 'critics' knew and knows exactly what I meant. They are taking this as yet another opportunity to say, 'Whoa! Limbaugh wants America to fail!' and that's such BS. I want this country to succeed, and it won't happen if he succeeds with his agenda."[54] But his comment—"I hope it prolongs the recession"—revealed his true meaning. Conservative thinkers knew that his new excuse was a deception. Journalist David Frum wrote, "Notice that Limbaugh did not say: 'I hope the administration's liberal plans fail.'"[55]

Back in 1993, Limbaugh had a very different approach to Democratic failure when writing his second book: "I sincerely don't want Bill Clinton to fail, unless failure is defined as the defeat of his current economic policies."[56] Limbaugh never made any similar qualification about Obama. So it's clear that Limbaugh wants far more than the failure of Obama to pass his policies. Limbaugh wants Obama's economic policies to cause financial ruin in America so that liberalism will be discredited.

OPERATION LIMBAUGH

As Limbaugh stepped up his rhetoric against President Obama, the White House spoke against him by name. In January 2009 Obama tried to persuade some House Republicans to support the Democratic stimulus package and told them: "You can't just listen to Rush Limbaugh and get things done."[57] Proving that appeasing their shrinking base of Dittoheads is more important than getting anything done, not one House Republican voted for the stimulus plan.

Call it "Operation Limbaugh." According to Politico.com, "The strategy took shape after Democratic strategists Stanley Greenberg and James Carville included Limbaugh's name in an October poll and learned their long-time tormentor was deeply unpopular with many Americans, especially younger voters."[58] Rahm Emanuel on CBS's *Face the Nation* called Limbaugh "the voice and the intellectual force and energy behind the Republican Party." Carville noted, "His positives for voters under forty was 11 percent," and said: "It's great for us, great for him, great for the press. The only people he's not good for are the actual Republicans in Congress."[59]

"I was named the head of the Republican Party by the White House, by the Obama White House," Limbaugh declared. "What they were trying to do was get Republicans—elected Republicans—to throw me overboard, disavow me. . . . If they could have gotten a couple of Republicans to go out and say, 'Yeah, Limbaugh is off the reservation. He's a nut. He's a wacko,' it would have been a success and a home run."[60]

Sadly, the extent of Limbaugh's influence in the Republican Party is not a myth invented by the Obama administration. The Republican Party has become defined by Rush Limbaugh. In 2009 reporter Howard Fineman went even further in asking, "Why limit it to the Republican Party? You know, he thinks he's a leader of a movement. He thinks he's a leader of the planet."[61]

HATING MICHELLE

Rush Limbaugh seemed particularly offended at the idea of Michelle Obama being First Lady. He claimed during the 2008 campaign, "Michelle Obama called room service and ordered lobster hors d'oeuvres, two whole steamed lobsters, Iranian caviar, and champagne" and then repeated the story, declaring "it's hypocrisy."[62] It was a completely fabricated tale, and the *New York Post* quickly retracted it and apologized for spreading it. Two weeks later, he briefly mentioned that the story was false, without apologizing or mentioning his role in spreading the lie.[63]

Not satisfied with making up only one story, Limbaugh also said there was a video showing Michelle Obama using racial language: "They're waiting to use it in October, of Michelle going nuts in the church, too, talking about 'whitey' this and 'whitey' that."[64] The videotape never surfaced because it didn't exist; Michelle never went "nuts" in a church talking about "whitey," despite Limbaugh's fantastic racial imagination. He never offered an apology or a correction.

Limbaugh has repeatedly claimed about Obama, "He had to get his wife a no-show job at Chicago hospital."[65] He asserted, "Michelle Obama did not have to show up for her hospital job."[66] Michelle Obama always showed up for her job at the University of Chicago Hospitals. There is no evidence, not even an allegation, to support this lie that Limbaugh said over and over again.

In addition to making up stories denigrating her career, Limbaugh also made up quotes to attack her. According to his Web site, Rush claimed about Michelle's trip to Copenhagen to promote the Olympics: "She said, 'It is a sacrifice for her to fly over there and make a pitch for the Olympics, that it is a sacrifice for her husband to fly over there to make a pitch for the Olympics, but that they are doing it for the kids.' While American soldiers are being shot at and dying in Iraq and Afghanistan because of inaction and indecision and probably apathy on the part of President Obama, they have the audacity to say that they are making a huge sacrifice to go to Copenhagen."[67]

In reality, Michelle Obama said nothing like this. She told the people who had been working on the Chicago 2016 Olympic bid committee, "As much of a sacrifice as people say this is for me or Oprah or the president to come for these few days, so many of you in this room have been working for years to bring this bid home."[68] In other words, Michelle was denying that it was a huge sacrifice to go to Copenhagen, the exact opposite of what Limbaugh claimed she said and quoted her as saying.

Limbaugh hates everything about the Obamas, and expresses it openly, even critiquing Michelle Obama's sweaters and accusing the woman widely admired as the most fashionable First Lady in decades of having a "classless wardrobe"—quite a feat for a man whose sole contribution to fashion has consisted of selling loud, overpriced ties designed by one of his former wives.[69]

THE OBAMA PRESIDENCY

Even after Obama became president, Limbaugh continued to repeat lies about him. Limbaugh claimed about the 2008 presidential election, "We would have won this race if we had had a million or three more voters."[70] In reality, Obama beat McCain by 9,522,083 votes. But by lying about the numbers, Limbaugh was trying to minimize the overwhelming majority who voted for Obama.

At the Conservative Political Action Conference in 2009, Limbaugh referred to "the Messiah's house, purchased by Tony Rezko."[71] Rezko, a political fund-raiser later convicted on corruption charges, never purchased Obama's house. In fact, Rezko didn't provide any money at all for Obama's house. Rezko bought a smaller property next to Obama's house, and then sold Obama a small strip of it at a market-rate price. Rezko ultimately turned a profit on his real estate investment.[72]

Claiming that Obama's undergraduate thesis had been discovered, Limbaugh went on a tirade that Obama hated the Constitution: "How many times have you people sent me e-mails, 'Rush, be very careful when you start saying the president of the United States looks at the Constitution as an obstacle'? He doesn't like the Constitution! I've said it over and over again, and now here are his own words."[73] Limbaugh didn't bother to read the original blog, written by a conservative, about Obama's "thesis," or see the "satire" tag on it. The whole thing was fake. When Limbaugh's mistake was quickly discovered, he still claimed to be right: "But we know he thinks it. Good comedy, to be comedy, must contain an element of truth, and we know how he feels about distribution of wealth."[74]

The "Maha Rushie" had to issue another correction the next week. After Fox News Channel falsely reported that Obama had watched a documentary about himself rather than the 2009 election returns, Limbaugh went on a lengthy attack against Obama without bothering to check the story.[75] Even after learning that Obama had already seen the documentary and wasn't watching it on election night, Limbaugh claimed that Obama was so infatuated with himself that he was "watching the rerun, 'Boy, boy, do I look good! Do I look good!' "[76]

For Limbaugh, it doesn't matter what Obama actually says or does; the fictional stories are more true than the truth.

LIMBAUGH AT WAR

As a man who evaded the Vietnam War draft with the help of an anal cyst, Limbaugh is a chickenhawk fond of making hyperbolic attacks on the Obama administration's foreign policy: "We are dangerously close to being at greater risk from a foreign attack than we have ever been."[77] Really? We are at greater risk than before the attack on Pearl Harbor or during the Cuban Missile Crisis or the Cold War?

Limbaugh also questioned Obama's commitment to veterans: "I would ask those of you who have served in the military or are serving in the military, can you name anything—anything Obama has done prior to running for president to show his support for you? . . . Did he speak to veterans groups? Did he do interviews with veteran- and military-related media? Did he visit military hospitals and shake hands with the wounded? No."[78] Obama served on the Senate Committee on Veterans' Affairs throughout his U.S. Senate career, did an interview with the *Military Times* three months before Limbaugh's accusation, and frequently visited troops, including meeting with five hundred soldiers at an American Legion conference in 2005 and visiting soldiers in Iraq and Kuwait in 2006.[79] Beyond being factually wrong, Limbaugh missed the fact that as a senator, Obama had helped pass several bills to aid veterans.[80]

Rush Limbaugh falsely claimed that Obama had not voted to fund troops: "Did he vote to fund the troops? To send them the armor and the bullets and the reinforcement they needed while they were on the battlefield? No . . . He spoke out against it. All of it."[81] In reality, Obama repeatedly voted to provide funds for fighting in Iraq and Afghanistan. Obama made a symbolic vote against one funding bill because it lacked a timetable for withdrawal, but Republicans had also opposed a funding bill because it included a timetable.

Rush particularly likes to push false smears about Democrats; he said, "They will not receive anything from the Democrat Party along the likes of 'Job well done. We're proud of you.' And this is highly distressing. Not only will Democrats not say, nor leftists, say to any returning troops from Iraq, 'Good job. Job well done. We honor your service.' No, they did just the opposite."[82] He was wrong again. Just two days before Limbaugh made this comment, Obama declared during a June 30, 2008, speech in Independence, Missouri: "The sacrifice of our troops is always worthy of honor" and noted, "No one should ever devalue that service, especially for the sake of a political campaign, and that goes for supporters of both sides. We must always express our profound gratitude for the service of our men and women in uniform."[83]

As a senator, Obama said: "We have asked so much of our brave young men and women. We have sent them on tour after tour of duty to Iraq and Afghanistan. They have risked their lives and left their families and served this country brilliantly. It is our moral duty as Americans to serve them as well as they have served us. This GI Bill is an important way to do that."[84] At a May 12, 2008, speech in Charleston, West Virginia, Obama said about American troops, "They deserve our admiration. They deserve our respect. They deserve our enduring gratitude," and added, "The true test of our patriotism is whether we will serve our returning heroes as well as they've served us."[85]

But Limbaugh repeatedly questioned Obama's patriotism: "We've got somebody in office who doesn't like this country."[86] He claims Obama "loathes America. He blames America. America's responsible for all that's wrong in the world."[87] Obama doesn't loathe America, and he's never even remotely blamed America for everything that's wrong in the world.

LIMBAUGH'S TOTALITARIAN FANTASY

Limbaugh has been comparing Obama to dictators from the first moment Obama garnered national publicity. After watching his speech at the 2004 Democratic National Convention, he said about Obama, "He may be Left as Mao Tse-Tung."[88]

Limbaugh has called Obama an "extremist, tyrannical president."[89] When Sean Hannity said socialism was Obama's vision for America, Limbaugh not only agreed but took it even further: "And fascism. We must not be afraid to use that word, either. It's a combination of the two."[90] To display his fearlessness, Rush repeatedly accused Obama of "imposing socialism and fascism"[91] and referred to "Obama's authoritarian fascism."[92] Limbaugh declared, "My use of the word regime is to connote an authoritarian government. And it fits. It is a regime! They're governing against the will of the people, the election be damned." He said, regarding using the term "Obama regime," "I'm thinking of Idi Amin Dada. I'm thinking of Hugo Chávez and Fidel Castro, governing against the will of the people."[93]

Limbaugh's Nazi Fetish

Limbaugh's rhetoric about Obama even reached the point of comparing him to Nazis and Hitler. This sparked criticism of Limbaugh, and his response was to deny that he had said what he had said. Rush complained, "I did not call Obama a Nazi. I called him a fascist. . . . What I did was I compared Obama's health care policies to the Nazis' health care policies. The Nazis did a lot of things besides the Holocaust. The Holocaust was the last thing they did. But stuff leading up to it, I mean Obama coulda written the playbook." He added, "Look at everything that guy did before you get to the Holocaust. You can't ignore just because of the Holocaust anything else he did. You gotta look at the total thing, and it's dangerously similar."[94] In other words, he claimed that Obama was a Nazi in every respect except the Holocaust. The Nazi policies before the Holocaust included dictatorial rule, abolition of habeas corpus and civil liberties, a ban on opposition parties, abolition of state and local government power, and the torture and murder of political prisoners. Nothing about Obama's policies resembles Nazi Germany in any way.

Limbaugh explained, "Now what are the similarities between the Democrat Party of today and the Nazi Party in Germany? Well, the Nazis were against big business. They hated big business and, of course, we all know that they were opposed to Jewish capitalism. They were insanely, irrationally against pollution. They were for two years mandatory voluntary service to Germany. . . . They were against cruelty and vivisection of animals but in the radical sense of devaluing human life, they banned smoking. They were totally against that. They were for abortion and euthanasia of the undesirables as we all know and they were for cradle-to-grave nationalized health care."[95]

With this comment, Limbaugh proved only that he knows nothing about either the Democratic Party (which has never called for banning smoking or "mandatory voluntary service," whatever that is) or Nazi Germany. By smearing the Democrats as anti-Semitic and claiming that "there are gazillions of similarities between National Socialism in Germany and Obama's health care plan," Limbaugh was resorting to the lowest form of argument.[96]

Yet Limbaugh said, "I never called him Hitler."[97] He merely compared Obama to Hitler. Limbaugh claimed, "The Obama health care logo is damn close to a Nazi swastika logo" and "Obama's got a health care logo that's right out of Adolf Hitler's playbook."[98] In reality, the two logos look completely different, with the only similarity being wings, and Limbaugh's comment about Hitler's "playbook" makes no sense.

"It is liberalism that's the closest you can get to Nazism,"[99] Limbaugh proclaimed. And he reserved his most crazed attacks for the president personally, claiming that Obama is "sending out his brownshirts to head up opposition to genuine American citizens" and saying that "Adolf Hitler, like Barack Obama, also ruled by dictate."[100] He also called one of his callers "crazy" for objecting to the comparisons of Obama to Hitler, and then he asked, "Why can we not use Hitler, who was the architect of National Socialism in Germany?"[101]

He repeatedly invoked Nazism: "When you're dealing with a guy like Obama and the Democrat Party, who are going to impose Nazi-like socialism policies on this country, you've got to say it!" Rush also maintained that the Obama White House was "sending out thugs to beat people up" at town meetings.[102]

The Backlash Against Limbaugh's Rhetoric

The Anti-Defamation League issued a statement about Rush Limbaugh from national director Abraham Foxman: "Regardless of the political differences and the substantive differences in the debate over health care, the use of Nazi symbolism is outrageous, offensive, and inappropriate. Americans should be able to disagree on the issues without coloring it with Nazi imagery and comparisons to Hitler. This is not where the debate should be at all. . . . It's off-center, off-issue, and completely inappropriate."[103]

National Review's Cliff May noted, "It is wrong, outrageous, and damaging for Rush Limbaugh to compare Obama to Hitler." Rabbi Marvin Hier, dean and founder of the Simon Wiesenthal Center, called Limbaugh's comments "shameful," "beyond the pale," and "unworthy of Americans."[104]

The American Jewish Congress also condemned him: "The Limbaugh comments comparing Obama (and Pelosi) to Hitler and the Nazis are grossly offensive and intolerable. They reflect a nasty and hyperbolic tendency on our political culture, one which makes reasoned discourse impossible, confuses disagreement with evil, and which makes it impossible to distinguish evil from ordinary politics."[105] Moderate conservative David Brooks said about Limbaugh's Nazi comments, "What he's saying is insane."[106]

Limbaugh defended his Nazi comparisons by claiming, "It was Nancy Pelosi who started it!"[107] and that "Nancy Pelosi called all of you and me and everybody showing up at these town meetings Nazis."[108] The radio host, again, was wrong. Here's what Pelosi said about right-wing protesters: "I think they are Astroturf—you be the judge: They're carrying swastikas and symbols like that to a town meeting on health care."[109] Pelosi was arguing that these protests were "Astroturf," or being manipulated by right-wing organizations to give the appearance of a grassroots movement. Obviously, it would make no sense for a carefully controlled Astroturf protest to include swastikas as if they were endorsing Nazi ideas. So Pelosi wasn't calling these conservatives Nazis; she was complaining that these people were using swastikas to falsely accuse the Democrats of being Nazis.

Of course, Limbaugh has compared liberals to Nazis for many years with little criticism, whether it's "the anti-smoking Nazis" or "environazis" or his legendary term "feminazis."[110] But it's Limbaugh who has the support of today's Nazis. The April 2009 issue of the neo-Nazi National Socialist Movement's *Stormtrooper* e-zine prominently quotes from Limbaugh to denounce Obama and the Democrats.[111]

THE LIMBAUGH MOVEMENT

Limbaugh imagines himself as the leader of a massive anti-Obama movement: "We fear—62 million Americans fear by virtue of those who voted against Obama—we love and we fear the loss of our liberty, the loss of our freedom. We fear a government tyranny. We fear any form of a dictator-ship."[112] Of course, most people who voted against Obama didn't fear him then, and don't fear him now—they simply preferred the other candi-date. Only a tiny fringe joins the Limbaughian despair over the Obama "dictatorship."

Obama was threatening and punishing conservatives, Limbaugh said: "People are so afraid of this guy that everybody shuts up. People are genu-inely afraid of whatever retribution might be heading down the pike."[113] Nowhere does he explain what "retribution" will come from Obama. Con-sidering that there are far more attacks on Obama in the mass media (largely because of right-wing talk shows) than any president in history, it's difficult to believe that anyone is shutting up because of fear.

To Rush, "Obama is the lead thug of the Chicago thugocracy."[114] Lim-baugh said in 2008, "He will drop thirty thug lawyers into Alaska trying to dig up dirt on Sarah Palin. He'll have thug hackers get into her private e-mail account and post whatever they find on the Internet to the glee and satisfaction of the AP."[115] In reality, Obama didn't send any lawyers, thug or otherwise, into Alaska to dig up dirt on Palin. Nor does Obama have any hackers.

Every Obama policy became synonymous with a totalitarian regime. Lim-baugh compared Obama's health care plan not only to Nazi Germany but also to Mussolini's Italy, the Soviet Union, and North Korea.[116] Limbaugh accused Obama of "Mussolini-type stuff,"[117] writing, "His education plan is Maoist (no surprise given the Ayers/Klonsky influence), and he is otherwise a Bolshevik. I'm also quite sure, given his character traits, that he would be a Stalinist if he thought he could get away with it . . . and he's working on that, too."[118] There is nothing Maoist about Obama's education proposals, and nothing "Bolshevik" about Obama, whatever Limbaugh means by that.

When Obama proposed to reduce financial waste and better manage defense procurement, a policy no one could reasonably object to, Limbaugh objected to it as a secret plot to "expand the Barack Obama police state"[119] and claimed, "Obama is asking citizens to rat each other out like Hitler did. Obama's the one that's got the snitch Web site right out of the White House, flag@whitehouse.gov, asking citizens to report people who are saying weird, odd things." He added, "This man who is losing our trust has started an enemies list—essentially, a snitch list."[120]

There was no "snitch" list Web site; it was an e-mail account used to find out about some of the false attacks on health care reform so that they could be refuted. Everywhere Limbaugh looks, he sees a conspiracy leading toward an Obama dictatorship, and every time he does, he is utterly wrong.

Rush proclaimed that any investigation of crimes committed by those in the Bush administration "is Stalinist. If you've ever wondered what the definition of is Stalinist, this would fit it."[121] Actually, this is the exact opposite of Stalinism. Stalinism is about creating a dictatorship run without respect for the rule of law. Investigating the Bush administration (an idea that Obama has largely opposed) would reject that idea entirely. But for Limbaugh, Stalinism (like Nazism) is just another evil term to associate with his political enemies, no matter how ridiculous the comparison. Investigating the lawbreaking of Bush administration officials is, in the mind of Limbaugh, considered the equivalent of a brutal dictatorship responsible for the deaths of millions.

He lamented the fact that his overblown charges were not believed by most Americans: "It's almost like back in the eighties, if you started throwing the word 'communist' around to describe certain Americans, it wouldn't persuade anybody because Americans didn't want to think there were communists running around in the country, with any power. So to say now there are these authoritarians that are out there trying to wrest control."[122]

Limbaugh sees every action, every verbal gaffe as proof of a secret communist conspiracy guiding Obama. During a TV appearance at the baseball All-Star Game in 2009, when Obama made a common Chicago mispronunciation of Comiskey Park as "Cominskey Field," Limbaugh instantly seized upon it as proof of communism: "What used to be 'Cominskey Field.' It's Comiskey Park. There's no 'n' in there, but this guy was brought up by communists, so all these inskys have made an indelible impression on his mind like Saul Alinsky, and so he thinks it's Cominskey Park."[123]

In Limbaugh's eyes, even the word "workers" is part of a communist plot: "'Workers' is a communist word. 'Workers' is a socialist word, it's a Karl Marx word. 'Workers of the world unite.' We don't have workers, we have citizens; we have employees; we have associates. . . . Workers. All this little leftist lingo trickling into our lexicon."[124] When Obama noted an increase in jobs for March 2010 by saying, "This month more Americans woke up, got dressed, and headed to work in an office or factory or storefront," Limbaugh attacked him as a Marxist: "Storefront? Factory? These are all Marxist and Leninist terms. So is 'worker.'"[125] There is nothing Marxist or Leninist about these words at all, unless Limbaugh himself must be a Marxist, since he has used the words *factory, worker,* and *storefront* hundreds of times on his own show.[126]

In reality, the most common term popularized by Marx is Limbaugh's favorite word, "capitalist."[127] Limbaugh associates Obama with everything Russian—even when his history is all wrong. He declared, "If we want to compare Obama to the Russian Revolution, he's got czars! Only the Russians have czars!"[128] Limbaugh apparently hasn't read much history, or he might have recalled that the Russian Revolution overthrew the czars rather than creating them. But he should have recalled the fact that the first American "czar" came during the Reagan administration when the "drug czar" position was anointed. For Limbaugh, no fact (even when it is erroneous) is ignored in the quest to smear Obama as "an authoritarian socialist."[129]

Limbaugh speaks about Obama's "ultimate objective (which is the expansion of federal government, a totalitarian state, or however you want to characterize it)."[130] Any expansion of government regulation or assistance is tantamount to a "totalitarian state." He warned of "Obama camps, reeducation camps"[131] and declared, "We have descended into a nation that loves the concept of soft tyranny."[132] There are no reeducation camps, except in Limbaugh's deluded brain. There is no "soft tyranny," whatever that means.

Smearing the president in the most exaggerated terms possible is a daily event on Limbaugh's show. Rush has openly called Obama a "dictator" and compared him to a "big cockroach."[133] However, Limbaugh's evidence of a dictatorship is comical at best.

Limbaugh slammed Obama as being like Fidel Castro for giving a long speech against torture: "We got Castroed! We got Castroed by Fidel—uh, Barack Obama. . . . I felt like I was watching a Castro speech. It just went on and on and on and on and on and on and on."[134] How long was Obama's "Castro" speech? Fifty minutes.[135] Even a day later, Limbaugh was still referring to "that Castro-like speech that never ended."[136] By contrast, Limbaugh's 2009 speech at CPAC, scheduled to last for thirty minutes, went on for eighty-five minutes.[137] In fact, there is no evidence on record that Barack Obama has ever given a speech in his entire life as long as Rush's CPAC address. Of course, rambling for eighty-five minutes is no sweat to Limbaugh: He routinely speaks that long, uninterrupted except for commercial breaks, on every single show. Yet a fifty-minute speech by the president was too grueling for Limbaugh's limited attention span and worthy of comparison to a dictator.

Running out of actual dictators for his smears, Limbaugh compared Obama to a fictional dictator, 1984's Big Brother: "For those of you who read the book 1984, Big Brother was everywhere no matter where you went. Big Brother was on television, on the radio, didn't matter where you went."[138] Of course, such a comparison is odd coming from someone who is on the media far more than Obama every day, and unlike Obama, Rush has total control over the media airwaves he uses. Yet Limbaugh complains, "He's everywhere. He's Big Brother."[139]

Limbaugh was appalled when a few leftists made ridiculous comparisons of George W. Bush's administration to totalitarianism. But at least those critiques were based on policy. Limbaugh actually called Obama a totalitarian dictator because he was on television communicating with the public—which is exactly what a good president in a democratic society should be doing. But to Limbaugh, everything happening was part of a vast conspiracy: "This is part of the long-term plan. We are being organized to serve Obama."[140]

Taking his hatred to theological heights, Rush even imagines himself as Jesus and Obama as the devil. Limbaugh said, "How do you compromise good versus evil? How do you compromise victory with defeat? As I said last week, should Jesus have made a deal with Lucifer? Should Jesus have made a deal with Satan?"[141]

The list of imagined Obama crimes even includes torture: "Who's going to vote for torture, who's going to vote for tyranny, who's going to vote for dictatorship? But we did. We did. And you see it slowly encroaching."[142] It's no small irony that Limbaugh, an avowed endorser of torture under George W. Bush, describes Obama as committing torture, albeit without bothering to mention who has been tortured. It doesn't matter to Limbaugh that he doesn't have a scintilla of evidence to support his hyperbolic claims of torture, tyranny, and dictatorship by Obama. He doesn't need evidence if he feels it strongly enough.

When Obama ordered the release of Bush administration memos condoning torture, Limbaugh condemned him as a dictator: "This is not American. This is not America. This is not what America does. . . . This is Banana Republic kind of stuff."[143] In the upside-down world of Limbaugh, a secretive government deserves praise (if it's Republican), while a Democratic president who releases information is running a Banana Republic.[144]

The African Dictator

The lies Limbaugh tells about Obama are often tinged with racism. In one of his regular failed attempts at humor, Rush referred to the president as "a well-known Kenyan named Barack Ogabe," comparing him to brutal Zimbabwe dictator Robert Mugabe.[145] This kind of hilarious wordplay is common for Limbaugh, who also referred to Obama as "Barack Peron" to compare him to the late Argentine dictator and called him "Saddam Hussein Obama."[146]

Limbaugh particularly likes calling Obama a third-world dictator to raise the issue of race. In June 2008 he said: "Barack Obama is no different than any other African colonial. Meaning he's a despot." According to Limbaugh, "Barack Obama is nothing more than an old-school African colonial who is on his way to turning this country into one of the developing nations that you learn about on the National Geographic Channel."[147]

Two weeks later, Limbaugh returned to the same attack: "Obama wants to govern like an African colonial."[148] Why would he choose the phrase "African colonial," a term used for foreigners ruling over another people? Limbaugh was suggesting that a black man in charge of a predominantly white country is just like the white men who ruled over black Africans.

At times, Limbaugh has made openly racist attacks like "We've elected somebody who is more African in his roots than he is American."[149] This kind of bigotry plays well with Limbaugh's "birther base" and his xenophobic fans. The old accusation that liberals are un-American gets merged with a new racism toward Obama's African heritage.

Obama's race has motivated Limbaugh's frequent references to slavery: "The man who speaks to you of sacrifice is speaking of slaves and masters and intends to be the master."[150] Perhaps it's just coincidence that Limbaugh invokes the racially charged language of slavery to describe Obama's presidency. But he also said, "I had a dream that I was a slave building a sphinx in a desert that looked like Obama."[151]

Racist wordplay is common on the radio host's show. After mistakenly thinking that New York governor David Paterson would appoint the successor to Representative Eric Massa after his resignation in March 2010, Limbaugh took the opportunity for a race-baiting play on words: "So, David Paterson will become the massa who gets to appoint whoever gets to take Massa's place. So, for the first time in his life, Paterson's gonna be a massa." It's clear that Rush enjoyed using the stereotypical slave's pronunciation of "master" to mock the idea that a black man could be in the position of a "massa."[152]

"Authoritarianism" is another of Limbaugh's favorite terms to describe Obama. In August 2009 Limbaugh said about the health care plan, "We're talking about authoritarian imperialists,"[153] and in the spring of 2009 he said about Obama, "You've got to think in terms of authoritarian tyrants." He also accused Obama of "pure totalitarian politics,"[154] calling him "a guy who is an autocrat, who is an authoritarian."[155]

Obama's black heritage marked him as evil to Limbaugh: "I think he has natural sympathies toward authoritarians. He has sympathy for dictators. He relates to them. He inherited his father's Marxism."[156] Limbaugh never explains how someone could "inherit" Marxism from an absent father he barely knew. Nor does Limbaugh offer any evidence of Obama ever expressing any "sympathies" for authoritarians and dictators.

When the Obama administration updated lighting efficiency standards in June 2009, Limbaugh denounced it as "dictatorial, statist crap coming out of this administration,"[157] saying also, "These people are autocrats" merely because Vice President Joe Biden said the government would try to accelerate the distribution of the stimulus money allocated by Congress.[158]

Although the questionable election of George W. Bush in 2000 was relentlessly defended by Limbaugh, he questioned the legitimacy of the election Obama won by almost 10 million votes: "There's a parallel going on in the world right now to this bunch that's running this country and the parallel is Iran. They supposedly had a fair election. The people of Iran didn't think it was fair. They think it was a fraudulent election and they started protesting in the streets."[159] Limbaugh has stated, "Obama is vote fraud, voter intimidation."[160]

Much of what Limbaugh says about Obama and dictatorship seems merely crazy. But there are more disturbing hints Limbaugh makes about how conservatives should rise up and overthrow a tyrannical leader. He declared, "Before Obama's through, folks, we're all going to have a mug shot one way or the other."[161] It was a typical kind of Limbaugh paranoia: Barack Obama will arrest all the conservatives in the country. Or, he seemed to hint, the patriots would be arrested for taking up arms against the "dictator" in office. Limbaugh is never explicit in urging violent revolution. Instead, he always communicates his message with a wink and a nod.

Speaking about the 2009 military coup in Honduras that overthrew the democratically elected president, Limbaugh noted, "The coup was what many of you wish would happen here."[162] A few days later, he again endorsed the idea of an American military coup against Obama: "If we had any good luck, Honduras would send some people here and help us get our government back."[163] Of course, Limbaugh will never do more than dream about a military coup against President Obama. But the fact that he does dream about a coup, and constantly refers to Obama as a dictator, reflects how far from reality Limbaugh has strayed and how he is encouraging violence by his listeners.

To justify a military coup to overthrow Obama, Limbaugh proclaimed that Obama planned to violate the Constitution and make himself president for life, which was the very same justification for the coup in Honduras: "I think anybody who thinks that he intends to just constitutionally go away in 2016 is nuts. . . . These are people who seek power for reasons other than to serve. They seek to rule."[164] A few days later, Limbaugh repeated the bizarre idea that Obama would simply break the law to stay in power: "I don't know that he would have to change the Constitution to do it," and said about Obama, "His vision is emperor. His vision is all-empowered leader for life."[165]

Limbaugh was endorsing a violent revolution against the Obama administration: "Do you realize, ladies and gentlemen, what we are living through right now is exactly why the Revolutionary War was fought?"[166] Considering how obedient and deranged some of Limbaugh's listeners are, Limbaugh's comments about dictators and coups are not just idle chatter. They're dangerously irresponsible at a time when death threats against the first black president are skyrocketing.

Limbaugh's Obama Conspiracies

Limbaugh regularly fabricates stories to push the idea that the Obama administration is leading a vast government conspiracy. When the Securities and Exchange Commission (SEC) announced a civil suit against Goldman Sachs in 2010, Rush saw an Obama plot: "This whole thing was organized, with Goldman probably involved in it," all agreed to "in exchange for being in bed with the Obama administration." According to Limbaugh, "There aren't any coincidences in politics."[167]

Although Rush has spewed a lot of insane conspiracy theories, this one is over the top even for him. Limbaugh actually believes that Goldman Sachs wanted to be sued by the SEC to help make Obama look good. There's no evidence that Obama had any influence on the SEC decision, and there's certainly no evidence that Goldman Sachs persuaded the SEC to go after them. The proof offered by Limbaugh turned out to be dead wrong: Revealing that the Obama group Organizing for America had purchased an ad to run on Google search results for "Goldman Sachs SEC," Rush concluded: "This plan has been in the works for months is what this means. This has been in the works for months."[168] Unfortunately for Limbaugh, he understands nothing about the Internet: Buying an ad on search engine results doesn't require months of preparation; it was done hours after the SEC investigation had been announced.[169]

Every massive conspiracy imagined by Limbaugh has zero basis in reality. The plots he sees never exist. After racial and sexual insults were yelled at members of Congress during the passage of health care reform, Limbaugh immediately saw a conspiracy: "They wanted to provoke an incident and when it didn't happen, they made it up. This strategy was hatched right along with the signing of the bill."[170] In Limbaugh's view, walking in public on a nice day is a secret plan to "provoke" an incident, and four members of Congress conspired to pretend that they all heard the "n" word.

Mr. Limbaugh even lied about trivial issues concerning Obama. Limbaugh falsely claimed that Obama's first pitch at the 2009 All-Star Game hit the dirt, and then refused to admit his error despite irrefutable video evidence: "We got the story right on the first pitch."[171]

Six months into the Obama presidency, Limbaugh still claimed: "This guy's got a career of 150 days in the Senate and community agitation in Chicago."[172] Obama was a U.S. senator for four years (more than fourteen hundred days), and he spent eight years in the Illinois senate (over twenty-five hundred days), in addition to his work as a community organizer, a lawyer, and a law professor—all of it reflecting far greater accomplishments than George W. Bush or Sarah Palin had before they ran on a presidential ticket. Yet Limbaugh was so convinced of the false "150 days" claim that he repeated it five times. He went even further to compare Obama to terrorists, saying, "If Al-Qaeda wants to demolish the America we know and love, they better hurry, because Obama is beating them to it."[173] Limbaugh believes not only that his political opponents are evil, but also that anyone who supports Obama is deranged: "Being brainwashed or mentally deranged is the only way anyone could possibly think Obama is good for this country."[174]

The only mental derangement in evidence stems from Limbaugh's visceral hatred of Obama. After years of condemning liberals who dared to criticize George W. Bush, Limbaugh sees nothing hypocritical about his crazed attacks on Obama. To Rush, no attack on Obama is too harsh or dishonest.

4

THE LIMBAUGH CONSPIRACIES: KILLER CLINTONS, TREASONOUS DEMOCRATS, AND THE BIRTHERS

Rush LIMBAUGH IS HIS own lunatic fringe, if a man speaking to millions of people every day can be considered part of the fringe. He is one of the biggest promoters of conspiracy theories in the entire mass media, and his influence is particularly pernicious not only because he spreads falsehoods about his political enemies but also because he trains his listeners to become conspiracy thinkers. Conspiracy thinkers tend to view every event through a prism of malign intentions and hidden meanings, and Limbaugh is the master of imagining and explaining such conspiracies.

Yet Limbaugh is rarely identified publicly as a conspiracy theorist. His conspiracy theories are almost always ignored by the press and his sympathizers. Conspiracy theories are one key sign of a failing political ideology, and when crackpots like Limbaugh become the ideological leaders of the conservative movement, it reveals a crisis far deeper than simply being unpopular or marginalized. Limbaugh has helped move conservatism into the shadows of irrational thought.

THE VINCE FOSTER "MURDER"

Limbaugh has been a conspiracy theorist throughout his career, imagining a vast left-wing cabal everywhere he goes. He united with the far-right conspiracy nuts most notably in 1994, when he claimed that the Clintons were involved in a secret murder. In 1993 the deputy White House counsel Vince Foster, a close friend of Hillary Clinton, committed suicide in Virginia's Fort Marcy Park. He was suffering from depression and had been regularly attacked by *The Wall Street Journal* and other conservatives.

On March 10, 1994, Limbaugh announced to his listeners a remarkable secret: "Brace yourselves. This fax contains information that I have just been told will appear in a newsletter to Morgan Stanley sales personnel this afternoon. . . . What it is is a bit of news which says . . . there's a Washington consulting firm that has scheduled the release of a report that will appear, it will be published, that claims that Vince Foster was murdered in an apartment owned by Hillary Clinton, and the body was then taken to Fort Marcy Park." Limbaugh got the allegations in the newsletter wrong, and the story was completely false to begin with. The false story was that Foster's body had been moved; Limbaugh added the even more ludicrous fictions that Foster had been murdered and that Hillary Clinton owned this apartment. After he returned from a commercial break, Limbaugh began referring to the story as a "rumor," but he continued to claim that "the Vince Foster suicide was not a suicide."[1]

When a pediatrician from Memphis called to criticize Limbaugh for spreading false reports about Foster's death, Rush was upset: "One thing I'm not is a rumor-monger." He later went on to imply that the pediatrician had been calling from the "West Wing of the White House" (even though the doctor had also attacked the Clinton health care plan). "I think that what is going to happen during the course of this year," Limbaugh said, "is that a bunch of people are going to call this show that have been given marching orders. . . . What's going to happen is there will be numerous attempts, and they've gone on all the time, to discredit what occurs on this program."[2] It was typical of Limbaugh that when a caller challenged his White House conspiracy theories, Limbaugh assumed the man was part of a White House conspiracy.

Limbaugh believes Foster was a murder victim: "The Vince Foster death—and I say death, not suicide. I'm choosing my word very carefully there. I really think there's something really rotten here."[3] He referred to it as a "crime scene."[4] Fairness and Accuracy in Reporting noted, "On February 3, 1994, he devoted most of a TV show to evidence that Foster was a homicide victim."[5]

Roger Ailes, Limbaugh's friend and TV show producer (and now head of Fox News), celebrated the fact that Christopher Ruddy, one of the leading proponents of the Foster conspiracy theory, "for the first time on *The Rush Limbaugh Show* said that . . . he did not believe it was suicide." Later, Limbaugh lied about what he had done: "Never have I suggested that this was murder."[6] When you report (and even exaggerate) a story about how someone was "murdered," and repeatedly say that it was not a suicide, that probably qualifies as suggesting that it was a murder.

Limbaugh has never apologized for smearing Hillary Clinton, nor did he ever offer a correction. In fact, he regularly returns to this lie by invoking "Fort Marcy Park" whenever he thinks someone is annoying Hillary Clinton and will be killed as a result. The casual listener may miss its meaning, but most Dittoheads understand what Limbaugh is saying: Hillary Clinton will stop at nothing, even murder, to get what she wants.

More than a decade after he first falsely and maliciously accused Hillary Clinton of murder, Limbaugh was still joking about it. In 2004 he said, "Whoever briefed Janet Reno, start searching Fort Marcy Park."[7] Limbaugh said that the Clintons are "pretty confident Kerry is going to lose and if Kerry wins there's always Fort Marcy Park."[8] Later that year, he said about President Clinton's national security adviser, Sandy Berger, "Sandy Burglar, stay away from Fort Marcy Park."[9] In 2005 Limbaugh warned that antiwar protester Cindy Sheehan would be murdered by the Clintons for daring to criticize Hillary: "Do the words 'Fort Marcy Park' mean anything to you?"[10] He added the next day that Cindy Sheehan "will not mention her again, ladies and gentlemen, unless she wants to end up in Fort Marcy Park. Mark my words on it."[11] In 2007 Limbaugh warned CNN's Wolf Blitzer, "We know Wolf's already got a reservation he's not aware of to Fort Marcy Park."[12] In 2008, after Barack Obama's campaign plane had to make an emergency landing due to mechanical problems, Limbaugh twice referred to it as "Fort Marcy Airlines."[13]

It's crude enough that the radio host regularly jokes about a tragic suicide. But the fact that he still spreads the right-wing myth that it was a murder committed by Hillary Clinton is sick. Normally, a broadcaster who falsely reported that the First Lady was involved in a murder would be permanently discredited as a crackpot and shunned by everyone in the mass media. But he benefits from a double standard for right-wing stars. Instead of being marginalized, he is a celebrity.

DEMOCRATIC CONSPIRACIES

Unlike many antigovernment crackpots who imagine conspiracies everywhere from Waco to 9/11 run by the Trilateral Commission and the Federal Reserve, Limbaugh is highly selective about when he imagines the government is out to get us. Every Democratic administration and liberal viewpoint is the enemy, but Republican administrations are invariably good. The result is an odd roller coaster of conspiracy. Under Obama and Clinton, the government is and was out to get you; under Reagan, Bush, and Bush, the government bureaucrats were still out to get you, but the conservative Republicans stopped it in its tracks. Under Republican leadership, there was a Democratic conspiracy to destroy all Republicans; under Democratic leadership, there's a government conspiracy to take over the country. Limbaugh's only consistency is ideology and partisanship.

When Democrats emerge victorious, Limbaugh sees a conspiracy. He declared of Al Franken's 2008 election to the Senate, "We did not elect Al Franken. He stole the race."[14] Later, after several courts found that Franken won the most votes, Limbaugh was still denouncing "that clown Senator Franken, who stole a Senate seat."[15] Franken didn't steal a Senate seat. He won a Senate seat.

After a scandal came up before the 2006 elections involving a Republican congressman, Mark Foley, and his sexual messages with congressional pages, Limbaugh asserted without evidence that "these emails were planted by a liberal."[16] Perhaps realizing that Foley actually did write the messages, Rush had to concoct a conspiracy that went to the top of the Democratic Party: "Nancy Pelosi knows the person who planted the story about Foley five weeks before the election. . . . She knows the person because this—these emails were held by a liberal, they were planted by a liberal, and they were timed to the 2006 election cycle by a liberal."

Rush even declared that Pelosi was part of a vast liberal conspiracy to undermine the Republicans by bribing an underage page to seduce Foley: "How do you get a kid to do this? You threaten 'em or you pay 'em. I don't know. You know, how do these pages get into the page program? How does this happen? One way is through political connections, political patronage. So who are these pages and who sponsored these kids to become pages and, and for, for what reason? Is there a political party that would stoop this low? Yes, there is. We know that there is a political party that would stoop this low to set somebody up this way. What I'm suggesting here is that a lot of people knew of Foley's proclivities and arranged to amass evidence of it for this very reason."[17]

Naturally, the "Maha Rushie" had no evidence to support his claims. Yet he pushed the idea of a conspiracy based on threats and bribery: "What if somebody got to the page and said, you know, we want you to set Foley up. We need to do a little titillating thing here. Keep it and save it and so forth. How would you get a kid to do that? Yeah, who knows? You threaten him or pay him. There's any number of ways given the kind of people that we're dealing with and talking about here."[18] And then Limbaugh had the audacity to complain, "There's no concern about the kid—no concern about the children," right after he baselessly accused a kid of being paid to seduce a congressman.[19] If Limbaugh was really worried about children, perhaps he might have avoided falsely claiming that they were political prostitutes willing to sell themselves sexually.

And, of course, the conspiracy did not end with the Democratic Party. The media was part of this vast Foley conspiracy, too: "This is so obviously a planned, orchestrated release—timed release of information that's designed to keep the story going. I know how these people in the drive-by media work. I know how they coordinate with the Democrat [sic] Party. They're all excited."[20] None of this was true. ABC News reporter Brian Ross noted that "to the extent that I know the political parties of any of the people who helped us," they were Republicans.[21]

Rush even sees a conspiracy theory in the Democrats' use of PDF files: He believes that Democrats in 2009 tried to keep the stimulus bill a secret, by "reformat[ting] the bill—they've made it a PDF file when they posted it.

Now, for those of you that don't use computers, basically what that means is that it cannot be keyword searched. A PDF file is essentially a picture of a page. And, so, you can read every page, but you cannot keyword search it. It's not a text file as legislation normally is as posted on these public websites. They don't want anybody knowing what's in this."[22] In reality, using the Find tool or the Search window, it's very easy for anyone except Limbaugh to search for any word in a PDF, or to save the document as text.

Limbaugh also sees pollsters as part of the vast liberal conspiracy, because he thinks they secretly raise Obama's approval ratings: "They're doing everything they can—they're upping the sample to black Americans—to keep him up at 50% in the Gallup poll."[23] As Frank Newport, Gallup's editor in chief, noted, "This statement is a complete and inexplicable fabrication."[24] When polls showed support for health care reform, Limbaugh declared that it was a conspiracy of the media to fake polls in coordination with the Obama administration: "So USA Today/Gallup is totally making it up. Now, yesterday I shared with you all these unscientific polls being touted by liberals to substantiate the popularity of Obamacare, and USA Today/Gallup is one of them. Just like the *Star Wars* bar scene setting for the signing of the bill yesterday, this is all staged. All of this is being staged by the administration to make Obamacare look and feel like America really wants it."[25]

When car dealerships were being shut down, Limbaugh saw another vast liberal conspiracy: "Do you think maybe Obama and his administration are targeting dealerships happened [sic] to be run and owned by Republicans?"[26] When Obama forged a coalition of carmakers, politicians from both parties, and environmental groups to support raising fuel standards, Limbaugh again perceived a conspiracy: "They had no choice . . . it's this or jail."[27] Jail? Exactly how would Obama put anyone in jail for opposing fuel standards? In fact, if Obama had ever threatened to do such a thing, it would have imperiled his presidency once the news was made public. But as usual, Rush was making things up. Absolutely no one involved in this decision made an allegation that they were threatened with jail time. Perhaps more important, he was a lone nut among conservatives in making such an accusation. No one else asserted that anyone would be locked up in prison for opposing higher fuel standards.

After Toyota's problems with sudden acceleration became public, Limbaugh blamed it on an Obama administration conspiracy, even though the government had failed to regulate Toyota: "Look, they own General Motors and Chrysler. They're using the power of government ownership here to go after a competitor on the basis the competitor is killing its customers, and, (sigh) yep, they're not unionized. It's out there for one and all to see. This is Chicago thug politics."[28]

But the greatest victim of the vast liberal conspiracy is Limbaugh himself. He claimed in August 2009, "They are starting in the White House now to replicate the failed attempts by Bill Clinton to get rid of me."[29] Clinton never tried to "get rid of" Limbaugh, nor has Obama. But in Limbaugh's paranoid imagination, any criticism he receives amounts to a government conspiracy to silence him. He said, "I've got the government preparing to make a law to shut me up."[30] But no such law has been created. Still, his devotion to this and his other conspiracy theories is remarkably consistent, even in the face of all contrary evidence.

Conspiracy on Wall Street

Wall Street is another of Limbaugh's conspiratorial targets. He said the cap-and-trade pollution bill was a conspiracy to benefit Wall Street, which supposedly would profit from the trading system: "This is the 'trade' aspect. This brings Wall Street into this, which I think explains these Republican votes." Limbaugh declared, "My suspicion is that being in the Northeast, some of them, they've got ties to Wall Street with donations, contributions, and so forth, and that talks. That talks. So here I am ripping Wall Street."[31] But out of the eight House Republicans voting for the bill, only one represented New York, and he came from the far northern part of the state with no connection to Wall Street. Limbaugh's unusual denunciation of rich people came only because it enabled him to attack liberal legislation, and ascribe evil motives to the Democrats and moderate Republicans who supported it.

Rush also complained about the cap-and-trade bill, "There is a requirement that the bill being voted on be in the well of the House. It was not there because it hadn't been written, much less read."[32] In reality, the bill had been written, and was available to anyone online.[33]

Limbaugh's Obama Conspiracies

Under the Obama administration, Limbaugh has begun to lose his temper on the air and reveal more of his true beliefs. The election of Obama has turned his occasional invocation of conspiracy theories into a daily barrage of imagined plots formulated in the Oval Office. The most mundane actions of the Obama administration have prompted paranoid ravings from Limbaugh. When the Department of Homeland Security announced plans to hire up to one thousand new cybersecurity experts, Limbaugh said: "Department of Homeland Security to hire up to one thousand new Obama spies."[34]

Limbaugh also declared that smart meters, which measure a home's energy use, are "tyranny, pure unadulterated tyranny" from the Obama administration.[35] After a caller criticized his dismissal of such a valuable device, Limbaugh declared: "I simply listened to what Obama said. He talked about it in a White House meeting with one of these groups that he then sent off into work groups. He said: 'And we're working on new thermostats that will report your electronic usage and will let you know when you are over your limit.' I said, What? Now a lot of people are saying that talking about this is just—that this is conspiracy kooks that believe in this. Obama said it!"[36] Obama never said it. Obama actually said, "We could set up systems so that everybody in each house have [sic] their own smart meters that will tell you when to turn off the lights, when the peak hours are, can help you sell back energy that you've generated in your home through a solar panel or through other mechanisms."[37] There was no talk of government monitoring or limits, except in the minds of Limbaugh and other "conspiracy kooks."

He often imagines conspiracies that don't even follow any internal logic. When two uninvited guests crashed a state dinner at the White House in 2009, Limbaugh instantly saw a plot. "It all begins to make sense," he concluded, when you realize that the couple was trying to get on a Bravo TV show, Bravo is owned by NBC, NBC is owned by General Electric, and GE head "Jeffrey Immelt is in bed with Obama on 'green' technology and government grants to GE." Limbaugh believes Immelt and Obama conspired to create a "giant distraction" while "Obama's, you know, sneaking around with his other agenda while nobody's looking."[38]

According to Rush, the Obama administration "wants us all living as wards of the state."[39] Obama is "actively seeking to expand the welfare state in this country because he wants to control it."[40] Limbaugh also claimed that Democrats want to destroy cities so that Republicans will move out and Democrats will control them: "It's all about turning as many cities into Detroit as they can."[41] This is one of Limbaugh's numerous conspiracy theories that doesn't have an internal logic. Since Democrats already dominate urban politics, why would they want to drive out of Detroit the wealthy Republicans who help provide funding for all of those Democratic programs?

When Obama supported Chicago's bid for the 2016 Olympics, Limbaugh immediately imagined a conspiracy: "It was Mayor Daley and it was Valerie Jarrett and all these corrupt Chicagoans who were going to sell property they owned to the Olympic committee or to whoever for big profits to build the now-never-happening Olympic village."[42] The Olympic village was going to be built on public land and the site of a former hospital. Mayor Daley and Valerie Jarrett never had any property to sell to the Olympic committee.

In another of his conspiracy theories, Limbaugh claimed that the Obama administration would impose "mandatory service."[43] But every proposal from Obama has been for a voluntary system where students would be paid for community service to reduce their student loans. Rush has even said, "They're going to take your 401(k), put it in the Social Security trust fund."[44] There has never been any proposal to take people's money from their 401(k) accounts and use the money for Social Security. It would be illegal to do so. Still, the fact that Limbaugh imagines that such a thing is not only possible but "going" to happen indicates how far his conspiracy theories go.

In 2009 he claimed, "There are two conflicting polls on the whole concept of universal health care" and decided that the poll he didn't like (which showed strong support for a public option) was part of a conspiracy to manipulate poll results: "The Reuters Thomson poll purposely found stupid, uninformed people." The only stupid, uninformed person was Limbaugh himself, since he falsely claimed that a Rasmussen poll showing 62 percent opposition to single-payer health care was about "the public option."[45] He even imagined that the Obama administration was plotting to "outlaw the Republican Party, rewrite the Constitution, require redistribution of wealth, get rid of talk radio."[46]

The Treason of the Democrats

Every policy disagreement, in Limbaugh's eyes, has turned into a plot to destroy America: "This investigation of the CIA, this is designed to weaken us." He regards Democrats as committing treason: "They have aligned themselves with the enemy. They continue to align themselves with the enemy. They won't admit it, obviously. The enemy kills more soldiers, their spokesmen here in the U.S. are the Democrats. . . . The Democrats assume the role of media PR spokespeople for Al Qaeda."[47] It's bad enough that he endorsed the failed policies of George W. Bush that proved to be the greatest recruiting tool for Al Qaeda, and even celebrated the torture of prisoners that gave Al Qaeda a PR victory. But when he falsely accuses Democrats, without any basis, of being the spokespeople for terrorists, it makes Limbaugh no different from the left-wing lunatics who think the Bush administration conspired with Al Qaeda.

These conspiracy theorists, who call themselves the 9/11 Truth movement, or 9/11 Truthers, assert the loony theory that the Bush administration was secretly involved in blowing up the Twin Towers with explosives on 9/11 to justify the Patriot Act and the War on Terror. But the difference between the 9/11 Truthers (who also include crazy people on the far right) and Limbaugh's right-wing conspiracy theorists is that the leftists are completely marginalized. Even within the tiny realm of left-wing media in America, the 9/11 Truthers are entirely dismissed. They're banned at Daily Kos and dismissed by leftist magazines such as *The Nation* and *In These Times*.

By contrast, the conspiracy theories of the right wing are endorsed by the biggest media stars in the conservative movement. Although Limbaugh is the most enthusiastic proponent of far-right conspiracy theories, he is far from alone; Sean Hannity, Michael Savage, Glenn Beck, and many more Limbaugh imitators share his formula of using conspiracy theories to gain an audience among the conservative base. Limbaugh has never had to pay a price in his prestige or credibility despite routinely spouting completely implausible conspiracy theories.

OBAMA AND THE ENEMIES LIST

One of Rush Limbaugh's conspiracy theories is that Obama is plotting to destroy him. Limbaugh even invoked Richard Nixon's infamous Enemies List to claim that Obama is far worse: "This administration has gone far beyond what Richard Nixon even contemplated! This administration is targeting individual private citizens and a network. This administration is doing everything it can to silence and put out of business its opposition or its critics. Nixon was just trying to get a fair shake. It's amazing."[48] Limbaugh's defense of Richard Nixon "trying to get a fair shake" is even more contemptible because history has proved that Nixon was doing far worse things than the media ever reported at the time.

It's amazing that anyone could dismiss Nixon's Enemies List while attacking Obama. White House counsel John Dean described in an August 16, 1971, memo to top Nixon advisers "how we can use the available federal machinery to screw our political enemies" and recommended "how we can best screw them (e.g., grant availability, federal contracts, litigation prosecution, etc.)"[49] The original Nixon's Enemies List included comments about targets such as Common Cause executive Morton Halperin ("a scandal would be most helpful here") and Representative John Conyers ("has known weakness for white females"). White House counsel Charles Colson compiled the ever-growing list of enemies, and wrote a 1972 memo to Dean about a tip on tax problems with a leader in the Teamsters union, even asking if an "informer's fee" could be paid.[50]

There's not the slightest indication that the Obama administration is using litigation, prosecution, or control over federal contracts to punish their critics, let alone digging up interracial sex scandals. There is no Obama enemies list, and there is no conspiracy to screw political enemies . . . only an effort to criticize the powerful forces attacking Obama in ways that Nixon could have never imagined.

Complaining about media coverage is one of the great American presidential traditions, and what the Obama administration says about Limbaugh, Fox News Channel, and talk radio is no different from what any politician does in response to harsh criticism. Far from "doing everything it can to silence and put out of business its opposition," the Obama administration is doing absolutely nothing to silence its opponents. The fact that Limbaugh can defend the criminal activities of Nixon and his cronies as he besmirches Obama for mere criticism of conservatives shows his remarkable political bias. In his eyes, no Republican crime is too large to ignore, while every Democrat is smeared for no reason at all.

Rush even imagined that an Obama press conference was being delayed so that Obama could react to what Limbaugh said: "There's clearly one reason why. He had to wait for his staff, or maybe he listened himself, to tell him what I said before going out and making comments. . . . No, Snerdley, I'm not joking and I'm not being pompous. I'm never pompous and I'm not being braggadocios. You're not bragging if you can do it."[51] You're not bragging if you think that the president of the United States rearranges press conferences based on your comments: You're delusional.

"Their enemies list is the private sector of this country where you work,"[52] Limbaugh said about Obama and his campaign staff. While there is no enemies list in the Obama administration, Limbaugh isn't simply personally paranoid in imagining that Obama is out to get him; he thinks Obama is trying to destroy the entire country.

THE OBAMA MOB

Limbaugh regards the government as a kind of mob family under Obama: "Tony Soprano has taken over the U.S. government and the private sector is an opposing family. He's going to wipe it out."[53] Limbaugh claimed about Obama, "He kneecaps people to get them to cooperate."[54]

The radio host must have been a big fan of *The Sopranos*, because he relies on the mob metaphor for a lot of his stories. He explained the impact of the Employee Free Choice Act in this way: "You are a small business employee. Your boss has a shop that is not union. After this legislation passes, one day Tony Soprano will walk in, with a lead pipe, and he will start beating people upside the head to vote to unionize, because you cannot vote in private."[55] Of course, unions are rarely concerned about small businesses, since the dues can barely pay for their large supply of lead pipes. There are several states where some employees can already unionize via card check, and no stories of lead pipes have been uncovered. Limbaugh isn't actually afraid that

Obama and mafia hoods will start busting heads; he's afraid that workers want to join unions, and might do so unless the system is stacked against them.

Limbaugh has a lot of peculiar ideas about unions. He has claimed that massive pro-immigration protests were "rent-a-mobs" created by unions forcing people to attend, and added, "And they pay people."[56] So he thinks hundreds of thousands of people showed up on the streets because the unions forced them to be there or paid them, even though there were no reports to support either claim. Limbaugh cannot conceive of the possibility that a large number of Americans hold views that he abhors, such as wanting to increase legal immigration, so he imagines a plot must be behind it all.

When a union doesn't exist, Limbaugh simply makes one up to serve as a punching bag. After the 2010 Massey Energy disaster killed twenty-nine coal miners in West Virginia, he immediately blamed the unions for failing to protect workers at the nonunion mine. After getting e-mails that pointed out he was wrong, he refused to relent. Citing a 2009 case where Massey Energy was ordered to rehire eighty-five coal miners who had been discriminated against for joining a union, Limbaugh claimed, "So there were union workers there, and so the United Mine Workers should have been overseeing their safety." In fact, Limbaugh took the opportunity to remind his listeners that he is always right and must never be doubted: "You people, it's been twenty-one years. At some point you are going to learn: If you go up against me on a challenge of fact, you are going to be wrong."[57] On this challenge of fact, Limbaugh was completely wrong. The case of the eighty-five coal miners was at a different mine, and there is absolutely no doubt that the mine where twenty-nine people died had no union.[58]

He claimed that Obama's administration is "literally a thugocracy that is operating out of the White House" and said that he was the victim of Obama: "They came after me."[59] In Limbaugh's paranoid imagination, being criticized by Obama officials was the same as a conspiracy to destroy him.

NUTS OVER ACORN

The Association of Community Organizations for Reform Now (ACORN) is a favorite source of conspiracy theories for Limbaugh and other conservatives. After reading reports of executives at hedge funds getting death threats, Rush concluded that it was an Obama-run conspiracy: "[It's] probably ACORN people. I'm sure it's coordinated. Obama has the network to do this."[60] There is no "network" of Obama minions threatening to kill people. But Limbaugh does not hesitate to accuse an organization and even the president of ordering death threats.

He also claimed: "Do you know that in the Obama stimulus package, $4.19 billion is going to ACORN? . . . Would somebody explain to me what in the name of Sam Hill $4.19 billion to a voter-fraud organization has to do with stimulus? I'll tell you what's going on here. We, ladies and gentlemen, we are funding Obama and the Democrat [sic] Party's army on the street. We are funding the forces of the Democrat Party's re-election."[61] Limbaugh's facts were all wrong. There was no $4.19 billion grant to ACORN. It didn't exist. There was a $4.19 billion program in the stimulus package for "emergency assistance for the redevelopment of abandoned and foreclosed homes."[62] ACORN, like any other organization, is perfectly free to submit competitive contracts for this funding. But there was nothing granted to ACORN. Even if ACORN did receive funding, this money would go to housing assistance, not to fund any "Democrat [sic] Party's army on the street."

Yet Limbaugh repeated this false claim a few weeks later: "But their objective is to see to it they're never defeated again. Why do you think ACORN's getting all this money? Why do you think Obama's reelection machine is getting all this money starting in 2010? Federal money going to campaign coffers for Democrats in the guise of a stimulus bill."[63] This was a complete fabrication. There was no federal money in the stimulus bill going to Obama's reelection campaign. That would be illegal, and Rush was simply inventing the allegation, knowing that his listeners would never hear the truth.

Limbaugh asserted that the housing bubble caused by deregulation was the result of ACORN: "But all of this happened because Democrats from Bill Clinton forward, Barney Frank, and Chris Dodd, demanded—and ACORN—demanded that people that could not ever pay a loan back or even qualify for one, be given one, essentially be given a house. They were threatened by Janet Reno and others. And regulators that tried to stop this were in turn threatened by people like Barney Frank and Chris Dodd."[64] Nobody was demanding a free house for people who couldn't afford one and nobody was threatened for trying to stop it. The housing bubble and its collapse had nothing to do with the Community Reinvestment Act (CRA). More than 84 percent of the subprime loans in 2006 were made by financial institutions not covered by the CRA.[65] In fact, because the CRA encouraged more lending to minorities by banks rather than exploitation by subprime lenders, the CRA probably reduced the mortgage problem. As Media Matters for America noted, "Frank supported bills to *increase* regulation of Fannie Mae and create a government regulatory agency that would supervise and have authority over some aspects of the company."[66]

Arguing that Obama was part of a vast, three-decade conspiracy to teach black people to hate America, Limbaugh opined: "But as you study more and more of this ACORN stuff, you find that it has been part of an entire movement that has been going on for two, maybe three decades, right under our noses . . . and Barack Obama is smack dab in the middle of it, they have been training young black kids to hate, hate, hate this country, and they trained their parents before that to hate, hate, hate this country. It was a movement. It was a Bill Ayers, anticapitalist, anti-American educational movement. ACORN is how it was implemented, right under our noses. It has been a movement, it has been a religion, and Obama and Jeremiah Wright and William Ayers were all up to their big ears in it."[67] Limbaugh is so obsessed with race that he refuses to see how inequity and discrimination is a reality for many African Americans, and must instead posit that they are all indoctrinated to hate America and invent all of these problems. He apparently imagines a scene thirty years ago where a teenage Barack Obama, attending high school in Hawaii, meets up with Reverend Jeremiah Wright and Bill Ayers while he was still on the run underground as a wanted man, and plots this decades-long plan to destroy America and capitalism by teaching black kids to hate everyone, utilizing some kind of secret curriculum no one has ever discovered, all of it carefully coordinated by ACORN without a whisper of the truth being revealed to anyone.

Limbaugh imagines that the vast ACORN conspiracy reaches even further, that ACORN is part of a conspiracy to steal elections for Democrats. He claimed, "Pelosi and Reid can say, 'No, no, we'll send ACORN in there, we'll have enough voter fraud, we'll run enough commercials that your constituents won't matter.' That's what they're going to be told."[68] Limbaugh even insinuated that Obama (and ACORN) stole the 2008 election: "Like I always say, folks—and I've been saying it since the primaries—Obama cannot win in a fair vote," and later, "Who's better at vote-stuffing than the Obama [*sic*]?"[69]

There have never been any elections stolen by ACORN (or Obama), no voter fraud that ever affected an election result. But Rush Limbaugh's ravings have a powerful effect on his fans. A 2009 survey by Public Policy Polling found that 52 percent of Republicans believe it's possible that "ACORN stole" the 2008 election for Barack Obama.[70]

Limbaugh claimed, "By now everybody should understand that a Republican will never win a close or contested vote in a state with a Democrat as secretary of state,"[71] though he offered no evidence of a Democrat stealing an election. Of course, numerous Republicans have won close elections with Democrats in charge of the vote counting. But Limbaugh's trust in his stunning exaggerations and conspiracy theories make him believe that every single Democrat will steal an election.

OBAMA'S BIRTH CERTIFICATE

Limbaugh has embraced one of the dumbest conspiracy theories about Obama: the belief that he was secretly born in Kenya and therefore ineligible to be president. This theory, pushed by "birthers," has been completely discredited from the beginning. Obama was born in Hawaii, and a birth announcement was printed in the Honolulu newspaper. His birth certificate is real, and has been publicly released showing that he was born in Honolulu at 7:24 P.M. on August 4, 1961. The original birth certificate has been seen and verified by numerous independent observers.[72]

Less than two weeks before the 2008 election, Limbaugh said: "This birth certificate business, this lawsuit that a guy named Philip Berg filed in Philadelphia in August for Obama to produce his genuine birth certificate and he still hasn't replied. You've got a deathly ill grandmother, you are going to rush to her side a few days from now, when you first announced this, you're going to rush, you're going to hurry, you're going to make tracks, you're going to get over there because you don't want your grandmother to die before you got there like your mother did, but somehow you keep campaigning, you take three days to get over there, if he's left yet, and this birth certificate business, I'm just wondering if something's up. . . . There are a lot of people now that are starting to speculate and be curious about this."[73]

Limbaugh's peculiar conspiracy theory was proven wrong a few days later when Obama's grandmother died. Nothing about Rush's theory made any sense. It was perfectly reasonable that a presidential candidate near the end of a campaign would need some time to rearrange his schedule for a flight to Hawaii. Nor is it possible to imagine what Obama could do, under constant press surveillance, to hide the truth about his birth certificate. Only the craziest of the birther nuts imagined this "dying grandmother" was a cover for a conspiracy about Obama's birth certificate, and Limbaugh was their leader.

Being proven wrong once again didn't bother Limbaugh at all, and after Obama became president, Rush raised the birth certificate business over and over again in a desperate attempt to delegitimize the president. In June 2009 he joked, "What do Obama and God have in common? Neither has a birth certificate."[74] Later in the same show, Limbaugh got a call from a man criticizing him for this, and silenced the caller to avoid being challenged: "I did cut your mike, Joe. Nobody can hear you. Now, I don't hate anybody. I criticize Obama, and I'm one of the few who does, and that's what outrages you."[75]

Limbaugh discussed Obama's birth certificate many times, with great seriousness. In April 2009, he discussed how Obama had been talking about his own country and asked, "Is he talking about Kenya or the United States of America?"[76] In the middle of a discussion of Mark Sanford in June 2009, Limbaugh suddenly brought up the birth certificate again: "A friend of mine said, 'Where was Obama born?' And I don't know. He's not a native Hawaiian. Where was he born? I don't know. Supposedly Hawaii, but we don't have independent confirmation of it. I don't want to go there. God doesn't have a birth certificate, either, so it's no big deal."[77] Limbaugh proclaimed on June 20, 2009, "Barack Obama has yet to have to prove he's a citizen. All he'd have to do is show a birth certificate. He has yet to have to prove he's a citizen."[78] In declaring that Obama was not a native Hawaiian, Limbaugh was embracing the nutty theory that Obama was secretly born in Kenya.

In July 2009 Limbaugh was still endorsing the birther movement by referring to Obama as having "no birth certificate."[79] Rush linked his birther theory with other conspiracy theories about Obama's academic work in college and law school: "He hasn't released his law school records, his law review records, his Columbia records, his university records. He hasn't released a lot of things. This thing could easily be shut down if Obama would just release the birth certificate."[80]

And Limbaugh denounced the liberal media for failing to pursue the story, complaining that "nobody's interested in the fact that he hasn't shown anybody his birth certificate."[81] The radio host even blamed Obama for the birthers: "Obama could shut it down. There has to be some reason he doesn't want people to see that birth certificate. Maybe it's dual citizenship, who knows."[82] Of course, Obama—unlike anyone else who has ever run for president—actually did show his birth certificate to the entire world. The "dual citizenship" theory promoted by some birthers doesn't make any sense—not only was it untrue, but "dual citizenship" would not appear on a U.S. birth certificate.

Limbaugh said, "You people run around and you talk about the birthers and how irresponsible and off their rockers they are? The global warming believers are just as wacko as the birthers, if you want to look at them as wacko."[83] Notice how Limbaugh was unwilling to call the birthers "wacko," a term he uses without reservation for environmentalists and scientists who believe the facts about global warming. The real analogy here is between the birthers and the antienvironmentalists on the right wing, who share an indifference to facts and scientific reality.

Limbaugh's embrace of the birthers legitimized their conspiracy theories among Republicans. Birthers form the base of Limbaugh's audience. A 2009 Public Policy Polling poll of conservatives in Arkansas found that twice as many conservatives view Limbaugh favorably as believe that Obama was born in the United States.[84] If Limbaugh had spoken out against the birther conspiracy theory, he would have helped to stop the spread of this insanity. Instead, he became one of the leading figures promoting the idea, by repeatedly declaring his doubt about Obama's birth. Limbaugh even endorsed a 2010 Arizona "birther" law that requires presidential candidates to show a birth certificate: "This works for me. The states hold the key of getting us out of this mess we're in here."[85] WorldNetDaily editor in chief Joseph Farah (ghostwriter of Limbaugh's second book and leader of a campaign to put up "Where's the Birth Certificate?" billboards around the country) noted the importance of Limbaugh's stand with the birthers: "What that did is beyond

Rush's impact. It also gives other talk show hosts license to talk about this issue. . . . Rush is kind of the standard of talk show hosts. A lot of people emulate what he does. He crossed the Rubicon on that show, and I'm very proud of him for doing it."[86]

By repeatedly raising the birth certificate issue, Limbaugh has appeased the crackpot fringe that are the core of his audience.

PARANOIA ON THE NET

Net neutrality is yet another topic where Limbaugh manages to see the darkest plots hidden in the most innocuous of ideas that have broad support, even among conservatives: "What's coming way beyond this, what's coming in the fall is the deceptively named Net neutrality. The easiest way to understand this is to think of a Fairness Doctrine for the Internet. Now, how would this work? Let's say that you want to go Google or Bing, you want to search the mating habits of the Australian rabbit bat. Net neutrality would require that every search engine produce an equal number of results that satisfy every disagreement about the issue. Yep."[87]

Nope. Net neutrality means that Internet service providers must treat all websites equally, and can't ban or slow down certain sites for their customers. Among all the critics of Net neutrality, only Limbaugh is dumb enough to imagine that it has anything to do with search engine results. Showing how little he understands about the Internet, a month later Limbaugh was telling the opposite story: "Net neutrality was going to really reward Google if that ever happens."[88]

Limbaugh painted a picture of secret government control exerted over the World Wide Web: "So in the era of Net neutrality—and this is where the Google–White House partnership comes into play—the results of any search, let's say you want to search abortion, or you want to search the health care bill, they want to control what you see." He even imagined that the Obama administration conspired with Google to produce search results critical of him: "The White House and Google are bedmates, Google, largest search engine. Already, if you do a search of me on Google and you look at the crap that comes up, it's by design and on purpose."[89]

It takes a remarkable level of paranoia for anyone to imagine that a search engine is conspiring against you with the help of the government. Limbaugh also explained that faster broadband Internet is just a conspiracy by the Obama administration "to control the content as best they can. Just think of it as Fairness Doctrine for the Internet. I'm not making this up. I guarantee you that's what's coming."[90] There is no Fairness Doctrine for the Internet, and no government control of Internet content. But Rush has no problem offering his personal "guarantee" behind a conspiracy theory no one else believes.

THE OBAMA PLOT TO DESTROY AMERICA

The biggest conspiracy ever imagined by Limbaugh, a conspiracy theory he has repeated on almost a daily basis, is his belief that Obama is intentionally destroying the economy in order to increase dependence on government. He has said, "President Obama and the Democrats are destroying the U.S. economy. They are purposely doing it, I believe. I think the real reason he wants health care is because, when he gets it, that is the single greatest power the government will have to regulate every aspect of our lives—and that's what Obama is; and that's what the Democrats, the liberal wing of the Democrat Party today is: total control."[91]

The conspiracy theory has been repeated over and over again by Limbaugh. "This is wrecking the U.S. economy for the express purpose of remaking America and getting rid of the wealthy." He has also said, "The whole private sector is being dismantled in front of our eyes on purpose,"[92] and called it "a massive socialist takeover of the country."[93]

Obama's willingness to cause "suffering" proves how evil he is in Limbaugh's view: "I don't think people understand that this kind of pain and suffering fits somebody's master plan, and it's hard to convince people of that."[94] Rush never questions his assumption that all liberals are simply lying in pursuit of their policies. He imagines that there is a "master plan" to destroy America led by the Democrats, indicating the depth of his paranoia.

Such was Limbaugh's paranoia that he imagined a massive conspiracy linking Obama to the financial collapse that caused the Bush recession: "Somebody had to tell him what was coming in 2007, meaning the crash in 2008. He didn't have any experience to know. Somebody had to know, somebody had to tell him, for that somebody to know they had to have a hand in it. Can anybody say George Soros? Pulling the marionette strings here of our leader of the regime."[95] Limbaugh saw Soros as the puppeteer secretly controlling Obama, who ordered him to run for president and then staged the collapse of the housing bubble in order to help Obama win. Limbaugh said, "George Soros has said that one of his goals in life is to bring about the world financial crisis and profit from it" and added, "Soros may be running Obama."[96] Everything about this conspiracy theory is absolutely untrue. Soros had nothing to do with Obama's decision to run for president. Soros never said what Limbaugh claimed he did. And Soros could not have possibly caused the housing bubble and the Bush recession. Limbaugh's Web site featured an illustration of Soros standing above Obama, holding a manipulator to control the president's actions. Limbaugh would have us believe the Obama administration intentionally destroyed the economy in order to increase unemployment and produce more support for health care reform: "Proof of my point here that the joblessness is on purpose: If your number-one signature issue is health care—and his is—and if, which is true, health insurance is not portable when you lose your job; what's the best thing you can do for yourself? Create unemployment. The more people unemployed, the more people losing their health insurance, the more people scared to death, the more people clamoring for it."[97]

The health care debate brought Limbaugh's conspiracy theories to new heights: "They can deny people coverage based on their lifestyles. They can dictate what you can eat, what you don't eat, if you're going to get this precious health insurance."[98] This was pure insanity. No one can control what people eat, even if they care enough to try. But it's a particularly strange charge to make because the plan being pushed by Obama would prohibit denying coverage to anyone who sought it. The possibility of denying people coverage based on lifestyle exists only in the private system admired by Limbaugh; the Obama plan prohibits exactly what Rush claims it would impose.

Reading a story about declines in donations to universities, Limbaugh immediately saw a conspiracy: "That's just what Obama planned. That's just what Obama planned. He wants the government to be in charge of all charities."[99] So Rush thinks that Obama plotted to destroy the U.S. economy with a recession that began more than a year before he took office, in order to reduce donations to higher education. Like many of Limbaugh's conspiracy theories, this one is not only factually impossible, but it also lacks any internal logic. How, exactly, is the government taking over charities? Why would Obama want to see funding reduced for higher education? And how could Obama secretly destroy the economy just to hurt charities?

Crackpot theories dominate Limbaugh's thinking, such as his certainty that Osama bin Laden, despite regularly putting out tapes, is dead: "He's not alive! Don't doubt me on this."[100] Even Limbaugh admitted that his ideas should cause him to be perceived as a wacko: "Obama loves this chaos, he's tried to destroy the United States economy, he's trying to destroy the institutions and traditions of this country, it's purposeful . . . this is something you just, as an American, you don't expect that this can happen here, so when somebody says it is they might be a kook or they might be wacko."[101] Yet Limbaugh's deeply influential kook ideas rarely receive any critical attention in the media.

5

LIMBAUGHNOMICS: THE STRANGE ECONOMIC IDEAS OF RUSH

On almost any topic, from science to medicine to economics to history, Limbaugh is dead wrong, over and over again. Rarely has so much ignorance sustained such certainty of genius. When it comes to economics, he is almost illiterate. He seems blissfully unaware of mainstream economic thinking, preferring instead to imagine that right-wing economic theories are the only ones that exist. But even among the fringe group of extremely conservative economists, Limbaugh's theories would be considered nonsensical.

What's most appalling about Limbaugh's ignorance of basic economic concepts is his absolute belief that he understands everything about economics and that anyone who disagrees with him is an idiot. Rush said about the Obama administration plans, "Anybody with a brain, ladies and gentlemen, anybody sane has to admit that this is not being done to revitalize an economy. Everybody with a brain knows this."[1]

In reality, Obama's stimulus plan and approach to the economy followed the advice mainstream economists have offered for more than a half century. It's well known that during a recession, private demand for goods declines, and standard Keynesian economic theory supports increasing government spending to fill in the gap. By contrast, cutting spending to balance the budget only deepens the recession by reducing demand for goods and increasing unemployment. There was nothing crazy at all about Obama's economic plan. Yet Limbaugh claimed, "I maintain to you that nobody who is economically literate—economically experienced and understanding—would dare do what we are doing if their objective was growth and jobs."[2]

Many of Limbaugh's objections were based on pure misinformation. He declared, "You don't raise taxes in a recession. You don't do anything he's doing in a recession."[3] Rush neglected to mention the fact that Obama hadn't raised any taxes; he cut taxes for the overwhelming majority of Americans.

But the radio host has repeatedly claimed that Obama was intentionally trying to destroy the U.S. economy with his stimulus plan: "Folks, I know it's hard to understand that we've elected somebody who is willingly, purposely setting out to deplete the capital in the private sector, to destroy the U.S. economy."[4] Rush is so completely convinced of his right-wing economic views that he cannot even conceive of the possibility of a sincere dissent from his ideas; anyone, such as Obama, who wants even a modest increase in government programs during a recession must be knowingly plotting the destruction of capitalism.

This insane theory reflects the kind of ideological bubble Limbaugh lives in. After years in which no one is allowed to challenge his views, where he gets adulation and constant "dittos" praising his views, Rush has reached the point where he cannot imagine anyone disagreeing with him unless they have ulterior motives.

In reality, many economists have pointed to the success of the Obama stimulus bill. Dean Baker noted, "The stimulus probably added 2.5 to 3.0 percentage points to the growth rate for the quarter" in the spring of 2009.[5] Niall Ferguson, a senior fellow at the conservative Hoover Institution, wrote: "According to Moody's, the ratings agency, the stimulus package has saved more than 500,000 jobs. Without the jump in government spending, GDP would still be in a nosedive."[6]

Although other economists might dispute the size of the effect, no economist has come forward to embrace Limbaugh's theory that the stimulus bill actually caused the recession to worsen, that "thanks to Obama-Pelosi-Reid's stimulus bill, we are losing millions of jobs."[7] The idea that a stimulus bill could actually cause millions of jobs to disappear is so absurd, so contrary to every single theory of economics, that anyone who posits such a concept should be regarded as a complete buffoon on the topic. Limbaugh, of course, never explains how his theory of the stimulus bill could possibly be true. Is it the case that companies, upon learning that the government is spending money to replace the absent private sector investment, would decide to start laying off workers to deal with the anticipated increase in demand? Exactly how is it possible for government spending during a recession to cause a short-term economic decline leading to the loss of millions of jobs?

Yet Limbaugh returned over and over again to his conspiracy theory about the intentional destruction of the U.S. economy by the Obama administration, saying, "Nobody's this dumb, nobody is this economically illiterate. They have to be doing this on purpose,"[8] and maintaining, "Obama's stimulus bill is working exactly as intended: rising unemployment, crisis. This is what they want."[9] According to Limbaugh, "Obama, he's not telling people that he's destroying the economy, he's not telling people of the pain this is all causing, that it's intentional,"[10] and, "Obama is purposely destroying the middle class—purposely destroying it."[11] Limbaugh's crazy conspiracy theory isn't some verbal gaffe made in the heat of an off-the-cuff tirade; it is his fundamental theory about the Obama administration repeated with absolute certainty on almost a daily basis.

His conspiracy theory even reached the point where he projected his own hopes for financial disaster, claiming that the Obama administration "hopes this country fails." When jobless claims increased, Limbaugh imagined "Obama with a big excrement-eating grin on his face."[12]

Conservative talk show host Michael Medved called the idea of Obama intentionally destroying the economy "paranoid delusions."[13] But Medved (who didn't challenge Limbaugh by name) was rare among both conservatives and the mainstream media, where the radio host is either feared or admired.

The constant repetition of Limbaugh's conspiracy theories has had a substantial impact on public opinion. A poll by the Beemer Report found that in 2009, after the stimulus package passed, 12.1 percent of Americans feared President Obama was trying to ruin the U.S. economy. By March 2010, the pollster found that 35.8 percent believed Obama has a plan to damage the U.S. economy so he can implement more government control. C. Britt Beemer, author of the Beemer Report, noted: "Never in thirty-one years have

I seen so many people question the integrity and motives of a U.S. president."[14]

IMAGINING AN OBAMA RECESSION

On November 6, 2008, just two days after Obama was elected president, Limbaugh was naming Bush's recession after him: "Speaking of Obama, by the way, the Obama recession is in full swing, ladies and gentlemen. Stocks are dying, which is a precursor of things to come. This is an Obama recession. Might turn into a depression. It's—he hadn't done anything yet, but his ideas are killing the economy. His ideas are killing Wall Street."[15] On November 11, 2008, Limbaugh again referred to the "Obama recession."[16] It was inconceivable that Obama could have caused the recession that began in 2007 when he was still considered a long shot for the presidency. Inconceivable, that is, to anyone but Limbaugh.

Less than a week after Obama became president, Limbaugh was again blaming him for unemployment, declaring about massive layoffs that "casualties are mounting across the United States" and attributing it to the "Obama war on prosperity."[17]

At the Conservative Political Action Conference in February 2009, Limbaugh denounced Obama for being too negative about the state of the economy: "Barack Obama portrays America as a soup kitchen in some dark night in a corner of America that's very obscure. He's constantly telling the American people that bad times are ahead, worst times are ahead."[18] Limbaugh accused Obama of "talking down the economy."[19] A month earlier, the radio host had proclaimed, "There's no reason to . . . tell the American people that their future is bleak. There's no reason, as the administration is doing, to depress their hopes. There's no reason to insist that recovery can't happen quickly, because it can."[20]

But once Obama had passed the stimulus plan, Limbaugh immediately stopped his complaints against people saying the economy was in a crisis, and started declaring that the economy was in a crisis. After complaining about "media attempts to create a crisis mentality where the economy is concerned," Limbaugh switched to complaining that the media was ignoring the economic crisis, which he depicted in particularly stark terms.[21] By the summer of 2009, Limbaugh was leading the crusade to emphasize that bad times were ahead, in order to blame it on Obama: "We are on the cusp of an unmitigated national disaster."[22]

Limbaugh repeatedly claimed that under Bush, "Unemployment was at 4.7 percent, an all-time record low,"[23] and added, "It was just two years ago we were at record employment at 4.7 percent, after coming out of a mild recession that Clinton left us with."[24] In reality, the 4.7 percent unemployment rate wasn't a record; the record was set in 2000 under Clinton at 4.0 percent.[25] And the "recession" Limbaugh blamed on Clinton led to only a 4.8 percent unemployment rate in 2001, barely higher than the 2007 employment levels that Limbaugh falsely claimed were a record low.

But it's curious that Limbaugh was willing to blame a recession on Clinton that occurred at the very end of his presidency, while completely refusing to blame Bush for a recession that was far deeper and started much earlier in his presidency. Rush even claimed, "The recession began in 2008. They say 2007, so they can blame all this on Bush."[26] Does Rush really imagine that people will somehow forget who was president during all of 2008?

No aspect of economic data was immune from Limbaugh's distortions. He declared on July 31, 2009, "This economy has shrunk twice as much as it did with George W. Bush in the trailing end of 2008."[27] Once again, Limbaugh was wrong. He was misreading a Bloomberg news report that noted that the gross domestic product fell 1.9 percent from the fourth quarter of 2007 to the fourth quarter of 2008, a dramatic worsening from the previous estimated decline of 0.8 percent. The report also said that GDP shrank "3.9 percent in the past year." The 3.9 percent decline referred to the previous year, including the last half of 2008 (which was the "trailing end of 2008"). In reality, the quarterly GDP declines reported were 2.7 percent in the third quarter of 2008, 5.4 percent in the fourth quarter of 2008, 6.4 percent in the first quarter of 2009, and 1.0 percent in the second quarter of 2009.[28] So the GDP decline in the last half of 2008 was actually bigger than the decline in the first half of 2009, the exact opposite of what Limbaugh claimed. More important, the revised figures showed that the recession under Bush was far worse than had been reported, while the economy under Obama was improving better than expected by economists.

After getting all of his economic facts dead wrong, Limbaugh complained, "This is a great example of what state-controlled media is," citing the positive headlines about the lower-than-expected decline in the GDP.[29] But the mainstream media was right; in fact, the story proved that the media had been far too optimistic about the U.S. economy under Bush. It was Limbaugh, not the "state-controlled media," who was guilty of distorting the truth about the economy by taking news that proved how bad the Bush recession was and claiming it meant the exact opposite.

Limbaugh even turns good economic news into evidence for his conspiracy theories. Upon learning that the decline in the GDP during the second quarter of 2009 was only 0.7 percent, not the original projection of 1.0 percent, he declared: "There is no recovery from the recession! And that is by design. . . . The economy is not rebounding."[30] When the GDP increased substantially in the third quarter of 2009, he claimed it wasn't real because the government spending from Obama's stimulus plan was responsible for most of the increase. This logic was particularly odd because Limbaugh claimed the stimulus had no effect on the economy: "There aren't any roads being rebuilt, not with stimulus money."[31] Limbaugh falsely asserted that only 4 percent of the stimulus had been spent, when by September 28, 2009, over $100 billion had been spent, along with $63 billion in tax cuts, which made up 21 percent of the stimulus (and an additional $140 billion of spending was already in process).[32]

When a report in December 2009 indicated an improvement in jobs, Rush immediately dismissed the possibility of any good news: "No matter how you do the math on this there aren't new jobs being created, and there really isn't any slowdown in jobs being lost. Zilch, zero, nada."[33] The very next day, a decline in both the unemployment rate and the underemployment rate was announced as job losses slowed to almost zero.[34]

LIMBAUGH'S SHIFTING STANDS

When the economy was headed toward a deep recession under Bush, Limbaugh was relentlessly optimistic and in complete denial. Then, as the economy began to make a recovery under Obama, Rush became relentlessly pessimistic, emphasizing its dire state. In 2008, when the recession had already begun, Limbaugh raised no objection when Dick Cheney declared on Rush's show, "We don't believe we're going to have a recession, though."[35]

In January 2008, at the very moment when the United States was already in a recession, Limbaugh claimed it was all media bias: "The drive-by media is doing its damnedest to create an economic depression."[36] After many months of denying any recession when Bush was president, Limbaugh suddenly discovered the existence of a recession only when he could blame it on a Democrat.

When CNN reporter Ali Velshi dared to question Limbaugh's positive view of the economy, Limbaugh responded on his own show: "Mr. Velshi, you are incompetent. You are a disservice to your business. Except you fit right in at CNN. Disinformation, character assaults. This economy is nowhere near as bad as it was in 1982."[37] Only a few months later, Limbaugh denounced the Obama administration for a 5.7 percent decline in GDP that occurred in the first quarter of 2009, a decline (under the Bush administration's policies) that happened at the very time when he was attacking Velshi for accurately portraying a terrible recession.

The odd thing is, Limbaugh's argument that 1982 was a worse recession than 2008 undermines his admiration of Ronald Reagan's beneficial impact on the economy. Whether 1982 or 2008 was a worse recession should not matter to Limbaugh because both happened under conservative presidents. But Limbaugh was desperately trying to stop Obama's $789 billion stimulus package from passing, and he calculated that if the depth of this recent recession could be denied, it would remove the need for government stimulus. Speaking of the two recessions, Limbaugh said, "When Obama talks about past economies, he somehow always leaves out the recession of the eighties as worse than this one. Why does he leave it out? Because you know why he leaves it out, America? He leaves it out because we got out of that recession with tax cuts."[38] The 1982 recession wasn't ended by tax cuts. As Bernard Sherman, a self-made billionaire who praises Reagan's 1986 tax reform, noted, "The Reagan 1981 tax cut neither caused the 1983 recovery—other factors deserve the credit—nor boosted tax revenues. It did cause a significant increase in the Federal budget deficit."[39]

In his first book, Rush Limbaugh defined the Reagan era as "the period from 1983 to 1989, the years of full-blown Reaganomics."[40] So Limbaugh claimed that Obama was responsible for the economy months before he was inaugurated, whereas Reagan's responsibility for the economy didn't start until two years after he became president, conveniently omitting one of the worst recessions of the twentieth century. This kind of dishonest, partisan economics is typical of Limbaugh's analysis.

As Limbaugh increasingly tried to blame Obama for Bush's recession, he changed his mind about which recession was worse. Comparing the 2008–2009 recession to the 1982 one, Limbaugh claimed, "Teenage employment, 23 percent. It's 52 percent today!"[41] He even repeated the claim days later: "Teenage unemployment is running over 50 percent."[42] And then he repeated it again the next day: "There's a 52 percent unemployment rate among America's youth."[43] But it wasn't true. The actual teen unemployment rate was 25.9 percent in September 2009, or less than half of what Limbaugh said it was.[44]

THE TAX-CUTTING FETISH

Cutting taxes is the solution to every problem, according to Limbaugh: "In 1981, Ronald Reagan when he was inaugurated, the top marginal income tax rate was 70 percent. And the annual take, the federal budget, was around $500 billion. In 1989 when Ronald Reagan left office, the top marginal rate was 28 percent, the tax take had doubled, almost doubled. It was $950 billion, after reducing tax rates from 70 percent to 28 percent."[45]

Limbaugh's numbers are wrong because he fails to account for inflation and omits the fact that Bill Clinton raised the top tax rates and saw bigger economic growth than during the Reagan era. The federal government had $511 billion in revenues in 1980, and $909 billion in 1988. When Bill Clinton took office, the top marginal tax rate was 31 percent, and the annual tax take in 1992 was $1.091 trillion. When Bill Clinton left office in 2001, the top marginal tax rate was 39.6 percent, and the tax take was $2.026 trillion.[46] So Clinton raised taxes and increased revenues. In constant (2000) dollars, the 1980 revenues were $1.028 trillion, and the 1988 revenues were $1.236 trillion, an increase of only 20 percent. By contrast, 1992 revenues were $1.283 trillion, and 2000 revenues were $2.026 trillion, an increase of 58 percent. In constant (2000) dollars, the deficit under Reagan was $147 billion in 1980 and $211 billion in 1988. But under Clinton the deficit was $341 billion in 1992 and the surplus was $236 billion in 2000.[47] So the deficit under Reagan increased by 44 percent, while Clinton took a much larger deficit and turned it into the largest surplus in American history.

But the clearest evidence of how Limbaugh's economic theories are wrong is George W. Bush's record: Tax revenues in constant dollars went from $2.026 trillion in 2000 to $2.006 trillion in 2008, a decline of 0.3 percent, and the $236 billion surplus turned into a $364 billion deficit, all while the top marginal tax rate was cut from 39.6 percent to 35 percent.[48]

These simple facts should establish once and for all that anyone such as Limbaugh who says that reducing the top marginal tax rates inevitably increases tax revenues and that raising these tax rates inevitably reduces tax revenues is simply ignorant of economic reality. But Limbaugh often claims, "We all know that lowering taxes would be the correct way to generate more revenue."[49] The idea that lower taxes leads to more tax revenue is one of the holy writs of conservative economics, but it has no basis in reality. If lowering taxes always generates more revenue, then we could create the highest possible revenue by lowering taxes to zero.

Rush Limbaugh is fond of distorting statistics about Reagan's tax cuts and their influence. To prove how Reagan helped African Americans, for example, Limbaugh offered these figures: "Between 1978 and 1982 the number of poor blacks rose by more than 2 million; between 1982 and 1989 the number of poor blacks fell by 400,000."[50] Limbaugh twisted the numbers by ignoring the fact that Ronald Reagan was already president when black poverty skyrocketed from 1981 to 1982 by more than five hundred thousand. According to the Census Bureau statistics, there were more poor blacks when Reagan left office than when he entered. The contrast with Bill Clinton is clear. In 1993 there were 10.877 million blacks in poverty; by 2000, the last year of Clinton's presidency, the number stood at fewer than 8 million.[51]

Rush tried to claim that "during the Reagan years" the poor got a 540 percent tax cut, while the wealthiest got the smallest tax cut of only 7.9 percent, according to the Census Bureau. As Al Franken revealed, Limbaugh was simply being deceptive. First, Limbaugh got the source wrong (the U.S. Census Bureau doesn't provide tax data). Second, Limbaugh fudged the dates of the "Reagan years" to extend them to 1992 in order to include Bush 41's tax hikes and the Earned Income Tax Credit, both of them liberal policies denounced by Limbaugh. Third, Limbaugh omitted payroll taxes. Taking this all into account, Franken calculated that the poor got a 15 percent tax hike during the Reagan era, while the rich got a 15 percent tax cut.[52]

LIMBAUGH'S ECONOMIC FORECASTS

Nearly every economic prediction Limbaugh makes is wrong. He wrote in 1993, "The maddening thing is that in a few years, when it becomes clear that Clinton's plan has not reduced the deficit, he and his congressional conspirators will simply say that if they hadn't done something, the deficit would have been worse."[53] Limbaugh denounced the Clinton administration and "the inevitable failure of their programs"[54] and wrote, "I have predicted that when Bill Clinton serves out his first and only term as president . . . the era of Reagan will stand alone as clearly one of the most prosperous periods in American history."[55] As usual, Limbaugh turned out to be dead wrong, and the economic success of the Clinton administration far exceeded the Reagan administration's record by any measure: economic growth, unemployment, poverty rates, and budget deficits.

Limbaugh was completely confident about his economic theories, though: "Is there any real likelihood that Clinton's program can work? I must tell you that I am confident that the plan will not work, for a number of reasons. As I said, tax increases retard economic growth and, other things being equal, accentuate the deficit problem."[56] But economic growth under Clinton was far greater than under Reagan, and the deficit disappeared under Clinton while it hit record levels during the conservative presidencies of Reagan and George W. Bush.

Back when Clinton was president, Limbaugh was willing to bet on failure: "I'll put my money where my mouth is. I'll bet the Democratic National Committee that after this economic plan has been implemented—if it is, by 1995 or 1996, you take your pick—unemployment will be higher than the day the plan was passed, the inflation rate will be higher than the day the plan was passed, and the deficit and interest rates will be higher, too. And Bill Clinton's approval rating will be at 45 and falling."[57]

The unemployment rate steadily declined from 7 percent in 1993 to 5.67 percent in 1995 and 5.47 percent in 1996.[58] Inflation dropped from 3.0 percent in 1993 to 2.8 percent in 1995 before rising back to 3.0 percent in 1996.[59] In 1993 the deficit was $255 billion, which dropped to $164 billion in 1995 and $107 billion in 1996.[60] Out of forty-six Gallup polls in 1995 and 1996, Clinton had below 45 percent approval in only three of them, and his ratings steadily increased in 1996.[61] Limbaugh was only correct about interest rates, which increased slightly while the GNP skyrocketed. Limbaugh would have lost his million-dollar bet.

Yet Limbaugh in 1993 was convinced that liberals were pushing a plan to fail: "They know this plan won't work. But they don't have the guts to say so—not the people in the Democratic National Committee or anybody else."[62] He would use almost the exact same words in 2009 to denounce Obama's economic plan.

When George W. Bush was named president, Limbaugh turned from a perpetual pessimist into an optimist. In 2005 he declared: "There are new numbers in on the ten-year projection for the deficit. It's down a trillion dollars. The projection was $2.3 trillion, or $2.2 trillion, the deficit projection for the next ten years is down to $1.2 trillion. Well, it's bad news, but it's better news than what the projection was! We've cut it in half! We're growing. The point is, the only reason the deficit comes down, because the economy is growing."[63] All those projections were dead wrong. The Bush administration added trillions to the national debt through a combination of wasteful spending and massive tax cuts for the rich. The Bush deficit for 2009 alone (without the Obama stimulus package) almost reached the ten-year fantasy Limbaugh believed in.

After years of ignoring the massive deficits under George W. Bush despite a bubble economy, Limbaugh was quick to blame Obama for the large deficit increases caused by the Bush recession. By June 2009 Limbaugh had proclaimed that Bush was entirely blameless for the record deficits under his presidency: "Let me tell you where 100 percent of the deficit belongs, blame Obama and Congress."[64] According to Limbaugh, "This man has spent more deficit money in one year than the Bush eight years in total."[65] But from 2002 to 2008, the United States ran a total deficit of $2.13 trillion, far more than the $1.4 trillion deficit in 2009.[66]

The bigger lie spread by the radio host is that this is "Obama's budget deficit." As Reagan Treasury official Bruce Bartlett noted, "According to the Congressional Budget Office's January 2009 estimate for fiscal year 2009, outlays were projected to be $3,543 billion and revenues were projected to be $2,357 billion, leaving a deficit of $1,186 billion. Keep in mind that these estimates were made before Obama took office, based on existing law and policy, and did not take into account any actions that Obama might implement." Bartlett noted the Congressional Budget Office found that fiscal year 2009 "ended with spending at $3,515 billion and revenues of $2,106 billion for a deficit of $1,409 billion."[67] Under Obama, the federal government spent slightly less money than budgeted, but because the Bush recession was worse than expected, the drop in revenues caused a slightly larger deficit than predicted.

Yet Limbaugh ignored all of these economic facts: "Barack Obama continually, childishly, immaturely blames predecessors for all of the mess that he and he alone has compounded."[68] In the childish world of Rush Limbaugh, Obama deserves the sole blame for the Bush recession, even though it began long before Obama ever took office. We all know exactly what Limbaugh would say if a Republican had followed a Democratic president during economic troubles; he would invariably blame the Democrat. We know this because it's exactly what Limbaugh does for Ronald Reagan.

Limbaugh claimed the 1982 recession that began well into Reagan's presidency directly because of Reagan's policies "was the result of four years of Jimmy Carter."[69] By contrast, after only a few months of Obama's term, Rush gave "sole" blame to Obama for a recession that began under his predecessor. And after making his hypocritical attack on Obama for Bush's recession, Limbaugh had the gall to call Obama "childish" for accurately pointing to the Bush administration's policies that led to the recession.

BLAMING THE DEMOCRATS

Limbaughnomics is a particularly crazed and uneducated type of right-wing economics. Rush has said of Obama, "He inherited the strongest economy in human experience."[70] There are many ways to describe the disaster Obama inherited in January 2009—"the worst recession inherited by a president since the Great Depression" comes to mind—but "the strongest economy in human experience" is not one of them.

There is no economic problem that Limbaugh does not blame on the Democratic Party. He blamed high gas prices on Democrats: "These gas prices didn't start going through the roof till your buddies took over the House in 2006. . . . Through six years of the Bush administration, oil was low, gas was low for the most part. Only when the Democrats got in there did the world markets panic and start going through the roof."[71] Limbaugh's bizarre suggestion that the world market for oil was in a panic because Democrats controlled the House of Representatives falls somewhere in that shady area between insanity and stupidity, where he prefers to roam. No one imagines that U.S. election results control the price of oil. Moreover, if they did, under Rush's theory we should have seen a sudden rise in oil prices right after the 2006 elections, which didn't happen. In fact, oil prices had steadily increased since 2001, dropped sharply for a short time in 2006, and then skyrocketed in 2008 under the Bush administration before plummeting due to the global recession. The only consistent factor during this period was Republican control of the presidency, but no economist imagines that Bush was personally responsible for oil prices.[72]

In Limbaugh's world, Democrats are to blame for every economic downturn: "I want to thank President Bush for saving or creating between 1.6 and 2.4 million jobs as well, which he genuinely did—and he took the unemployment rate down to 4.7 percent. It started skyrocketing up the moment Nancy Pelosi and the Democrats took control of the House in 2007."[73] Actually, the unemployment rate when Bush took office was 4.2 percent; when he left in 2009, it was 7.7 percent. Nor is it plausible to blame the Democrats. The unemployment rate when the Democrats took control of Congress in January 2007 was 4.6 percent. By May 2007, it had actually declined, not skyrocketed, to 4.4 percent.[74] Only when the housing bubble burst did the unemployment rate rise dramatically during the Bush recession.

For Limbaugh, facts are an inconvenient barrier to his true task of indoctrinating and entertaining his audience. He is fond of tossing out bizarre statistics, although his books, like his radio show, are free of evidence to substantiate his claims. "Health care, that's one-sixth—one-sixth!—of the U.S. economy, one-sixth of our GDP," he declared in July 2009. "You take that out of the private sector. That means the private sector has shrunk by one-sixth. That means there's less capital for people to compete for and earn, and there's less opportunity for that remaining five-sixths (and it's going to be less than that because all this other stuff's going to take even more of the private sector) to grow."[75]

Once again, Limbaugh is not afraid to display his ignorance of economics. First of all, the Obama plan maintains the private health insurance system and private health care providers. Second, even if the private health care sector magically ceased to exist, it would not reduce the amount of capital available in the rest of the economy for investment and opportunity. So everything Limbaugh has said about the economics of Obama's health care reform is not merely wrong but completely illogical.

While the economy was already recovering from the Bush recession, Limbaugh claimed that an economic recovery was impossible: "How in the world can any sane, credible economist or financial analyst predict an economic recovery with cap and trade lurking to be passed and nationalized health care about to be passed? Folks, there will be no such thing as a private sector economic recovery if either or one [sic] of these two pieces of legislation gets signed into law."[76] No economist imagined that the passage of these plans would put the economy in a permanent recession. The fact that Limbaugh actually believes this—and regards any dispute with it as insane—reflects how little he understands about economics.

When he is being particularly irrational, Limbaugh likes to proclaim the certainty of his beliefs: "This is not left economics versus right economics. Economics is economics. It's science. There are left–right disagreements in it obviously, but what Obama is doing here, there is nobody that can say, 'This is an honest attempt at really doing what they think is best.' "[77] What Obama was doing was not only an honest attempt at doing what he thought was best, it was mainstream economic policy. Much like the claims of his idol, Ronald Reagan, who predicted economic disaster and socialism from the passage of Medicare, Limbaugh's overblown rhetoric has no basis in economic reality.

THE OBAMA STOCK MARKET

On January 15, 2009, Limbaugh contended that Obama was responsible for the Dow Jones Industrial Average dropping during his speech on the economy, arguing that the stock market is "giving him a failing grade."[78] He declared, before Obama was even inaugurated: "It's entirely fair to call this Obama's stock market because it's reacting to what Obama's plans are for the economy," adding, "Financial markets are a rough predictor of future economic performance, and based upon what the markets know of Obama's plans, it's giving him a failing grade."[79]

If the stock market results were used to grade presidents, Obama would be considered a remarkable success. Limbaugh decried "the absolute fall, the fallout on the market, in the market since Obama was elected. It's down over 2,000 points. You can chronicle each plunge with stated, announced, or completed Obama policy. The market is plunging."[80] But Limbaugh suddenly stopped talking about the Dow Jones Industrial Average as "the Obama Daily Tracking Poll" when the numbers for Obama looked good.

As the stock market began to recover from the Bush recession in April 2009, Limbaugh had an immediate explanation: "Have you seen the Dow Jones Industrial Average today? It's up 252 points, and Obama is out of the country! If there's just a way to keep him over there for a while, the market might come back sufficiently to start the rest of the economy coming back."[81] He said months later, "I maintain this is because President Obama is out of the country. The market loves it when Obama leaves," and, "Remember when Obama left, the markets skyrocketed. The markets know Obama is coming back and so the markets are plummeting."[82]

When the stock market continued to rise despite Obama's presence in the country, Limbaugh quietly abandoned that crackpot theory. But that didn't stop Limbaugh from repeatedly invoking the stock market as a judge of Obama exclusively on those rare days when it dropped. He claimed on May 28, 2009, "How can the economy said to be back from the brink, folks, when the market tanked 200 points yesterday?"[83] So what did Rush say the next day, after the Dow Jones jumped sharply? Well, nothing. For Limbaugh, any facts that refute his theories are simply ignored.

As the stock market soared under Obama, Limbaugh changed his message: "What's happening is that the industriousness of the American people is dealing with the damage that Obama has wrought. The stock market is still down, gang. It peaked up at over 14,000. It's down 16 points today."[84] To Limbaugh, all increases in the stock market were caused by the industrious American people, while the 5000-point decline during the Bush administration was the fault of Obama.

On Obama's inauguration day, the Dow Jones stood at 7,949. By June 5, 2009, the Dow was at 8,763, an increase of more than 10 percent. By October 2009, the Dow had jumped above the 10,000 mark, but Limbaugh still mentioned the stock market exclusively on days when it dropped. Of course, if the Dow Jones measured the success of a presidency, then Bill Clinton and

Barack Obama were more successful than Ronald Reagan or any other Republican president, and George W. Bush was the worst president since Herbert Hoover.[85]

The "Maha Rushie" celebrates every momentary dip in the stock market as a repudiation of Obama's policies: "The market was on its way to 11,000 when Obama attacked the banks, promised to tax them for repaying TARP money with interest. Then he released his economy-killing budget. The market's voting and it isn't even November. These are people with skin in the game."[86] When the stock market surged past 11,000 a few weeks later, Limbaugh said nothing. Amazingly, Limbaugh has complained that the media failed to imitate his own practice of blaming Obama for stock market declines during the massive increase in the Dow Jones during the Obama administration: "At no time will the stock market decline ever be attributed to Obama. It can't be. The stock market going down when Obama's in the White House is just not possible."[87]

Listening to Limbaugh is like watching a stock market ticker that can only move in one direction. Every downturn in the Dow Jones is reported with breathless anxiety, while the more frequent increases disappear into an ideological memory hole: "Obama can manipulate the jobs numbers all he wants. But he cannot manipulate the real money on Wall Street. The Dow Jones Industrial Average is down 107. They are not buying this unemployment number. Look, anybody with half a brain knows it's bogus."[88] Limbaugh never explains how the stock market could rise so dramatically during the Obama administration if the Dow Jones is immune to Obama's manipulations. Perhaps it might have something to do with the booming economy under Obama.

Yet Limbaugh continues to blame Obama for all of the economic problems caused by the Bush recession, often exaggerating the economic downturn to suit his purposes: "American families have lost 20 percent of their wealth since January of this year, some families more than that. This is the average. Twenty percent! I mean, there are trillions of dollars of wealth that have been lost in 401(k)s, pension plans, stock portfolios, people being fired."[89] It's true that American families lost 18 percent of their wealth, but that happened in 2008 under George W. Bush, not in 2009.[90] In Rush's view, Obama was secretly controlling the economy while George W. Bush was still president. That would be a remarkable achievement, but unfortunately for Limbaugh, there's not the slightest evidence to support this allegation.

ATTACKING THE STIMULUS PLAN

Limbaugh even believes that the Obama administration's bailouts and stimulus plans made the financial crisis ten times worse than it originally was:
"What we've done in response to whatever financial crisis there was, was
compound the crisis by a multiple of ten if we'd have just left it alone."[91]
Limbaugh's belief that the government should do nothing is not shared by
anyone in the Republican Party, except perhaps a small fringe group of
radical libertarians. There are many flaws in the bailouts begun by George
W. Bush, but doing nothing would have been a disastrous alternative.

Rush's ignorance of economics is reflected in his attacks on the Obama
stimulus plan. Limbaugh said, "Skateboard parks, streetscrapes [sic], up-
grades of park facilities, bike trails, parking garages? That's what's being
built with stimulus money. Stimulus money was to stimulate the economy."[92]
Apparently he doesn't understand the basic economic fact that government
spending on parks employs people and does stimulate the economy. Limbaugh concluded, "Everybody knows the stimulus plan bombed!"[93] He has
declared, "The economy has dropped at 5.7 percent in the first quarter—5.7
percent! Folks, that is phenomenal. After all the stimulating, after all of the
spending, after all of the pep talks, after all of the bailouts! Washington's
solutions are not working."[94] But the 5.7 percent decline in the first quarter
happened almost entirely before the stimulus plan passed, and certainly before
it had time to work. The fact that GNP only declined 0.7 percent in the second
quarter indicated the success of the stimulus plan in helping the economy
recover and restoring economic stability.

Limbaugh asked, "Where are the 'shovel-ready jobs'? Where's all the
work on the infrastructure? It ain't happening. Caterpillar is still laying
people off."[95] Ironically, his remark came just two days after Caterpillar's
stock soared when it reported second-quarter profits that nearly tripled
analysts' expectations, and CEO Jim Owens declared, "We are seeing signs
of stabilization that we hope will set the foundation for an eventual recovery."[96] Of course, Caterpillar depends upon a global market, so even an
increase in government infrastructure work in America wouldn't offset
worldwide losses or the dramatic drop in private construction. But Lim-

baugh's misunderstandings about the global economy and the stimulus plan don't change the fact that he cited Caterpillar as evidence of the economy getting worse at the very moment when Caterpillar was seeing evidence for optimism.

On January 8, 2009, Limbaugh asserted, "Recessions come out of their cycles in twenty-four-month periods if you just leave them alone."[97] Perhaps recognizing that a two-year recession wouldn't allow him to blame Obama, a few weeks later Limbaugh decided to cut that number to less than half of what he earlier claimed it was: "The average recession will last five months to eleven months."[98]

A common myth among conservatives promoted by Limbaugh is that "the New Deal did not fix the Great Depression; it made it worse. The New Deal prolonged it."[99] Limbaugh's version of Hooverism did not end the Great Depression; by contrast, the New Deal was a success at helping limit the terrible effects of the Great Depression. The worst mistake Roosevelt made was in 1937, when he gave in to conservative thinkers and cut government spending in order to balance the budget, which resulted in a severe recession.[100]

Rush's ignorance about economics makes him imagine the worst about his political enemies. On almost a daily basis, Limbaugh told his audience in 2009 that Obama was intentionally destroying the economy to increase his power: "If you wanted more people to demand a government health care program, wouldn't you want to drive their bills through the roof? . . . This is by design, folks! . . . There isn't an economist anywhere who would suggest doing this and keeping it up."[101]

Not one leading liberal commentator ever suggested that George W. Bush tried to destroy the U.S. economy in order to enhance his power, even though Bush, unlike Obama, actually helped cause one of the worst economic collapses in American history. In fact, it would be difficult to find a single random left-wing blogger who made such a bizarre suggestion. But for the leading conservative voice in the country, spouting such a crazy conspiracy theory was considered so unexceptional that no one in the mainstream media reported on it.

Plenty of conservatives criticized Obama's economic plans, but only Limbaugh imagined a vast conspiracy to destroy America's economy: "That's so hard for people to grasp. It's so difficult for people to put their arms around, a U.S. president that wants to destroy the economy."[102] Perhaps the reason why it's difficult to grasp is because it's insane. In the strange, twisted world of Limbaughnomics, mainstream capitalist economic theories are evidence of a secret plot to destroy America.

6

"TRUTHINESS" ON PARADE: LIMBAUGH'S LIES, ERRORS, AND DISTORTIONS

Rush Limbaugh's show is a monument to the notion of "truthiness"—the belief that feeling you are telling the truth matters more than the truth itself. As Stephen Colbert (the person, not the character) noted, "It used to be, everyone was entitled to their own opinion, but not their own facts. But that's not the case anymore. Facts matter not at all."[1] This attitude is particularly true of Rush.

In Limbaugh's imagination, he is the last bastion of truth against an onslaught of liberal lies: "You know, folks, the two universes here—the Universe of Lies, the Universe of Reality—they don't overlap anymore." He claimed, "If you live in the Universe of Lies, the last thing that you are governed by is the truth. The last thing you are governed by is reality. The only thing that matters to you is the advancement of your political agenda. And you tell yourself in the Universe of Lies that your agenda is so important the world will not survive without it and therefore you could lie, cheat, steal, destroy whoever you have to to get your agenda done—because your opponents are eeevil, and in fighting eeevil, anything goes. There are no rules when you're in a fight with the Devil."[2]

What Limbaugh said about Obama actually applies to himself: "He exists in the Universe of Lies."[3] It's Rush who occupies the Universe of Lies, it's Limbaugh who thinks his agenda is so important that the truth doesn't matter, and it's he who imagines his political enemies are "eeevil" and therefore anything goes.

Oblivious to the irony, Rush has said about liberals: "They live in an emotional cocoon that they've constructed for a safe worldview, plus you couple it with the fact that they think they are the smartest people in the room. All they are is arrogant and condescending."[4] Limbaugh occupies an emotional cocoon of his Dittoheads, all while being condescending toward anyone who disagrees.

In October 2009 Limbaugh told the *Today* show, "Do I think I ever cross a line? Yeah, probably. Look, fifteen hours a week, no script, no guests, some phone calls thrown in. Anybody who does that is going to say some things, 'Oh, wish I hadn't said that,' but you just come back and apologize for it."[5] However, he almost never apologizes for anything he says, nor does he correct the seemingly endless factual errors that he makes. In fact, Limbaugh boasted in 2005: "We don't retract anything we do here because we never lie and make things up on this program."[6]

Yet Limbaugh is defensive about any criticism, blaming it on a vast left-wing conspiracy: "All you need to do is grab a radio or get to the Web site and turn it on. And yet never am I quoted by what I actually said on the radio. It's always, 'And according to Media Matters for America,' or 'according to the Daily Kos,' or 'according to this or that,' and the only explanation of this, this is purposeful. We're the enemy. We have to be discredited and destroyed. The left can't engage in open debate."[7] Media Matters for America directly quotes what Limbaugh says, and he has never presented a single example where Media Matters for America has written something inaccurate about him, despite thousands of cases where they quote him. In Limbaugh's eyes, any criticism of him quoting his words is an attack on open debate, while his own refusal to engage critics is the essence of open debate.

For a man whose job consists largely of giving his opinions about current events, it's remarkable how often Limbaugh gets basic facts wrong. It would be very easy for him to simply read the day's news and give his conservative view on it. Instead, he seems to have a compulsive desire to twist the facts and distort reality to fit his ideology.

Limbaugh claimed in 1993 that his show "*never* betrays the truth."[8] In 2009 he still claimed that he makes "zero mistakes."[9] But everyone makes mistakes. Rush's claim that he never retracts anything means that he refuses to admit any errors. As he declared, "I don't apologize. Ever. Of course, it helps that I'm never wrong."[10] On the rare occasions when Limbaugh's mistakes receive any media attention, he bizarrely proclaims that this is proof of his near-perfection: "You see, I am right so often that when I make a mistake it is glaring and people just loooove to run in and correct me."[11]

Even some of Limbaugh's fans admit that he is often less than accurate. Limbaugh sympathizer James Rainey wrote in the *Los Angeles Times,* "I enjoyed his barbs at hypocritical 'green' Democrats who flew a squadron of private jets into D.C. for the big day. But that hardly forgives the whoppers he spins out for his listeners, some of whom seem willing to believe that Obama really did cause the recession all by himself."[12]

Limbaugh's style contributes to his propensity for errors. One journalist reported, "Limbaugh works without notes, just his infamous 'stack of stuff.' As Rush told one reporter: 'At noon today I had no idea what the first thing was I was going to say until about twenty seconds into the theme music. It's improv. Stream of consciousness. That little pressure improves my performance. I do my best, most expansive thinking when I am speaking. I get on a roll.' "[13] Limbaugh doesn't need much preparation or planning because he pays so little attention to the facts. His listeners will believe almost anything he tells them, so getting the facts right is unimportant to his show.

He repeatedly says things that no rational person could believe in order to smear liberals. He makes the same error, invokes the same conspiracy theory, over and over again. And unlike the audience of a late-night comedy show, Limbaugh's listeners believe what he tells them—sometimes to his annoyance when he really is engaged in parody.

When the focus is on policy, the radio host's errors grow even more numerous. According to Limbaugh, "Somebody is putting the news out there, folks, that Social Security is going to be in default in two years. Yeah, Social Security in default in two years."[14] No, that was not even remotely true. A Republican, Representative Spencer Bachus (R-AL), accidentally said "default" when he meant to say "deficit."[15] But Limbaugh spread the falsehood that Social Security will be in default in two years.

Ironically, one of Limbaugh's most frequent deceptions is his claim to accuracy. For almost his entire career as a talk show host, Limbaugh has claimed to have a highly specific measure of his accuracy, declaring in 1992 that he is right "97.9 percent of the time."[16] By 2009 Limbaugh was claiming,

"I have an official opinion auditing firm, the Sullivan Group in Sacramento. They just last week released an audit of my opinion since the election. As you know, I went into the election documented to be almost always right 98.9 percent. I have jumped a full tenth of a point. I have not been wrong since the election, according to Sullivan Group, the opinion audit now documented to be almost always right 99 percent of the time."[17] The Sullivan Group is an investment brokerage firm started by Limbaugh's friend Tom Sullivan, who hosted a show at Limbaugh's original station KFBK in Sacramento. The Sullivan Group, which Sullivan sold to Prudential Securities in 1986, would have no expertise in documenting opinions, and the entire reference is an inside joke by Limbaugh. There is no audit of Rush's accuracy by the Sullivan Group or anyone else, and the whole idea of auditing opinions rather than facts is silly. It's simply a way of mocking his enemies and even his own audience by getting them to think there is some kind of statistical basis to his claim to being right.

Limbaugh explained, "They only audit opinions. They don't audit whether I misspeak on a fact or something like."[18] He added, "It is a massively complex—I mean the server farm to handle all this, folks, fills rooms at the Sullivan Group. I mean this is even more complicated than trying to explain my diet."[19] Obviously, there is no computer program that could measure the accuracy of opinions, nor is there any "server farm" filling rooms that would be needed to run it. In this unique instance, Limbaugh was detailed enough about the "audit" to reveal to a careful listener what a fraud it was.

But on most of his shows, Limbaugh simply declares that he is "documented to be almost always right 99.8 percent of the time."[20] Magically, his error rate dropped from 1 percent to 0.2 percent in less than a month. Limbaugh's claims to be almost perfect in his accuracy have grown precisely when his dishonesty and inaccuracy on the air has reached new heights.

LIMBAUGH'S FIGHT WITH FAIR

In 1994 Fairness and Accuracy in Reporting (FAIR) issued a lengthy report on Limbaugh's mistakes.[21] Limbaugh responded with his own detailed defense.[22] Although this debate is more than fifteen years old, it is notable because it was the first, and last, time he ever responded in detail to any criticism. It reveals how Limbaugh approaches his work, and how he rationalizes his mistakes. And it is also worthy of examination because Limbaugh has not altered his views at all, nor has he changed his tactics. He refused to respond to half of FAIR's critiques, but he did try to defend himself against some of their attacks. In his twenty-two responses, Limbaugh displayed a remarkable degree of mendacity, and a near-total refusal to admit an error under any circumstance.

Twisting History

In his first book, Limbaugh quoted James Madison: "We have staked the future upon the capacity of each and all of us to govern ourselves, to control ourselves, to sustain ourselves according to the Ten Commandments of God."[23] FAIR showed that the quote was a fake. Limbaugh admitted, "The quote is not Madison's. But the misattribution of this statement (an error, not 'a lie') has been made by many over the years."[24] Then Limbaugh offered a series of quotes by Madison that he claimed support the view in the fake quote, including one supporting separation of church and state that directly contradicted Limbaugh's idea that Americans should be governed by the Ten Commandments.[25]

Distorting American history is a common motif for Limbaugh: "There are more American Indians alive today than there were when Columbus arrived or at any other time in history. Does this sound like a record of genocide?"[26] FAIR noted: "According to Carl Shaw of the U.S. Bureau of Indian Affairs, estimates of the pre-Columbus population of what later became the United States range from 5 million to 15 million. Native populations in the late 19th century fell to 250,000 due in part to genocidal policies. Today the U.S.'s Native American population is about 2 million."[27] Limbaugh responded, "The facts support me," citing a Heritage Foundation report that says, "Some Indian groups are more populous today than in 1492."[28] Some groups are more populous, and others are not. That's why we have math to add them all up. Whether genocide was involved is a hotly debated issue, but the numbers are quite clear, and Limbaugh was wrong.

To condemn the environmental movement, Limbaugh wrote, "Do you know we have more acreage of forest land in the United States today than we did at the time the Constitution was written?"[29] FAIR noted: "In what are now the 50 U.S. states, there were 850 million acres of forest land in the late 1700s vs. only 730 million acres today."[30] Limbaugh tried to refute this by declaring, "In 1952, the U.S. had 664 million acres of forest land. In 1987 the number had climbed to 731 million acres."[31] But that reflects, in part, the success of the environmental movement in preventing deforestation. More important, such numbers have nothing to do with Limbaugh's original false claim about America in 1787.

Denouncing All Democrats

Attacking Jimmy Carter is a longtime favorite sport of Limbaugh's, even when the facts aren't true: "Those gas lines were a direct result of the foreign oil powers playing tough with us because they didn't fear Jimmy Carter."[32] FAIR noted: "The first—and most serious—gas lines occurred in late 1973–early 1974, during the administration of Limbaugh hero Richard Nixon."[33] Limbaugh responded, "I wasn't discussing the 1973 gas lines. I was discussing the gas lines that Jimmy Carter was responsible for—because he ran such a pathetic foreign policy operation."[34] But Rush still didn't explain why there were worse gas lines under Nixon, if bad foreign policy is the cause of gas lines.

Limbaugh trumpeted any attack on the Clintons, even inaccurate ones: "You know the Clintons send Chelsea to Sidwell Friends private school . . . a recent eighth-grade class assignment required students to write a paper on 'Why I Feel Guilty Being White.' My source for this story is CBS News."[35] In reality, the source was CBS Morning Resource, a clipping service for talk show hosts that got the story from *Playboy* and has no connection to CBS News. The title of the assignment, it turned out, was also wrong. It was, according to the reporter's source, "Should White People Feel Guilty and Why?"[36] In another example, opposing the Clinton administration's efforts to stop genocide in Bosnia, Rush claimed: "For the first time in military history, U.S. military personnel [in Bosnia] are not under the command of United States generals."[37] But FAIR noted, "In World War I, France's Marshal Ferdinand Foch was in overall command of Allied troops."[38] Still, that didn't stop Limbaugh from simply repeating his mistake in his rebuttal:

"U.S. military personnel have served with forces from other countries throughout history, such as in World War I and II, but U.S. generals have always been at the top of the command structure."[39] Attacking the Democrat-controlled Congress, Limbaugh declared: "You better pay attention to the 1993 budget deal because there is an increase in beer and alcohol taxes."[40] FAIR wrote: "There were no increases in beer and alcohol taxes in the 1993 budget,"[41] and Limbaugh responded, "Beer and alcohol taxes were indeed considered for the 1993 budget deal. FAIR gives no context to the quote, nor a date on which I supposedly said it."[42] Then Limbaugh wrote about what he "could have been referring to." But FAIR listed the date and noted, "When Limbaugh made this statement, different budget packages had passed both the House and the Senate, and neither package included tax increases on beer or alcohol."[43]

On the Persian Gulf War, Limbaugh said, "Everybody in the world was aligned with the United States except who? The United States Congress."[44] FAIR stated, "Both houses of Congress voted to authorize the U.S. to use force against Iraq."[45] Limbaugh declared on his radio show: "When I said it, it was true."[46] But as FAIR responded, "Limbaugh made the statement on April 18, 1994—more than three years after the vote."[47]

Limbaugh, in one of his early conspiracy theories, claimed that the Democrats tried to "sabotage" President Bush with the 1990 budget deal: "Now, here is my point. In 1990, George Bush was president and was enjoying a 90 percent plus approval rating on the strength of our victories in the Persian Gulf War and Cold War."[48] FAIR noted: "In October 1990, when the budget deal was concluded, the Gulf War had not yet been fought."[49] Limbaugh responded, "My point, that George Bush was riding high in the polls on the strength of his handling of foreign policy."[50] But Rush did get the facts wrong, and Bush never reached 90 percent approval until after the 1991 Persian Gulf War.

Rush on Race and Gender

In his attack on feminism, the radio host didn't let the facts stand in his way: "Women were doing quite well in this country before feminism came along."[51] FAIR stated: "Before feminism, women couldn't even vote,"[52] to which Limbaugh responded, "I was referring to contemporary militant feminism, not women's suffrage."[53] The problem is that his modified claim doesn't hold water, either. Before the feminist movement of the 1960s, women routinely faced massive discrimination and exclusion from leading colleges and workplaces. If Limbaugh really believes that women had full equality in 1960, he doesn't prove it. Instead, he quoted a number of people criticizing feminism, which has nothing to do with the accuracy of his comment.

Limbaugh was the loudest defender of Clarence Thomas (who later presided at Limbaugh's wedding) and felt free to make up false claims to smear the woman who accused him of sexual harassment: "Anita Hill followed Clarence Thomas everywhere. Wherever he went, she wanted to be right by his side, she wanted to work with him, she wanted to continue to date him. There were no other accusers who came forth after Anita Hill did and said, 'Yeah, Clarence Thomas, he harassed me, too.' There was none of that."[54] FAIR noted: "Hill could not have continued to date Thomas, since they never dated. Two other women, Sukari Hardnett and Angela Wright, came forth in the Thomas case with similar charges."[55] Limbaugh responded by writing, "My comment about Hill dating Thomas actually demonstrates my recall of the Thomas-Hill episode—specifically that the record shows Anita Hill had a genuine affection for Clarence Thomas and repeatedly invited him to her apartment for drinks (a fact Thomas, not Hill, offered for the record)."[56] Limbaugh has an interesting interpretation of what dating means. An assertion that Hill "followed Clarence Thomas everywhere" and "wanted to continue to date him" is not proven by the fact Hill invited Thomas into her apartment for a beer once after he gave her a ride home. Both Hill and Thomas denied that Hill ever tried to date him.[57] Amazingly, Limbaugh thinks his incorrect statement proves how good his recall is. For him, it's almost inconceivable to admit an error.

Defending the police officers who beat Rodney King, Limbaugh said: "The videotape of the Rodney King beating played absolutely no role in the conviction of two of the four officers. It was pure emotion that was responsible for the guilty verdict."[58] FAIR wrote: "'Jury Foreman Says Video Was Crucial in Convictions,' read an accurate Los Angeles Times headline the day after the federal court verdict (4/20/93)."[59] Rush responded, "I discounted the role of the videotape in the jury's decision, despite the jury foreman's claims." Limbaugh cited a *Wall Street Journal* article that said that in the first hung jury, "the notorious eighty-one-second videotape of Mr. King's beating had been perceived as ambiguous in places by the first jury,"[60] as well as various articles about how stressful the jury hearing had been. But none of these articles support an accusation of "pure emotion" deciding the verdict and dismissing the most compelling evidence as completely irrelevant.

Revealing his hatred of government, Limbaugh declared about the quick rebuilding of a freeway destroyed in an earthquake, "There was one key element that made this happen. One key thing: The governor of California declared the [freeway] a disaster area and by so doing eliminated the need for competitive bids . . . Government got the hell out of the way." He added, "They gave this guy [contractor C.C. Myers] the job without having to go through the rigmarole of giving 25 percent of the job to a minority-owned business and 25 percent to a woman."[61]

FAIR noted, "There was competitive bidding: Myers beat four other contractors for the job. Affirmative action rules applied: At least 40 percent of the subcontracts went to minority or women-owned firms. Far from getting out of the way, dozens of state employees were on the job twenty-four hours a day."[62] Limbaugh responded, "FAIR's 'edit' of my statements amounts to misrepresentation," then proceeded with a lengthy but irrelevant discussion praising Myers as "an American hero" without ever challenging anything FAIR wrote, or explaining how it was a misrepresentation.[63]

Media Bashing

Attacking the mainstream media is a favorite Limbaugh hobby, even when the facts don't agree. He describes journalist Michael Gartner as "portraying himself as a balanced, objective journalist with years and years of experience faking events, and then reporting them as news—and doing so with the express hope of destroying General Motors in one case and destroying businesses that cut down trees, the timber industry, in another."[64] Limbaugh responded to FAIR by citing the fact that Gartner was president of NBC News when it staged a video about General Motors.[65] But as FAIR noted, Limbaugh never offered any evidence that Gartner was directly involved, or that he had the "express hope of destroying General Motors."[66]

Smearing his favorite foe, *The New York Times*, Limbaugh declared about the Whitewater scandal: "I don't think *The New York Times* has run a story on this yet. I mean, we haven't done a thorough search, but I—there has not been a big one, front-page story about this one that we can recall. So this has yet to create or get up to its full speed—if it weren't for us and *The Wall Street Journal* and *The American Spectator*, this would be one of the biggest and most well-kept secrets going on in American politics to-day."[67] This wasn't true. Limbaugh didn't apologize for misleading his listeners, but instead claimed, "My point, that as of February, much of the mainstream press had not played up Whitewater details while conservative publications had covered the scandal prominently and advanced the story, is correct. I plainly state that I don't recall if *The New York Times* has run a front-page story."[68] But FAIR wrote, "Limbaugh did not overlook one front-page *New York Times* story on Whitewater, he overlooked half a dozen."[69]

While he obsessed about Whitewater, Limbaugh denied the existence of Republican scandals such as Iran-Contra: "This [Special Prosecutor Lawrence] Walsh story basically is, we just spent seven years and $40 million looking for any criminal activity on the part of anybody in the Reagan administration, and guess what? We couldn't find any. These guys didn't do anything; but we wish they had so we could nail them. So instead, we're going to say, 'Gosh, these are rotten guys.' They have absolutely no evidence. There is not one indictment. There is not one charge."[70] But FAIR noted that there were fourteen indictments,[71] to which Limbaugh responded, "I obviously misspoke when I said there were no indictments—I clearly meant to say there were no convictions, a point I have made on many occasions."[72] But he was wrong once again. As FAIR stated, "eleven were convicted or pleaded guilty" (some convictions were later overturned on appeal due to technicalities).[73]

Resisting Reality

In his desire to praise everything about America, Limbaugh lives in a world of denial; take, for instance, his view of poverty: "The poorest people in America are better off than the mainstream families of Europe."[74] After FAIR challenged him on this statement, he quoted an analyst at the Heritage Foundation: "'Poor' Americans live in larger houses or apartments, eat more meat, and are more likely to own cars and dishwashers than is the general population in Western Europe."[75] Only Limbaugh could claim that owning a dishwasher and eating Big Macs makes you rich. In reality, the purchasing power of the average Western European was and is far above that of the poorest Americans.

FAIR criticized Limbaugh for defending the use of private banks that profit from federal-guaranteed student loans. Rush responded, "Banks do take risks in issuing student loans and are entitled to their profits." What are the risks in these government-guaranteed loans? Limbaugh quoted a PR person for the bank industry: "If banks don't follow the guidelines precisely, they won't be reimbursed by the government and they are left high and dry. That is risk."[76] By that logic, any government contractor takes a risk because they won't be paid if they don't follow the proper procedures. Real "risk" means the risk that a borrower won't be able to pay, a risk that banks don't have with these guaranteed student loans.

Dr. Limbaugh

American health care, Limbaugh claimed in 1999, was the best: "If you have any doubts about the status of American health care, just compare it with that in other industrialized nations."[77] FAIR did this, and noted that the United States ranked poorly in infant mortality and life expectancy. But Rush simply responded, "America's health care system is the best in the world."[78] However, FAIR wrote, "The U.S. also has the lowest health care satisfaction rate (11 percent) of the ten largest industrialized nations."[79] Foreshadowing his later distortions about health care, Limbaugh claimed: "Most Canadian physicians who are themselves in need of surgery, for example, scurry across the border to get it done right; the American way. They have found, through experience, that state medical care is too expensive, too slow and inefficient, and, most important, it doesn't provide adequate care for most people."[80] When FAIR pointed out that this was groundless, Limbaugh claimed it was "an obvious humorous exaggeration to be sure, but it is hardly 'groundless.'"[81] He then cited an article about Canadian doctors moving to America to work for more money, apparently unaware that he was changing the topic.

Some of Limbaugh's antiscientific views can have a dangerous effect if his listeners believe him, such as this view: "The worst of all this is the lie that condoms really protect against AIDS. The condom failure rate can be as high as 20 percent. Would you get on a plane—or put your children on a plane—if one in five passengers would be killed on the flight? Well, the statistic holds for condoms, folks."[82] FAIR noted that condoms have a failure rate of 2 percent or less, not 20 percent,[83] to which Limbaugh responded, "My point is that because condoms can have such a high failure rate, they are not good protection against contracting HIV and AIDS. That is distinctly different from saying that condom users have a one-in-five AIDS risk."[84] But Limbaugh simply invented the 20 percent condom failure rate.[85]

Indeed, he often disputes basic medical and scientific information: "There is no conclusive proof that nicotine's addictive . . . And the same thing with cigarettes causing emphysema, lung cancer, heart disease."[86] When FAIR pointed out the overwhelming medical consensus, Limbaugh responded, "My point, made over and over again in recent months, is that if nicotine is really a terrible drug then Congress should just call it a terrible drug and ban it outright. The fact is that nicotine's addictiveness and whether or not it is a drug is, contrary to FAIR's assertion, a source of tremendous controversy."[87] Perhaps that was his point, but it had nothing to do with what he said. There was a controversy over regulating nicotine as a drug, but not over whether it was addictive or harmful.

The truly outrageous part of Limbaugh's antiscientific stand about nicotine was revealed many years later. In 2009 he finally admitted (without mentioning his past denials), "Nicotine is the most addictive substance on earth." Interestingly, his reasoning had nothing to do with scientific evidence, but was instead an observation he must have made long ago: "The proof in this is that nobody has a pleasant first experience with it. Have you ever seen somebody take a drag on their first cigarette? *(coughing)* Some of them head into the bathroom thinking they're going to throw up. And within seconds they're lighting the second cigarette. Now, most other substances, when you take a hit, you get a high or you get a mellow or whatever. But with this it's pure agony the first time you do it, and yet that doesn't dissuade people." Why did Limbaugh change his mind? In order to make yet another argument against government regulation: "If they're going to reduce the amount of nicotine per cigarette they're just going to increase the number of cigarettes people smoke."[88] By declaring in 2009 that nicotine is a terribly addictive drug, Limbaugh contended that government regulation to reduce nicotine levels would simply cause more smoking. Rush is willing to change any of his views about science so long as it serves his hatred of government regulation.

Rush's Reign of Error

Limbaugh concluded his response to FAIR by writing, "People take me seriously because I am effective. And in my pursuit of the truth, I am an exceptionally accurate commentator."[89] If this collection of lies, smears, and evasions is what Limbaugh regards as "exceptionally accurate," it may explain why nearly every show of his is riddled with mistakes and false allegations. As FAIR noted in its "Reply to Limbaugh's Non-Response," Limbaugh's reply rarely confronted the issue: "Mostly it changes the subject, dodges and wastes thousands of words on tangents and what-I-really-meant-to-say digressions."[90] And, FAIR added, "Limbaugh ignores almost half of the errors that we pointed out."[91]

Among FAIR's critiques that the radio host never answered was the fact that he falsely claimed that income inequality didn't grow during the Reagan administration, incorrectly said that inequality was greater in the 1950s, and wrongly asserted that the public housing budget increased under Reagan.[92] Limbaugh claimed, "Bill Clinton is the first president in modern history to have both houses of Congress," somehow missing seven out of the eleven previous presidents.[93]

In his book *See, I Told You So*, Limbaugh claimed a biblical basis for low taxes, citing the story in Genesis about "the lowering of tax rates on grain from 90 percent to 20 percent, giving seven fat years during the days of Pharaoh in Egypt. . . . You can trace individual prosperity, economic growth back to the Bible, the Old Testament."[94] As FAIR noted, "Genesis 41 is about the wisdom of instituting taxes, not cutting them." After dreaming about seven fat years followed by seven lean years, the pharaoh imposed a 20 percent tax during good times to sustain his empire during a recession. The 90 percent tax existed only in Limbaugh's vivid imagination.[95]

Limbaugh wondered, "Why were people better educated before the

American Revolution with no public funding than in 1993, when we are spending in excess of $100,000 per classroom?"[96] He, of course, was wrong. The twelve years of schooling common today in America were extremely rare in colonial America, and literacy was lower, though New England had the highest literacy rates in the world. The key reason why Americans then were so well educated, contrary to Limbaugh's ideology, was public schooling: A 1647 Massachusetts law required towns with fifty or more families to support a primary school.[97]

And Limbaugh asserted, "Now I got something for you that's true—1972, Tufts University, Boston. This is twenty-four years ago—or twenty-two years ago. Three year study of five thousand co-eds, and they used a benchmark of a bra size of 34C. They found that the—now wait. It's true. The larger the bra size, the smaller the IQ."[98] However, apparently no one at Tufts or anywhere else did any study like this. Fifteen years later, Limbaugh again invoked this mythical study, but claimed that it proved "the larger the bust size, the higher the IQ."[99]

In 2010 Limbaugh complained that he had been criticized for talking about this study that no one has ever been able to find: "It's one of the things that's constantly pointed at as something I lie about, I just made up. I didn't make it up." He then reversed his position again on what this nonexistent study proved: "The smaller the bust size, the higher the IQ."[100]

These and many more evasions were part of Limbaugh's record, but he didn't bother to respond to FAIR's analysis. Instead of confessing to his errors, Rush made every possible excuse and irrelevant argument to distract attention from his own words. And in the rare case where Limbaugh admitted an error, such as repeating the fake Madison quote, he seemed utterly unconcerned about it, and defended it as a common mistake.

Anyone who communicates for many hours every week is likely to make some mistakes. But FAIR and other Limbaugh critics don't denounce him just for slips of the tongue (which Limbaugh commonly has) or erroneous statements that he quickly retracts. Limbaugh's errors go to the core of his arguments.

After being humiliated by FAIR, Limbaugh continued to hold a grudge and looked for ways to respond. On April 5, 1995, Limbaugh announced that he was going to "nuke FAIR" with some new information on forests:

"This, of course, is an area about which I've come under severe and fallacious attack by this media watchdog bunch of homies called Fairness &
Accuracy In Reporting."[101] To prove his claim, Limbaugh quoted an op-ed
quoting a book by conservative Gregg Easterbrook: "In the mid-nineteenth
century, Vermont, Massachusetts, and Connecticut were about 35 percent
wooded; now they are 59 percent wooded." Limbaugh concluded that there
is "more forest land today than two hundred years ago."[102] It's not surprising that wooded lands increased in a few small Northeastern states as
clear-cut agricultural areas were replaced. However, three states are not a
representative sample of the entirety of America. Nor was the mid-nineteenth
century "two hundred years ago," as Limbaugh claimed. So Limbaugh's original statement was still wrong; the facts that he thought would "nuke FAIR"
were irrelevant to the debate.

But to conservatives, Limbaugh can do no wrong. Ann Coulter claimed
in her book *Slander* (which has a foreword written by Limbaugh), "There
are plenty of denunciations of Rush for being inaccurate, but it turns out,
liberals lie even when accusing conservatives of lying."[103] Coulter then de-
votes two pages of her book to delineating one criticism of Rush by FAIR
that she claims was inaccurate. It's a curious kind of logic, to assert that everything Limbaugh says is right because one criticism out of thousands
might be inaccurate. Coulter obviously read the FAIR report, but she chose
to ignore 99 percent of its criticism of Limbaugh.

Coulter concluded, "But on the off chance that anyone ever does locate
some minor inaccuracy by Rush Limbaugh comparable to those regularly nur-
tured by the major media, the point is this: Rush Limbaugh is not the president, the vice president, or a Massachusetts senator. He's not the *New York
Times*. He's not ABC, NBC, or CBS. Arguably, the satirical commentary of a
noted polemicist should not be treated with the earnest indignation better
reserved for the invasion of Poland."[104] It's no surprise that Coulter, infamous
for her racist remarks as well as her regular errors of fact and logic, would
like to use "satirical commentary" to provide immunity for right-wing lies
and smears.[105] But her double standard for conservatives, her assertion that
Rush Limbaugh should not be held as accountable for his mistakes as the
mainstream media should be, is not an intellectually honest approach. A falsehood is a falsehood, whether it's spread by a president or a talk show host.

Coulter exposed her own hypocrisy when she praised Limbaugh's vast political importance: "He's not the leader of the Republican Party. He's something much bigger than that."[106]

Yet the exposure of Limbaugh's lies has not reduced his popularity, nor has it affected his propensity for telling falsehoods to his audience. On April 27, 1995, Limbaugh read examples of "liberal hate speech" by Pacifica Radio host Julianne Malveaux and CBS reporter Eric Engberg from the right-wing Media Research Center's newsletter, unaware that he was reading fake quotes from the April Fool's edition published almost a month earlier.[107] The next day, the radio host admitted the quotes were false but heroically refused to apologize to the journalists he had falsely smeared: "Given some of the things liberals actually do say, it's not too tough to believe they would say the things [Brent] Bozell makes up."[108] Limbaugh's error was even more amazing because he had made the exact same mistake one year earlier when he had read the newsletter's fake quotes as if they were real.[109]

Since that FAIR report, Limbaugh's penchant for making things up has only become more frequent and outrageous. However, Limbaugh no longer deigns to respond to his critics when they expose a falsehood.

LIMBAUGH'S CONSTITUTION

Throughout his career, the self-proclaimed "Doctor of Democracy" has displayed a remarkable degree of indifference to and ignorance of what's in the U.S. Constitution. While calling himself a Constitutionalist, Limbaugh prefers to imagine that the Constitution says exactly what he thinks it should.

In his introduction to Mark Levin's book *Men in Black,* Limbaugh claimed, "Constitutionalists like Mark (and me) believe that the judiciary should stay out of politics and policy matters."[110] Oddly enough, Limbaugh immediately went on to complain that "it was the Court that upheld slavery and segregation, setting back race relations in America for more than a century."[111] Limbaugh seemed unaware that demanding the Supreme Court prohibit segregation—as it did in *Brown v. Board of Education*—was a complete contradiction of his view that the Court must stay out of policy matters.

Limbaugh claimed about the Bible under liberalism, "You wouldn't legally be allowed to read it in a school."[112] There are no books banned in school, particularly not the Bible. In fact, there are public school classes about the Bible.

Even conservative theories of jurisprudence are incomprehensible to Limbaugh, who declared: "Remember Obama believes that the Bill of Rights is a set of 'negative' rights.' This is a concept that's being taught in law schools and has been for a lot of years. Negative rights. They look at the Constitution, people who believe in negative rights, as obstacle. The Bill of Rights says what Congress can't do to you—and statists, authoritarians like Obama look at that, that's a negative."[113] As usual, Rush didn't understand what he was talking about. The idea of the Bill of Rights as a set of "negative rights" is a conservative concept. It means that the role of the Constitution is to prohibit the government from violating specified rights, such as restricting the rights of free speech and freedom of religion. So Obama stands with the conservatives in opposition to a leftist belief that the Bill of Rights should be expanded to include "positive rights"—such as an enforceable right to receive health care. Rather than praising Obama, though, Limbaugh imagines that Obama is an authoritarian using the word "negative" to mean a bad thing rather than seeing it as a descriptive term favored by conservatives.

Limbaugh goes even further in misunderstanding the Constitution: "So what Obama wants are things in the Constitution that say what the government can do, either for you or to you, which totally bastardizes the founding of this country. It turns the Constitution upside down and renders it irrelevant."[114] Obama's proposals on health care were exactly how conservatives think politics should be decided: by the elected representatives, rather than the courts. Contrary to what Rush claimed, Obama wants a political solution rather than a constitutional amendment or reinterpretation of the document. Still, Limbaugh declared that Obama's health care proposals violate the Constitution: "Aside from the bastardization of the Constitution that the Obama plans are that TARP is, it's not constitutional,"[115] though he has never explained exactly what in the Constitution prohibits these policies.

Unable to understand the constitutional law professor's legal ideas, Limbaugh reduced Obama to a cartoon: "He doesn't like the Constitution. [Doing an Obama impression] 'I didn't vote for the Constitution. The Constitution was put together by a bunch of slave owners. I don't like that. I didn't vote for that.' If they could trash it in front of our eyes, they would."[116] Of course, Obama has never said anything like this.

But Limbaugh understands nothing about slavery in the Constitution. He claimed, "When the Founders wrote the Constitution, they put the prescription in the Constitution for ending slavery, in the amendments, and in our founding document, the Declaration of Independence."[117]

There was nothing in any amendments by the Founders about ending slavery (it was the Thirteenth Amendment in 1865 that finally prohibited slavery). Every provision about slavery in the Constitution defends and protects slavery. Importation of slaves was explicitly permitted in Article 1, Section 9. Article 4, Section 2 prohibited any assistance to escaped slaves and compelled Americans to return slaves back to their owners, which meant that a ban on slavery would have required a Constitutional amendment. And Article 5 explicitly prohibited any amendments banning importation of slaves until 1808.[118] Thomas Jefferson's original draft for the Declaration of Independence included a provision strongly condemning slavery as "this execrable commerce," but it was removed.[119] The final Declaration of Independence says nothing about slavery.

Almost everything Limbaugh says about the Constitution and American history is wrong: "When they wrote the Constitution, they provided the mechanism for all of these things that were wrong at the founding to be fixed. This was the first country, the Brits were close behind, to actually get rid of slavery."[120] In reality, Britain enacted the Slavery Abolition Act in 1833, thirty-two years before the Thirteenth Amendment banned slavery in America; France, Romania, Mexico, Guatemala, El Salvador, Honduras, Nicaragua, Costa Rica, Ecuador, Colombia, Panama, Venezuela, Argentina, Chile, Portugal, Japan, Sweden, Hungary, Denmark, Peru, Moldavia, and Russia also banished slavery before the United States did.[121]

Shortly before the 2008 election, Limbaugh declared that "Barack Obama was an anticonstitutionalist professor. He studied the Constitution, and he flatly rejected it. He doesn't like the Constitution, he thinks it is flawed," and added, "I don't see how he can take the oath of office" because "he has rejected the Constitution."[122]

Obama has never rejected the Constitution. Limbaugh was referring to a 2001 interview Obama did on public radio where Obama said that the Constitution "reflected the fundamental flaw of this country that continues to this day," but also said that the Constitution is "a remarkable political document that paved the way for where we are now."[123] Obama was talking about slavery, which Rush apparently didn't consider much of a flaw.

It is ridiculous to believe that anyone who has criticized the Founding Fathers and pointed out any inadequacies in the Constitution should be banned from holding office (in fact, the idea would be unconstitutional), but Limbaugh declared, "How is he gonna place his hand on the Bible and swear that he, Barack Hussein Obama, will uphold the Constitution that he feels reflects the nation's fundamental flaw. Fundamental. When he talks about a fundamental flaw, he's not talking about a flaw that can be fixed. Fundamental means that this document is, from the get-go, wrong."[124] The Constitution's embrace of slavery was wrong from the get-go, but that doesn't mean it can't be fixed. In fact, it was fixed, although the effects of slavery continue.

Limbaugh has repeatedly smeared Obama, claiming that he wants to "desecrate the Constitution," without the slightest evidence to support such a charge.[125] Limbaugh even referred to "Obama's burning of the Constitution," but he has never explained exactly what parts of the Constitution Obama is destroying.[126]

When Obama criticized a Supreme Court ruling on campaign finance, Limbaugh declared: "Why would a law professor oppose a Supreme Court decision on a matter of constitutional law and not respect the authority of the Court and honor our system of separation of powers? Why? Of course it's easy. Because he doesn't like the Constitution."[127] Of course, everyone (including Limbaugh) has criticized Supreme Court rulings they don't like. But only Limbaugh imagines that anyone who disagrees with the Supreme Court must hate the Constitution.

Limbaugh's inability to understand the Constitution extends to the crackpot belief that income taxes may be illegal: "There is actually an article in the Constitution prohibiting the transfer of funds from one individual to another."[128] Once again, he is wrong. The original Constitution required "apportioned" taxes but didn't prohibit any kind of "transfers," whatever that means. The Sixteenth Amendment explicitly allows income taxes.

When he's not making up parts of the Constitution, Limbaugh is inventing wild stories about how liberals view it: "The way liberals are interpreting the First Amendment today is that it prevents anyone who is religious from being in government."[129] Of course, Limbaugh never cites a single liberal who thinks this. The First Amendment would prohibit any ban on religious people in government (as does the Constitution's ban on religious tests)—not that anyone has ever proposed such nonsense.

But Limbaugh's most embarrassing gaffe revealing his ignorance of the Constitution came during his 2009 speech at the Conservative Political Action Conference, when he proclaimed: "We believe that the preamble to the Constitution contains an inarguable truth that we are all endowed by our creator with certain inalienable rights, among them life, liberty, freedom, and the pursuit of happiness."[130] The correct phrase is "life, liberty, and the pursuit of happiness"—and these words don't appear anywhere in the Constitution. They're from the Declaration of Independence. For someone claiming to be so devoted to the Constitution, who had just received CPAC's "Defender of the Constitution" award, perhaps Limbaugh should try reading it sometime.

History is not Limbaugh's forte, considering how often he distorts the lives of the Founding Fathers of America: "You can't read a speech by George Washington, you can't read his inaugural address, you cannot read them without hearing him reference God, the Almighty, and how this nation owes its existence to God and our thanks to God for the vision in founding this nation with people treated as he made them, the yearning spirit to be free and so forth."[131] PolitiFact.com declared Limbaugh's claim "false" and noted several speeches by Washington without a mention of God: "Washington's second inaugural address, the shortest on record, had no references to God, direct or indirect." PolitiFact also noted, "In Washington's private writings, there's not one specific reference to Jesus."[132]

Despite his lack of historical knowledge and his misunderstandings of the language in our founding documents, Limbaugh did not hesitate to condemn others who shared his ignorance: "thirty percent of office holders did not know that 'life, liberty, and the pursuit of happiness' are the inalienable rights referred to in the Declaration of Independence."[133] In 2010 he repeatedly laughed at Representative John Conyers for accidentally saying "good and welfare clause" rather than the Constitution's actual language about promoting "the general welfare."[134] According to Limbaugh, "Conyers is making up a clause" in the Constitution. It takes some hubris for a man who misquoted a clause in the Declaration of Independence (and claimed it was in the Constitution) to laugh at anyone for stumbling over their words about the Constitution.

SHAMELESS SHAKING

One of Limbaugh's most infamous mistakes came in October 2006, when actor Michael J. Fox, who suffers from Parkinson's disease, appeared in a campaign commercial for Missouri Democratic Senate candidate Claire Mc-Caskill because she supported stem-cell research. Limbaugh declared that Fox was faking his Parkinson's disease symptoms: "In this commercial, he is exaggerating the effects of the disease. He is moving all around and shaking. And it's purely an act. This is the only time I have ever seen Michael J. Fox portray any of the symptoms of the disease he has. . . . This is really shameless of Michael J. Fox. Either he didn't take his medication or he's acting, one of the two."[135] On his "dittocam," showing him in his studio, Limbaugh was gyrating back and forth in a mock tremor, displaying how he thought Fox was faking the symptoms of his disease.[136]

Fox was a liar in Limbaugh's eyes: "I've watched him on *Boston Legal,*" he declared as proof that Fox didn't shake very much from his disease.[137] As Fox pointed out, he can never be sure how his medication will work on a particular day, and television shows have multiple takes and editing. Limbaugh kept digging himself in deeper to defend his mistake: "I did some research today, and I found his book that was published. It's *A Lucky Man,* 2002 I think, but he admits in the book that before a Senate subcommittee on appropriations in, I think, 1999, September of 1999, he did not take his medication, for the purposes of having the ravages and the horrors of Parkinson's disease illustrated, which was what he has done in the commercials that he is running for Claire McCaskill and Jim Talent."[138] It's true that Fox testified without taking his medication to show the effects. But he didn't lie about it. And it's not what he did during the commercial, according to Fox.[139]

As usual, Limbaugh saw a conspiracy and claimed that Democratic strategists "worked with Michael J. Fox on deciding how they wanted him to appear. . . . They wanted it to appear this way but I just—the idea that you're fooled by it is what bothers me."[140] Rush also claimed there was a media conspiracy against him: "Some networks have sped it up to try to enhance the spasticlike nature of it. They are all saying that I was 'mocking, making fun of. How low will Limbaugh go now and next? This is unconscionable.' It is absurd and ridiculous for them to make this charge that I would make fun of somebody in this circumstance."[141] Of course, Limbaugh offered no evidence to support his ridiculous charge that multiple networks had all sped up the footage of him mocking Fox. And if he wasn't really trying to mock Fox, Rush certainly was doing a very good job pretending to be someone mocking a man with Parkinson's disease.

Limbaugh is a huge liability for the Republicans and the conservative movement when people in the mainstream pay attention to what he says. As much as he mobilizes the conservative base, Rush also alienates the majority of Americans. As Fox noted, "He did us a great favor because he put a lot of attention on the conversation. We could hijack the last two weeks of the political season."[142] Partly because of Limbaugh's bumbling, Claire Mc-Caskill won the Senate seat in Missouri.

And Limbaugh still refuses to admit that he was wrong. The online "Limbaugh wing of the Museum of Broadcasting" created in 2008 on his Web site carries the statement, "It turns out that Rush was right," repeating the old claim that Fox in his book admitted to "faking" his illness before Congress.[143] Even years after he was proven wrong and helped bring down the candidacy of a Republican for the U.S. Senate, Limbaugh still thinks he was right.

LIMBAUGH ON DRUGS

The biggest scandal of Limbaugh's life, and one that Limbaugh has never fully answered questions about, is his abuse of prescription drugs. Suffering from back problems, Limbaugh tried surgery. But he rejected a surgical approach that would go through the back of his mouth, fearing it might damage his vocal cords. The alternative procedure didn't work, and Limbaugh began taking massive amounts of pills to deal with his back pain.[144]

Rush learned that his housekeeper Wilma Cline's husband had a prescription for the painkiller hydrocodone, which he'd been prescribed after falling off a ladder. She began supplying Limbaugh with the drug, but he asked for stronger drugs. Limbaugh and the Clines exchanged sandwich bags filled with OxyContin pills for a cigar box stuffed with cash. Cline told the *National Enquirer* that she delivered enough pills "to kill an elephant." In just one year, from July 2001 to June 2002, Limbaugh purchased more than thirty thousand hydrocodone, Lorcet, and OxyContin pills.[145] Cline even accused Rush of bullying her to provide more and more painkiller pills, which he called his "little blue babies."[146]

Limbaugh was giving vast amounts of money to his drug dealers. He made thirty to forty withdrawals of $9,900 from his bank account, just below the mark where authorities must be notified.[147] Roy Black, Limbaugh's lawyer, reported that Limbaugh "paid substantial amounts of money" to Wilma and David Cline before she demanded a $4 million payment and he refused because she had "bled him dry."[148] Cline turned Limbaugh in to the authorities, and sold the story to the *National Enquirer* for $250,000.[149] However, it wasn't the purchase of massive amounts of illegal drugs from the Clines that got Limbaugh in legal trouble; since the Clines were accused of blackmailing Limbaugh and had sold their story to the *National Enquirer,* prosecutors considered them unreliable witnesses against Limbaugh.

But Limbaugh's addiction was so massive that he needed multiple sources for his pills. In addition to buying tens of thousands of pills from the Clines, a police affidavit showed that Limbaugh obtained more than two thousand pills from four doctors over a six-month span, and was taking about a dozen pills per day, including OxyContin, Lorcet, Norco, hydrocodone, Kadian, and Xanax. Florida law punishes doctor shopping by up to five years in prison. Limbaugh's lawyer declared, implausibly, "Mr. Limbaugh and I have maintained from the start that there was no doctor shopping, and we continue to hold this position."[150]

There's no doubt that Limbaugh was doctor shopping to fuel his addiction. As *The Washington Post* reported, "In May 2003, a prescription for fifty tablets of Lorcet was filled for Limbaugh at the Zitomer Pharmacy on Madison Avenue in New York. The tablets were to be taken at a rate of two a day, and at that pace the prescription should have lasted twenty-five days. Three days later, a prescription was filled for Limbaugh at the same pharmacy for another fifty tablets. A third prescription for ninety-six tablets of Norco was filled about the same time at the Lewis Pharmacy in Palm Beach, according to the court documents."[151] Limbaugh was taking as much as fifty times the medically prescribed dose of OxyContin.[152] Prosecutors reported finding "evidence that would support in excess of ten felony counts."[153]

LIMBAUGH'S REHAB

When he returned from five weeks of drug rehabilitation, Limbaugh told his listeners: "I can no longer anticipate what I think people want and try to give it to them. I can no longer live my life by making other people happy. I can no longer turn over the power of my feelings to anybody else, which is what I have done a lot of my life."[154] Limbaugh may be one of the few people to come out of successful rehab even more of an egomaniac than when he entered. A few months later Limbaugh's third marriage ended in divorce, perhaps because his wife realized that she no longer wanted to be married to a man who had stopped trying to make her or anyone else happy.[155]

Rehab had no discernible impact on Limbaugh's show. After his short declaration of self-centeredness, he continued his relentless attacks on liberals and defense of the Republicans. Limbaugh later recounted, "The rehab was in Arizona. A spartan place called The Meadows. Not one of these half-assed places for celebrities. It was five weeks and I really got into it. Very educational for me to learn about myself. It was inspiring. I can't imagine taking a pain pill now. It holds no attraction. I haven't had a relapse or craving since then. I had to talk to a therapist for eighteen months afterwards. Never done that before. Thought it bunk. Actually that helped."[156] Despite the success of rehab for himself, Limbaugh has never argued for making it an alternative to the massive prison complex in America, where drug addicts like Rush are locked up by the hundreds of thousands.

The radio host told his audience that due to the criminal investigation, he couldn't talk about how he acquired drugs: "This is something I am not able to be as blunt and open about now as I'd like to be. That day will come, and it will come soon."[157] That day has never come; Limbaugh never came clean about what exactly he did, even though he no longer faces prosecution: "I am not going to dignify the details in that stupid story."[158]

Evading the truth about his addiction is a common response for Limbaugh, who said, "I had a problem. I admitted it. I went and dealt with it."[159] Actually, he admitted his problem and dealt with it only after the *National Enquirer* revealed that he was an addict and that he was facing criminal charges for doctor shopping. The charges were finally reduced in 2006 to a single count of illegally obtaining forty pills.[160] Ultimately, Limbaugh got the kind of plea bargain common for rich people with expensive lawyers. As Black argued, "There should be a recognition that people like Rush really should not be prosecuted."[161]

After Limbaugh pleaded not guilty, Black arranged a deal where a single charge of doctor shopping would be dropped after eighteen months as long as Limbaugh didn't break the law and continued to see a doctor for his addiction.[162] He was subject to random drug tests for eighteen months, paid thirty thousand dollars for the cost of the investigation, and also was prohibited from owning a gun as part of the deal.[163] Limbaugh declared victory: "Case closed. Story's over. I won."[164] Limbaugh did win, but the story's not over. To this day, Limbaugh has never explained what he did.

The worst impact of Limbaugh's drug use may have been on his hearing. Dr. Jennifer Derebery, who treated Limbaugh for his hearing loss, said that his addiction to prescription painkillers may have caused it, though no one can be sure. Derebery told *Good Morning America,* "What we do know is that Mr. Limbaugh had a very rapidly progressive hearing loss, a textbook picture of autoimmune inner ear disease." Derebery said that "prescription drugs can attack hearing" and added, "We don't know why the immune system goes haywire in some people and attacks their inner ear. We don't know why some people, but apparently not most, who take large doses may lose their hearing."[165] Fortunately for Limbaugh, his doctors were able to help him regain some of his hearing.

LIMBAUGH'S DRUG HYPOCRISY

Limbaugh's drug abuse has nothing to do with his ideas. It is the realm of gossip, not refutation of what he thinks. But the story does reveal his hypocrisy: a proponent of law and order who complains when he's caught breaking the law, a stout defender of the war on drugs who thinks his drugs don't hurt anyone, a devoted defender of the Bush administration's illicit spy program and violations of privacy at the very moment he complains about the government investigating his medical records for evidence of his doctor-shopping crimes.

In his first book, Limbaugh emphatically attacked illegal drug use: "Can a woman choose to steal, using her own body? Of course not. Can she choose to do drugs? Not according to the law."[166] Limbaugh clearly expressed his opposition to legalizing drugs: "Besides, the people who are inclined to use drugs are going to do so regardless of its illegality. But the fact that people are going to ignore and break laws is not a valid argument for decriminalization."[167] He specifically denounced drug users, too: "If someone becomes an irresponsible human being and a worthless citizen, he is directly or indirectly affecting everyone who is willing to live up to the responsibilities of citizenship."[168]

Limbaugh also wrote: "There is no basis in the Constitution for the privacy right."[169] Yet his lawyers invoked the right to privacy when it came to protecting his medical records, even though there's nothing in the Constitution that explicitly says medical records can't be read by the government. Limbaugh, however, had earlier been clear about his belief that no one had a right to take illicit drugs in their home: "The 'right to privacy' is not a right, but rather a protection granted by the government. The 'right to privacy' does not allow you to take drugs in your car or home with impunity."[170]

Limbaugh condemned anyone who supported legalizing drugs: "I'm appalled at people who simply want to look at all this abhorrent behavior and say, 'Hey, you know, we can't control it anymore. People are going to do drugs anyway. Let's legalize it.' It's a dumb idea. It's a rotten idea, and those who are for it are purely, 100 percent selfish."[171] Limbaugh even mocked the use of illicit drugs by the Clinton administration: "Did you know that the White House drug test is multiple choice?"[172]

Limbaugh repeated his tough law-enforcement view of the war on drugs in 1995: "We have laws against selling drugs, pushing drugs, using drugs, importing drugs. And the laws are good because we know what happens to people in societies and neighborhoods, which become consumed by them. And so if people are violating the law by doing drugs, they ought to be accused and they ought to be convicted and they ought to be sent up. What this says to me is that too many whites are getting away with drug use. Too many whites are getting away with drug sales. Too many whites are getting away with trafficking in this stuff. The answer to this disparity is not to start letting people out of jail because we're not putting others in jail who are breaking the law. The answer is to go out and find the ones who are getting away with it, convict them and send them up the river, too."[173]

Even in 2003, while Limbaugh was deep into his addiction, he defended harsh treatment of drug users: "These tough sentencing laws were instituted for a reason. The American people, including liberals, demanded them. Don't you remember the crack cocaine epidemic? Crack babies and out-of-control murder rates? Liberal judges giving the bad guys slaps on the wrist? Finally we got tough, and the crime rate has been falling ever since, so what's wrong?"[174] In his 1993 *Playboy* interview, he mocked the idea of legalizing drugs: "By legalizing drugs, all you're going to do is define further deviancy downward. Freedom has to have some limits."[175] That same year, he declared that he wanted the United States to "send the people who want to do drugs to London and Zurich."[176]

Limbaugh's addiction wasn't the end to his drug problems. Limbaugh laughed on the air about his short detention for bringing Viagra through U.S. Customs at Palm Beach airport without a proper prescription: "I had a great time in the Dominican Republic. Wish I could tell you about it."[177] Limbaugh had had the prescription issued in his doctor's name to protect his privacy, and suffered no consequences beyond a short delay.

Hypocrisy is part of Limbaugh's unprincipled nature. He is a man who demands that politicians (or at least the Democratic ones) be held accountable and answer to their misdeeds while he continues to conceal what he did.

Limbaugh's drug abuse ultimately says little about his character. Plenty of people, liberal and conservative, have gotten addicted and been caught up in the war on drugs. But Limbaugh's whining about being held accountable for his crimes, his belief in a conspiracy to punish him because he's a conservative, and his refusal to alter any of his beliefs, all reflect his lack of moral fiber. Rush may have been strongly addicted to painkillers, but he has an even more powerful addiction to his wealth and fame.

LIMBAUGH'S WEAPONS OF MASS DECEPTION

After the invasion of Iraq in 2003, Limbaugh trumpeted Iraq's nonexistent weapons of mass destruction: "We're discovering WMDs all over Iraq. . . . You know it killed NPR to report that the 101st Airborne found a stockpile of up to 20 rockets tipped with sarin and mustard gas. . . . Our troops have found dozens of barrels of chemicals in an agricultural facility thirty miles northwest of Baghdad."[178]

Long after the Bush administration had admitted that there were no WMDs in Iraq, Limbaugh in 2006 announced his plan to "get out the truth on weapons of mass destruction," blaming "the obdurate stubbornness and blindness of the Democrats and the drive-by media" for the failure to promote what Limbaugh claimed was "the discovered news of weapons of mass destruction in Iraq." He said, "We've had a three-year propaganda program on 'no weapons of mass destruction, none have been found.' This is just settled in now as fact. It is not fact. It is propaganda. The facts are coming out, and there's probably a lot more to be unclassified if somebody will just do it."[179] The facts did come out, and Limbaugh was wrong once again. By 2009 he eventually admitted the truth when it no longer mattered: "No weapons of mass destruction of significance were found," but he did it to blame the Democrats for the war in Iraq: "All of these Democrats, remember how eager they were to go in there and take out Saddam, Hillary and all that bunch."[180]

Even though his claims about WMDs were proven false years ago, and he admitted none were found in Iraq, Limbaugh continues to believe in them. Talking about the WMDs in Iraq, he declared in 2009, "A lot of people believe they were there."[181] Rush was not speaking in the past tense, about the many who mistakenly bought into the Bush administration's lies about Iraq before the war began. Limbaugh believes in the unsupported theory that Saddam Hussein had WMDs in Iraq, but secretly moved them elsewhere, without anyone noticing them.

When evidence revealed how misinformation was spread to start the war in Iraq, Limbaugh dismissed it: "The Downing Street memo doesn't say anything, and it may be a fake. It may be a forgery."[182] The memo was real; it records the minutes of a July 23, 2002, British Cabinet meeting, including British intelligence chief Richard Dearlove's statement that in Washington, "the intelligence and facts were being fixed around the policy" to promote a war in Iraq.[183]

Limbaugh also tried to rewrite history about the predictions of the war. In 2005 he claimed, "Nobody ever said that it's gonna be like walkin' in and playin' baseball the next day. That's in your dreams. This has always been portrayed as something that's gonna be hard; it's part of the war on terror and no end date was ever given, and the ease with which all this was gonna happen was never stated."[184] But in 2003 Vice President Dick Cheney said the war would last "weeks rather than months,"[185] and declared that same day, "My belief is we will, in fact, be greeted as liberators."[186] Donald Rumsfeld declared that the war in Iraq "could last six days, six weeks. I doubt six months."[187]

When he wasn't ignoring evidence, Limbaugh was simply misreporting it. Limbaugh said about the 9/11 Commission, "The report said that Mohamed Atta did meet with an Iraqi Intelligence Agency, or agent, in Prague on April 9th of 2001. We've known this for a long time."[188] The 9/11 Commission staff report concluded about the 9/11 plotter, "We have examined the allegation that Atta met with an Iraqi intelligence officer in Prague on April 9. Based on the evidence available—including investigation by Czech and U.S. authorities plus detainee reporting—we do not believe that such a meeting occurred."[189] Just five months later, Limbaugh was claiming that it was a "myth" that anyone ever suggested a link between Iraq and the 9/11 terrorists: "The fact that there's no—no relationship to Iraq and—and 9/11—nobody ever said there was. You guys just believed the myth out there that was—that was—that was promulgated. Nobody ever said there was."[190] Nobody, that is, except Limbaugh and his conservative friends.

By falsely linking Iraq to 9/11, Limbaugh promoted the war for years. In August 2002 he called for an attack on Iraq to fall on the first anniversary of the September 11 attack: "I think it would be fabulous. I think a 9/11 act on Saddam . . . you talk about getting this country up!"[191] For Limbaugh, American soldiers should be sacrificed for a "fabulous" war to celebrate some sick anniversary; soldiers are just pawns in a political game. Under Republican presidents, he defends every war, no matter how unjustified and costly in human lives. Under Democratic presidents, Limbaugh attacks every military action. But in a classic case of projection, Limbaugh claimed: "It's the Democrats who have always politicized war."[192]

Limbaugh uses soldiers as a marketing device to fuel his personal profits. His Rush 24/7 Adopt-A-Soldier Program encourages people to give him $49.95 and sponsor someone in the military to receive a free subscription to the Limbaugh Letter and Rush 24/7.[193] If Limbaugh were really concerned about the troops, he could easily donate his program free of charge to every soldier, with a minimal cost to himself. Instead, he manipulates his audience's concern for soldiers to create a faux charity program that costs Limbaugh nothing and actually makes money for his program.

Limbaugh uses these soldiers to gain positive publicity. When Representative Jack Kingston (R-GA) introduced a resolution in Congress "commending

Rush Hudson Limbaugh III for his ongoing public support of American troops serving both here and abroad," the resolution specifically praised Limbaugh "for providing free subscriptions for active-duty servicemembers."[194] Limbaugh gets credit for helping soldiers while he pockets most of the money donated by his listeners.

As someone who has never served in the military, Limbaugh shows little concern for the fate of its members. Limbaugh declared about the war in Iraq, "What is the imperative in pulling out? What's in it for the United States to pull out? I don't think they have an answer for that, other than, 'It's gonna bring our troops home. Save the troops. Keep the troops safe.' Or whatever. It's not possible intellectually to follow these people."[195] When saving the lives of American soldiers is intellectually incomprehensible to Limbaugh, it indicates how little interest he has in their lives.

But Rush had a completely different perspective when a Democrat was president and considering a foreign invasion. In 1993 he wrote about Bosnia: "There is no justification for risking American lives in a Vietnam-scale quagmire."[196] Only three American soldiers were killed in the effort to stop genocide. The notion that Bosnia was a "Vietnam-scale quagmire" is laughable. Obviously, Limbaugh would praise any Republican war while denouncing any war started by a Democrat.

A decade later, Limbaugh tried to delete from history the opposition of leading Republicans and himself to the war in Bosnia: "We have had Kosovo, which, I mean, it went without any casualties. There was no—you know, Republicans didn't raise a lot of hell about that. Didn't try to divide the country over it."[197] House Majority Whip Tom DeLay denounced it as "the Clinton war" and other Republican leaders called it "the Democratic war."[198] Senate Republican Policy Committee chair Larry Craig, before his toilet toe tapping made him famous, called the Kosovo operation the "Clinton-Gore war."[199] Admittedly, no leading Republican went so far to divide the country as Limbaugh did in calling it a "Vietnam-scale quagmire" with "no justification," but the Republican opposition was clear.

Bosnia inspired Limbaugh toward a position of nonaggression that he would later ignore completely. Limbaugh declared in 1993 that the United States should only invade a country in a situation such as the Persian Gulf War, which offered a strategy that "permitted victory to be clearly defined, and thus a definite conclusion to the mission could be achieved, which would allow us to exit the region."[200] Yet Limbaugh completely rejected his own theory when it came to George W. Bush's war in Iraq, and instead beat the drum for an attack. In his 1993 book Limbaugh had warned, "There's a lot of evil in the world. There's a lot of bad guys out there. Americans must accept the fact that there's nothing they can do to rid the world of mean people and evil behavior." He also said, "All the good intentions in the world are not worth losing the lives of even one platoon of courageous American soldiers. You can't just send troops willy-nilly across the world without a clear end in sight."[201] But a decade later he embraced the war in Iraq.

Whether it's war or domestic politics, Rush Limbaugh has a clear record of hypocrisy and deception. He will smear anyone, even the victims of terrible diseases, if they dare to take a stand he opposes. Limbaugh will tell any lie, and distort any fact, if he thinks it serves his argument for conservative values.

7

HOT AIR AND GLOBAL WARMING

Rush Limbaugh, more than any other individual, is responsible for shifting conservative opinion to deny the existence of global warming. As he himself noted: "I normally don't pat myself on the back, but today global warming is an issue that has the concern of 30 percent of the American people, and years ago it was over 50 percent. . . . That's because somebody spoke up day in and day out and said, 'This is a hoax, this is BS.' That somebody was me."[1]

While Limbaugh constantly pats himself on the back, in this case he deserves all the credit.

Other influential conservatives, such as George W. Bush and Newt Gingrich, eventually caved to scientific reality by embracing the truth of global climate change (albeit while doing nothing to ease the problem). But Limbaugh has held firm from the very beginning. According to Steve Forbes, "He has been wonderful in skewering the most fantastic fantasy of our era—global warming."[2] Because of Rush, the number of Americans who believe in the existence of global climate change has sharply declined while the evidence keeps getting stronger for it. In 2010 48 percent of Americans believed that the seriousness of global warming is generally exaggerated, up from 41 percent in 2009 and 31 percent in 1997. And 19 percent believe that the effects of global warming will never happen, more than double the number who believed that in in 1997.[3]

Limbaugh has been denying the existence of climate change for almost his entire career in talk radio. As the country's leading denier of global climate change, he quickly became the unofficial spokesperson of the global warming deniers in the early 1990s. Ted Koppel invited Limbaugh to appear on *Nightline* in 1992 and debate Senator Al Gore about the existence of global warming.[4] Limbaugh claimed, "If you listen to what Senator Gore said, it is man-made products which are causing the ozone depletion, yet Mount Pinatubo has put five hundred seventy times the amount of chlorine into the atmosphere in one eruption than all of man-made chlorofluorocarbons in one year."[5] This false statement marked an improvement from Limbaugh's first book, which made the even more outrageous claim that Pinatubo caused a "thousand times the amount of ozone-depleting chemicals in one eruption than all the fluorocarbons manufactured by wicked, diabolical, and insensitive corporations in history."[6]

A 1994 report from the Environmental Defense Fund noted in response, "Cumulatively speaking, Pinatubo's destructive effect on the ozone layer has been about fifty times less than that of CFCs, rather than a thousand times greater, as Limbaugh claims. Thus, his estimate is off by a factor of fifty thousand."[7]

Limbaugh must have gotten the 570 number from Dixy Lee Ray's *Trashing the Planet,* which the radio host called "the most footnoted, documented book I have ever read."[8] But Ray's book attributed the 570 multiple to the 1976 Mount Augustine eruption, not Pinatubo, and if Limbaugh had read the original source in Ray's footnotes, a 1980 *Science* article, he would have discovered that this scientific analysis was actually about a much larger eruption in California seven hundred thousand years ago.[9]

However, none of these factual mistakes really mattered anyway, because the chlorine compounds in CFCs are different from those spewed by volcanos. As the journal *Science* noted at the time, "Chlorine from natural sources is soluble, and so it gets rained out of the lower atmosphere. CFCs, in contrast, are insoluble and inert and thus make it to the stratosphere to release their chlorine."[10] So Limbaugh had the numbers wrong, the date wrong, the location wrong, and all of the science wrong.

In the 1990s Limbaugh denounced the "so-called ozone hole" as a myth without mentioning the fact that the ozone layer is returning to normal levels thanks to international agreements to limit the use of CFCs that harm the ozone layer.[11] His error about ozone also disproves his fundamental belief that nothing humans do can affect the environment. By proving that global regulation can help save the planet, the international agreement on ozone depletion points the way to global cooperation on climate change.

More than a decade later, Limbaugh continued his denials about ozone depletion. In 2005 he declared: "We couldn't destroy the ozone layer if we—we would have to put out the sun. We would have to find a way to send fire trucks to the sun and put it out." A rare critical caller got through and asked him, "Then what was the point of the Reagan signing the Montreal Protocol, you know, ending CFC production? Or restricting it at least?" Rush, confused, simply responded, "It's all irrelevant to me."[12] For him, scientific reality is always irrelevant.

THE ENVIRONMENTAL CONSPIRACY

In his 1992 debate with Al Gore on *Nightline,* Limbaugh asserted that a secret conspiracy, unknown even to Gore, controlled the environmental movement: "There are those who want to shut down business, who want to blame American business for the problems that we have, and they want to go back to the Stone Age. . . . I think you may not be aware of just some of the hideous leadership that—we don't even know the names of these people, I mean, they're not public, I know who they are."[13] Limbaugh has never revealed who is part of this secret "hideous leadership" that runs the environmental movement.

While refusing to acknowledge his own errors, Limbaugh condemns others in the harshest terms when he disagrees with them. He said about Al Gore, "Gore is a liar. There's no question about it."[14] He said in 2009 about global climate change, "Gore knows it's a hoax. They all have to know it's a hoax."[15] Limbaugh sees environmental plots everywhere; he claimed in his first book, "What they really want to do is attack our way of life"[16] and, "The Sierra Club wants to limit the number of kids you can have to two."[17] But there was no Sierra Club conspiracy to ban people from having children.

Still, Limbaugh frequently invokes this evil environmentalist conspiracy. When an oil rig in the Gulf of Mexico exploded in 2010, he declared, "It wasn't just a spill, a break, but maybe something that was done purposefully" by environmentalists who murdered eleven workers: "What better way to head off more oil drilling, nuclear plants, than by blowing up a rig?" Limbaugh didn't need any evidence to believe that "this could well have been on purpose."[18] When Chris Matthews criticized his sabotage conspiracy theory, Rush was irate: "He has not listened to this program nor read the transcripts. I didn't assign any sabotage on this until the regime sent SWAT teams in there—and I never accused the administration of blowing up the rig. I said it appears the regime may be open to some sort of attack."[19] Matthews never said that Limbaugh had accused the Obama administration; Matthews accurately said, "Here's this blowhard saying it might have been sabotage by the environmentalists."[20] That's exactly what Limbaugh had said when he called it "one oil spill which might have been intentional" and linked it to a conspiracy by environmentalists around Earth Day.[21] He claimed, "And the left, of course, loves to take these little on-air think pieces out of context and try to say that we said things on this program that we haven't said."[22] When Limbaugh was caught making up yet another implausible conspiracy theory, he simply attacked everyone in the media and denied his own words.

Environmentalism is the cause for every problem Limbaugh sees: "Politics is why you can't get a car you really, really like or why they don't make as many as you really, really like because they're being forced to keep the Gestapo off their back. They're forced to manufacture cars that people aren't buying to keep the Gestapo off their back."[23] No one is forcing car companies to make cars people don't like. In recent years, the only shortages of vehicles have been the fuel-efficient hybrids that Limbaugh despises.

He is equally dismissive of mass transit: "The automobile, so cursed by Algore [sic], has reduced the heavy need for timber required by the rail industry."[24] Even if there were fewer automobiles and more rail travel, this would not have a dramatic effect on the amount of timber being used on existing rail lines (which also service freight trains). The notion that we should encourage the use of automobiles rather than railroads because of an erroneous theory that it would save a small amount of wood used in railroad ties requires a remarkable twisting of environmental logic.

National disasters, too, are the fault of environmentalism: "EPA rules actually may have caused the shuttle Columbia disaster . . . a lot of people are beginning to think that the banning of Freon actually caused the shuttle accident, the Columbia shuttle accident, two flights ago. And I'm inclined to believe it when I hear this."[25] NASA had an exemption from EPA rules, and a NASA study determined that Freon was used on the shuttle Columbia foam that caused the accident.[26] Limbaugh is inclined to believe any lie he hears that smears the environmental movement. He even calls environmentalists "terrorists" because "they're terrorizing everybody."[27]

Limbaugh regularly denounces what he calls "the left's totally concocted hoax of global warming."[28] However, it's Rush, not the environmental movement, who is guilty of perpetuating a hoax about global warming. In 2007 he even promoted a study that appeared on a fake Web site falsely claiming that bacteria caused global warming, despite having gotten an email alerting him to the hoax.[29]

Limbaugh claims, "Man-made global warming is a 100 percent, full-fledged, undeniable hoax."[30] This kind of brute certainty in the face of all contrary evidence is typical of him. It's not enough for him to question the solid science on global warming; instead, he knows with "100 percent" certainty that it's an "undeniable hoax." Not even the most extreme among the small group of scientists still skeptical about global warming would put their opposition in such absolute terms.

Limbaugh's opposition to global warming isn't based on any facts or any evidence, and therefore it hasn't changed as the evidence for global warming has accumulated. Instead, his view of the environment is entirely faith-based: based on his faith in a God whose planet cannot be affected by men, and his faith in conservatism. He has said, "We don't have the power to make cold weather warm. We can't make warm weather cold. We can't produce rain clouds. We can't steer hurricanes, we can't produce diddly squat and the idea that only advanced democracies are doing this with their automobiles is absurd."[31] In Limbaugh's fallacious reasoning, because humans can't control the weather, it must mean that nothing they do affects the weather. A simple contrary example is smog: although humans don't control the weather, it's quite clear to everyone that smog is created with human pollution.

SCIENTIFIC ILLITERACY

Rush Limbaugh is legendary for his scientific illiteracy, such as his claim in 1991 that Styrofoam was biodegradable and paper wasn't.[32] When the average ocean temperature in June 2009 set a new record, warmer than the previous record by more than one degree, he was quick to dismiss its importance: "They're blaming the ocean for falling global temperatures. The sun warms the oceans, so any fluctuation comes from the sun. There is no other heat source for the ocean."[33] The idea that the sun is the only variable involved in heating the ocean displays a staggering level of scientific ignorance. Obviously, the atmosphere traps heat (which is why Venus is hotter than Mercury, even though it's farther from the sun). To deny global warming is ignorant, but scientifically possible. To claim that only the sun can affect the ocean's temperature is pure idiocy.

Limbaugh said about one environmentalist, "This guy is an absolute brain-dead narrow-minded idiot. There is no 'science.' There is none that confirms that there's even any warming, much less that it is caused by man. The warmest year in the last ten was 1998, or I guess last eleven years was 1998. The warmest year was 1998! We've got early cold records and snowfall records being made all over this country. Narrow-minded critics? I'll tell you, the narrow-minded bubbleheads are all on the left. They are the most closed-minded ideologically rigid, live-in-a-cocoon bunch of brain dead . . . I've gotta stop there because I don't want to say the word."[34] Limbaugh had to stop himself from swearing on the air about people who believe in global warming, but he was dead wrong about the facts. According to NASA's data on the global average land and ocean surface temperatures, the warmest year ever recorded was actually 2005, with 1998 ranking second. Although data sets vary, the NASA data indicates that every year from 2001 to 2008 was warmer than every year on record (going back to 1880) except 1998.[35]

Limbaugh routinely ignores all of the evidence showing global warming is a fact, while misrepresenting the rare evidence that could be used to question the extent of global warming. In 2005 he tried to explain global warming as being unrelated to human beings: "Global warming has finally been explained: the earth is getting hotter because the sun is burning more brightly than at any time during the past 1,000 years, according to new research."[36]

He based this on a London *Telegraph* article describing research by Sami Solanki. However, Limbaugh did not read to his listeners another part of the article: "Dr Solanki said that the brighter Sun and higher levels of 'greenhouse gases,' such as carbon dioxide, both contributed to the change in the Earth's temperature but it was impossible to say which had the greater impact." Solanki added, "The increased solar brightness over the past twenty years has not been enough to cause the observed climate changes."[37]

After trumpeting the false claim that the sun has caused global warming, Limbaugh quickly returned to his preferred theory that there is no warming at all. In 2006 he proclaimed, "The Antarctica ice is actually increasing. This—just this hysteric global warming is unsupportable by facts. It's not even supported by these wacko computer models anymore."[38] By 2009 he was convinced, "The world is not warming, it's cooling."[39]

One example of Limbaugh's scientific illiteracy is his inability to comprehend what carbon dioxide is. He told his audience in 2009, "With this cap-and-trade business they're gonna start taxing carbon. You realize they're even going to be able to raise taxes on Coke and Pepsi? Carbonated beverages that makes it fizz."[40] No one had ever proposed environmental regulations on soda, because carbonation has nothing to do with carbon emissions. A few days later, Limbaugh announced that the government would be regulating our breathing: "Do you realize what a big business trading carbon credits is going to be when virtually every one of us has carbon? We're a carbon-based life form. We exhale what is now going to be traded, carbon dioxide."[41] None of this was real, but he uses his pseudoscience mish-mash to spread fear among conservatives. For Limbaugh, the truth about carbon dioxide is revealed by your yard, not the global measurements of scientists: "The more CO_2, the more the jungle loves it, the more your yard loves it, the more your garden loves it."[42]

Limbaugh's Scientific Consensus

In 1993 Limbaugh blamed the news about global warming on "the hysterics of a few pseudoscientists."[43] On *Nightline* he falsely claimed, "There are as many scientists, maybe even more, on the opposite side of all of these doomsday predictions, and I think that they need to be listened to." He reiterated this lie in his second book: "A Gallup poll of scientists involved in global climate research shows that 53 percent do not believe that global warming has occurred, 30 percent say they don't know, and only 17 percent are devotees of this dubious theory."[44] The Environmental Defense Fund noted, "The Gallup poll found that a substantial majority of the scientists polled, 66 percent, believed that human-induced global warming was already occurring. Only 10 percent disagreed, and the remainder were undecided."[45]

In nearly twenty years, the scientific community has become more completely convinced about the reality of global warming. But Limbaugh denies that any consensus can exist. In 2009 he declared: "You can have no consensus in science. It's not up for vote, it's not up for an opinion."[46] Just three days later, he said, "The consensus has fallen apart."[47] If a consensus cannot exist in science, then how can it fall apart in only three days? There is always consensus in science, as Thomas Kuhn's *Structure of Scientific Revolutions* makes clear. Consensus doesn't prove scientific truth, and a scientific consensus can be wrong. But science functions through consensus. If politicians ignored scientific consensus, then any crackpot theory could become the basis of public policy.

Limbaugh often points to the rare scientist who questions aspects of global climate change theories as proof that they have been disproven, such as, "Professor Richard Lindzen, MIT," who "says that 'carbon dioxide is irrelevant in the climate debate.' Lindzen, nobody disagrees with this man to his face. He has instant credibility, MIT."[48] Actually, many scientists disagree with Lindzen's claims.[49] If MIT has "instant credibility," then Limbaugh should believe the much larger group of Lindzen's colleagues, who run the MIT Integrated Global System Model and now predict that by 2100, the rise of global temperatures will be 5.1 degrees Celsius, more than double the previous estimate, in part due to the global growth in emissions.[50]

Rush wasn't just declaring victory in this scientific debate; he ordered his audience never to read anything from a scientist supporting the existence of climate change, and to suppress any scientific evidence in the schools: "Do not read anything written by any 'scientist' who tells you there is man-made global warming. Demand, in writing, that schools cease and desist from advancing the agenda of environmentalist wackos. Get it out of the textbooks."[51]

While there are always critiques to be made of scientific theories, no one can reasonably claim that there is no scientific evidence for global warming. But Limbaugh claimed, "There's no scientific basis for the theory of man-made global warming."[52] He has said, "These guys just believe it. There's no curiosity, there's no doubting."[53] For Limbaugh, science requires doubt rather than certainty, no matter what the scientific evidence says. And he is absolutely certain, without any doubt, that global warming cannot exist.

GOD AND SCIENCE

As the scientific evidence has piled up about global climate change, Limbaugh's rejection of the facts has not altered at all. This is because he has never had a scientific approach to global warming; evidence does not matter in the least to him. His angry opposition to the possibility of climate change is ideological. Therefore, no amount of scientific evidence, no matter how overwhelming, could ever change his point of view. According to him, "Global warming is the latest liberal trick."[54]

Limbaugh has also claimed, "The average third world country does more to pollute this world than any citizen of an advanced country."[55] Technically, Rush is right: An entire country does pollute more than a single individual. But what Rush meant to say, that people in the third world pollute more than Americans, is largely false. The United States ranks first in the world in per capita creation of municipal waste and carbon dioxide.[56] According to the Environmental Performance Index, the United States ranks 39th out of 147 countries, behind several third world countries such as the Dominican Republic and Malaysia.[57] Of course, America is less polluted than many impoverished countries, but there's a simple reason for that: environmentalism. Thanks largely to the environmental movement, the United States has stricter environmental regulations to prevent pollution than most of the third world. The solution to pollution in the third world isn't the free market, it's government involvement.

Rush believes that the earth is magically capable of resisting any harm caused by humans. He wrote in 1992, "The earth is a remarkable creation and is capable of great rejuvenation. We can't destroy it. It can fix itself."[58] Limbaugh never lets the facts get in the way of confirming his fervent belief that the earth cannot be harmed by humans. In 2008 he claimed about the 1989 Exxon Valdez oil spill in Alaska: "The sea eats oil alive. That place up there, nature cleaned it up faster than we ever could."[59] In fact, the Exxon Valdez spill surprised scientists because "very little of the oil actually disappeared," according to research chemist Jeffrey Short.[60] Despite cleanup efforts, in 2006 the government's Exxon Valdez Oil Spill Trustee Council concluded, "The coastal and marine ecosystems in the oil spill region have not fully recovered at this time from the effects of the oil spill."[61]

Limbaugh believes it is impossible for humans to affect the earth: "Global warming relies on the theory that we are destroying ecosystems. There is no evidence that we could destroy ecosystems."[62] Limbaugh has expressed his own absolute certainty that nothing can be done about global warming: "Even if it's warming up, we can't cool it off."[63]

The theological part of Limbaugh's denials about global warming reflect his religious belief that only God, not man, can fundamentally change the world: "My views on the environment are rooted in my belief in Creation."[64] God makes global warming unthinkable: "I simply cannot accept the fact that we would be created to do things that would destroy our own environment, life-sustaining environment."[65] According to Rush, "We couldn't destroy the earth if we wanted to."[66] This fanatical religious belief would seem naive even to the most faithful believers.

While invoking religion as his primary basis for rejecting global warming, Limbaugh claims that supporters of the theory are working on faith alone: "Global warming is a religion. It has what all religions have which is faith, because no one can prove their religion. It has a Garden of Eden element, destruction brought by humanity then redemption for our sins by paying higher taxes and getting rid of our cars and planes."[67] He doesn't explain which passage in Genesis offers redemption in exchange for higher taxes, but Limbaugh has total faith in his hatred of global climate change: "I instinctively know this . . . I believe in God. As such, I don't believe that progress in human beings God created destroys the planet."[68] He has said, "I refuse to believe that a God who created the universe would create creatures who, by virtue of improving their lives and making progress, would destroy another part of His creation."[69]

Limbaugh's ferocity on the issue is aided by his indifference to scientific facts. For him, global warming is fundamentally a religious issue. To admit to the possibility of global warming is, according to Limbaugh, the same as confessing that man can affect God's creation. It is blasphemy. Rush decried environmentalists because "they are pantheistic; their God is an impersonal god."[70] Pantheism and an impersonal god are completely different religious concepts, and it is untrue that all environmentalists fit either description. But because Limbaugh relies purely on faith to oppose global warming, he assumes that everyone else does the same.

It's not clear if Limbaugh sincerely believes in religion, since he doesn't attend a church, he rarely talks about his faith, and religion usually doesn't seem to influence his thinking. The only meaningful god in the radio host's universe is himself. When Rush talks about religion, is he revealing his personal faith, or just using the language of his believing listeners for his convenience?

HOW LIMBAUGH AFFECTS POLITICS

Limbaugh has a powerful influence on the global warming debate. In June 2009, when he began naming members of Congress and ordered his listeners to "call [their] member of Congress" over the cap-and-trade bill, H.R. 2454, Congress members' phone lines were jammed with Dittoheads.[71] But Limbaugh's claims about the bill were fictional. He said, "When you sell your house, environmental experts have to come in and do a survey to find out if you've got leaky windows, if all the environmental systems are correct, if you have relatively new appliances, and until you modernize in the way they say, you can't sell—that's in the bill."[72] He even repeated this claim the next day. But FactCheck.org noted, "We've combed through the portion of the House-passed bill pertaining to residential buildings and found no point-of-sale mandates for owners of existing homes. Major trade groups representing home builders and real-estate brokers also say these claims are false."[73]

Yet the imaginary provisions of this bill continued to roll off of Limbaugh's tongue: "You won't be allowed to sell an energy inefficient home. Before you can sell it you're going to have to modernize it, according to

Obama's standards, with the proper kind of windows and drains, even if you've got a microwave oven that's not energy efficient, or a stove, you may not be able to sell the house until you make these improvements."[74] Considering that homes are often sold without a microwave oven, it's inconceivable that anyone would be banned from selling a house with an inefficient one.

Along with these fictional proposals came a fantastic price tag: "If cap-and-trade goes through . . . Your annual electricity bill goes up minimum two thousand dollars."[75] Considering that the average household electric bill is about one thousand dollars per year, it's absurd to imagine that electric rates will more than triple because of this bill.[76] The Natural Resources Defense Council estimated that the average American household would actually save seventy dollars per year from H.R. 2454.[77]

In addition to his power to command millions of Dittoheads, Limbaugh also has direct political influence. Marc Morano, one of Limbaugh's former producers, who later worked for one of the leading Republican global warming deniers, Senator James Inhofe, was instrumental in getting Inhofe to denounce a 2006 UN conference on global warming as a "brain-washing session."[78] Many in the conservative movement worry about the effect of Rush's antiscience ideology. As conservative David Frum noted, "You don't have to accept Al Gore's predictions of imminent gloom to accept that it cannot be healthy to pump gigatons of carbon dioxide into the atmosphere."[79] The problem is not that Limbaugh criticizes environmentalism; the problem is that he completely denies science.

Limbaugh defended the Bush administration's manipulation of scientific data on global warming: "Anybody that suppressed data that said there was man-made global warming was doing us a favor. They knew it was a hoax, and they were not spreading lies."[80] By contrast, Limbaugh called his enemies criminals: "This global warming hoax, this climate change stuff borders on criminal corruption."[81] He even urged the death penalty for scientists he claimed were manipulating data, and called for "making sure that every scientist at every university in this country that's been involved in this is named and fired, drawn and quartered."[82]

New York Times columnist Thomas Friedman wrote, "I absolutely do not understand why Rush Limbaugh and other conservatives would make climate-change denial a conservative Republican plank."[83] The reason is simple: If Limbaugh admits that climate change is real, then he would have to admit that capitalism is flawed and that government regulation is sometimes necessary. Most rational people already recognize that government regulation is essential in certain circumstances, but Rush lives according to an article of faith that the government is always evil.

More important, he is psychologically incapable of admitting he is wrong. Limbaugh was a climate change denier from the very beginning, and he has maintained that view for two decades. During that time, the evidence for climate change has gone from strong to overwhelming, and fewer scientists than ever doubt its existence. But for Limbaugh to admit this would require him to repudiate thousands of his diatribes against global warming. It is far easier for him to proclaim, "There is no global warming" and ignore all evidence to the contrary.[84]

8

DEATH PANELS AND PROHIBITED POPCORN: LIMBAUGH'S LIES ON HEALTH CARE

The democrats' health care reform plan in 2009 spurred Limbaugh to an unprecedented level of crackpot theories about how the plan would establish a totalitarian state where every aspect of life was monitored by the government.

Back in 1993, Rush was an essential part of the right-wing campaign to kill the Clinton health care plan. It wasn't Harry and Louise who killed health care reform during the Clinton administration; it was Rush and his buddies in talk radio. Newt Gingrich regularly faxed memos to the radio host dictating strategy, and admitted that there was a "very close symbiotic relationship" between Republican Party leaders and Limbaugh.[1] Republican consultant Mary Matalin noted at the time, "You cannot underestimate, and you cannot overstate, the power of Rush Limbaugh. What he's saying is sinking in out there."[2] In a survey of members of Congress and their staffers, 46 percent said talk radio was the most influential source of information during the 1990s health care debate, more than all of the newspapers combined.[3]

In 2009 Limbaugh again mobilized his listeners to contact Congress to oppose health care reform: "I want you to ask your senators and your member of Congress, point-blank: 'Are you going to opt out on the health-care plan you have to join the public option health plan you are going to write for the rest of us?' Don't accept anything other than a yes or no answer."[4] Considering that his question literally made no sense, giving a yes or no answer was a little difficult. Congress already has government-provided health insurance, and a public option is not going to be imposed on anyone (as shown by the word "option"). The government already provides Medicare, and no one demands that members of Congress must utilize Medicare in order to prove that it's a worthwhile program.

Limbaugh complained about the health care proposals, "Just because he says it, we're supposed to believe it. Problem is, we've read it."[5] But he did not seem to have read the bill himself; instead, he copied some false charges against it from right-wing emails being sent around the Internet to attack the plan.[6] "You will lose your private insurance and your doctor. It's on page 16 in the House plan," Limbaugh declared in one instance,[7] and in another, "On page 16 of the House bill, it's right there, and you've heard people quote from it. I'm going to summarize it, page 16: private insurance will become illegal. Insurance companies cannot write new policies, people will lose their existing policy if they change jobs, if they change coverage, or if they change prices. Once any aspect of your private health insurance changes after this bill goes into effect, you can't renew it. You have to go public option."[8] It's notable that Limbaugh first said he was going to quote from the provision, and then decided to "summarize" it. None of this was true. Page 16 was an obscure clause for "grandfathered" health insurance plans that didn't have to meet the new requirements (such as a ban on discrimination for preexisting conditions) because they were not enrolling new people or changing coverage. Private insurance will still be completely legal, contrary to Limbaugh's paranoid misreading of page 16.

The falsifications by Limbaugh expanded with every word he spoke; he completely invented claims that specific pages of the health care proposal required audits of employers, rationing of health care, Medicare cuts, and mandatory national ID cards. None of this was true, but Limbaugh's listeners trust his claims even when a simple glance at the bill would have showed that he was dead wrong.[9] He even claimed that the Obama health reform would result in "direct deposit access to every individual's bank account."[10] Rush is unclear on the concept of direct deposit: It gives someone the power to deposit funds, not to withdraw them.

One of his most outrageous lies about health care spread the myth that "death panels" were part of Obama's plan. Limbaugh claimed, "Page 427: Government mandates program that orders end-of-life treatment. Government dictates how your life ends."[11] Absolutely nothing on page 427 (or anywhere else in the bill) says that government will dictate how a person's life ends; in fact, it explicitly protects "enabling orders for life sustaining treatment." The provision allowed for Medicare to pay for end-of-life counseling such as living wills. Nothing will be compelled.[12] After a conservative doctor (who urged the abolition of Medicare) called into the show supporting the plan to have end-of-life discussions with patients, Limbaugh remained oblivious to the facts: "I will be damned if it's going to become federally mandated law that the government hires a bunch of counselors that has these death care—as you call it, death care—discussions, 'end-of-life discussions.' " He continued, "That's what the counselors are preparing these people for: end of care . . .'cause they're getting old and it isn't going to be worthy of investment. It's right in the House bill! People want to try to deny all these things that are right there. People have read it. They're in the bill."[13] Once again, Rush was lying. There was nothing about hiring counselors in the House bill. There was nothing about imposing "end of care."

Yet Limbaugh persisted with the fake story of death panels: "Page 429: Advanced care planning consult will be used to dictate treatment as patients' health deteriorates. This can include an order for end-of-life plans. The order will be from the government."[14] Nothing on page 429 says that the government can order death. In fact, it requires that a doctor's order "effectively communicates the individual's preferences regarding life-sustaining treatment."[15] Republican senator Johnny Isakson of Georgia, who has sponsored legislation similar to what was in the bill, noted: "How someone could take an end-of-life directive or a living will as that is nuts. You're putting the authority in the individual rather than the government. I don't know how that got so mixed up."[16]

When a woman at a town hall meeting told Senator Arlen Specter that the House bill would let a seventy-four-year-old man with cancer die without treatment, Limbaugh agreed: "She's reading from the bill. She's got it there, and he says it's a 'malicious rumor,' and it's not."[17] Limbaugh knew that this little dystopian fantasy wasn't anywhere in the bill, but he doesn't care about the truth.

Not only did Limbaugh repeatedly invoke the falsehood about "death panels," but he saw in it an Obama conspiracy to murder old people: "This is what dictators do . . . there's a reason, if you go back to world history, you go back to Cambodia, you go back to Mao Tse-tung in China, you go to Cuba, you go to old Soviet Union, one of the things they did was target— Hitler, health care—target the elderly. Target them. Why? Because they vote, they are more likely it [*sic*] vote, and they're more educated, they have more experience, they know more, they have been alive longer. You get rid of the people who know the past. You get rid of people who know how great the eighties were with a conservative economic policy, get rid of those people."[18] It's just crazy to imagine that Obama is planning to murder millions of senior citizens in order to keep the mediocre economic growth of the Reagan era a secret.

But not too crazy for Limbaugh, who claimed about the Obama administration, "They want old people to die. . . . I totally believe it. It's in the bills."[19] There was nothing in the "details" of the bills that would ban "lifesaving health care for people with certain diseases at a certain age." But Limbaugh has a conspiracy theory for every occasion: "It would save a whole lot on Social Security . . . they are looking to save money to spend it elsewhere in society in cultivating younger people to become wards of the state." He compared the Obama plan to the movies *Soylent Green* and *Logan's Run,* where the elderly are killed (and even made into food) to save society money.[20]

After health care reform passed, Limbaugh still insisted that the nonexistent "death panels" were real: "They knew they couldn't talk me out of the death panels because the death panels were in the bill!"[21] The mythical "death panels" made regular appearances on Limbaugh's show, even when his comments made no sense. New technology to delivering proper drug dosage was, in his eyes, part of a conspiracy to murder patients: "They want to set up a device connected to your skin where your doctor via the Internet can regulate the dosages of whatever medications they have you on. Can you say, death panels, anybody?" But Limbaugh had long since stopped pretending to cite specific parts of the health reform law to support his health care hallucinations, and almost every single specific example he cited as evidence that there was an evil plan behind the health care bill was dead wrong. On September 10, 2009, Limbaugh declared, "The bill in the House legalizes health care for illegal aliens!" and "He lied about coverage for illegal aliens." Limbaugh repeated it: "Barack Obama was lying through his teeth," and spoke of "Obama's lie on illegal immigrants."[22] So what was Obama's "lie" about health care? According to Limbaugh, "It will cover undocumented aliens. Now, it may not specifically say so in the bill. But we have to know that what's coming is amnesty. They're going to be made legal. We're going to have all of this. If Obama gets his way we're going to legalize 12 to 20 million illegals, and they're going to become citizens and they're going to get coverage."[23] Of course, there is no amnesty bill. And as Limbaugh admitted, there was nothing about illegal immigrant coverage in the health care bill. What Rush called "Obama's lie" was nothing but his own lie, repeated over and over again.

HEALTH CARE HORRORS

It sounds like the plot of a bad science fiction movie: The government tracks all your medical data, spies on you everywhere, and even tells you what you can eat and drink and do. Although a movie critic would probably deem it lacking in believability, Rush Limbaugh calls this terrifying dystopia "The Obama Health Care Plan."

Limbaugh has spread every possible conspiracy theory about health care, including that "centralized, digitized health records won't be any more confidential than our military secrets leaked to the media."[24] The military already has a centralized record of health and other records about individual soldiers, and there's never been a case of these military health records being leaked to the media and published.

Part of Limbaugh's antigovernment conspiracy theory is an assertion that a vast army of IRS agents will impose a reign of terror on America: "The people fear the government right now, 16,500 new IRS agents to enforce whatever the hell is in this health care bill that we do not yet know."[25]

Limbaugh was certain that he was right: "All these thousands of agents have been hired."[26] In fact, no such agents had been hired, primarily because they didn't exist. The number represented an exaggerated guess from a right-wing think tank about how many new agents would be needed under the health care bill. However, the new law doesn't include an enforcement mechanism, so any additional agents would be handing out tax credits, not tyrannizing taxpayers.

One of his most remarkable conspiracy theories is that Obama will murder Republicans: "There are people who are actually fearful that if they are
Republicans they will be discriminated against in terms of health care because this is such an ideologically political administration that does have a
bunch of enemies."[27] The Obama administration directly provides health
care to millions of veterans, the elderly, the disabled, and the poor through
various programs. How many cases are there of anti-Republican discrimination in health care? None. But Limbaugh asserts, "You are going to get treatment based on how much some government agency or bureaucratic thinks
you're worth. Who knows how that's going to be decided, the degree to which
you have a sickness or an illness or a disease, your age, are you working or not,
are you a drag on the system anyway? Did you vote for Obama?"[28]

Obama's proposal to make more health records electronic in order to
improve efficiency, reduce paperwork costs, and prevent dangerous medical
errors was the least controversial part of his health care plans, an idea that
everyone could endorse. Everyone, that is, except the cunning mind of Limbaugh, who saw through the smoke screen of this obviously beneficial policy to reveal the "secret" plan.

As the Obama health care plan moved through Congress, Limbaugh's
ruminations about the secret plot behind it grew more alarming: "This kind
of fear that's arrived, invasion of privacy, they'll know everything about me.
They're going to know that when they get your medical records digitized,
which is going to be part of national health care under the guise of facilitat-
ing your care. But the purpose will actually be for them to know and to be
able to blackmail you or use whatever information they have about you and
your treatment."[29] For Rush, no conspiracy theory about the government is
too implausible to discuss with millions of dutiful listeners.

Wild speculation replaced any facts as Limbaugh wondered, "How
many people want their tax returns available and their medical records
available to anybody in government for any reason at all?"[30] Nobody does,
which is probably why no one is planning to do this. It's ludicrous to imagine that "anybody in government" would be able to look at a person's tax
and medical records, but Limbaugh does much more than imagine it: He
declares it with total certainty.

The conspiracy theories didn't end with medical blackmail. Limbaugh also contended that the government soon would be videotaping everyone in their bathrooms: "What aspect of your private life aren't they going to be into? Well, I don't imagine they'll be in your bathroom. Not with cameras. They might be, who knows."[31] He imagined an amazing, alarming tale of government bureaucrats blackmailing Americans over their diseases and videotaping them in their own bathrooms. His hyperbolic rhetoric about the health care bill even included a prediction of tyranny: "The United States of America ceases to be a representative republic and turns into a veritable tyrannical dictatorship, which is essentially what's going to happen if this health care bill passes."[32]

THE POPCORN CONSPIRACY

Rush Limbaugh sees health care reform as a secret plot to regulate everything people do, from wearing polyester to eating popcorn. He declared, "National health care is the single biggest intervention in liberty this government could conceive. Because every aspect of your life can be regulated on the theory that it will control costs of health care."[33] He told Sean Hannity, "If they get nationalized health care, they are going to be able to control every aspect of our lives because you get in a car the wrong way, it can impact health care costs. If you eat popcorn with coconut oil, it could impact health care costs. If they get that, then people have no idea the control over their lives the government will exert." Limbaugh added, "Think of virtually any activity you engage in with your kids that might put them at risk. You take them outside and play. You drive on a snowy road without chains. You fly in an airplane. Anything that could risk injury, which is practically everything you do, could be regulated or taxed because of the impact your behavior will have on the cost of health care."[34]

Under Obama's health care reform, Rush said, the government will order people not to eat certain foods: "You have the public at large, mom and pop, Joe Six-Pack, Mary Botox, and they're out there living their lives and they're going to have all these restrictions on what they can eat, what they can't eat."[35] The health care reform bill contains no restrictions on eating certain foods, and no mechanism for compelling it. Of course, no one has even remotely suggested a ban on eating popcorn or getting in a car the wrong way or letting kids play outside. It doesn't make any sense: Such bizarre rules, in addition to being incredibly unpopular and pointless, would be impossible to enforce.

Insurance companies would be destroyed, Limbaugh told his audience, if they supported the Republicans: "It depends on how the insurance company voted. If the insurance company voted for Obama, then they'll probably get some sort of a participatory role in administering the whole government-run health care plan."[36] It's absurd to imagine that an insurance company's status under Obama's health care plan would depend on how much it supported Obama. Insurance companies don't vote. Individuals vote with a secret ballot. So there's no way an insurance company could "[vote] for Obama," and no way of knowing how a company's employees vote.

Beyond insurance, Limbaugh imagines that every health issue is a disguise for a secret liberal plot. He claimed that concern about the swine flu was a conspiracy by the Obama administration to conceal some unspoken evil deed: "What are they doing with the other hand when you're not watching?"[37] Limbaugh was still complaining about "the nonexistent swine flu epidemic" after the Centers for Disease Control estimated that ten thousand Americans had died from H1N1.[38]

Limbaugh's accusations grew even crazier. He endorsed Sarah Palin's bizarre claim that "death panels" would decide whether to kill her son: "Sarah Palin has rocked 'em with that one because she's dead right. They are death panels."[39] Later, Rush tried to backpedal from his lie: "I have not used the word 'death panels' except quoting Sarah Palin."[40] Of course, that wasn't true.

In response to a caller, Limbaugh declared about the House bill, "The government will be able to dictate when you can and when you can't have children." He posited that it was part of a conspiracy to stop Republicans from having children: "The real reason they want to control family planning, you could throw in, yeah, they want to limit the number of potential Republicans born."[41]

Imagining a vast new government power, Limbaugh even asserted that "They're gonna be able to regulate, call you a risk based on, do you smoke, do you not smoke, how far do you drive to work, do you wear polyester—

it's more flammable—It could get ridiculous."[42] When the leading radio show host in the country claims that health care reform will lead to a ban on wearing polyester, it's already ridiculous.

In Limbaugh's opinion, the government would control everything once health care was passed: "This health care bill, if it ever passes in this present form, gives them unlimited power to regulate lifestyles and behavior, in every way possible."[43] How can Limbaugh claim that a bill that gives the government zero power to regulate lifestyles and behavior actually provides "unlimited power"? Limbaugh never quotes from the actual bill whenever he makes these absurd assertions, perhaps because he knows that the words do not exist.

Fortunately, the health care bill did pass, and now we know that everything Limbaugh promised about it was wrong. But he continues to make up false accusations about the health care law that no one imagines to be true: "I guarantee you with the new health care bill it's going to become a mandate that women are going to have to breast-feed."[44] There is absolutely nothing in the health care law compelling breast-feeding, and no one has ever proposed such an unconstitutional (and impossible) idea.

Imaginary prohibitions on children, flat-screen TVs, eating, and polyester aren't the limit of Limbaugh's political hallucinations. He has also repeatedly claimed that Obama's health care proposals will be used to murder the elderly: "We're going to get rid of your old clunker grandparents with Obama's health care. Cash for clunkers. Death for clunkers."[45]

Limbaugh has also posited that it would be the Republican elderly who would particularly be in danger of murder by Obamacare: "I've heard this fear from so many people who have called this program, that whatever the rules in this bill are, that if you're a Democrat it's going to be a little easier for you to be massaged through the system, you're going to be punished less, your wait list will be shorter if you're a Democrat. A lot of people have this fear. It tells me that people know who this guy is and what he's all about."[46]

When a caller claimed the Obama plan was "generational genocide," Limbaugh declared, "You're damn right."[47] Days later, he said, "There are provisions galore for factoring your death when you reach a certain seasoned citizen age. There are facts and proposals and pages galore of how health care is going to be rationed."[48] There are no provisions for murdering people who reach a certain age. There are no facts and no pages at all that say health care is going to be rationed. Limbaugh was simply making it all up.

Limbaugh endorsed a caller's fear that Republicans would be denied health care under Obama: "If you want to look at yourself as perhaps being discriminated against, it's that you're elderly first and then maybe Republican second."[49] He also declared: "What the Obamacare plan contains is end of life. Forget end-of-life counseling. It does have end of life. It's right there in the bill. He said it himself a number of times."[50] But Obama never said that. When Obama held a press conference on health care, Limbaugh claimed it "was chock-full of some of the most blatant lies a president has told the country or the press corps, and he was not called on one of them."[51] But Rush didn't identify a single lie told by Obama; he simply assumed that his audience would believe him without evidence and made up his own lies about how "Obama admitted he's going to wipe out private insurance."[52]

HEALTH CARE RANKINGS

To justify his attacks on health care reform, Limbaugh proclaimed America's health care system to be the best in the world and invented all kinds of excuses for its poor global ratings: "About the World Health Organization rating French health care at the top and United States thirty-fourth. I did some digging on this, and let me tell you the two interesting factors that go into the World Health Organization's rating of health care. One thing they take into account is military people killed in action. [snorts] When you start comparing United States troop commitments around the world to those of France, you'll find that the frogs are in very few places getting shot at."[53]

The WHO rankings don't give any special bias to military deaths, although life expectancy is one factor. The latest WHO rankings, where the United States was rated thirty-seventh in health care performance, not thirty-fourth, came in 2000, when America had not lost a substantial number of troops in military operations for a quarter century.[54] So Limbaugh's argument about the WHO ratings was entirely fictional.

Global statistics on health care seem to confuse him: "The government says that life expectancy in the United States has risen to a new high, un-expectedly so. It stands at seventy-eight years. How can this possibly be with our horrible health care system, I ask you? How can our life expectancy be up seventy-eight years, unexpectedly so?"[55] Life expectancy of seventy-eight years isn't "unexpectedly" high; America ranks number fifty in the world, which is a terrible result for a country that spends far more than any other country on health care.[56] In Canada, with the socialized medicine and "ration-ing" decried by Limbaugh, life expectancy is eighty-two years, ranking it number eight in the world. The United States ranked number eleven in life expectancy in 1984, and number forty-two in 2004, according to U.S. Census Bureau statistics, indicating that the current health care system is failing.[57]

A 2003 study by the Commonwealth Fund found that the United States ranked dead last among nineteen industrialized countries in the rate of deaths that could have been prevented by proper health care, a decline from Amer-ica's rank of number fifteen in 1998.[58] America's rate of preventable death is 70 percent higher than that of France, which spends far less money on health care; if America could improve its health system to the level of France, one hundred thousand American lives would be saved every year. These life ex-pectancy results show how flawed the American health care system is, the exact opposite of what Limbaugh claims.

In his attempt to deny the high cost of health care, Limbaugh claimed: "Obama said, 'We spend more on health care than any other country in the world.' Well, guess what, folks? We also spend more on public education than any other country in the world. And we spend more on food stamps than any other country in the world. We spend more on welfare than any other country in the world. We spend more on unemployment than any other country in the world. What is this mantra we spend more on health care than any other na-tion?"[59] It's not a mantra, it's a fact—unlike what Limbaugh said. In educa-tion spending, the United States is not the top in the world. America spends only 5.7 percent of the GDP on education, ranking thirty-seventh in the world.[60] When it comes to the welfare state, America is far below the stan-dards set by Europe and ranks twenty-sixth with 14.8 percent of the GDP.[61] But when it comes to health care, the United States is easily the biggest spender, with 13.9 percent of the GDP, far above No. 2 Switzerland at 10.9 percent.[62]

THE HEALTH CARE CRISIS

Limbaugh refuses to listen to any contrary viewpoints. When a caller challenged his defense of the status quo on health care, accurately pointing out the high cost of insurance premiums, he was immediately cut off after referring to Rush's drug addiction following failed back surgery. Limbaugh declared later on in the broadcast that "he was a fraud all the way around. . . . His point was trying to discredit me. He was probably calling from Rahm Emanuel's office, maybe from the Oval Office."[63]

Rush also imagines that Democrats' plots include "assigning doctors regionally, assigning them geographically. It went so far in Hillary's health care bill as to assign what specialty they would learn. Doctors were going to be totally controlled. And it would be no different in this health care bill if Obama and Reid and Pelosi and Waxman get what they want."[64] There is absolutely nothing in any of the health care proposals about "totally controlled" doctors who would be told where they can work and "what specialty they would learn." Absolutely nothing in any health care proposal would tell doctors where they can go and ban them from moving elsewhere.

Limbaugh has also declared about the health care reform proposal in the House, "After this bill becomes law, nobody in the insurance business can offer anybody and you can't buy private medical insurance."[65] In reality, the provision does not ban private health insurance at all. This is just another right-wing conspiracy theory Limbaugh is spouting without bothering to read the actual legislation.

Perhaps recognizing that he had been spreading an obvious lie, Limbaugh changed to a different argument that private health insurance would disappear because "you can't stay in business if you're competing against somebody that doesn't have to make a profit."[66] That's an odd sentiment from someone who successfully competes with noncommercial public radio stations on a daily basis. Although Rush has to play annoying commercials and make enough money for massive profits, he probably has a bigger audience in his time slot than all of the noncommercial radio stations in the country combined. Limbaugh believes that public competition in the realm of health care insurance (which already exists with Medicare, Medicaid, and the Veterans Administration) would simply destroy private companies.

Have libraries destroyed all bookstores? Has PBS destroyed Fox News and every other network?

Yet Limbaugh promises "the utter destruction of the United States private sector as a result of President Obama's health care plan."[67] Considering that the primary left-wing critique of Obama's plan is that it maintains the private health insurance system, it's hard to see how Obama's proposals would destroy the existing system. Even if America went to a single-payer, government-run health care system, how could that possibly destroy the entire private sector?

Grasping at anything to oppose health care reform, Limbaugh claimed: "This health care plan is nothing more than the subprime mortgage debacle ready to happen all over again."[68] It's this kind of reasoning that exposes how little he understands about economics. The subprime mortgage crisis was the result of a bubble: Too many people bought houses they couldn't afford justified by speculation about rising prices. By contrast, health care will never cause a bubble; you can't sell your own good health to another person. It's not a transferable good. The money spent on health care is a necessity, but it's not an investment. No one ever goes into a hospital expecting to come out richer, unlike with real estate.

So what is Limbaugh's explanation for the high cost of private health insurance? According to him, "People are going to the doctor too much."[69]

A few months later, he found himself in the emergency room during his 2009 Christmas holiday in Hawaii, suffering from chest pains. Nothing was wrong with him, but he declared, "Based on what happened to me here, I don't think there is one thing wrong with the American health care system. It is working just fine, just dandy."[70] Hawaii is one of the most progressive states in health care reform, and Limbaugh was treated at Queens Medical Center by unionized nurses, proving that his alarmist lies about the consequences of progressive health care reform were all wrong.[71]

Yet Limbaugh said, "You don't have to be a millionaire to be able to pay for what I was charged for my hospital stay in Hawaii. . . . To the vast majority of people this would be affordable. It's just a choice. I mean, this was more affordable than a car. This was more affordable than a house."[72] Limbaugh displayed just how out of touch he is. The "vast majority" of Americans can't afford to spend tens of thousands of dollars on a medical false alarm.

Limbaugh famously threatened to leave for Costa Rica to seek medical treatment if health care reform was implemented: "I'll just tell you this, if this passes and it's five years from now and all that stuff gets implemented—I am leaving the country. I'll go to Costa Rica." While Limbaugh angrily decried the misinterpretation of his comment as a promise to move out of the country, he missed the larger point: Costa Rica has a much more "socialist" health care system than Obama has ever proposed, but that doesn't prevent private hospitals from providing treatment.[73]

Rush is particularly ignorant of what causes health care expenses: "There's only one way to save money in our current health care system, and that's: Stop spending as much money on the sick, because we don't spend any money on the healthy."[74] He has it all wrong. One important way to save money on health care is to spend money on basic health care and prevention, rather than waiting until an illness progresses to the point where treatment is much more expensive.

Without offering any evidence, Limbaugh also claimed, "It has been established that there is no cost-benefit to preventive care."[75] The opposite is true. As Newt Gingrich Twittered, "Preventive care has largest benefits relative to cost for those most likely to suffer from specific medical problem."[76]

However, Limbaugh was effective at spreading misinformation among a large number of Americans. He spread so many obvious falsehoods that it's almost inconceivable to believe that he didn't understand what he was doing. And his listeners, repeating his lies, had enormous influence lobbying Congress and protesting at town hall meetings.

A rational person, hearing about such secret government plans, might imagine that the speaker belongs to a tinfoil-hat wearing club of people who think that aliens give them anal probes. But the typical Limbaugh listener nods thoughtfully at another worrisome trend toward dictatorship. And everyone else ignores it: There was nothing reported in the mainstream media (or even the tiny left-wing press) about Rush's nutty ideas about health care cabals. One of the leading voices for conservatism in America can spout utter lunacy about the leading public policy issue of our time to an audience of millions, and nobody even noticed.

9

THE KING OF TALK RADIO: LIMBAUGH'S MEDIA EMPIRE

K̲ARL ROVE, THE LEADING Republican strategist, declared: "Ask Americans who they think of when they hear the words 'talk radio,' and chances are they'll say 'Rush Limbaugh.' For twenty years Rush has been the leader of a very long parade of listeners—educating, engaging, energizing, and even occasionally outraging some of them in a way no other talk-radio show host ever has." Rove is right: Limbaugh's name is synonymous with talk radio, and all its flaws. Rove continued, "But Rush did much more than define and shape the genre of talk radio, rescuing the AM band in the process. His greatest accomplishment was to completely remake American politics by offering an alternative to the three major networks: CNN, *The New York Times*, and *The Washington Post*."[1]

Limbaugh helped to transform not just talk radio but the entire media landscape in America. He has been called "the man who saved AM radio."[2] But Rush didn't save AM radio; AM radio saved him. The shifts in the radio industry occurred at an opportune moment for Limbaugh to strike it rich. Talk radio was an inevitable development for AM radio to compete against the superior sound of FM radio and CDs.

Still, right-wing control over talk radio wasn't inevitable, and Limbaugh deserves some of the credit (or blame) for making it possible. AM radio could have moved toward high-quality news programming, but that would have been expensive. Limbaugh made AM radio cheap and profitable. He built up the audience by eliminating the pretense of objectivity found in conventional news radio, and he drove down the cost of radio through syndication. Instead of paying for a host during the less lucrative midday period, radio stations could run Rush, often for free in his early years, in exchange for a barter agreement to give up some of the commercial time.

Of course, talk radio existed long before Limbaugh hit the airwaves. But it was local and not particularly ideological. He made talk radio national and explicitly political. Just as we cannot completely dismiss Limbaugh's contribution to talk radio, we should not invent some kind of mythical nostalgic past where we imagine deep, intellectual conversations once took place on the airwaves. Radio was a vast wasteland long before Limbaugh ever sat behind a microphone. And he helped make political discussion a commercially viable model for radio at a time when it was boring, apolitical, and unimportant.

Stations could have adopted a more balanced approach, with nearly equal numbers of liberal and conservative hosts. But Limbaugh filled a desire on behalf of a certain segment of the conservative audience to hear the right-wing point of view without constraints or contradictions. And he did it cheaply. As he put it, "The reason my show was successful was that so many people with a conservative viewpoint did not think it was being reflected in the media. I validate what they already think."[3] By giving conservatives what they already believe, Limbaugh can be a success precisely by rejecting critical thought.

The overwhelming power Limbaugh has over his audience is a point of great pride for him: "I have total credibility with the audience. It's an audience that continues to grow despite all of the new conservative shows on radio and television, and all of us in conservative media have that bond with our audience. The effort to discredit us is always going to fail. It will always fail as long as we remain true to who we are and don't disappoint our audiences in any way in terms of substance and being serious about what we really believe."[4]

Rush accurately describes the ideological bond between the conservative host and his audience. It's a bond that is not affected by lies and inaccuracies; he can spout almost any factual falsehood to his audience and have it be believed. That's because his audience doesn't come to him looking for accurate information; they come to him for right-wing ideology and the confirmation of what they already think.

But Limbaugh does far more than simply reinforce the conservatism of his audience. He also extends it into new territory. He tells his listeners how to apply their conservative ideology to every policy. For many of his listeners, he isn't critiquing the media, he's replacing it. As a chapter title in *The Way Things Ought to Be* puts it, "Who Needs the Media When They've Got Me?"

The success of Limbaugh's show created a slew of right-wing imitators who have helped fill the airwaves. Rush leads the cheerleading squad of the far right. And his influence extends far beyond radio: Limbaugh's syndicated TV show ended after a few years, but he helped change the course of cable news by setting an example for the Fox News Channel to follow.

There's no reason why cable news had to turn into an endless train of pompous ideologues; instead, it imitated the model set by Limbaugh, especially Fox News Channel under the leadership of Limbaugh's former producer Roger Ailes.

Ironically, Limbaugh sometimes seems less powerful today only because he has so many imitators. From Bill O'Reilly to Sean Hannity to Ann Coulter to Glenn Beck to dozens more on radio, TV, and print, Limbaugh has provided the template for a right-wing media revolution that has transformed the flow of information about politics.

THE MYTH OF THE LIBERAL MEDIA

The mass media in America lean in a conservative direction. This idea is anathema to the millions of people in the audiences of right-wing programs who constantly rail against the liberal media, but that very antipathy helps prove the point. If the media were really controlled by liberals, you would never have Rush Limbaugh and his imitators proclaiming that fact to a mass audience. The argument for a liberal bias in the media requires omitting talk radio and Fox News from any calculation, even though they form a substantial chunk of the mass media in America.

There are always arguments about the tilt of mainstream media in America. Conservatives point to the Democratic dominance among journalists; liberals point to the Republican dominance among media owners, and the bias found in mainstream coverage. A FAIR study of the media in 2008 found that only 21 percent of the citations of think tanks in the U.S. media were of liberal groups, compared to 31 percent of right-wing think tank citations.[5] This was actually a substantial improvement in balance over previous years, when conservative think tanks dominated even more.

Both sides can select anecdotes to try to prove their case, but the primary bias of mainstream media is toward the center. The far right and especially the far left are shut out of the mainstream press, and journalists tend not to question the status quo in power while striving, however imperfectly, for objectivity and balance. Whatever biases exist in the mainstream press (and sometimes they exist on both sides), it cannot compare to the massive right-wing bias found in talk radio, which has enormous influence over millions of people without even making an effort to restrain its bias. A 2007 study by the Center for American Progress noted that 91 percent of talk radio is conservative.[6]

The weaknesses of the conservative critique of the "liberal" media are revealed in Limbaugh's regular attacks on the press. Limbaugh is oblivious to what the media are actually reporting, preferring to rely upon his instinctual condemnation of liberal bias. While the mainstream media was filled with stories about the economic downturn and its dire impact on Americans, Rush absurdly claimed in 2009 that not one story about the recession's impact could be found in the press: "I don't see one sob story. . . . I don't see any of the stuff that we usually get when a Republican's in the White House and the economy is roaring!"[7] While the news reported on a daily basis about the devastating effects of the Bush recession (without ever blaming it on Bush), Limbaugh asserted that none of these stories existed: "If you are a steady consumer of the traditional media, the establishment media, you would not know that there's hardly anything wrong in the country. Everything is hunky-dory and wonderful."[8]

Limbaugh often sees liberal bias where none exists, even making up words to prove his point. After Judy Woodruff on *PBS Newshour* asked a guest, "If the Kennedys were so influential, how do you explain the many years of Ronald Reagan, of the two Bush presidencies, the fact the country is so divided. Does that mean the Kennedys weren't so influential after all?" Limbaugh claimed, "Judy Woodruff says, 'What are we doing here? All this influence of the Kennedy family and look what we've got to put up with, eight years of Reagan. We've had to put up with twelve years of a Bush in the White House.' [laughing] These people are just wringing their hands.

They're so filled with angst."[9] Of course, Woodruff never said what Limbaugh claimed; she wasn't "filled with angst." She was simply a straightforward journalist questioning the influence of the Kennedys and pointing out the strong power of conservatism in America, which is the exact opposite of a liberal bias.

Limbaugh claimed about journalists, "Most of them are liberals. Eighty percent of them will admit it in the latest press poll."[10] In reality, a 2004 poll by the Pew Research Center for the People & the Press found that only 34 percent of national journalists (and 23 percent of local journalists) identified themselves as liberal; most called themselves moderate. The overwhelming bias of opinionated mass media in America is conservative, and Limbaugh himself is the clearest evidence of it. As he said, "Who has been the loudest, most consistent voice in criticizing Obama policies? It would have to be me and all of the conservative media thrown together. It's working. It is working in terms of causing people's attitudes and opinions on his policies to be majority negative."[11] Limbaugh was correct: He is the most consistent and most effective voice who has been changing public attitudes against Obama.

Not only do Rush and friends control a vast swath of the media landscape, but they help shape how the rest of the media is perceived. On a daily basis, the mainstream media is denounced as a liberal institution, even when the accusation seems ridiculous in retrospect. In 2003 the radio host attacked an article in *The Washington Post* quoting defense officials who said the war in Iraq could go on for "months": "If you read that, you conclude we're losing this war, that we've got no way out, that we are hemmed in and we are hopelessly lost. Now, I have to say that even I thought it would take the mainstream media more than a week to attempt to undermine the war effort. I didn't think it would happen this soon."[12] Limbaugh's alleged proof of the liberal, traitorous media was merely that they reported the view of some military leaders that the war in Iraq would last for "months" rather than days.

Rush also said about the press, "They lied about Bush's National Guard records. Did worse than lie; they created forged documents. When it was proved they were forged, they circled the wagons around Dan Rather and gave him [a] Pulitzer Prize or Peabody Award or whatever."[13] Dan Rather didn't receive a Pulitzer or a Peabody for his poor work on the Bush National

Guard story. He was forced out of his job by CBS, which has never happened to Limbaugh despite the routine lies he tells. And although the documents were forged, the story was true, and it was Limbaugh who lied in defense of Bush.[14]

Limbaugh also has strange ideas about the Pulitzer Prize: "Many people ask me over the course of my sterling and starring broadcast career if I'm ever upset that I can never win a Pulitzer. No. If I won a Pulitzer I would be embarrassed, I might resign."[15] He would be embarrassed? The entire journalism industry would be embarrassed. It's particularly unlikely because the Pulitzer Prizes are usually given only for writing (assuming that Limbaugh doesn't draw cartoons or take photographs for a newspaper). There are no Pulitzer Prizes for broadcasting.

Revealing his egomaniacal tendencies, Limbaugh then asked himself, "Well, Rush don't you think you ought to get a Nobel?" His answer: "Yeah, I think I do qualify for a Nobel prize."[16] It's not clear what Nobel Prize he would want to get. Literature, for his ghostwritten books? Chemistry, for his self-medicating experiments with OxyContin? In 2007 the Landmark Legal Foundation (run by Limbaugh's friend Mark Levin, with the "Maha Rushie" himself sitting on the board of directors) announced that it had nominated Rush for the Nobel Peace Prize. Contrary to Limbaugh's subsequent claims, he was never legitimately nominated for the prize because the Landmark Legal Foundation doesn't fit the broad nominator qualifications for the Nobel Prize.[17] Nevertheless, he trumpeted his fake nomination, and even sells T-shirts featuring his face on a fake "peace prize" medal.

The Drive-By, State-Controlled Media

To express his hatred of the mainstream media, Limbaugh began to call them the "drive-by media." Here's how Rush explained the term: "The drive-by media. It's like a drive-by shooter except the microphones are the guns, and they drive into groups of people, they report a bunch of totally wrong libelous stuff about people. They create a giant mess. Sometimes people get really harmed. They go out and try to destroy people's careers."[18]

The irony is that Limbaugh, not the mainstream press, is more often guilty of "drive-by" media, giving listeners a superficial, distorted picture of

reality. A typical half-hour news program has far more substance and reporting than an entire three-hour chunk of his show. It's Limbaugh who per-
forms the drive-by, blowing by news stories with only a fleeting connection
to the facts before pounding in hatred of liberalism no matter what the story
is. He is the drive-by shooter, maliciously attacking his enemies and attempting to destroy their careers with "totally wrong libelous" smears. Limbaugh
is far worse than the most superficial "drive-by" reporters in the mainstream
media.

With the election of Barack Obama, Limbaugh shifted his rhetoric about
the press. Instead of calling them drive-by media, he decided to name them
the State-Controlled Media. Rush said, "I think the whole concept of reporting has gone out the window. I call them the *state-controlled media*
because it's what they are. They're just repeaters. They take dictation from
Rahm Emanuel for the most part, and they simply run with it."[19]

The irony is that Limbaugh literally took dictation from the Republican
Party, repeating the talking points of Newt Gingrich and Republican leaders
for many years. And when the media fail to repeat the lies of Limbaugh, he
claims that they're controlled by the government.

Of course, the press often functions as a transcription service for those
in power, and there's no better example of this than the Bush administration, when the post–9/11 coverage of Bush ran the gamut from fawning to
sycophantic, and the myth of weapons of mass destruction in Iraq was promoted by *The New York Times* and other "liberal" media with hardly any
words of dissent.

But Limbaugh isn't criticizing the tendency of the American press to
serve as transcription machines for those in power. He makes a purely partisan attack on the media. Rush imagines some vast conspiracy of media
to work with Democrats, referring to "their media puppets in the state-
controlled media."[20] That was the entire purpose of his shift in rhetoric: "So
forget drive-by media. Forget mainstream media. It is now state-controlled
media."[21] It would have made no sense for Limbaugh to refer to the "state-
controlled media" when a Republican president ran the state. The election
of a Democratic president allowed Rush to update a tired old phrase. Limbaugh said, "Obama is a far more dangerous president than Bush or Clinton or even Jimmy Carter, because there's no media check on what he says
or what he does. The media is now state-run, government-controlled."[22]

Despite a complete lack of evidence for his charges, Limbaugh routinely denounced the "government-controlled Associated Press" and "government-controlled Reuters" and "government-run *Los Angeles Times*." He referred to "government-controlled reporters" and claimed, "This is no different than Pravda during the days of the Soviet Union."[23] Of course, Limbaugh never points to a single example of the Obama administration controlling reporters.

When Rush started referring to the mainstream media by the bizarre term "state-run media," Republican politicians quickly followed in lock-step. A group of forty House Republicans formed the "Media Fairness Caucus" and sent a letter to ABC News denouncing it as "a state-run television network" for holding a prime-time town hall meeting with Obama about health care reform, before the program even aired.[24]

His purpose in calling the media state controlled is much more than to smear a Democratic president. Limbaugh is reinforcing the myth of the liberal media in a particularly radical form. The phrase "State-Controlled Media" is meant to declare a vast left-wing conspiracy between a Democratic administration and the press.

The Obama Media

Nothing upsets Limbaugh more than the media coverage of Obama: "The press has met their Waterloo, and it's Obama. They have sacrificed whatever integrity, character, professionalism, ethics that they've had. It's all gone. Their total reason, most of them, for existence, is propping this guy up. . . . The mainstream media has cashed in its chips. They have become nothing more than stenographers for Rahm Emanuel, in large part, and it's just breathtaking to see. They willingly sacrifice every characteristic that makes quality journalism."[25] But the American press has been far more critical of Obama than they were of Bush in the run-up to the war in Iraq, when *The New York Times* and other leading outlets were stenographers for the Bush administration and its lies about weapons of mass destruction.

Rush Limbaugh imagines that journalists and Democrats conspire together on a constant basis. He claimed about a journalist's question on racial profiling at an Obama press conference, "It has to have been a setup."[26]

Obama had no idea what questions would be asked, and absolutely no control over them.[27] But Limbaugh actually thinks that the Obama administration secretly controls all the journalists and tells them what questions to ask, even when the result is terrible publicity for Obama.

During the 2008 campaign, the radio host claimed about Obama, "Lenin, Stalin never got this kind of coverage from their media," which he blamed on the "chickification of our culture and our news business."[28] After Obama won the presidency, Rush attributed his victory to "blatant imbalance and unfairness" in the media.[29] According to his analysis of the media in the 2008 election, "So they were going to cover up Jeremiah Wright and all these things that give indication of radicalism of Obama."[30] If the mainstream media were trying to conceal Reverend Jeremiah Wright during the 2008 election, then it was the worst cover-up ever, because the mainstream press was saturated with news about him and the conservative media was obsessed with the topic.

In fact, the bias in the media is strongly conservative. Even if the milquetoast mainstream press had a liberal bias (something that's hotly debated but never really proven), it could not balance out the relentlessly partisan work of Limbaugh and his imitators on talk radio and Fox News Channel.

The failure of the conventional media to misreport facts the way Rush does is his primary evidence of liberal bias. Citing one notoriously inaccurate estimate of the crowd at an anti-Obama protest, Limbaugh declared: "There were more people at that event on Saturday, according to the British press, than there were people who showed up at Obama's immaculation back in January. You will not find that reported anywhere in the State-Controlled Media in this country, but in the UK press, the British press, it's all over the place."[31] The Washington, D.C., fire department estimated that sixty thousand to seventy thousand people were at the Tea Party protests.[32] The Obama inauguration had crowds more than twenty-five times as large, with 1.8 million people.[33] Reality, not conspiracy, explains why the "State-Controlled Media" wasn't reporting an obvious falsehood. Yet Limbaugh declared, "The crowd Saturday was two million people," an exaggeration of roughly 3,000 percent.[34]

One effect of Rush and his imitators is to undermine the public trust in their competitors, the news media. Early on, he told his listeners not to read the newspapers: "I will do all your reading, and I will tell you what to think about it."[35] In 1985, before he began his show, 55 percent of Americans believed that newspapers and broadcasters generally got their facts right. By 1999 this number had dropped to 37 percent in the Pew Research Center for the People & the Press poll, and by 2009, only 29 percent believed in the credibility of news media, while 63 percent felt that news stories are frequently inaccurate.[36] Although many factors contributed to the increasing distrust of the media, Limbaugh and his followers in talk radio played a key role in undermining confidence in the press. The irony is that one of the most inaccurate and frequently discredited members of the mass media in living memory has convinced millions that his competitors cannot be trusted.

The Limbaugh Times

The media outlet that Rush hates most is *The New York Times,* and he often charges the newspaper with omitting some vital piece of antiliberal information that, upon quick investigation, it turns out was prominently mentioned.

He declared in 2009, "Did you know the other day Congressman William Jefferson of Louisiana was convicted? In *The New York Times* they never once mentioned his party. . . . They never put his party affiliation."[37] *The New York Times* referred to Jefferson as a Democrat in the second paragraph of its story.[38] So what was Limbaugh's response to his embarrassing mistake? He repeated it five days later: "I don't think *The New York Times* has yet identified Congressman Cold Cash as a Democrat. [laughing] I don't think they have."[39]

Why does Limbaugh make so many mistakes about *The New York Times?* The primary reason is that he doesn't bother to read it. He admitted, "I must be honest. I can only read so many paragraphs of a *New York Times* story before I puke."[40] Apparently that number of times is one, since he seemed unable to get through the second paragraph of this story.

Limbaugh consistently sees liberal media bias in *The New York Times,* even when the evidence says otherwise. In 1995 he claimed that the media had tried to suppress the Republicans' "Contract with America": "*The New York Times* never ran anything on the contract 'til after the election. The rest of the news media hardly talked about it at all."[41] But Fairness and Accuracy in Reporting discovered, "In the 42 days between the announcement of the 'Contract with America' and the November 8, 1994, election, *The New York Times* published 45 articles that mentioned the contract—more than one a day. The Nexis computer database reports that more than 1,400 pieces mentioning the contract were published before the election."[42]

Right before the 2002 elections, Limbaugh claimed that *The New York Times* was suppressing a story about Republican candidates being likely to win key races in Congress: "In fact, you can't find this story. You know where I found this *New York Times* story? In some little paper, like the *Oshkosh Gazette* or something. But it's an Adam Clymer story. . . . I can't find it in the *Times,* but the *Times* guy wrote it. It's so good for the Republicans, I don't think it made the *Times,* and went out on a *New York Times* wire service or news service, I think."[43] Clymer's story, "Control of House Expected to Stay in Hands of G.O.P.," was printed on the top of the front page of *The New York Times* on the very day Limbaugh was complaining about its absence.[44]

At other times Limbaugh resorts to bizarre smears. In 2006 he said: "I think 80 percent of their subscribers have to be jihadists. If you look at *The New York Times* and the kind of stories they're leaking and running and the information they're getting, it's clear that they're trying to help the terrorists. They're trying to help the jihadists."[45] This strange accusation made no sense, and the idea that *The New York Times* is pro-jihadist by reporting factual news is contrary to the traditional American conception of a free press.

Limbaugh's refusal to pay attention to the mainstream media causes him to make major errors. When William Mark Felt's Watergate "Deep Throat" fame was revealed, Rush declared: "We had the news on the program yesterday that Felt had been pardoned, and I found it interesting that for most of yesterday and last night, no major media outlet or even cable news show mentioned his conviction for ordering illegal break-ins."[46] All of the major media (including NBC, MSNBC, CNN, ABC, PBS, *The Washington Post, The New York Times,* and the *Los Angeles Times*) mentioned Felt's conviction.[47]

Limbaugh's hatred of *The New York Times* is also personal. He routinely complains about bias and errors in the paper, especially when its reporters write about him: "Marta Fitzgerald is my wife; met her on CompuServe. And by the way, it was not—listen, *The New York Times,* which never gets

anything wrong, quoted my chief of staff, H. R. Kit Carson, who never spoke
to them, and they quoted him as saying that we met on a computer dating
service. This is why I don't want the press knowing anything about it. They
purposely go out of their way to try to get things wrong where I'm concerned."[48] *The New York Times* actually reported that Carson spoke to the
Associated Press, and the article never said anything about a computer dating
service. Instead, it accurately noted, "The couple met through the computer
bulletin board CompuServe."[49]

Despite his hatred of the paper, *The New York Times Magazine* ran a
glowing profile of Limbaugh in 2008 that almost entirely ignored his record
of errors and bigotry.[50] Rush would never have allowed a *New York Times*
reporter such wide access without being completely assured that the article
would be written from a sympathetic, conservative approach, which the reporter, Zev Chafets, provided, since he is a prominent critic of Palestinians
(and former director of Israel's government press office), and had written a
column on the right-wing Web site Townhall.com.[51] Limbaugh even referred
to Chafets as a "friend" on his show.[52] Chafets shared that friendship, declaring about Rush, "I'm a little bit defensive because I think that the liberal
media takes such an unfair view of him."[53] If *The New York Times* has run
articles written by a reporter who is a "friend" of Limbaugh and denounces
the "liberal media," how can anyone take seriously Limbaugh's accusations
of bias against him?

Limbaugh would never admit it, but he has received fawning treatment
from the mainstream press, and especially *The New York Times*. That paper
gave him his first big media coverage in a 1990 article, and in 1994 it used
him as a spokesman for their ad campaign, which prompted Limbaugh to
declare: "Who is the liberal bible using to advertise their sheet? Me. So I've
come and I've conquered. They can't do it without me."[54]

Chafets's 2008 profile lavishly praised the radio host, comparing him to
"the great black singers of his generation" and calling him "the first white,
Goldwater Republican soul shouter." Bob Garfield of NPR's *On the Media*
observed to Chafets, "Your piece on Limbaugh was very generous, I would
say even flattering. You seem to give him a pass for his excesses."[55] When
Garfield confronted him with the infamous Limbaugh quote "The NAACP
should have a riot rehearsal, they should get a liquor store and practice rob-

beries," Chafets responded, "Not my sense of humor, but it's not a lie."[56] Really? It's not a lie to link the NAACP to riots and liquor store robberies?

Chafets is a relentless defender of Rush. He has written, "A lot of Limbaugh's critics dismiss him as a buffoon or a fanatic. These are people who don't listen to his show. Limbaugh is not only a brilliant communicator, he is a smart political strategist."[57] A *Columbia Journalism Review* blog noted, "It seems Chafets was distracted by all the bling in Rush's World, so that the piece reads more like an episode of *MTV Cribs*."[58] Chafets reported proudly, "Limbaugh informed me that I was the first journalist ever to enter his home."[59]

It's notable that Chafets, with the full cooperation of Limbaugh, turned his article about Rush into a biography published in 2010 by Sentinel, "a dedicated conservative imprint" of Penguin Books created for explicitly "right-of-center books."[60] When the in-depth coverage of Limbaugh in *The New York Times,* that bastion of alleged liberal bias, is written by a conservative soul mate, it shows how much Limbaugh benefits from favorable coverage even in a newspaper that he falsely condemns on a regular basis.

ANATOMY OF A LIMBAUGH SMEAR: TRASHING BRIAN ROSS

Despite the fawning coverage of Rush Limbaugh in much of the media, he still complains about "their devilish, demonic portrayal of me all of these years."[61] He was particularly offended that his comparisons of Obama to Nazis were mentioned in an ABC News report by Brian Ross, and he saw a conspiracy between the White House and ABC News: "This whole thing is calculated to divide and distract. It indicates just how unhinged and out of whack the White House is on this." According to Limbaugh, "This story is likely a White House plant."[62]

In addition to smearing Ross as a servant of the Obama administration, Limbaugh falsely claimed there was a double standard in Ross's coverage: "I never hear word one from Brian Ross at ABC or the Southern Poverty Law Center about Khalidi or Jeremiah Wright or Bill Ayers or any of the rest of them."[63] In fact, Ross directly confronted Ayers during the 2008 campaign and asked him, "What is it you're hiding?"[64] Ross also did a story on Wright showing his most inflammatory rhetoric, pointing out that he "regularly mocks black Republicans as sellouts."[65] Media Matters for America even criticized Ross for failing to mention that Obama had disavowed Wright's remarks about 9/11.[66]

Rush also falsely smeared Ross and gave him the nickname "The Repeater" for allegedly repeating what his Democratic masters want him to say: "Brian Ross also played a role in helping Pelosi become Speaker a few years back with Mark Foley, don't forget. He was spoon-fed information, held it back until the most critical time in the 2006 elections."[67] This is a lie. Ross never held a story to help Democrats (it was Hurricane Katrina that delayed him from pursuing what he thought was a minor story for a few weeks). Ross had nothing to do with Pelosi becoming Speaker, and his sources were Republicans, not Democrats.[68]

The Foley scandal launched Limbaugh into yet another series of wild conspiracy theories. In 2006 he told his guest, Republican Speaker of the House Dennis Hastert, "It's clear to me that what the Democrats are doing here in some sort of cooperation with some in the media is to suppress conservative turnout by making it look like you guys knew this all along, but because you're so interested in holding the House rather than protecting children that you've covered it up."[69] In reality, Hastert and the House Republican leaders had done exactly that for those exact reasons. But Limbaugh wasn't satisfied with denying reality. He had to imagine an entire media–Democratic conspiracy seeking to reduce conservative votes.

To attack Ross's credibility, Limbaugh also declared: "Has Brian 'The Repeater' Ross ever gone out there and done a report on left-wing hate groups? No!"[70] He was wrong again. In 1996 Ross ran a report on *ABC World News* in which he declared, "Over the years, Earth First! has been best known as a violent group." FAIR criticized Ross for his misleading coverage, such as talking about Earth First! violence over video of a man attacking a peaceful Earth First! protester. Ross also misleadingly linked Earth First! to the Unabomber, Ted Kaczynski: "Authorities believe Kaczynski was at a meeting attended by top Earth First! members." In reality, it was an environmental conference also attended by government officials and representatives of the timber industry that Earth First! had no role in organizing.[71] In addition, Ross has been criticized by FAIR for promoting the myth that Saddam Hussein had weapons of mass destruction long after the story had been discredited.[72] So Ross did report on left-wing hate groups, and his reporting in favor of conservatives was deeply flawed. His reporting on right-wing hate groups, by contrast, was straightforward and factual, and Limbaugh never identified any errors.

So when Limbaugh accused Ross of conspiring with Democrats on the Foley story, he was lying; when he accused Ross of failing to report on controversial statements by Obama's associates, he was lying; when he accused Ross of never reporting on controversial left-wing groups, he was lying; and when he accused Ross of reporting "100 percent total manufactured BS," he was lying.

But Limbaugh's lies have a powerful effect on the mainstream media. His deceptions help promote the myth of the liberal media. And corporate media outlets, fearful of Limbaugh's wrath, are much more reluctant to engage in reporting that might offend "El Rushbo."

THE MEDIA CONSPIRACY

"I believe that I," said Rush, "am responsible for the mainstream media's behavior today because they think I am the one who destroyed their monopoly beginning in 1988 when I started my show."[73] Of course, Limbaugh did not personally destroy the mainstream media monopoly. Cable networks such as CNN preceded him, and the Internet did far more damage to the mainstream press.

Limbaugh's show often plays the message, "Members of the media, do not panic. Your show prep will continue."[74] If the media are biased against Limbaugh and other conservatives, why would they be using him for show prep? Limbaugh still imagines that he controls the public debate: "This is how we get things in the drive-by news cycle. There will be discussions on this with me being proposed as a lunatic, but yet they will discuss my idea [laughing]. They'll call them the rantings of a madman and then they'll start talking about it seriously and they'll get two or three days out of this on the cable networks. They ought to be paying me."[75] Limbaugh not only imagines that he controls all of the mainstream media, he also has a persecution complex that the media is attempting to destroy him and all other conservatives.

One crazy conspiracy theory Limbaugh offered came when he predicted that a government takeover of banks would lead to control of media outlets that get loans from banks: "When the government owns the radio company . . . they will be able to tell radio and television stations what their programming should be."[76] Later, he added, "We could reach a point where Obama controls radio and TV, because he will own it. By virtue of the banks he controls owning it. This is a very stealth way. You don't need the Fairness Doctrine. . . . So if you think that the media in this country cannot also be owned by Barack Obama, think again."[77] But the government doesn't control the lending decisions of the banks, and the banks don't control the programming decisions of radio and television stations.

THE MYTH OF THE FAIRNESS DOCTRINE

The Fairness Doctrine, a long-abolished and never-enforced policy of the Federal Communications Commission, has long been part of Limbaugh's media conspiracy theories. He claimed that the abolition of the Fairness Doctrine made his success possible: "When I began my national talk show in 1988, no one, including radio industry professionals, thought my syndication would work. There were only about 125 radio stations programming talk. And there were numerous news articles and opinion pieces predicting the fast death of the AM band, which was hemorrhaging audience and revenue to the FM band. Some blamed the lower-fidelity AM signals. But the big issue was broadcast content. It is no accident that the AM band was dying under the so-called Fairness Doctrine, which choked robust debate about important issues because of its onerous attempts at rationing the content of speech."[78]

The Fairness Doctrine had absolutely nothing to do with the death of ratings on AM radio. The Fairness Doctrine had been around without any enforcement for many years, and certainly there was no fear of it being enforced against conservative talk radio under Ronald Reagan in the 1980s when AM ratings were plummeting. The death of AM radio wasn't caused by government censorship; it was caused by the desire for better-sounding music.

Limbaugh and his imitators weren't successful because radio station managers were suddenly freed from onerous government control; they became dominant because they offered cheap labor.

The fact that Limbaugh was a conservative was a bonus, not a barrier. It helped him get slots at stations owned predominantly by conservative businessmen. And station managers rightly believed that a pro-corporate host would attract advertising more easily than a liberal. There was also a big market for conservative talk radio that didn't exist for liberals. Liberal listeners were more likely to seek out contemporary music on FM, which conservatives tended to dislike, and liberals interested in politics would listen to NPR stations, which offered appealing, in-depth, commercial-free news coverage.

It's doubtful that vigorous enforcement of the Fairness Doctrine would have ever been possible politically, and, if it had been, the Supreme Court would have almost certainly overturned any attempt by the federal government to impose it. In 1969 the Supreme Court did uphold the Fairness Doctrine in *Red Lion Broadcasting Co. v. FCC,* but warned that any restrictions on free speech would be unconstitutional.[79] During its entire history, from its beginnings in 1949 until the FCC under Reagan overturned it in 1987, no radio or television station was ever denied a license due to the Fairness Doctrine or compelled to alter its content by government order.

Congress attempted to reinstate the Fairness Doctrine in 1987, but Reagan vetoed it. However, there was bipartisan support for the law, which passed by an overwhelming margin with the votes of such notable conservatives as Representative Newt Gingrich (R-GA) and Senator Jesse Helms (R-N.C.), who, along with some White House officials, opposed getting rid of the doctrine, arguing that it constrained the "liberal" media from openly attacking conservatives.[80]

Limbaugh, however, called efforts to reinstate the Fairness Doctrine the "Hush Rush" bill.[81] He has been declaring himself the victim of a liberal censorship crusade for more than fifteen years. In 1993 he even proclaimed, "I, Rush Limbaugh, the poster boy of free speech, am being gang muzzled."[82]

Why the Fairness Doctrine Is a Bad Idea

Some on the left have urged a return to the Fairness Doctrine. Writer Steve Almond argued in *The Boston Globe,* "The Fairness Doctrine would *not* stop talk radio hosts from spewing the invective that has made them so fabulously wealthy. All it would do is subject their invective to a real-time reality check." However, we should always be wary of government-imposed reality checks. Almond claimed that the purpose of the Fairness Doctrine is "not to silence extremists who broadcast inflammatory lies, but to force them to share their microphones with those who beg to differ, in reasoned tones."[83] Who do we trust to decide which broadcasters are lying extremists and which are reasoned dissenters?

Advocates of the Fairness Doctrine have exaggerated notions of what it can achieve. Almond wrote, "If Obama and his congressional counterparts don't have the guts for that fight, Americans of all political persuasions will continue to seek out 'news' and opinions that merely reinforce their biases, rather than forcing them to question those biases."[84] The Fairness Doctrine wouldn't prevent people from seeking out programs to reinforce their views. Nor would it do anything to bring reasoned debate to broadcasting.

The only example of government regulation similar to the Fairness Doctrine being enforced was when Kenneth Tomlinson, the conservative chairman of the Corporation for Public Broadcasting under George W. Bush, was unhappy with Bill Moyers's show NOW and hired a right-wing consultant to monitor ideological balance on the show and several others.[85] Tomlinson also forced PBS to broadcast low-rated conservative shows hosted by Tucker Carlson and The Wall Street Journal editorial board by threatening to withhold $22.5 million in funding.[86] This right-wing abuse of public broadcasting shows how dangerous it could be to have a Fairness Doctrine imposed by a Republican administration.

PBS commentator Bill Moyers noted, "The Doctrine is a throwback to a time when there were a lot fewer ways to hear news and opinion than there are in today's universe of websites, blogs, and tweets," and, "fairness is not a doctrine to be enforced, but a choice to be made, a responsibility to be honored." He added, "The two new commissioners to the FCC expressed their strong opposition to its restoration. The new FCC chairman is opposed, too."[87]

The Obama Conspiracy Against Radio

Barack Obama has been explicit in opposing the Fairness Doctrine, but that hasn't stopped Limbaugh from imagining the worst. He believes that

Obama dreams of silencing radio stations: "Hugo Chávez just shut down thirty-four radio stations, and I'm thinking, 'Obama is looking at that and saying, "Damn! Someday, someday."' "[88]

According to Limbaugh, "The way they're going to try to get rid of conservative talk radio is with localism, and what they want is to divest ownership and have more minorities own radio stations. I mean, folks, there is a civil rights component to virtually everything Obama's doing, and the civil rights component is angry. This guy is an avowed Marxist socialist. This guy praises Hugo Chávez's takeover of the media in Venezuela."[89]

There are no "content rules for diversity and fairness" being proposed by the FCC; it's a fantasy made up by Rush and the right wing. Nor has Obama ever praised Chávez's actions in Venezuela. Because there is no movement to reinstate the Fairness Doctrine, Limbaugh had to imagine other conspiracies to destroy him: "They can't go Fairness Doctrine because it's too obvious. So they're trying to do this backdoor route with 'diversity' and ownership, a 100 percent tax on operating in order to pay public radio because they're supposedly fair."[90] There is no "100 percent tax" proposed on operating costs.

OPPOSING FREE SPEECH FOR LIBERALS

The principle of freedom of speech is not something that Limbaugh supports for liberals. After a caller bragged about helping to disrupt a speech by Howard Dean where they "booed and heckled him so badly that he was not able to get up and give his ten- or fifteen-minute speech," Rush declared, "You should be proud of yourselves."[91] In 2005 he said, "Wouldn't it be great if anybody who speaks out against this country, to kick them out of the country? Anybody that threatens this country, kick 'em out. We'd get rid of Michael Moore, we'd get rid of half the Democratic Party if we would just import that law. That would be fabulous."[92] Limbaugh believes in free speech for himself and no one else.

But no one should seek to silence him. As Deepak Chopra wrote, "Rush Limbaugh may represent a toxic form of entertainment—and the bile he spews bears no resemblance to true morality—but the fact that America makes room for him is something to be proud of."[93]

Unlike any journalist, Limbaugh has near-complete freedom to say anything he wants on any subject. He bragged, "I've never had one meeting to do this radio show."[94] Indeed, the only person who ever silenced a show with "Rush" in the name was Limbaugh himself, since his companies filed a $20 million lawsuit in 1994 against Aaron Harber, a liberal radio host who tried to market an "After the Rush" show to respond to conservative talkers.[95]

PUBLIC AND PRIVATE RADIO

Conservatives often cite the radio host as a necessary counterbalance to liberal radio. Stuart Stevens, a media adviser for Mitt Romney, noted about Limbaugh: "He's like the NPR for conservatives."[96] But there's a fundamental difference between NPR and Rush. NPR aspires to have fair-minded, objective news broadcasts. Rush aspires to be the voice of the conservative movement. The fact that Limbaugh has a conservative bias is freely admitted by all, including himself. But the evidence of liberal bias at NPR is weak at best. You'll look in vain for any conservative groups monitoring and exposing the bias at NPR, because it's so rare and insignificant; conservatives prefer to proclaim that there's a liberal bias at NPR rather than actually proving it. In fact, leftists have regularly bemoaned the conservative bias of NPR (a 2003 study by Fairness and Accuracy in Reporting found that Republican guests outnumbered Democrats on NPR, 61 percent to 38 percent), but no one listens to them.[97]

National Public Radio allows virtually no commentary on the air. One may question whether NPR's news coverage is biased (as seen above, both liberals and conservatives have claimed that it is), but it is categorically different from the kind of bias found in Limbaugh's program, which is all bias and opinion without any attempt at providing real news. In a 2008 Roper Poll, NPR and its television counterpart PBS were less likely to be regarded as "liberal" by the public than any other network except Fox News. (PBS was trusted more than any other news outlet and most often regarded as "mostly fair".)[98]

The biggest liberal bias about NPR is the attitude of its listeners. Because there are no national, liberal talk radio programs available on the same scale as Limbaugh and his imitators, liberal listeners are drawn to

NPR for its substantive news and lack of commercials. Conservatives, on the other hand, boycott NPR in favor of hearing conservative talk show hosts confirm their point of view.

The audience for NPR (41 percent Democrats, 24 percent Republicans) is the inverse of talk radio (41 percent Republicans, 28 percent Democrats).[99] This has had an important impact on the culture of the two parties. Talk radio, led by Limbaugh, is full of misinformation and unsupported opinions, where the conservative viewpoint is relentlessly pushed, often without an opposing view. NPR, by contrast, strives to be balanced and moderate, with fact-checked news reports presented by professional journalists and very little opinionizing by reporters.

Limbaugh took credit for NPR's audience, and claimed in 1993, "Even among public radio stations, the Limbaugh Effect has been profound. In 1989 there were only eleven noncommercial stations in the entire country devoted to all-news programming; in 1993 there were 184. Isn't it rich? I have helped to revitalize even the boring pseudointellectuals of public radio."[100] But the rise of news in public radio was partly an anti-Limbaugh effect: Radio listeners accustomed to hearing objective news from commercial stations were searching for legitimate news outlets instead of the wave of right-wing talkers who had taken over.

In fact, NPR is vastly more efficient than Limbaugh and produces a far superior product. With a weekly audience of 20.9 million in 2008, NPR news reaches more people than Limbaugh does.[101] Yet the entire annual budget for *Morning Edition* and *All Things Considered* is less than Limbaugh's salary alone.[102] It's notable that NPR serves a larger audience than his, creates real substantive news coverage from around the world, and does it all without the massive costs involved in his show.

With Rush Limbaugh setting the tone for the Republican Party, the party has shifted far to the right, and removed any concern for moderation, facts, intellectual debate, or dissenting opinions. Limbaugh has helped to change the Republican Party for the worse. But the damage Limbaugh has done extends far beyond the conservative movement.

With Roger Ailes leading Fox News Channel, it became the cable equivalent of talk radio, modeled on Ailes's friend and former syndicated TV host, Rush Limbaugh. In the media landscape, the far right has seized control of a large sector of the mass media.

The Absence of Liberal Talk Radio

In the vast majority of the country, there is literally no liberal talk radio. In Missoula, Montana (the most liberal city in the state), the only progressive talk radio station, KMPT, was converted in 2009 to conservative talk radio, joining two other right-wing talk radio stations in town.[103] GapWest Broadcasting, which owns all three talk radio stations, decided to change the station due to a lack of advertising revenues.[104] This reveals an important bias in talk radio: It's not enough to have listeners; progressive talk radio needs to have advertisers, which is difficult for a liberal station with hosts who might be critical of corporate America. Limbaugh, on the other hand, never has to worry about selling out his principles to corporate America, because his principles are directly in line with corporations. Because of his conservative views, he has had remarkable freedom in corporate radio: "I have had people that I've worked for who have been just fabulous, who got out of my way, let me try it the way I thought it ought to be done. They invested trust and faith in me."[105] As FAIR noted, if Limbaugh "beat up every day on major corporations and other monied interests—getting his facts wrong time and again. . . . It's clear he wouldn't have survived in a small market like Sacramento, let alone nationally."[106]

The success of *The Rush Limbaugh Show* is partly due to Limbaugh's savvy with advertisers: "I don't think they have, as liberals, the slightest understanding of the commercial aspects of the success that it takes in radio, particularly talk radio."[107] And Rush has been explicit that this commercial success requires support for the pro-business agenda of media owners; Limbaugh has criticized journalists because "they demand exemption from bottom-line concerns and openly criticize the owners (risk-takers and investors) of the very companies which employ them when those people make decisions to keep the business running profitably."[108] To him, satisfying corporate America is both an ideology and a highly profitable business model.

AN ADVERTISER'S DREAM

Perhaps no one in radio is more devoted to selling products than Rush Limbaugh, and that accounts for much of his success. Limbaugh declared in the early 1990s, "A turning point in my career came when I realized that the sole purpose for all of us in radio is to sell advertising."[109] He recalled, "I realized out there that if I was ultimately going to succeed I had to get myself actively involved in the revenue stream of the radio station. I had to be able to put my hand, my finger on X-number of dollars I was generating. That would buy me insurance against the occasional ratings fall. You know, rating books or the vagaries of these things back then were crazy, could go up or down and it was dependent on diary replacement, the market, and a number of other things."[110]

Limbaugh understood that he could have control over his program if he had his "hand on a certain amount of the revenue stream."[111] Since his talk show began, Rush has been obsessed with his advertisers; early in his radio career in Sacramento, he even tried to demand that he could decide what advertisers would be allowed on his show.[112] He understood from the start that his advertisers would determine the fate of his career and that selling products was "ratings insurance."

In the 1990s Limbaugh had to stop himself from doing almost every commercial spot on his show: "I wanted to hold on to my credibility and my believability. And I didn't want any of that to be watered down, nor did I want to be perceived as a huckster, nor did I want the audience to believe that I perceived them as customers."[113] Biographer Paul Colford wrote about Limbaugh, "He feared that listeners were unable to tell the difference between his own remarks about a product and the prepared text that he read."[114]

Limbaugh no longer has that fear. He has realized that his believability stems from his listeners' devotion to him. Nothing he does, no amount of pandering to his advertisers, would ever affect his credibility in their eyes, and so Limbaugh has merged advertising with his program to an unprecedented level.

The Rush Limbaugh Show runs millions of dollars in ads every week, and Rush courts his advertisers aggressively. He meets personally several times a year with all of the advertisers who hire him to voice their ads. He noted, "It's a total involvement and deeply personal. It's something we request."[115] As Ty Shay, an executive with Hotwire.com, put it: "Before Rush even took our business, we had an hour-long conference call with him. He wanted to understand our business. . . . That process was really important because Rush became a true evangelist for our business. He cares about how we're doing and how consumers are interacting with our business."[116]

Limbaugh's syndicated television show ultimately failed not merely because of mediocre ratings, but primarily because of the difficulty in finding advertisers for his controversial views. Kevin Goldman in *The Wall Street Journal* noted, "advertisers don't want to offend anyone, pinko or redneck."[117]

After Glenn Beck declared that Obama has "deep-seated hatred for white people or the white culture," activists persuaded dozens of companies to drop their advertising from Beck's show on the Fox News Channel.[118] Similar boycotts have been tried against Limbaugh over the years, and have been largely unsuccessful. However, he has been hurt by some of them. In the 1990s Limbaugh lost advertising for Florida orange juice after the National Organization for Women, the National Education Association, the National Association for the Advancement of Colored People, and other groups led a boycott of the product. In 2003 RadioShack and Amtrak dropped their advertising, claiming that they avoid political shows and only advertised due to a mistake.[119] Some mainstream advertisers were lured by Limbaugh's success, including General Motors, Johnson & Johnson, Pfizer, and Schering-Plough.[120] Premiere Radio Networks president Charlie Rahilly noted in 2008, "*The Rush Limbaugh Show* enjoys an unprecedented platform of radio affiliates. Plus, advertisers harness the intensity of listener engagement. No one's word of mouth about a product or service delivers more impact than Mr. Limbaugh's."[121]

Boycotts can't affect Limbaugh because many of his advertisers are not major retailers, but midsize online companies that rely on Limbaugh loyalists for a substantial part of their business. As *Crain's New York Business* reported, "A good portion of the show's inventory is sold to direct-response advertisers who aren't worried about their corporate image."[122] Limbaugh's audience is so big that Dittoheads alone can sustain a substantial business.

Limbaugh is fiercely loyal to his advertisers, even to the point of making up implausible stories about them. When a decline in phishing attacks was reported, he explained it was the result of one of his advertisers: "The reason the number of phishing emails is going down is because the bad guys aren't getting away with it, thanks to LifeLock."[123] But no one could possibly believe that one small company dealing with identity theft was personally responsible for a shift in data-stealing techniques, especially since there wasn't a decline in identity theft, just a change in tactics. The Federal Trade Commission and thirty-five state attorneys general (some of them Republicans) charged LifeLock with deceptive advertising, and in March 2010 LifeLock paid a $12 million settlement due to the violations.[124]

The conspiracy theories that fill Limbaugh's show also extend to his advertisers, since he believes that the government is out to get them. After one of Limbaugh's advertisers faced a warning from the Food and Drug Administration, Limbaugh jumped to their defense: "This silly ban on Zicam, for example, 130 people in trumped-up legal cases claim their sense of smell was destroyed? You wouldn't believe the number of cases that Zicam entered, had to defend, and was victorious in. And because Zicam kept winning—Matrixx is the company—kept winning the cases the FDA finally said, 'Okay, a sponsor of Limbaugh's, well, let's zap 'em.'"[125] Contrary to Limbaugh's imagination, the FDA's action against Zicam was not due to "nattering nabobs" at the FDA but because of allegations that it was a product that caused the loss of sense of smell in some patients.[126]

Radio has always been the medium of selling out, with hosts routinely making extra money by lending their voices to commercials or doing live reads of ads during their show. Limbaugh observed, "I always say my real purpose is to attract the largest audience I can, and hold it for as long as I can, so I can charge confiscatory advertising rates."[127] He regularly takes what he calls an "obscene profit timeout," but that's only a part of his revenue stream. Limbaugh also weaves advertiser messages into his regular program commentary, which advertisers pay a premium for. Product placement has become a routine part of his show.

And no radio host is more devoted to product placement than Rush Limbaugh. To a caller who said he took two showers after voting for Hillary Clinton during Operation Chaos, Limbaugh responded: "If you had followed my advice and gotten a Rinnai tankless water heater, you wouldn't have needed to take two showers. And I'll tell you why."[128] Limbaugh takes calls specifically in order to turn them into product placement advertisements for Carbonite and other products.[129]

On April 2, 2009, Limbaugh declared that he was "continually amazed that the Heritage Foundation" produced its right-wing analysis. Not convincingly, he added, "I'm not saying this because they're a sponsor."[130] Of course, he was saying that precisely because they're a sponsor. In fact, he charged them an enormous amount of money for what he said. The next day, the first caller asked a question and then asked about the Sleep Number bed. Rush declared, "I love sharing my passion."[131] Limbaugh's passion isn't mattresses, it's selling advertising. He provides right-wing conspiracy theories on a firm foundation of mattress ads. The easiest way for a caller to get on Limbaugh's program is to announce intense devotion to one of his advertisers.

Remarkably, in the middle of one ad, Rush proclaimed, "I, my friends, am a long-time member of the Heritage Foundation, I'm not a comp member, either, I pay for it, I don't accept comps, I don't want to be obligated, I don't like conflicts of interest."[132] To Limbaugh, taking something for free is a conflict of interest, but getting paid to promote an organization is not.

But there are limits to his devotion to advertisers. The first rule of Limbaugh's show is that no one can contradict him. In 1994, when conservatives Pat Buchanan and Phyllis Schlafly made ads opposing the GATT (General Agreement on Tariffs and Trades), Limbaugh's radio and television shows refused to run the spots. Schlafly, who had no problem running two anti-Clinton ads on Limbaugh's shows, said the ban on her ad was "unusual."[133]

Boycotting Government Motors

Limbaugh is so powerful that he can even attack his own advertisers. One of his biggest national advertisers was General Motors (GM), but when GM went bankrupt in 2009 and was bailed out by the federal government, Limbaugh started denouncing "Government Motors" even while it was running ads on his show. He declared that GM was "in the toilet" and insulted the company: "GM already makes these kinds of worthless little ecocars."[134]

After a caller who had been a GM customer for thirty-nine years announced that he was boycotting GM, Limbaugh strongly agreed: "I think everybody's relationship with General Motors has ended. Those who continue to buy cars from General Motors are not really buying from General Motors. We're buying from Obama."[135] Yet listeners could still hear Rush's prerecorded commercial for GM, declaring, "They are not just rebuilding their company, they're reinventing it."[136]

A few days later, he claimed he hadn't said what he said: "I urged no boycott of GM. General Motors is a sponsor here."[137] He added, "All I did, to clarify, was report a poll that said X number of Americans—what was it, 18 or 20 percent—say they are not going to buy a GM car anymore, after this bailout."[138]

But Limbaugh did far more than report—he actively praised his listeners who said they would boycott GM. A caller said to Limbaugh, "What you were just talking about there about not buying GM products because of Obama, it's exactly how I feel . . . I won't even look at another one right now, and I just want to say thanks. At least somebody understands what's going on here." Limbaugh responded, "I appreciate that."[139] Rush told one caller who participated in Cash for Clunkers, "I think it's even great you bought a Hyundai and screwed Obama's car company."[140] According to Rush, "Buying a General Motors or Chrysler car is a campaign donation" to Obama.[141] Limbaugh also smeared GM's union workers as thugs and warned his listeners that they would be physically assaulted at GM dealerships: "When people come in and want to test-drive a car and drive it, if they don't buy it, you're going to have some guy walking around threatening the potential buyer's kneecaps."[142] This may be the first time a corporation advertised on a show on which the host reading its commercials was simultaneously encouraging a boycott of the company.

The Ad Man

Limbaugh's "obscene profit time-outs" have been tremendously successful because of his loyal audience. His listeners are willing to sit through the commercial breaks to hear what he has to say. Perhaps most amazing of all, one study found that he had a bigger audience during the commercial breaks compared to the show itself.[143] Rush's listeners are so devoted to him that they pay more attention to his commercials than to his ideas. And Limbaugh has merged advertising into his show content so completely that his listeners barely distinguish between the two.

Of course, Limbaugh's show is one big advertisement for the conservative movement, a constant marketing tool for right-wing politics. During election season, it becomes a tool of the Republican Party. Limbaugh may sometimes attack Republican ideas (such as when he turned against George W. Bush's immigration proposal and his Supreme Court nominee Harriet Miers), but he always returns to the fold when voters go to the polls. Before an election, his only criticism of Republicans is tactical: He invariably argues that his party needs to be more conservative in order to win elections, all evidence to the contrary. For Limbaugh, the conservative movement is just another product he believes in, to be promoted relentlessly until his audience will buy it just as they buy the other products he sells.

THE LIMBAUGH DESERT

Advocates for better food choices created the term "food desert" to describe neighborhoods where there are no supermarkets or farmer's markets, where people without cars must go to the corner liquor store to buy overpriced groceries.

Vast swaths of American territory are a radio desert with few options. They may be bombarded during the middle of the day by Limbaugh intoning at them from several different stations, but they have no real alternative to conservative talk radio. After Limbaugh signs off, he is replaced by his friends, other conservative hosts such as Mark Levin, Sean Hannity, Laura Ingraham, and Michael Savage. You could drive across the country and never lose contact with a right-wing talk radio station playing Limbaugh and his imitators. At the same time, unless you managed to find a tiny, static-filled station in a major urban area, you could easily go through every state and never hear a progressive talk radio host.

The same exclusion of liberal views has occurred on cable news. MSNBC, the leading cable network for progressives now with Keith Olbermann, Rachel Maddow, and Ed Schultz, came to its liberal format (in the prime-time slots) only by accident after desperately trying to be a right-wing network; it never wanted to have progressive hosts. MSNBC had even fired Phil Donahue (host of its highest-rated show) in 2002; an internal NBC memo called Donahue "a tired, left-wing liberal out of touch with the current marketplace" and claimed that Donahue presented a "difficult public face for NBC in a time of war. . . . He seems to delight in presenting guests who are antiwar, anti-Bush, and skeptical of the administration's motives."[144]

MSNBC at first tried to become another imitator of the Fox News Channel, hiring former Republican congressman Joe Scarborough to host a prime-time show along with conservatives such as Tucker Carlson in 2005, and even bringing in the most vicious right-wing talk show host in the country, Michael Savage (who was fired in 2003 after his ratings were lousy and he told a caller to his radio show, "Oh, you're one of the sodomites. You should only get AIDS and die, you pig"[145]).

MSNBC turned to sports broadcaster Keith Olbermann in 2003, hoping that he could bring a lighter touch and provide some balance. Olbermann, almost by accident, turned into one of the most outspoken liberals in the mass media. After the right-wingers MSNBC had hired failed miserably in the ratings, in 2008 the network added Rachel Maddow and Ed Schultz, who helped improve MSNBC's notoriously low ratings. The shift angers the right. Limbaugh falsely complained about "MSNBC, whose content is produced almost entirely by Media Matters for America and MoveOn."[146] Ironically, MSNBC's status as a mildly progressive channel (its news programming during the day is neutral, and it maintains conservative Joe Scarborough as a morning host) developed due to the unwillingness of conservative viewers to watch anything but conservatives. Conservative viewers preferred the monolithic right-wing approach of Fox News, and so they never strayed.

Limbaugh is doing much more than preaching to the choir. He's leading the choir, calling the tune, and telling them how to sing it. He helps to shape the political debate. Limbaugh's audience is also much more than the choir. One key problem for left-leaning radio in America is that liberals don't share the same kind of ideological isolation that conservatives do. Almost one million self-identified Democrats listen to his show every week, making him more popular among liberal listeners than almost any left-wing talk show host. Liberal radio fails partly because conservatives refuse to listen, while far more liberals are willing to tune in to conservative hosts.

There's a fundamental difference between Rush Limbaugh's refusal to have any guests who might contradict him, and Rachel Maddow on MS-NBC pleading for Republicans to come on her show to debate ideas. The success of *Democracy Now,* an hourly radio and TV show that provides solid news and guests who debate different viewpoints in addition to progressive advocacy, reveals the differences between right-wing and left-wing media. But in many places around the country, Limbaugh is the only option on the radio for news analysis.

THE PRO-LIMBAUGH MEDIA

Limbaugh has complained that "the vast majority of journalists who write about me never call me" and "their purpose is not to get it right."[147] How often does he call people to get his facts right? Considering his vast earnings, Rush could easily hire a team of researchers to fact-check every issue before he discusses it. But he never lets accuracy stand in the way of a good story.

Even his claim that "no journalist ever calls me to say, did you say what they say?" is patently untrue.[148] Numerous journalists contact him to comment on some issue involving him, but Limbaugh rarely deigns to reply. In 1995 he bragged about the thousands of articles where he was mentioned without having to give a single interview.[149] Limbaugh did not respond to any requests for information for this book.

Fox News Channel is a strong ally of Limbaugh's, and he regularly appears on the network's shows to be praised and delicately questioned. Limbaugh even gets advance notice of some Fox News Channel stories; Limbaugh once noted that Fox News Channel's Bill Sammon alerted him about a story defending Limbaugh: "Rush, I'm working on a piece here, I hope to have it ready by the time your show starts, and here it is."[150]

Limbaugh has even translated his fame into numerous TV and film appearances, despite a complete lack of any acting talent. He made cameos on TV shows such as *Hearts Afire* and *The Drew Carey Show,* appeared in the Billy Crystal film *Forget Paris,* and starred in animated form on *Family Guy.* Far from being banished by the media, Limbaugh is a celebrity.

Some of the most powerful media owners in the world welcome Limbaugh. He appeared in 2009 at a fund-raiser for Congressman Michael Mc-

Caul (R-TX), a rare act of generosity perhaps motivated by the fact that Rush works for the radio giant Clear Channel Communications, which was founded by McCaul's father-in-law.[151]

Before right-wing media mogul Conrad Black was sentenced to six and a half years in prison for fraud, Limbaugh sent a letter to the judge praising Black's good character. As the *London Telegraph* reported about Limbaugh's office, "On the walls of the corridor there is evidence of Limbaugh's considerable power and influence, and his friends in high places. . . . Here a framed picture of him with George Bush. Here one of him with Donald Rumsfeld. Here he is with Hamid Karzai, the president of Afghanistan."[152]

In 2009 Limbaugh introduced his "good friend" Roger Ailes, head of Fox News Channel, when Ailes received the "Good Scout Award" from the Boy Scouts of America. Limbaugh called Ailes "one of the greatest Americans who has ever lived,"[153] and said proudly of him, "He's created this culture where everybody there is on the same page."[154] This is the model of a media company to Limbaugh: a culture where conservative views are imposed on everyone.

MEET THE MAINSTREAM PRESS

Limbaugh's influence also goes far beyond the conservative media. Though he uses a handful of progressive hosts on MSNBC to smear the entire NBC network—"NBC is not a credible source with me"[155]—over the years, Limbaugh has been consistently welcomed on NBC and MSNBC. In 2000 Chris Matthews told him, "Rush Limbaugh, it's an honor to have you with your legions of supporters around the country who do believe you are the last great patriot. Please come back."[156]

Limbaugh claimed he was banned from appearing on NBC on election night: "The last time I was on there was 2002. Tom Brokaw had me on and they're not going to do it again."[157] This was another lie. Limbaugh told his audience in 2004, "I was invited back again this year by NBC to be part of their coverage with Tom Brokaw and Tim Russert. . . . They were as accommodating as they could be, but as I allocated my time and ways to spend it on election night, they basically said, 'We'd like you for two three-minute to four-minute shots between eight P.M. and two or three A.M.' . . . I have better things to do on election night."[158] Even when Limbaugh was given the opportunity for unlimited time on MSNBC, he refused: "They offered, 'Well, go over on MSNBC all you want.' And so forth. I said, 'I appreciate that,' but I turned it down."[159] There has never been any liberal pundit offered eight minutes on a major network during election night along with unlimited time on a cable news outlet.

Russert was particularly friendly toward the radio host and frequently had Limbaugh on his CNBC show, and even complimented him in a 1998 appearance: "You look terrific."[160] In 2004 Limbaugh returned the favor by making his friend Russert one of the rare guests on his show: "We don't often have guests on this program, but we made an exception, here, for our friend, Tim Russert of NBC News." Limbaugh declared, "You will eventually become president of the news division of NBC." Russert said it was "an honor" to be on Limbaugh's program, and playfully suggested nominating him as the next host of *Meet the Press*. Limbaugh said, "I always enjoy talking to you, and I appreciate our relationship over the years."[161] Limbaugh had told Russert earlier in 1997, "You guys have done some amazing things on your show and Brokaw. I think—I think most of the mainstream press has dug up the facts."[162]

Brian Williams was also a fan of the "Maha Rushie." Less than a month after Williams became anchor for *NBC Nightly News* in 2004, he was publicly expressing his fondness for Limbaugh in a C-SPAN interview: "I do listen to Rush. I listen to it from a radio in my office, or depending on my day, if I'm in the car, I will listen to Rush. And he will tell you I've been listening for years. I think it's my duty to listen to Rush. I think Rush has actually yet to get the credit he is due, because his audience for so many years felt they were in the wilderness of this country. I think Rush helped to give birth to a movement. I think he played his part in the Contract with America. So I hope he gets his due as a broadcaster."[163] It would be difficult to find any major network anchor who has similarly praised a left-wing commentator with such enthusiasm, and Williams has never reported it his "duty" to listen to any left-wing talk show host. In 2002 Williams on MSNBC even referred to "our friend Rush Limbaugh," and Limbaugh was a frequent guest on *The News with Brian Williams*.[164]

LIMBAUGH JOINS THE MAINSTREAM MEDIA

Limbaugh has been embraced by every news network and mainstream media outlet. He was listed as one of *Time* magazine's 100 most influential people.[165] He made Barbara Walters's list of "the 12 Most Fascinating People" in 1993 and her list of "the 10 Most Fascinating People" in 2008 on ABC.[166] Limbaugh even appeared on *This Week with David Brinkley* and the *MacNeil/Lehrer NewsHour*.[167]

Ted Koppel of ABC praised Limbaugh as "extremely articulate" and invited him in 1990 on *Nightline* to argue about the Persian Gulf War with columnist Mark Shields, and again in 1992 to debate global warming with Senator Al Gore.[168] Koppel noted, "I was one of the first people here to say you've got to pay attention to this guy."[169] *Vanity Fair* reported about Limbaugh, "Ted Koppel is a Washington fan, if not a philosophical sympathizer, often laughing out loud as he rides to work; ditto Hollywood producer Don Simpson."[170] Richard Harris, a Limbaugh listener who worked for NPR and *Nightline*, noted: "He has the ability to get to the core of an issue without having an incendiary discussion with angry callers. You can have an honest debate with him, and you know he won't have his thumb perched on the cut-off button."[171] (In reality, Limbaugh routinely cuts off callers he disagrees with, although his listeners rarely notice this fact because he does it silently.) Also in 1990, CBS considered Limbaugh for a late-night talk show until he had a disastrous tryout guest-hosting Pat Sajak's show on March 30, which was interrupted by gay activists denouncing his homophobia. Lorimar Television did a *Talk Wrestling* pilot with Limbaugh and Gloria Allred, but it never went anywhere.[172] And Limbaugh auditioned for a role on the *To Tell the Truth* game show.[173] CBS News held talks with Limbaugh about having him join the launch of *60 Minutes II* in 1994, but the network ultimately decided against having a "point-counterpoint" segment.[174]

In 2006, during the first week of the *CBS Evening News* with Katie Couric, Limbaugh appeared as one of the commentators on her ill-fated "free speech" segment. Limbaugh agreed to do it because it was "an opportunity for me to express our views, my views without debate, without somebody coming on afterwards to refute it."[175] Limbaugh could appear on almost any mainstream news show in the country, anytime he wants to, but he demands no critical questioning and no contradiction from other guests.

Limbaugh appeared on Jay Leno's and David Letterman's shows in 1993 and 1994, and praised Letterman for having him on his show several times, noting: "He was very kind every time on those two or three returns."[176] He also appeared on Jay Leno's prime-time show in 2009, but apart from the superficial entertainment shows, he stays almost exclusively in the comfortable environs of the Fox News Channel, and never exposes himself to challenging questions.

The mainstream media elites treat Limbaugh with deference and admiration. When Walter Isaacson ran CNN, he tried to recruit Rush to be on the network. In 2001 Limbaugh reported on his show that he was being considered for a talk show on TV: "CNN is talking to me. I'm listening."[177]

As *Washington Post* media writer Howard Kurtz noted in 2002, "He's so mainstream that those right-wingers Tom Brokaw and Tim Russert had him on their Election Night coverage."[178] *Washington Post* columnist E. J. Dionne argued weeks later that Limbaugh's "new respectability is the surest sign that the conservative talk network is now bleeding into what passes for the mainstream media,"[179] and in 2009 *Chicago Tribune* columnist Clarence Page said, "I listen to Rush all the time. . . . And I've learned a lot from him."[180] Howard Fineman, *Newsweek*'s senior editor and chief political correspondent, also declared in 2010 that he "listens every day" to Rush.[181] Mark Halperin, the former director of the ABC News political unit and now Senior MSNBC Political Analyst, is an admitted Rush admirer: "Twelve o'clock for a normal person might be 'Let's think about having lunch,' but for me it's 'Rush Limbaugh is on.' " Halperin called Limbaugh an "American iconic" figure.[182] ABC News political director David Chalian even said on the air, "I'm not gonna pick a fight with Rush Limbaugh."[183]

Throughout Limbaugh's career, the mainstream media has treated him with kid gloves, refusing to report on his most offensive statements and craziest conspiracy theories. Their deference to Limbaugh partly stems from a fear of a right-wing backlash, but it also reflects the conservatism of many people in the so-called "liberal" media.

THE PRO-LIMBAUGH DOUBLE STANDARD

Conservative commentator Andrew Breitbart claimed that the media hate Limbaugh for taking away their audience and therefore they "bad-mouth him every chance they get."[184] However, Limbaugh isn't taking away most of the media's audience. The mainstream media's worst drop in audience is among the young, the demographic group where Rush has the fewest fans. More important, the media don't bad-mouth Limbaugh.

Conservatives also argue that Limbaugh is held to a higher standard than liberals. Andrew Klavan wrote, "Leftists—including the current administration and the mainstream media—have worked hard to demonize Rush by holding him to a different standard than liberal entertainers and commentators. If comedian Jon Stewart shouts the f-word on air at Governor Sarah Palin, he's just being outrageous and funny. If Bill Maher calls people racist for disagreeing with Barack Obama, he's thoughtful and interesting. But let Rush express himself through humor and sarcasm, and suddenly he's 'hateful,' 'racist,' 'ugly,' and all the rest."[185]

Bill Maher has never called people racist for disagreeing with Barack Obama (since Maher himself criticizes Obama on occasion, it's doubtful that he regards himself as a racist). And Jon Stewart is funny when he's insulting politicians, just as Rush often is. What makes Rush hateful and racist is the hateful, racist things he says, not his conservative ideology or his sarcasm.

The biggest favor the mainstream "liberal" press does for Limbaugh is to ignore him. His false claims, and his outrageous statements, are all communicated directly to his followers without any refutation by the mainstream media.

On the other hand, one reason why Limbaugh often gets positive coverage from the conventional media is that he threatens retaliation against journalists who dare to criticize him. In 2008 he said: "I think if the *Times* does a story on me they might actually worry about cancellations."[186] But he doesn't simply limit his threats to the possibility of boycott. As Michael Wolff of *New York Magazine* noted, Limbaugh's retaliation to him was announcing Wolff's e-mail address on the air: "Shortly after the war in Iraq began, when I was reporting from CentCom headquarters in Qatar, I asked an intemperate question of one of the military briefers in the daily televised news conference and, dissed by Rush for my lack of patriotism, got the full effect: more than twenty thousand e-mails in forty-eight hours, shutting down my mail server."[187] The fear of offending Limbaugh, or his legion of fans, makes mainstream journalists wary of any criticism toward "El Rushbo."

Limbaugh is particularly ruthless toward anyone who might criticize him personally. In 2007 he recounted how a reporter had been writing "a cover story on me coming out of one of the big news magazines, and it was going to totally mischaracterize me and what I do and how I do it." He went on to declare: "We found out who was writing it and made a couple phone calls to the person writing it. And we said, 'You know what? We're going to find out where your kids go to school. We're going to find out who you knocked up in high school. We're going to find out what drugs you used. We're going to find out where you go to drink and do—we're gonna find out how you paid for your house. We're going to do—and we're going to do exact—and we're going to say that, you know what? You are no different than Al Goldstein. You both masturbate.' "[188]

This sleazy tale of blackmail was reported with delight by Limbaugh: "And the guy started screaming on the phone, just went—'You can't do that.' We said, 'Watch us.' And it changed the tone of the story by about 60 percent, I would say, from what it was going to be. But nobody does that to these people. Nobody does it to them. And that would be so much fun. But I'd need to be wearing body armor every day. Oh, no question, these people are playing for keeps."[189]

This anecdote, and the fact that Limbaugh was willing to tell his audience about it, shows just how slimy Rush can be in attacking his critics. He actually threatened to stalk the children of a reporter and expose his sexual habits, all in order to force a journalist to be less critical of him.

This may explain how Limbaugh gets such fawning coverage from the mainstream press: because he threatens them. Those who dare to criticize him know that one angry word from Limbaugh on his show can cause the target to be pounded with an onslaught of nasty emails and even death threats.

10

LIMBAUGH'S WAR ON INTELLECTUALS, LIBERALS, AND BLUE BLOODS

In the war of ideas, Rush Limbaugh has been the leading figure dumbing down the conservative movement. He popularized a whole new kind of media, the right-wing talk show, where conventional media values such as objectivity were not only abandoned but actively opposed. Today's media environment is completely fragmented for the ideological satisfaction of the consumer. Conservatives listen only to conservative talk shows, liberals (to a much lesser degree) pay attention to progressive media, everybody goes to the websites that largely agree with them, and only a declining, aging fraction of the population still focuses on the mainstream media.

The result is a deep distortion in information about our political life. The mainstream press had many flaws, but a devotion to fairness and accuracy was one of its ideals. In the ideological media, particularly the conservative talk show, that value has been tossed out the window.

Limbaugh's influence on his listeners and the mainstream press shifts our entire media culture in a conservative direction. His success brought imitators such as Fox News Channel, which in turn put economic pressure on other media outlets to move to the right. Rush's ability to mobilize his listeners to attack anyone who questioned George W. Bush also helped discourage mainstream media outlets from criticizing the Bush administration in the wake of 9/11, particularly influencing the massive failure of the press to question the lies told about weapons of mass destruction in Iraq.

Limbaugh is often accused of incivility, of contributing to the coarsening of our discourse by demonizing his enemies. Interestingly, this accusation offends Limbaugh more than almost any other. He imagines himself to be a gracious and polite host, very different from the angry shock jocks and insult comics who demean others as part of their schtick. Insults aren't an act; they're a fundamental part of his radio success.

THE INSULT KING

Limbaugh isn't just dumbing down the conservative movement. He's also a leading force dehumanizing it. Rush has brought insults to an art form—a lousy art, but it serves his purpose. When he can't defeat liberal opponents with logic, he tries to humiliate them. Early in his radio career, he reported, "I found out I was really good, good at insulting people."[1] But Limbaugh quickly recognized the limits of an insult shock jock. So he turned his talents at insulting to the political sphere: Instead of insulting callers, he would insult politicians.

Most of Limbaugh's insults are juvenile, such as calling his enemies "pea brains." Limbaugh said about the Democrats in the House of Representatives, "Aren't they all liberal socialist jerks?" He also routinely calls his political opponents "idiots." Limbaugh said of Obama, "He is a lying idiot!" and, "This guy Obama is dangerous, because he's an idiot"; he referred to "that idiot Obama" and declared, "Obama's either a useful idiot, or he's worse."[2]

Limbaugh also extends the term to Obama's press secretary, "that idiot Robert Gibbs," his campaign manager David Plouffe ("You are an idiot, Mr. Plouffe"), Vice President Joe Biden (" a blooming idiot"), Speaker of the House Nancy Pelosi ("a dangerous, blithering idiot"), Obama's Supreme Court Justice Sonia Sotomayor ("she's the idiot") and, of course, "his idiot voters" and "his idiot supporters."[3]

Limbaugh routinely calls all liberals "idiots." He referred to "the stupid idiots of the American left" and has discussed "stupid, idiot teachers." He denounced Representative Henry Waxman (D-CA) for believing in global warming: "You're an idiot. You are a dangerous idiot." He attacked "a genuine idiot, David Letterman" for hosting Obama on his show and called Nobel Prize–winning economist Paul Krugman "a genuine idiot."[4]

These are just a few of the occasions when Rush calls his enemies idiots, taken from a span of only two years in time. Unlike Limbaugh, who uses "idiot" to baselessly smear people that he disagrees with, I do not believe that Limbaugh is an idiot simply because of his conservative ideology. Nor do I think that all conservatives are idiots. I lay out an extensive amount of evidence that Limbaugh is routinely wrong on simple factual matters, and fundamentally stupid in his ignorant views about science. Limbaugh's ignorance, and his pride in remaining ignorant, earns him the title of "idiot."

Limbaugh's Insult Humor

Crude, personal insults are Limbaugh's specialty, such as when he attacks Nancy Pelosi as "the Botox face of the Democrat Party"[5] or "the ferretlike Paul Krugman" (complete, on Limbaugh's Web site, with an image of Krugman's head photoshopped on the body of a ferret).[6] No one will ever call Limbaugh subtle.

Some of the derisive nicknames used by Limbaugh include Tommy Taxes (Tom Daschle), Richard "Little Dick" Gephardt, Chuck-U (Charles) Schumer, Nikita Dean (Howard Dean), Senator Dick Turban (Dick Durbin), Sheets Byrd (former KKK member Robert Byrd), Benedict Arnold or Dingy Harry (Harry Reid), The Haughty John Kerry ("Lurch" . . . "who by the way served in Vietnam"), The Swimmer (Ted Kennedy), Algore, Kathleen Sebortionist (Kathleen Sebelius), Leaky Leahy or Senator Depends (Patrick Leahy), Eleanor Squeal (Smeal), The Loser (Michael Dukakis), Nostrildamus or Nosferatu (Representative Henry Waxman), Queen Bee Nancy or Bela Pelosi (Nancy Pelosi), Banking Queen (Barney Frank), Timmy the Tax Cheat (Tim Geithner), Baghdad Bob Gibbs, Jack Crap (Chuck Todd), Tom "Dung Heap" Harkin, Walter Klondike (Cronkite), Rick "DUI, Leaving the Scene" Sanchez, the National Hemorrhoid (Jimmy Carter), and George Lakoff Rhymes With. Limbaugh also offers a couple of lame nicknames for the moderate Republicans who dare to violate conservative marching orders, such as David "Rodham" Gergen, Chuck "Senator Betray Us" Hagel, or Lindsey Graham-nesty.

Barack Obama has received a series of extremely lame names, even by Limbaugh's low standards of creativity. Limbaugh began in 2007 by making fun of Obama's big ears and calling him Barack O'Dumbo. Since then, he has tried Barack Fonda, Barack Marx, and Bamster.[7]

Limbaugh has called Pelosi and Obama "clowns." He denounced the Obama administration as "absolute inexperienced fruitcake nobodies" and attacked all Democrats as "a bunch of inexperienced little ninny socialist statists." Rush is particularly vicious toward anyone who criticizes him. After years of refusing to even mention his name, he referred to Senator Al Franken as a "genuine lunatic." After Limbaugh called MSNBC's Ed Schultz "a talking horse," Schultz invited Limbaugh to debate him on radio or TV: "But you won't do it. Cause you're a coward, Rush. I've always thought that."[8] To no one's surprise, Limbaugh never responded.

Denying that he ever said what his own Web site records as his exact words is a hallmark of Limbaugh's talent for rewriting reality. After Rahm Emanuel was quoted calling left-wing critics of Obama "retards," Limbaugh quickly agreed with him: "Our politically correct society is acting like some giant insult's taken place by calling a bunch of people who are retards, 'retards.'" He concurred with attacking "these retards on the left."[9] Facing a backlash of criticism, Limbaugh tried to deny he ever said what he said: "I never used the word. I never once used the word! It never crosses my mind to use the word."[10]

In the isolation of his radio studio, egged on by his adoring fans, Limbaugh finds it easier to deny his own actions and demean liberals rather than refute their arguments. He claimed in 2002, "I don't attack anybody. I defend."[11] Like many of his statements, this assertion was plainly false. His show is full of nothing but attacks, almost always directed at people who never go after Rush first.

Insulting Fatness

Insults about Limbaugh's fatness are common. Even Republicans make jokes about his weight. California governor Arnold Schwarzenegger declared,

"Look, I think they say that Rush Limbaugh is the eight hundred-pound gorilla in the Republican Party. But I think that's mean-spirited to say that because I think he's down to six hundred and fifty pounds."[12] But Limbaugh's weight is the least offensive thing about him. The fat jokes against Limbaugh are not only tiresome, they're insulting to overweight people (who don't deserve to be smeared in the anti-Rush tirades), and they ultimately fail to engage in a debate of ideas.

Of course, he deserves little sympathy for the fat jokes made about him because he makes the very same fat jokes about liberals he doesn't like. In the 1990s, when Ted Kennedy declared, "America needs health care reform," Limbaugh replied, "Ted Kennedy is fat."[13] In 2004 he insulted Germany's "big, fat foreign minister Joschka Fischer."[14] In 2008 he mocked a "humongously large, fat family" who appeared on an Obama infomercial during the campaign,[15] and in 2009, he referred to "the bloated bigot Michael Moore."[16] Rush said, "It's a common joke about how fat congressmen and senators are."[17] He even targeted Hillary Clinton for having "that big an ass."[18]

The famously overweight Limbaugh also mocked Rosie O'Donnell as "a killer whale"[19] and said, "I'm telling you, the deal was about the dog biscuits that they gave her on the floor in the dressing room were just the wrong flavor. They couldn't come to an agreement on the flavor of the Ken-L Ration that she eats."[20] In 2009 he said about the late feminist Andrea Dworkin, "She could be the poster child" for the obese.[21] It's appalling for Limbaugh to insult a dead woman for being obese when he weighed far more than her for most of his adult life.

In 2007 Rush even played Paul Shanklin's bad Al Sharpton impersonation, saying a series of "your mama so fat" jokes to Obama: "Obama, your mother is so fat, when she cuts, she bleeds gravy."[22] According to Limbaugh, "The stuff is hilarious. It is stuff, in my mind, that is cutting edge."[23] The only thing worse than a fat guy playing "mama so fat" jokes is a fat racist white guy playing them because that's what he thinks black culture is.

The worst aspect of the fat jokes directed at Limbaugh is that they reduce him to a punch line rather than a powerful political figure; Limbaugh needs to be critiqued for his bad ideas, not insulted for his waistline. But one aspect of his fatness is relevant to his ideas, because nothing better symbolizes Limbaugh's scientific misinformation than his hatred of exercise. In 2009 he said, "I'm too much an expert on this," citing his loss of fifty-four pounds in seventy-four days on a restricted-calorie diet,[24] and even claimed, "All you exercise freaks, you're the ones putting stress on the health care system."[25] Displaying his medical expertise, Limbaugh asserted in 2008, "Half the people who are obese have really great heart health. I've told you people, all this conventional wisdom about all this health stuff and exercise, I told you, don't buy into it."[26] He has no evidence to back up his assertion that half of all obese people have great heart health; obesity is *clearly* linked to heart disease and other ailments.[27] In another unfounded claim, Limbaugh links the obesity crisis to food stamps: "This is what happens when you let the left run things. . . . At least here in America, didn't teach them how to fish, we gave them the fish. Didn't teach them how to butcher a— slaughter a cow to get the butter, we gave them the butter."[28] Limbaugh's understanding of the obesity epidemic is about as accurate as his knowledge of how butter is made. But to him, it is an article of faith that every problem in America is caused by the government. Fatness, to Limbaugh, is just another thing to blame on liberalism.

THE LIBERAL ENEMY

Limbaugh's entire career in talk radio has been framed around his hatred of liberals. As he said, "My whole life has been spent researching liberals. That's what I do. I know them like every square inch of my shrinking yet glorious naked body."[29] For somebody who claims to know liberals so thoroughly, it's remarkable how ignorant he is. He has claimed, for example, "Liberals, period, by definition can't be happy. It's part of the ideology,"[30] and, "There's no intellect involved in liberalism."[31] It's these sweeping absurdities that show how little Limbaugh understands about liberals. To him, liberals are not real people capable of thinking; they are merely caricatures he uses to create a devilish enemy for his three hours of hate delivered every weekday against all things liberal.

In his first book, the radio host denounced what he called "the liberal compassion fascists."[32] He claimed about liberals, "They certainly do not subscribe to the basic work ethic common to this country."[33] Limbaugh even had a trash can in his library with the word *Liberals* on it.[34] He told *Play-*

boy, "To this day I do not own a pair of blue jeans" because he associates them with liberals.[35]

In the world of Limbaugh, everything conservative is good and everything liberal is evil. He says, "The brothers of liberals are Nazis, communists, socialists, and so forth."[36] His hatred of liberals also extends to moderates in the political center. He regards any deviation from conservatism as dangerous: "Centrism is a left-wing code word."[37] He said, "By definition, an organization or a person who is not conservative will be or will become a liberal."[38]

Conservatism was something Limbaugh was born into, yet he projects this onto liberalism: "Conservatism is not something you're born with. Conservatism is an active intellectual pursuit. Liberalism, there's nothing intellectual about it. It's all emotional. It's all feeling. It's all grievance and victimization. I can't answer if it's chosen or if you're born with it, but we need to find the answer. But trying to rationally explain it is a waste of time."[39] It's ridiculous to claim that any ideology, left or right, is "something you're born with." It's particularly ridiculous for him to say it because he was born into a conservative family and never rebelled; he has claimed, "Our whole family was born into Christianity."[40] Like everything else he believes, Limbaugh's religion was given to him by his father, and accepted without question.

Anyone who claims that there is nothing intellectual about liberalism (or conservatism) isn't an intellectual at all. That person is simply refusing to accept the reality that people with opposing viewpoints have a serious intellectual basis for what they believe.

Limbaugh has also said about liberals, "The liberals, you see, do not want to confront conservative ideas; they just attack conservatives as a group, and particularly their motives."[41] But when it comes to questioning the motives of his opponents rather than confronting arguments, no one can match Rush. In his view, no one can possibly disagree with him unless they're stupid or harbor some secret agenda.

Despite all of Limbaugh's claims about studying liberals, to him they are simply incomprehensible: "I don't know who they are, I don't know what they believe, but I can't relate. I can't possibly understand somebody who hates this country, who was born and raised here. I don't understand how you hate this Constitution. I don't understand how you hate freedom."[42]

Limbaugh sees liberals as psychotic: "I sometimes wonder if liberalism is not just a psychosis or a psychology, not an ideology. It's so much about feelings, and the predominant feeling that liberalism is about feeling good about themselves and they do that by telling themselves they have all this compassion."[43]

Liberalism, in Limbaugh's eyes, is the worst thing imaginable: "It is all a lie. It is a poison. It is corrupting decent people. It's corrupting the concepts of liberty and freedom this nation was founded upon. It stinks. It's insidious. It is a disease."[44] You don't argue with a disease; you eradicate it. In fact, Limbaugh imagines that liberals don't even have souls: "I mean, if there is a party that's soulless, it's the Democratic Party. If there are people by definition who are soulless, it is liberals—by definition. You know, souls come from God."[45] Limbaugh declared, "Conservatives are naturally happy," and "We don't burn our cars. We don't burn down our houses. We don't kill our children. We don't do half the things the American left does."[46] Of course, liberals in America don't do any of these things, either. But by imagining the left as the source of all evil things, he and his followers can refuse to engage any liberal ideas. By demonizing the opposition, Limbaugh tells his audience that any dialogue with liberals is impossible. And he demonstrates this on every show, attacking liberalism as evil rather than merely wrong, making statements such as "Liberalism is a rotting piece of scum, and everything it touches gets destroyed."[47]

Limbaugh's hatred of liberals enables him to ignore facts that come from any group he thinks is not conservative. He dismissed statistics from the World Health Organization because "any organization which has as its first name 'World' is a bunch of United Nations socialists."[48] Limbaugh orders his listeners to live in a little bubble of conservative ideas and never be corrupted by contrary views: "Be vigilant, folks. Be vigilant. We're being scammed. We're being spun. The Universe of Lies has us surrounded. We're in a little bubble here called The Universe of Reality. The Universe of Lies is all around us. We're just one little bubble in it. We're trying to stay pure and not be corrupted by it."[49] To live in this bubble isolated from contrary ideas is Limbaugh's goal.

In Limbaugh's mind, liberals are the equivalent of terrorists: "Chris Matthews, Keith Olbermann. We're talking about a jury of peers of these terrorists who hated this country so much they wanted to blow up the World Trade Center and did." Limbaugh added, "Senator Durbin sides with these guys."[50]

Limbaugh has always rejected the idea of bipartisanship: "Where is the compromise between good and evil?"[51] This Manichean logic is fundamental to his view of liberals, and explains his attitude toward Democrats: "We need to wipe them out."[52] Ironically, Limbaugh complained: "Of course, liberals need a villain; they need a demon. They can't win a debate in the arena of ideas. They need a demon, and they need somebody to demonize, and I'm it, and I'm happy to be it."[53] While Limbaugh demonizes all liberals, he imagines that he's the one being demonized.

Liberals are mass murderers, too, according to Limbaugh, who contended that Virginia Tech killer Seung-Hui Cho "was a liberal." Limbaugh said, "So it's a liberal that committed this act. Now, the drive-bys will read on a Web site that I'm attacking liberalism by comparing this guy to them. That's exactly what they do every day, ladies and gentlemen. I'm just pointing out a fact. I am making no extrapolation; I'm just pointing it out."[54]

Cho was mentally ill, but he had no apparent political ideology. He was raised as a devout Christian in a Republican state. But Limbaugh hates liberals so much that he must imagine that anyone who does an evil act is a liberal.

A few days later, Limbaugh claimed his critics "fell for it hook, line, and sinker" and said, "I was making a joke. . . . Although I do believe that it was liberalism that got ahold of this guy and made him hate things, professors and this sort of thing."[55] In other words, Limbaugh said he was joking, and then said he believed exactly what he had said.

The people who think Limbaugh is actually joking are the ones falling "hook, line, and sinker" for his shtick. His audience fully understands that he isn't joking, and that his mock apologies or denials are the real joke. Rush often confirms that by reiterating the same point that he had just claimed was a joke.

Limbaugh thinks liberals pose a threat to our country. In 1999 he claimed, "They are dangerous! Liberals, I believe, have destroyed or are in the process of destroying the culture of this country."[56] Ten years later he said that the "enemies of America are friends of the Democrat Party."[57]

Limbaugh likes to question the patriotism of his enemies: "These people have become the mainstream thought—thinkers, generators of the Democratic Party. It's who they are. They hate this country. They hate the military of this country."[58] He also said, "It's time for somebody to tell the people on the left, you're damn right we're questioning your patriotism."[59] Limbaugh views liberals as traitors, not political opponents.

Limbaugh often uses stronger language to describe his Democratic enemies: "We need to defeat these bastards. We need to wipe them out. We need to chase them out of town."[60] After Al Qaeda terrorists murdered civilians in Madrid in 2004, Limbaugh said that Democrats "celebrate privately this attack in Spain."[61] He added later, "You don't hear the Democrats being critical of terrorists."[62] Of course, liberals had denounced terrorists in the strongest terms. Limbaugh also said in 2004, "If you want the terrorists running the show, then you will elect John Kerry."[63]

Smearing liberals is Limbaugh's favorite hobby, as when he said Democrats believe "the more deaths in Iraq the better."[64] It was an appalling claim, and as usual he had no evidence. The only one who wanted more Americans to die in Iraq was Limbaugh, as when he celebrated the kidnapping and murder in Iraq of members of Christian Peacemaker Teams: "I like any time a bunch of leftist feel-good hand-wringers are shown reality. . . . I'm telling you, folks, there's a part of me that likes this."[65] Because Limbaugh wishes death upon those he disagrees with, he finds it easy to imagine that liberals want to see Americans die because they disagree with a president's decision to go to war.

RED-BAITING REDUX

The Berlin Wall fell in 1989, just a year after Limbaugh began his nationally syndicated program, and he has devoted twenty years to converting liberals into the role of evildoers once reserved for communists. Limbaugh demonizes liberalism much as previous generations of demagogues denounced communism. The twenty-first-century version of McCarthyism can be heard whenever Limbaugh associates all liberals with communism. When John Kerry quoted Langston Hughes's famous poem "Let America Be America Again," Rush said, "You've got a Democratic presidential nominee quoting from a poem written in the 1930s that is anti-America and pro-communist, Marxist-Leninist, what have you. . . . John Kerry either doesn't find anything wrong with the fact that Langston Hughes is a communist, or is banking on the fact that nobody will know it."[66] Rush sees any communist or anyone critical of America as so evil that even their poetry should be banished. Limbaugh claimed that Democrats moved "Pravda left" after the 2004 election.[67] After the dissolution of the Soviet Union, conservatives faced an ideological crisis: their paramount enemy, the communist threat, had essentially disappeared. But Rush was quick to find an even better enemy: liberalism.

Red-baiting is one of his favorite tactics: "*The Nation* is one of our favorite publications here, the far-left fringe publication of the liberal journal of opinion that is edited by well-known communist named Katrina vanden Heuvel whose husband is a well-known communist at Columbia. Well, I use the term advisedly. Stephen Cohen's his name. They're both big lovers of the old Soviet Union."[68] Neither vanden Heuvel nor Cohen are communists, nor did they love the Soviet Union.

The most important contribution of Limbaugh to the conservative movement was to give it a new enemy to fight. With the fall of the Soviet Union, conservatives could have simply declared victory and gone home. Instead, Limbaugh mobilized the right to pursue a new enemy, the enemy named liberalism.

Limbaugh wrote in his first book, "It is neither farfetched nor unfair to draw an analogy between the civil rights leadership and the Soviet Communist leadership, insofar as exploitation of their people is concerned. The leaders of both enjoy the privileges of class at the expense of the masses, who do all the work and whom the leaders purport to serve."[69] He saw a direct parallel between liberalism and communism in *See, I Told You So*: "Isn't it ironic that as America is celebrating its victory in the Cold War over communism, those same, tired, oppressive ideas are still winning the hearts and minds of millions of Americans."[70] In the book Limbaugh wrote about Bill Clinton: "How about that mysterious vacation to Moscow and Prague in the dead of winter."[71] Hinting that Clinton was some kind of secret communist sympathizer in his youth was the very same smear tactic Limbaugh used against Obama.

THE UNIVERSE OF LIMBAUGH

The universe of Limbaugh is a crowded place where there's only enough space for one point of view. His authority among his listeners comes, in part, from the air of certainty that he exudes. His bluster and swagger follows in the long tradition of DJs who ramble on alone in a studio, carefully controlling everything put on the air. Limbaugh wanted nothing to do with the constrictions of a news program or the tradition of having guests on a talk show. He desired total control.

Limbaugh cannot tolerate dissent. He once recounted what happened in 2009 when some friends dared to question him about Sarah Palin: "I had some people over for dinner last night, and it happened, I lost my temper, I started throwing a napkin, 'cause I got questions. These are my friends, people that listen to my show, these are people that I talk to a lot, and these guys, one of them, started spouting questions to me that just reflected every criticism of her that has been in the media. The Katie Couric interview and I said, 'Look, the—' well, I'm not going to tell you what I said 'cause it was waste. But I went on for five minutes, and I'm pounding the table and I'm throwing my napkin and picking it up and throwing it again."[72] If this is how Limbaugh treats his conservative friends, it's not hard to imagine how he regards liberals.

In Rush's alternate universe, Democrats are always evil, conservative policies always work, and he is always right. The key to maintaining the Limbaugh universe is to protect it from the intrusions of the real world. Every day of Limbaugh's show is devoted to carefully defending this universe, by dismissing all critics and imagining the facts that would support his worldview that America is a shiny beacon of perfection, where everyone is equal and opportunity is everywhere.

Rush Limbaugh has shaped American politics for the past two decades, stepping into the void left by Ronald Reagan's departure. Unfortunately, he's distorted politics in demeaning and destructive ways. He is the leader of the decline and fall of the conservative movement's principles and popularity, but not influence. With an ideologue rather than a politician guiding the party, the typical political norms of civility to opponents and moderation in order to appeal to independent voters have been thrown out, as Limbaugh has driven the Republicans much further to the right.

Ironically, as Limbaugh has become the voice of a decreasing proportion of Americans, his influence has grown ever larger. The smaller public support for the Republican Party means that it has become even more vulnerable to control by far-right voices such as Limbaugh's. It's a kind of death spiral for the conservative movement, where every election loss only increases the power of the fewer remaining Republicans, who occupy the more extreme end of the right.

Limbaugh, the Populist

Populism is one aspect of Limbaugh's ideology, despite his vast wealth and his constant defense of corporate America: "All of these rich guys—like the Kennedy family and Perot—pretending to live just like we do and pretending to understand our trials and tribulations and pretending to represent us, and they get away with this."[73] But it's Limbaugh who pretends to be one of the regular guys while he is completely out of touch. At the time of this quote, November 1993, Limbaugh was making $18 million a year and living a life of luxury. Limbaugh's salary, and his denunciations of rich liberals, only continued to escalate.

Limbaugh is clueless about the lives of everyday Americans. In 2009 he said, "This is the one country where, if you don't want to participate in a recession, don't. . . . You can create your own job."[74] In Rush's vivid imagination, unemployment is strictly a question of willpower. He thinks that anyone in America can be rich by trying hard.

Limbaugh presents himself as a populist who just happens to live the lifestyle of a wealthy man, saying, "I'm the one standing up for the little guy here."[75] But Limbaugh's idea of standing up for the little guy is rather odd, since he has also declared, "We need to raise taxes on the poor."[76]

Elitism is just a liberal attitude to Limbaugh: "I'm not an elitist. I don't have that kind of attitude or carriage," he claimed in 2009, adding, "The reason that I'm able to speak the truth to people is because I'm one of them."[77] Limbaugh drives a $450,000 Maybach 57S home to his twenty-four-thousand-square-foot home, one of five homes on his property.[78] A 1993 *Playboy* interview revealed that Limbaugh spent ninety thousand dollars a year on limousines.[79] His vast wealth has caused Limbaugh to forget his long struggle to make a living.

As Limbaugh has indicated, he believes poverty or even a middle-class lifestyle is the fault of the individual who refuses to earn more. He responded to one caller who dreamed of earning $250,000 a year by saying, "You want to earn 'two hundred fifty.' Do you know what? And I mean this from the bottom of my heart, Nathan. The only person stopping you is you. . . . Nathan, find out what you want to do. There's $250,000 out there for you if you want it."[80] Limbaugh thinks anyone can earn $250,000 if only they want it enough. His vision of levitating oneself into a penthouse apartment by one's own bootstraps is grotesquely out of touch with the average American's struggle to keep a job and stay afloat in a sea of debt during a severe recession. But his do-it-yourself philosophy is an essential component of his antigovernment conservatism.

Limbaugh always claims that he is celebrating the "average person."[81] But he has a strange definition of "average." When he first moved to New York City in 1988 to do his national radio show, Limbaugh worried about his salary because "$150,000 is not going to be enough to enjoy life in New York," and complained, "It was tight for about a year."[82] In 1993 he said, "I know families that make $180,000 a year and they don't consider themselves rich."[83] As Limbaugh has grown richer, his estimation of the amount of money necessary for survival has only grown. By 2009 Limbaugh contended that a couple in New York City making $1 million per year would wonder, "How do I live in this city?"[84]

Rush often imagines that he represents the regular people. He has said, "There are two sets of rules in America: one for elected Democrats. The other, for we the plebes, the peasants, the Great Unwashed, the Victims."[85] But this "peasant" is among the richest people in the world, with a $54 million Gulfstream G550 jet.[86] Meanwhile, Rush claimed, "I, of course, am not an elite. I'm not a country club, blue-blood Rockefeller type. I'm considered unsophisticated."[87] Limbaugh puts his populism in ideological terms: The "elitists" belong to the moderate wing of the Republican Party, while conservatives are the true representatives of the people. Thus, Limbaugh is not part of the elite even while he sits in a massive mansion counting his millions.

He is the strangest sort of faux-populist, one who openly flaunts his immense wealth while claiming to speak for the common people. He regularly drops the names of celebrity buddies ("one of my good friends is Al Michaels"),[88] and has bragged about his friendship with Cheryl Ladd[89] and about watching *Monday Night Football* at William Shatner's house.[90]

Limbaugh is a football fan, but he doesn't sit in the stands with the fans: He spends his games in skyboxes or receiving special access to the sidelines or the broadcast booth. But to his devoted listeners, Limbaugh is living their American dream. One caller told Limbaugh, "I live vicariously through you,"[91] admiring Limbaugh's trips on his private jet to go to a football game or go golfing. Indeed, Rush spends a great deal of time in private clubs, playing golf on courses where regular people can never dream of walking, even playing golf with both President Bushes.[92] But he is not one of the "country club" Republicans, at least in his own mind.

Elitism is Limbaugh's designated enemy, whether it's found in moderate Republicans or liberal Democrats. He claimed about Obama in June 2009, "He's totally caught up in the trappings of aristocracy or elite culture, taking the plane up to New York, flying the kids over to Paris."[93] But Rush regularly travels on his own private plane to New York and regales his audience with tales of flying around the country to benefits and parties. Limbaugh takes a particular pleasure in smoking very expensive cigars and bragging about them.

Limbaugh defines the Obama administration as elitist, even when his attacks are plainly hypocritical. He said about Obama, "These people are just pure downright elitists, up there at Marxist Vineyard, of all the places he could go, the richest places in the country with the whitest people in the country."[94] Moments earlier, Limbaugh had been bragging about a friend who owns the main golf course in Martha's Vineyard, and had invited Limbaugh to fly up and play a round while Obama was in town in order to taunt him.

Limbaugh even accused the Obama administration of being "elitist snobs advising us to sneeze on our arms."[95] Sneezing on your sleeve is universally considered a good way to reduce the spread of disease; this may have been the first time it was ever called "elitist."

Obama, unlike George W. Bush and Limbaugh, never came from a wealthy, well-known family. Yet Limbaugh claimed, "Obama cannot relate to an average person. He has no clue. He is above them! He is an elitist. He holds average people in contempt. He looks at them as stupid and malleable. He can make them do and think and believe anything he wants."[96] But Limbaugh arrogantly describes his power over his listeners, even bragging to *Playboy* in 1993 about swinging 20 million votes. *Playboy* asked him, "Votes you can control?" Limbaugh replied, "Yeah, if I choose to."[97] In 1994 Barbara Walters asked Limbaugh, "What influence do you think you have? Can you make people vote a particular way? Can you really change their views?" Limbaugh replied, "I can. I can."[98] Limbaugh said in 2009, "Radio is intimate, spoken-word radio that captivates the audience. You own that audience member."[99]

Columnist Kathleen Parker noted about Limbaugh: "Constant criticism of the 'elite media' is comical to most reporters, whose paychecks wouldn't cover Limbaugh's annual dry cleaning bill."[100] Rush is the most elite of the elite media: He's got the biggest audience, the biggest salary, and the biggest liberty to speak his mind. No reporter or anchor in the mainstream media could survive with even one day's worth of his distortions, errors, and opinions. But Limbaugh is the true media elite: He gets to call his own shots, and say whatever he wants without fear of retribution.

ATTACK OF THE BLUE BLOODS

Rush Limbaugh is obsessed with blood—in particular, blue blood. He regularly denounces the "blue blood" Republicans whom he regards as being the Northeast aristocracy of the party. In 2009 he declared, "The Republican Party is a mess right now" and blamed moderates (naturally, Limbaugh refused to take any responsibility) saying, "The big issue here that is keeping the Republican Party from unifying is the blue bloods. The country club types, the Northeastern, Rockefeller types never did like Ronald Reagan."[101]

Limbaugh has an almost fanatical hatred of the "blue bloods" that he believes are controlling the Republican Party. Limbaugh denounced "the old guard, country club blue blooders that are trying to define the party and run it," calling them "obedient" and "acting as oppressed minorities."[102] This animosity toward them stems from Limbaugh's deep insecurity about his third-rate education and lack of intelligence and sophistication.

Limbaugh is openly scornful of intellectuals, including conservative ones; as much as he hates liberal intellectuals, though, he reserves his deepest contempt for Republican intellectuals, condemning them as the "Wizards of Smart"[103] and "the Northeastern blue-blood Rockefeller country club types."

No matter what happens, Limbaugh always sees moving to the far right as the solution for the Republicans. He complained in May 2009, "The moderates run the Republican Party" and wondered, "How are we going to grow the Republican Party if more and more moderate Republicans are going to suck up to Barack Obama?"[104] To Limbaugh, moderate Republicans are not Republicans at all.

A Republican majority has never mattered to Limbaugh: "Tell us, why, again, Republicans need fifty-five senators? Why do we need fifty-five senators when we have so many malcontents and traitors in the bunch? And they all happen to be from the Northeast, and they all happen to be moderates, they all happen to be liberals."[105] Well, Rush got his wish, and the number of Republican senators dropped to a low of forty in 2009. As Limbaugh said about moderate Republicans in 2009: "If they all want to leave, let them leave."[106] He wants ideological purity, not a governing majority.

Republicans are in the middle of an identity crisis, and Limbaugh is the loudest voice in the room shouting about what they must do. But moderates are resisting his approach. Former secretary of state Colin Powell declared, "Can we continue to listen to Rush Limbaugh? Is this really the kind of party that we want to be when these kinds of spokespersons seem to appeal to our lesser instincts rather than our better instincts?"[107] Speaking to Larry King in July 2009, Powell noted, "The problem I have with the party right now is when he says things that I consider to be completely outrageous, and I respond to it, I would like to see other members of the party do likewise. But they don't." He added, "I know of several instances where sitting members in Congress or elsewhere in positions of responsibility in the party made like criticisms of Rush and within twenty-four hours they were backing away because there is a strong base of support for Mr. Limbaugh."[108]

Limbaugh tried to claim that Colin Powell had abandoned the Republican Party, denouncing Powell and proclaiming, "He voted for Clinton."[109] In reality, Powell had declared that he had voted for Republicans for president for twenty years before Obama's candidacy. Colin Powell answered, "Rush will not get his wish . . . I'm still a Republican."[110]

Limbaugh, the Anti-Intellectual

Rush Limbaugh's career has been based on his anti-intellectualism. He hates intellectuals: "For intellectuals, the last organ they're using is their brain."[111] When he first became successful, his belief in conservatism was an uneducated hunch, an ideology inherited from his family that he was too lazy and too poorly educated to challenge; Rush admitted, "If you're like me early on, I knew I was conservative, but I didn't know why. I mean I had the instincts but when it came time to explain it I was kind of lost."[112] According to Limbaugh, "I had a very fortunate thing happen to me: I was born a Limbaugh. And I learned starting at nine what liberals are, who Democrats are."[113]

He dreamed of becoming a DJ because he hated school, and the radio DJ he listened to while he was eating breakfast sounded like he was having fun. After being a failure as a music DJ and news reader, Limbaugh turned to talk radio because it brought him success. Limbaugh didn't get into his job because of his love of ideas and intellectual engagement; he got into radio precisely because he hated ideas and critical thinking.

Only once he had a highly profitable career did Limbaugh decide to fill in the gaps of his knowledge. After he became a radio star, with some guidance from William Bennett, he read a few conservative classics. But he's not a deep thinker, and he never talks about the concepts in these books. Limbaugh doesn't really discuss ideas; he discusses ideology. Bennett has called Limbaugh "very serious intellectually" and "our greatest living American."[114] But how could Limbaugh be a serious intellectual if he didn't read any important conservative books (or other serious books) until he was in his late thirties? Limbaugh is instead skilled at reducing conservatism to a sound bite and liberalism to a joke, without ever seeming to grasp the meaning of either of these ideas. Reading a few books hasn't changed Limbaugh's successful formula at all. He's still doing the same show, with an occasional right-wing book recommendation tossed in.

Limbaugh admits that he doesn't follow many of the events that he comments on: "I don't watch any of this stuff at night anymore. I can't handle it. It stopped being informative and educational a long time ago. So, as you know, I pay people to do this, to watch it so we can have the audio sound bites."[115] Limbaugh instead relies on his employees to compile a daily Stack of Stuff and audio clips that he uses for his show prep.

The Republican Party, for the first time since Barry Goldwater's 1964 nomination, is giving up on hopes of being a dominant political party and entrenching itself in ideology. Limbaugh claimed in 2008, "I know I have become the intellectual engine of the conservative movement."[116] And he's right; the problem is that it's a very small engine. Limbaugh wants to be an anti-intellectual intellectual. He aspires to be the intellectual force behind the conservative movement (evidenced by his penchant for recommending Hayek to any student), but at the same time he deeply despises intellectuals.

Limbaugh's lack of formal education has haunted him for decades. As a college dropout, he has always felt jealous of his better-educated peers, which is why he mocks the Ivy League graduates and anyone else who is well educated. However, the problem with Rush Limbaugh is not that he's uneducated but that he's stupid. There are plenty of stupid people with PhDs and plenty of smart people who never got a degree of any kind. In Limbaugh's case, he avoided an education because he resists having his views challenged; instead of learning about ideas different from what he already believed, Limbaugh preferred to live in a bubble of his own beliefs.

His show replicates that same model of learning: He seeks to encapsulate everything that his listeners might encounter, to inoculate them against dangerous liberal ideas, and to perceive everything through his own paranoid worldview.

Perhaps the most unusual part of Limbaugh's show is the absence of guests. He has said, "I didn't want guests. Every talk show in the world had guests. I couldn't get any different guests than anybody else got. I didn't care what the guests thought. I wanted people to know what I thought."[117] His hatred of guests is driven by the fact that most experts in most fields would disagree with him. Limbaugh can't bring academic experts, scientists, or authors on his program without exposing his audience to an opposing point of view, and he lacks the confidence in his own intellectual skills to defeat liberals in any one-on-one argument. By not having guests, he also establishes himself as the sole expert. Limbaugh is the only expert his listeners ever hear, and he almost never admits that he doesn't know what he's talking about. As

Limbaugh put it, "I'm the expert. I don't need to talk to somebody else to find out what's going on."[118]

Limbaugh was angry when Sam Donaldson told a forum on journalism at Michigan State University, "If you listen to Rush Limbaugh, you don't hear a lot of the other side." Amazingly, Rush claimed this was completely untrue: "I set up exactly what the other side's position is. I'm the only one who'll do it honestly. If I have a liberal guest on this program, I'm not guaranteed the liberal guest is going to be honest about what he believes."[119] Limbaugh keeps liberals off his show because he believes they're all dishonest, and that only he can be trusted to reveal the true liberal position. But Limbaugh once admitted the real reason why he avoids guests: "I don't have guests on my show because I don't care what other people think."[120]

Laziness has also played a strong role in his ruling out guests on the show. Booking guests is a time-consuming task, often requiring the help of a producer. And reading the books of guests would be a struggle for a poorly educated host like Limbaugh. Without any guests, Limbaugh can cut costs and spend less time preparing for the show. Such laziness has been a characteristic of Limbaugh since his youthful indifference to schooling. Ironically, Limbaugh never voted for his hero Ronald Reagan: He didn't register to vote until his midthirties, after he started his talk show, when a Sacramento newspaper columnist confronted him about it, he later attributed it to "pure and simple laziness."[121]

Because Limbaugh thinks he's the expert on everything, he is offended by any suggestion that he's superficial: "The media doesn't like me precisely because of my substance."[122] But Rush almost never gets any notoriety for his substance. On the rare occasions when he engages in substantive public policy analysis, no one pays much attention to him. He's just one of many conservative pundits, and less skilled at it than some of his competitors. If Limbaugh's substance was what really mattered about him, then he'd be writing columns and books, and his ideas would be studied by other conservatives. But he is the antithesis of an intellectual, and he prospers in the ephemera of radio, where his words go out on the airwaves and are quickly forgotten. No wonder he called Sarah Palin's lightweight memoir *Going Rogue* "one of the most substantive policy books I've read."[123] That statement reflects how little Limbaugh reads.

Limbaugh lives in a conservative bubble, where he never encounters criticism. As he declared, "Whenever I travel this country, and whenever I happen to make political remarks, I don't have people boo me. I don't have people run away. I don't have people say, 'You know, you need to tone this down 'cause it's really hurting.' I only hear this from so-called conservative people on television, so-called conservative people in media—and not all of them, just some. So I have become America's piñata."[124] Limbaugh lets only his fans get close to him, and he regards all of his critics on the right as "so-called conservatives" if they question his tactics.

At his 2009 Conservative Political Action Conference speech, Limbaugh opened with a lengthy, lame joke about how God "thinks he's Rush Limbaugh," and the speech became even more self-indulgent, featuring his analysis of the movie *Swing Vote* with Kevin Costner and his report about the audience's adulation for him: "People are just tired. They've been up and out of their chairs a hundred times here." Limbaugh accused Obama of having "a deranged psychology" and claimed, "Barack Obama portrays America as a soup kitchen in some dark night in a corner of America that's very obscure."[125] Of course, Obama has never portrayed America that way, in addition to the fact that America can't be a soup kitchen in a corner of itself, whatever that means. Yet Limbaugh's meandering, narcissistic, and often nonsensical speech was praised by right-wing pundits as some kind of glorious description of conservative ideas.

To Limbaugh, intelligence is a dangerous thing. He has condemned "arrogant egghead elites"[126] and denounced Obama because of the "Ivy League nerds and eggheads that populate his administration."[127] He calls his program "a graduate-level course in correct public-policy thinking,"[128] which indicates mainly how little Limbaugh knows what a graduate-level education is like. He even tries to discourage his listeners from getting an education, declaring that college is a "waste of time."[129] According to Limbaugh, college students "still arrive for the most part as individuals, and then it takes not but a split second and they get into these classes run by liberal professors and professorettes, and all the individualism is gone and they become sheep. They become little liberal marching robots."[130]

While condemning all colleges as "groupthink," Limbaugh himself embodies this idea. His show is an exercise in groupthink, where unanimity is expected and dissent denounced. Jim Derych, a former Limbaugh fanatic, described "the closed circle of the right-wing media. It's like a womb, safe and quiet, with no one disagreeing with you, and the only thing that gets in is what comes through the right-wing media's carefully monitored umbilical cord."[131]

LIMBAUGH'S IMPACT ON LISTENERS

It may be tempting to dismiss Rush Limbaugh as an innocuous crackpot, but he has a substantial effect on his listeners. In 2010 *Talkers magazine* named Limbaugh the most influential person on radio, calling him "the most-listened-to talk host and more relevant culturally than ever."[132] In their book *Echo Chamber: Rush Limbaugh and the Conservative Media Establishment*, scholars Kathleen Hall Jamieson and Joseph N. Cappella of the Annenberg School for Communication at the University of Pennsylvania noted Limbaugh's impact: "The opinion enclave in which Limbaugh listeners and Fox viewers reside protects their attitudes about Bush from assault by Kerry and increases the likelihood that Republican attacks on Kerry will be accepted."[133]

According to a 1996 study of non-Limbaugh listeners, mistrust of the government had no impact on voting and political activism. But for Limbaugh listeners, there was a strong association between lack of trust in the government and greater involvement in political activities.[134] Listening to the radio host causes people to hate their government, but it makes them even more committed to changing it. That's the remarkable power of Limbaugh: the ability to convince people to hate their government so much that they will do anything to help take it over. Limbaugh breeds cynicism but not apathy. That, more than anything else, is the magic that Limbaugh has brought to the conservative movement.

That attitude depends, however, on which party controls the White House. A survey in 2003, when George W. Bush was president, found that Limbaugh listeners were more likely to trust the government to operate in the public's "best interests."[135] So Limbaugh undermines trust in Democratic presidents, and enhances trust in Republican ones.

Limbaugh's show also helps inoculate listeners against liberal ideas that they might hear elsewhere in the media. Jamieson and Cappella noted, "Fox and Limbaugh insulate their audiences from persuasion by Democrats by offering opinion and evidence that make Democratic views seem alien and unpalatable."[136] David C. Barker, a professor of political science at the University of Pittsburgh who wrote an academic book titled *Rushed to Judgment: Talk Radio, Persuasion and American Political Behavior*,[137] surveyed Limbaugh listeners and nonlisteners and concluded: "If you take a group of people who never listened to talk radio before, and then look at their attitudes six months later, you'll see a clear change."[138]

One scholarly experiment in the 1990s asked supporters of Limbaugh about a policy issue such as increased prison spending. Those who listen to Limbaugh all or most of the time and were told that he supported the policy were twenty-two percentage points more likely to embrace it than those who were told that Limbaugh opposed it. For those who listened to Limbaugh some of the time, the difference was only six percentage points. Devoted Limbaugh listeners are easily swayed merely by what they think he believes, even without hearing a word from El Rushbo.[139]

Limbaugh sees the world as revolving around his all-encompassing vision of good (conservatism) versus evil (liberalism). "I know liberals," he has declared. "I know these cockroaches."[140] To him, liberals aren't human beings. They're the worst kind of insects who need to be exterminated. Limbaugh is completely devoted to demonizing his enemies, and he will sacrifice anything—civility, accuracy, and any sense of humanity—to accomplish his goals.

11

THE LEADER OF THE REPUBLICANS: HOW LIMBAUGH IS DESTROYING CONSERVATISM

Barack obama joked at the 2009 White House Correspondents' Association dinner, "Rush Limbaugh does not count as a troubled asset."[1] But that's exactly what he is for the Republican Party, which alternately fears his alienatation of moderates and trembles at criticizing him because of his enormous power to mobilize the conservative base.

Many conservative pundits love Limbaugh. Sean Hannity told Limbaugh, "You're the leading voice of opposition, conservative, and have defined conservatives for over two decades."[2] Some even regard Limbaugh with a godlike reverence: Steve Forbes wrote in 2008, "Rush Limbaugh will be constantly and happily showing us the way to secular salvation."[3]

In 2009 Representative Michele Bachmann (R-MN) declared on *Larry King Live*, "The American people are looking to voices like Sean Hannity, Rush Limbaugh, Mark Levin, Glenn Beck,"[4] and Karl Rove has noted: "He's a leader. If Rush engages on an issue, it gives others courage to engage."[5] *The Washington Times* in an editorial praised Limbaugh "for all he has done to inspire right-thinking people" and added, "One reason for a new conservative swagger is the work of radio talk-show host Rush Limbaugh."[6]

But all of this devotion to Limbaugh on the right conceals the damage he has done to the conservative movement.

THE WILLIAM F. BUCKLEY JR. OF TODAY'S CONSERVATIVE MOVEMENT

Limbaugh is named among the greatest conservatives in American history. In his 2008 article Steve Forbes wrote, "Rush Limbaugh is part of the trinity that made modern conservatism the most potent political and economic force in America" (with Ronald Reagan and William F. Buckley, Jr.).[7] Mark Levin noted: "Conservatism flourishes because a few pivotal individuals stepped forward and used their unique vision and gifts to champion the cause: William Buckley, Barry Goldwater, Ronald Reagan, and Rush Limbaugh."[8]

Such comparisons of Limbaugh to Reagan and Buckley are almost comical. Buckley's magazine, *National Review,* was the leading voice for conservative thought for decades. Limbaugh's "magazine," *The Limbaugh Letter,* is simply a device for profiting off his name, and it contains nothing but his musings and interviews. Buckley's talk show, *Firing Line,* featured numerous liberal guests engaged in a debate of ideas, something that is almost entirely missing from Limbaugh's show.

Although Buckley defended Southern segregationists (which he later regretted) and once called Gore Vidal a "queer" on TV and threatened to hit him in the face, he helped lead the conservative movement away from the John Birch Society crackpot wing.[9] Limbaugh, by contrast, embraces right-wing kooks and conspiracy theorists. Where Buckley enjoyed conversation and debate, Limbaugh slinks away from it. Michael Lind, executive editor of the *National Interest,* noted: "The William F. Buckleys and Irving Kristols who detoxified the right are being succeeded by a generation of Buchanans and Rush Limbaughs setting up a retox ward."[10]

Limbaugh imagines himself to be following in the footsteps of conservative intellectuals. He declared, "The genuine traditional conservatism, the Burkean conservatism, Goldwater, Buckley, that's going to have to become dominant once again."[11] But as Christopher Buckley observed, "Rush, I knew William F. Buckley, Jr.; William F. Buckley, Jr., was a father of mine. Rush, you're no William F. Buckley, Jr."[12]

LIMBAUGH'S POLITICAL POISON

Every Republican politician must respect Limbaugh's power over the conservative base. Kenneth Tomlinson, who ran the Corporation for Public Broadcasting under Bush and forced PBS to hire right-wing talk show hosts, declared that Limbaugh "represents conservative thought" and people "should not think they are on top of what is happening in America if they do not listen to Rush." According to Tomlinson, Senator Trent Lott, a Republican, said to him during the immigration debate: "Talk radio is running America. We have to deal with that problem."[13] Zev Chafets wrote, "The people who write the Republican talking points are getting their ideas, often as not, from Limbaugh. Listen to him on a daily basis and you know what Republican candidates are likely to be saying in a day or two."[14]

Limbaugh is undoubtedly influential, but among Republican politicians, his extreme right-wing views are often regarded as political poison; when challenged about them publicly, many Republicans seek to distance themselves from him. Representative Zach Wamp (R-TN) referred to Rush on CNN as an "entertainer" and said he didn't pay attention to Limbaugh.[15] Representative John Shadegg (R-AZ) said, "I think he is an entertainment personality who is an interesting factor in American politics. I agree with much of what he says on some issues, but not on other issues."[16] Representative Eric Cantor (R-VA) condemned conservatives comparing Obama with Hitler: "Do I condone the mention of Hitler in any discussion about politics? . . . No, I don't, because obviously that is something that conjures up images that frankly are not, I think, very helpful."[17] Congressman Jack Kingston (R-GA) said, "Rush Limbaugh, I don't think we want to look for solutions there, I think you gotta look for what is the best served for the most people."[18]

Asked about Limbaugh and Gingrich calling Sonia Sotomayor a racist, Senator John Cornyn (R-TX) said, "I think it's terrible. This is not the tone that any of us want to set when it comes to performing our constitutional abilities of advice and consent. Neither one of these men are elected Republican officials. I just don't think it's appropriate. I certainly don't endorse it. I think it's wrong."[19] Limbaugh was upset by this comment because he had once done a fund-raiser for Cornyn, and Cornyn's response showed how unpopular Limbaugh's approach was even among the politicians who had once embraced him.

THE FEAR OF LIMBAUGH

The Republican Party's fear of the self-proclaimed "Doctor of Democracy" is overwhelming. Back in the 1950s, it was President Dwight D. Eisenhower and other moderate Republicans who stood up to the demagogue Senator Joseph McCarthy and helped to end the worst repression of the anticommunist crusades in America. But today's Republican politicians all quake in fear of Limbaugh. Morton Kondracke noted about protests at 2009 town hall meetings, "I think that the leadership is afraid of Rush Limbaugh, frankly, because Rush Limbaugh is encouraging all this stuff."[20]

Such is Limbaugh's power that Republican politicians fear criticizing him. In 2009 a parade of Republican officials issued some mild critique of Limbaugh, only to quickly backtrack and apologize for daring to offend the Maha Rushie. As Obama's campaign manager, David Plouffe, noted in 2009, "But instead of rebuking the radio personality or charting their own course, Republican leaders in Washington are paralyzed with fear of crossing their leader."[21]

New York Republican congressional candidate Jim Tedisco said in 2009, "Rush Limbaugh is meaningless to me. The only constituency I'm worried about are the residents of the 20th Congressional District."[22] Then Tedisco's spokesperson issued a press release: "Jim's comments were in response to a question about what voters are asking him about on the campaign trail. So far, the concerns he has been hearing from voters on the campaign trail have been local in nature, such as his support for lower property taxes, fiscal responsibility, and his opponent's appalling support for the AIG bonus loophole. That was his point and any effort to characterize it otherwise is a distortion of the facts."[23]

Representative Phil Gingrey (R-GA) said that "it's easy if you're Sean Hannity or Rush Limbaugh or even sometimes Newt Gingrich to stand back and throw bricks. You don't have to try to do what's best for your people and your party."[24] Then the backtracking began: Gingrey called Limbaugh one of the "conservative giants [who] are the voices of the conservative movement's conscience." Gingrey also called Limbaugh's radio show and stated his "very sincere regret for those comments . . . I clearly ended up putting my foot in my mouth on some of those comments. . . . I regret those stupid comments."[25]

After Representative Todd Tiahrt (R-KS) described Rush Limbaugh as "just an entertainer," his spokesperson declared, "Nothing the congressman said diminished the role Rush has played and continues to play in the conservative movement."[26]

Governor Mark Sanford (R-SC), before he became a national punch line, said: "Anybody who wants [Obama] to fail is an idiot, because it means we're all in trouble."[27] Fearful of offending Limbaugh, Sanford's communications director said that "the governor was not referring to anyone" in particular, even though Rush Limbaugh was the only prominent figure saying that he wanted Obama to fail.[28]

In a 2009 interview on CNN with D. L. Hughley, Republican National Committee head Michael Steele argued that he, not Limbaugh, was "the de facto leader of the Republican Party" and proceeded to dismiss Rush's importance. Steele said about the "fail" comment, "Rush Limbaugh is an entertainer. Rush Limbaugh, the whole thing is entertainment. Yes, it's incendiary, yes, it's ugly."[29]

Limbaugh retaliated with an angry tirade against Steele: "I'm not in charge of the Republican Party, and I don't want to be. I would be embarrassed to say that I'm in charge of the Republican Party in the sad-sack state that it's in. . . . If I were chairman of the Republican Party, given the state that it's in, I would quit. I might get out the hari-kari knife because I would have presided over a failure." Limbaugh directed his next comment to Steele: "Why do you claim that you are leading the Republican Party when you are obsessed with seeing to it the President Obama succeeds?"[30]

Steele was quick to back down: "My intent was not to go after Rush—I have enormous respect for Rush Limbaugh. I was maybe a little bit inarticulate. . . . There was no attempt on my part to diminish his voice or his leadership."[31] Actually, Steele's problem was that he was *too* articulate on this point. Steele tried to blame a communications failure between his brain and his mouth: "I went back at that tape and I realized words that I said weren't what I was thinking. . . . It was one of those things where I thinking I was saying one thing, and it came out differently. What I was trying to say was a lot of people . . . want to make Rush the scapegoat, the bogeyman, and he's not."[32] It's not plausible to believe that Steele wanted to defend Limbaugh against attacks and accidentally called him "incendiary" and "ugly." Instead, Steele recognized that his political career was in jeopardy because of his remarks. Steele was already controversial among the far right, and if he dared to insult the leading conservative figure in the country, he might quickly find himself forced out of his job. So Steele called Limbaugh "a very valuable conservative voice for our party."[33]

Democrats quickly jumped at the opportunity provided by Limbaugh's divisive influence. Democratic National Committee Chairman Tim Kaine declared, "I was briefly encouraged by the courageous comments made my counterpart in the Republican Party over the weekend challenging Rush Limbaugh as the leader of the Republican Party and referring to his show as 'incendiary' and 'ugly.' However, Chairman Steele's reversal this evening and his apology to Limbaugh proves the unfortunate point that Limbaugh is the leading force behind the Republican Party, its politics and its obstruction of President Obama's agenda in Washington."[34]

White House chief of staff Rahm Emanuel said about Limbaugh, "Whenever a Republican criticizes him, they have to run back and apologize to him and say they were misunderstood."[35] The Democratic Congressional Campaign Committee even created a Web site called "I'm Sorry Rush" to document all of the Republican politicians apologizing to their leader for daring to question his authority and importance. In 2009 Kevin Stevenson was forced out as the spokesman of the Republican Party of Marathon County in Wisconsin after he wrote a column declaring that "Rush Limbaugh is hurting us more than helping us."[36] Stevenson observed in a statement after being pushed out, "Purging people who have differences from its ranks will ensure that it remains a minority party well into the future."[37] One anonymous GOP strategist, fearful of retaliation, said: "I don't need [Limbaugh] crawling up my ass any more than the president does."[38]

Because of the backlash Limbaugh can cause, Republican leaders are quick to praise him. Mitt Romney called him "a very powerful voice among conservatives. And I listen to him."[39] Rudy Giuliani said that "to the extent that Rush Limbaugh energizes the base of the Republican Party, he's a very valuable and important voice."[40]

But it's not just fear that leads many Republicans to avoid criticizing

Limbaugh. They also recognize that he can be useful to them in attacking liberals in ways that politicians can't. Charlie Cook, publisher of *The Cook Political Report,* noted, "Limbaugh can say outrageous things that [John] Boehner and [Mitch] McConnell can't or maybe wouldn't want to say but which will energize and motivate Republicans and conservatives. Plus, with him as the mouthpiece, the GOP doesn't pay a price or have to apologize. If they have to say anything, they should say, 'Rush is just being Rush.' "[41] Limbaugh is too powerful and too useful for Republicans to criticize him.

LIMBAUGH'S CONTROL OVER THE REPUBLICAN PARTY

Republicans also understand the power of Limbaugh in activating the conservative base of the party. Limbaugh's reluctant embrace of George Herbert Walker Bush in 1992 against Bill Clinton and Ross Perot came only after Limbaugh had, in his drive for ideological purity, supported the candidacy of Pat Buchanan in the Republican primary. With the radio host bashing the Republican president, Buchanan won a surprisingly strong second in New Hampshire. Buchanan's candidacy was doomed from the start, but it did weaken Bush. In 1992 Limbaugh wrote that Pat Buchanan accomplished "great things": "He moved the President demonstrably to the right."[42] Buchanan also alienated moderates at the Republican National Convention by proclaiming "a religious war going on in our country for the soul of America."[43] Limbaugh wrote, "I will always view Pat Buchanan as one of my mentors."[44] Rush would never take credit for it, but he helped make Bill Clinton president of the United States by pushing Bush to the right, where he won only 38 percent of the vote.

By the summer of 1992, Republicans had realized Limbaugh's importance. One Republican leader even urged Press Secretary Marlin Fitzwater to compile a tape of Rush speaking so that George H. W. Bush could imitate the talk show host.[45] Stroking the ego of the country's loudest conservative was critical to any get-out-the-vote effort.

On June 3 Limbaugh was the guest of the president at the Kennedy Center and spent the night at the White House in the Lincoln Bedroom, with the president carrying Limbaugh's bag up to the room.[46] As a result, Limbaugh biographer Paul Colford noticed, "Everything suddenly turned warm and rosy between the president and the commentator. A mutual admiration society took shape and its two members went out of their way to praise each other."[47] A few days after the meeting, Limbaugh appeared on the *Today* show to praise Bush as a "genuinely nice guy" while Katie Couric asked him the typical biased questions of the liberal media, like "Dinner at the White House? . . . That must have been very cool."[48]

Rush soon repaid the favor. On July 8, 1992, Dan Quayle was the guest on his show, where Limbaugh offered up his softball questions and defended him against the "malicious" attacks by liberals.[49] During the 1992 Republican National Convention, Limbaugh noted, "I'm in the Vice President's Box tonight." As one of his assistants put it, "The vice president kissing ass followed by the president tomorrow."[50]

On September 21, 1992, President Bush visited Limbaugh's show, calling himself "just one more fan sitting at the table." He helped Bush by raising the issue of Clinton's draft record, although Limbaugh's own avoidance of military service was never mentioned.[51] Limbaugh said about Clinton: "Never trust a draft dodger."[52] But Limbaugh himself was a draft dodger who avoided the war in Vietnam. He explained to *Playboy,* "I did have a student deferment because I was in college for that one year. And I had a medical deferment for what is called a pilonidal cyst. It's a tailbone cyst. I don't know if it's still something that disqualifies you, but it did then. If the thing flared up, which they are wont to do, it required major surgery. So I didn't do anything to avoid the war."[53] But as reporter David Remnick noted, "Limbaugh got out of the draft by taking the initiative of visiting his doctor, finding out he had a polonoidal cyst (which had never given him much trouble) and winning a 1-Y classification."[54]

Both Quayle and Bush returned to Limbaugh's show a second time to promote their reelection campaign on his friendly airwaves. Limbaugh wrote an opinion piece in *The New York Times* denouncing Clinton, and attacked Perot constantly when he returned to the race. Rush admitted to Charlie Rose, "This is like the Super Bowl. Nobody's favorite team is playing, so you root for somebody to lose." And on the crucial day before the election, Limbaugh was campaigning at Bush's side at a rally in New Jersey, and Bush spoke later in the day on Rush's show from Air Force One.[55] With the close embrace of Limbaugh, Bush received a smaller percentage of votes than any Republican since Alf Landon lost to FDR in 1936.

Limbaugh was obsessed with having power in the corridors of the White House. In January 1993 he arranged to have a note left for producers Harry Thomason and Linda Bloodworth-Thomason in the Lincoln Bedroom after Clinton was inaugurated: "I was here first, and I will be back."[56] Limbaugh's connections to the Republican elite grew closer with the Republicans out of power; in 1994 Justice Clarence Thomas even performed the ceremony at Limbaugh's third wedding—in Thomas's home.[57]

The Leader of the Republican Party

A March 2009 survey by the Pew Research Center for the People & the Press found that few people could name any person as the leader of the Republican Party. But Rush Limbaugh ranked second, at 5 percent, behind only former presidential candidate John McCain.[58] As Howard Fineman put it, "Why limit it to the Republican Party? You know, he thinks he's a leader of a movement. He thinks he's a leader of the planet."[59]

One poll found that far more Democrats (44 percent) than Republicans (11 percent) think that Limbaugh is the leader of the Republican Party.[60] The Democrats aren't wrong: By any objective analysis of the evidence, with the power Limbaugh wields and the fearful Republican officials who refuse to criticize him, Limbaugh is the leader of the Republican Party. It is equally clear that a strong majority of Republicans don't want him to be their leader. But Limbaugh's power within the Republican Party far exceeds his popularity. He holds the ultimate threat over Republican officials: a microphone he can use for three hours a day as he pleases against any dissenters, and a devoted core of millions of listeners who will help him take revenge against anyone who attacks him.

Excited over his power, in 2009 Limbaugh claimed that members of Congress were calling him to apologize for ever doubting his claim that Democrats are evil: "I'm hearing from more Republicans than ever the last two weeks wanting to keep me in the loop about what they're doing."[61] His influence on the right was also evident when James Dale Guckert, a former gay prostitute and columnist for the right-wing Web site Talon News who called himself "Jeff Gannon," was credentialed as a White House reporter and chosen to ask a question of George W. Bush during a major press conference.[62]

"Gannon" asked Bush, "Senate Democratic leaders have painted a very bleak picture of the U.S. economy. Harry Reid was talking about soup lines . . . how are you going to work with people who seem to have divorced themselves from reality?"[63] The line about Harry Reid was actually made up by Limbaugh himself. As Eric Boehlert noted on Salon, "That afternoon conservative talk show host Rush Limbaugh crowed that Gannon's question was 'a repeat, a rehash, of a precise point I made on this program yesterday.' However, Rush conceded that Reid had 'never actually said "soup lines."' That was simply Limbaugh's exaggerated characterization of Reid's concerns. Gannon either heard that phrase on Limbaugh's show or read it in Limbaugh's online column and then inserted it into his loaded question to Bush."[64] "Gannon" didn't just get his question from Limbaugh; he imitated Limbaugh's entire approach to "journalism," offering up softball questions to every Republican in sight while spreading lies about Democrats.

FAWNING OVER REPUBLICAN GUESTS

Limbaugh is legendary for his easy treatment of favored Republicans during interviews. Colonel Lawrence Wilkerson, the former chief of staff for Colin Powell, described Dick Cheney as "a vice president who speaks only to Rush Limbaugh and assembled military forces."[65] Cheney was a frequent guest on Limbaugh's program, even while Cheney refused to talk to most of the mainstream media. Cheney told Limbaugh at the end of an agreeable interview in 2002, "Great to talk to you, as always. Love your show. . . . You do great work."[66] Limbaugh answered Cheney: "It's always an opportunity and a thrill for someone like me to be able to talk to somebody like you."[67] Cheney told him again in 2008, "Love your show. It's a pleasure to talk to you again,"[68] and said in 2009: "Rush is a good friend, I love him."[69]

Less than a month before the 1996 election, presidential candidate Bob Dole came on the show, complete with the usual fawning from Limbaugh, who introduced him as "Senator Bob Dole, fresh off another stunning performance in last night's debate."[70]

While Rush sometimes challenges the Republican Party leadership when he feels it is compromising too much or straying too far from his core conservative audience, more often Limbaugh is devoted to protecting Republicans from attack. He is the rodeo clown of the conservative movement, distracting attention away from the Republican leaders who have fallen down on the job.

Mainstream Republican politicians come to his show when they're in trouble. In 2006 Representative Dennis Hastert, trying to save his job as Speaker of the House, called in to a sympathetic Limbaugh, who predictably blamed the Democrats for the scandal.[71]

Limbaugh rarely has any guests on his show, but when he does, they consist almost exclusively of those in the Republican establishment whom he is trying to help. In 2006 Secretary of Defense Donald Rumsfeld called in, and Rush was full of praise, even calling him a "sex symbol."[72] Limbaugh added, "You are in our estimation doing a terrific job" and "We're honored that you're serving as Secretary of Defense."[73] Rumsfeld told Limbaugh, "Thank you so much. I appreciate it a great deal," and Limbaugh replied, "Well, thank you, sir. I appreciate it. That's Secretary—it embarrasses me when I get thanked."[74]

Sometimes Limbaugh is so obsequious to his Republican guests, it's downright embarrassing. He told Karl Rove that he'd received "a bunch of e-mails" from listeners who wanted Rove to know that they love him. Limbaugh added, "We all do."[75]

Limbaugh's questions to his Republican guests are invariably fawning softballs lobbed easily in front of a sympathetic audience. In his entire career, he has never elicited an answer from these top Republican officials that was in the slightest degree newsworthy. His goal is the same as the Republican politicians: to assuage his conservative listeners who might be upset with the Republican Party. When Sarah Palin came on his show, Rush told her, "I tell you, I'm in a quandary here this morning. I admire you so much. I really don't even know what to ask."[76] Limbaugh eventually managed to come up with one of his easy questions, but his desire to turn his show into an outlet for serving the Republican Party is clear.

THE BUSH FRIENDSHIP

George W. Bush called Rush his "good friend" during a 2004 appearance on Limbaugh's show in the middle of the Republican National Convention.[77] After the 2004 elections, Limbaugh reported attending a holiday party at the White House: "Got a big hug from the president when I went through the line last night. It was just really cool."[78] In 2008 Limbaugh claimed to have inside information that Bush would attack Iran before leaving office: "I had talked to a bunch of his donors [who] said to me that they can't see Bush leaving office with Iran still a problem, a nuclear problem."[79] Rush was wrong, but the more important issue is that he was hanging out with Bush's financial donors.

Rush bragged about his intimate relationship with the president: "George Bush—I happen to know this personally—talked to the generals on the ground in Iraq weekly, sometimes daily."[80] Limbaugh said in 2009, "I love George W. Bush. He's a personal friend."[81] Rush was so influential that on August 1, 2008, President George W. Bush, along with George H. W. Bush and Jeb Bush, called in to mark the radio host's twentieth anniversary in national syndication.[82]

The election of Obama changed everything. In 2009 Limbaugh complained about his loss of access to power: "On Tuesday, before Obama is inaugurated, I'm invited to the White House for a birthday lunch by the president, and I'm toasted. Twelve weeks later, I am public enemy number one."[83] Limbaugh used the opportunity to brag about his connections to George W. Bush: "He brought out a chocolate birthday cake, a microphone, and stood beside me with Ed Gillespie and sang happy birthday. Photographers taking pictures."[84] When the president of the United States brings you a cake and personally sings "Happy Birthday" to you, it proves how powerful—and obedient—you are.

LIMBAUGH'S REPUBLICANS

Far from being a rebel, Limbaugh has deep ties to the most powerful people in the Republican establishment. In 1992 he described the House Republican Conference as "my soul buddies."[85] On June 18, 2004, Limbaugh announced on his show: "I talked to Senator Ted Stevens, folks, after the program yesterday. . . . He sent me a fax today with a revised amendment. They've gone in and they fixed the amendment. They—they've watered this thing down. Whatever the Harkin amendment was, it now doesn't mention my name. . . . Stevens did something yesterday to revise this and he sent me the—well, the—the—the—the new amendment and he said, 'Is this OK?' He said, 'Do you have any objections to this?' "[86]

Limbaugh was wrong: The Harkin amendment had never mentioned Rush. Senator Tom Harkin specifically stated, "I am not calling for American Forces Radio to pull Rush Limbaugh's commentaries from their talk radio service."[87] The example illustrates both Limbaugh's propensity for mistakes and his enormous power over Republicans in Congress. When a powerful Republican senator such as Ted Stevens asks Limbaugh for permission to sponsor legislation, it reveals that Limbaugh is just another branch of the Republican Party.

This incident shows not only Limbaugh's paranoid persecution complex, but also the enormous influence Limbaugh has with some of the most questionable politicians in the country. Alaska senator Ted Stevens, killed in a plane crash in August 2010, represented Republican sleaze and government waste more than any politician in Washington. Stevens was the king of pork, legendary for the Bridge to Nowhere, but he never faced any criticism from Limbaugh, even though Stevens stood for the budget-busting government spending that Limbaugh pretends to oppose. He even attacked the Bush Justice Department as "polluted with career liberals" because they dared to investigate Stevens.[88]

When Stevens's scandals finally caught up to him, Limbaugh was quick to defend him, complaining about Republicans, "We want to be first the throw our own people overboard."[89] Of course, he promptly attacked Stevens when it served his purposes in the 2008 campaign, declaring (falsely) about Sarah Palin, "She fought Ted Stevens,"[90] though Palin actually served as a director of the "Ted Stevens Excellence in Public Service, Inc." fundraising group on his behalf.[91] In 2009, when Stevens's conviction was thrown out by a judge, Limbaugh was back to praising him.[92]

To Limbaugh, all Democrats are corrupt and all Republicans (so long as they support his views) are perfect. He invents crimes for Democrats that never happened, while he defends and ignores the corruption of conservative Republicans. Rush is a party hack for the Republicans, and always has been. As Stephen Talbot noted, "Limbaugh is the national precinct captain for the Republican Party,"[93] and Limbaugh is very effective in that role. In 1996 those who listened to Limbaugh every day were 7.78 times as likely to vote for Dole over Clinton.[94]

At times, Limbaugh has openly admitted that he's been a stooge for the Republican Party. After the Republican losses in the 2006 elections, he proclaimed, "I feel liberated, and I'm going to tell you as plainly as I can why. I no longer am going to have to carry the water for people who I don't think deserve having their water carried."[95] His confession that he had been dishonest with his listeners about his true feelings was unusual. Limbaugh had been dutifully serving the Republican Party by defending its leaders and almost all of its policies, even though he didn't like many of them. This is why Limbaugh prefers to have a Democrat to attack as president: Instead of being stuck with Republican policies to defend relentlessly, he can choose his mode of attack against the Democrats.

RUSH AND NEWT

Even Newt Gingrich, who once represented the far-right fringe of the Republican Party and was ousted from his leadership role due to his deep unpopularity with mainstream America, now worries about the shift to the extreme right led by Limbaugh. After the right-wing *Weekly Standard* magazine featured Limbaugh, Glenn Beck, and Sarah Palin on its cover in 2009, Gingrich expressed concern about the trend of talk show hosts controlling the Republican Party: "You know, you can have a very, very intense movement of 20 percent. You can't govern."[96]

Gingrich recognizes that Limbaugh represents the far right of the Republican Party but alienates the remaining 80 percent of voters. When a hardcore conservative such as Newt Gingrich has become the voice of moderation and reason, it shows how far to the right Limbaugh has driven the GOP. What Gingrich understands is that Limbaugh and his friends will destroy the Republican Party as a mass movement that aims at majority status. But even though party elders such as Gingrich see the danger of Republicans becoming a permanent minority movement, they seem powerless to stop Rush and other far-right ideological conservatives.

When Gingrich criticized him, Limbaugh accused him of betrayal: "They will sell you out; they will throw you overboard to save themselves, faster than anything." Limbaugh added, "Next week Newt could come out and profess his total admiration and love for me if it would serve his purposes."[97]

But it's Limbaugh who admires Republicans only so long as they admire him. He declared that Gingrich was jealous of his success: "I am at the top of the mountain of what I do. Everybody underneath it wants what I've got. That's great. That's human nature. As such, they'll do what they can to take me down or to criticize me or what have you. It is beneath my dignity to be critical of those beneath me. . . . I know that Newt would give his whatever to have what I've got."[98]

The irony of this internecine battle for the soul of the Republican Party is that Gingrich once represented the political flipside of Limbaugh's radio revolution. Gingrich and his Republican Revolution of 1994 would have been impossible without Limbaugh, and they acknowledged his importance. In 1994, the day before the November elections, Rush called upon his listeners to "be ready at dawn tomorrow" to "gain Republican control of Congress."[99] A Republican leader in the House, Vin Weber, declared: "Rush Limbaugh is as responsible for what happened as any individual in America."[100]

The Republicans who won in 1994 were quick to praise Limbaugh. Representative Barbara Cubin declared, "Talk radio with you in the lead is what turned the tide, Rush. You were the voice everyone else could follow."[101] Representative Jon Christensen had campaign workers distribute pamphlets with RUSH WAS RIGHT stickers and noted, "He was a majority maker as much as any of the candidates or the campaign workers. He fueled the debate. He was a national sounding board for conservatives."[102] House Republicans named Limbaugh an honorary member. He bragged, "They thought I won about thirty elections."[103] In 1994 Limbaugh also mobilized his listeners to stop ethics reform in a bill that would limit gifts from lobbyists to members of Congress. A Gingrich spokesperson noted, "It wouldn't have happened without Rush Limbaugh."[104]

Limbaugh reached his apex of power along with the Republicans in the Congress he helped to get elected. Mary Matalin reported, "Senators and congressman all across the board on the Republican side call him all morning long before he goes on."[105] Gingrich faxed Rush his briefings for Republican leaders and noted, "Every day he educates about six million people around the country who then become centers of communication."[106]

Ultimately, Limbaugh played a role in Gingrich's undoing, and the decline of the Republican Party. By pushing Gingrich to the right, Rush egged him on toward some of his worst mistakes, such as shutting down the government. And Gingrich's biggest tactical error, the impeachment of Bill Clinton, was directly tied to Limbaugh's constant demands on the right for Republicans to take action.

Perhaps more than any other private individual, Limbaugh can claim credit for getting Clinton impeached. He not only helped to elect the Republican majority in the House of Representatives who made that vote possible, but he also aggressively pushed the story on a daily basis on his radio show, ensuring that his supporters would not ignore it, even after it became clear that a majority of Americans opposed impeachment. The result was a disaster for Republicans. They lost five seats in the 1998 elections after expecting a massive political gain; it was the worst performance in sixty-four years for the party out of power during an off-year election. The Gingrich/ Limbaugh crusade for impeachment was a total failure, and Gingrich gave up his position as Speaker of the House and resigned his seat.

Limbaugh, however, was immune from any political consequences for his mistakes because his audience formed the core base of the conservatives. To them, Limbaugh's crusade for impeachment was a great undertaking, no matter how much it alienated the majority of Americans.

HATING MCCAIN

The Republican most hated by Limbaugh is John McCain. Limbaugh played a critical role in helping George W. Bush defeat John McCain in the 2000 Republican primary. William Kristol noted that in 1999, "I think he helped rally conservatives behind Bush. He helped make it the orthodox conservative position that McCain was utterly unacceptable and also that Bush was fine, neither of which were intuitively obvious if you're a conservative."[107] Everyday Limbaugh listeners were 3.35 times more likely to support Bush over McCain in 2000 compared to Republicans who never listened to Limbaugh.[108]

Once again, Limbaugh's political judgment almost proved disastrous for the Republicans. John McCain probably would have won an easy victory if he had been the presidential nominee, by combining a reputation for integrity with a few moderate stands. Instead, Rush backed the hard-core conservative candidate with few qualifications other than his name, Bush. Al Gore won the popular vote over Bush, and an analysis showed he would have won the election in Florida if a complete recount had been permitted in accordance with legal rules.[109] Only the Republican-dominated Supreme Court saved Bush—and Limbaugh—from going down in defeat.

This hatred of McCain continued during the 2008 election. Limbaugh mocked McCain as "Saint John of Arizona" and denounced him explicitly: "Stabbed his own party in the back I can't tell you how many times."[110] How did McCain stab his party in the back? By supporting certain policies on immigration and campaign finance deemed too liberal by Limbaugh. But immigration is an example where McCain joined with his party, and President Bush, to push for reform. It was Limbaugh who stabbed the party leaders in the back by opposing it.

Limbaugh's hatred of McCain is fully reciprocated. McCain has called Limbaugh a "circus clown" and then extended "my apologies to Bozo, Chuckles, and Krusty" for comparing them to Limbaugh.[111] When McCain's ninety-seven-year-old mother, Roberta McCain, appeared on *The Tonight Show* in 2009, she denounced Limbaugh: "I belong to the Republican Party. What he represents of the Republican Party has nothing to do with my side of it. I don't know what the man means, I don't know what he's talking about." She added, "I think [Steele] was exactly right when he defined this man as an entertainer. To my horror, the Republican Party made him back up on it."[112]

On the eve of the 2008 Iowa primaries, Limbaugh declared about McCain, "The idea that he's a great conservative in this race is an affront to conservatives."[113] But Limbaugh didn't lead a crusade against McCain, nor did he embrace a conservative alternative. He made a strategic error in underestimating McCain's appeal despite his fading campaign. After McCain won the New Hampshire primary, Limbaugh went into overdrive to condemn him, and he had a substantial impact on his listeners' view of him. Among Limbaugh listeners polled before the New Hampshire primary, 50.7 percent thought that McCain was a conservative; among Limbaugh listeners polled in the month after the primary, only 38.9 percent called McCain a conservative. By contrast, people who didn't listen to Limbaugh consistently regarded McCain as conservative (59 percent) before and after the New Hampshire primary.[114]

A 2008 study by the Annenberg Public Policy Center determined, "Controlling for gender, race, education, party identification and ideology, Limbaugh listeners were 3.94 times more likely than non-listeners to know that *The New York Times* endorsed Sen. McCain and 3.75 times more likely than non-listeners to know that Sen. McCain had opposed some of President Bush's tax cuts."[115]

But Limbaugh had acted too late. With the victory in New Hampshire and the winner-take-all Republican primaries, McCain quickly secured the nomination in 2008. When that happened, Limbaugh threatened to oppose him, saying, "There's far more apathy or anger out there than the Republican establishment knows" and "One question I asked myself, if down the road you think that the election of Obama, Hillary, or McCain is going to result in very bad things happening to the country, who would you rather get the blame for it?"[116] Limbaugh said, "I also, I can see possibly not supporting a Republican nominee. And I never thought that I would say that in my life."[117]

Limbaugh toyed with the idea of refusing to support McCain but ultimately realized that he hated Obama—and perhaps feared the repercussions if he was blamed for a Republican loss—too much to continue his crusade against McCain. Instead, Limbaugh warned McCain, "If he picks a pro-choice running mate, it's not going to be pretty."[118]

McCain did his best to bow down before Limbaugh, and even told reporters: "I respect Rush Limbaugh. He is a voice that is respected by a lot of people who are in our party."[119] McCain's pick of Sarah Palin as his vice-presidential candidate was ultimately done in order to satisfy Limbaugh and the far right. Reports indicated that McCain would have preferred Joe Lieberman or another running mate, but he recognized that he could not withstand the opposition of Limbaugh and other talk show hosts.[120]

Palin ultimately hurt McCain's campaign, according to polls conducted shortly before the election.[121] But Limbaugh blamed the 2008 loss on McCain, saying in June 2009, "The Republican Party is changing and the reason the Republican Party lost is due to McCain, is due to Powell, and due to the moderates that are running it."[122] He touched on this again a month later: "There's no reason we should be losing elections. The only reason we are is because the Republican Party is dominated by people who think like McCain and Colin Powell. But this is a conservative country."[123] In the eyes of Limbaugh, the country is far to the right of moderate conservatives, despite the election results. But in trying to move the Republican Party to the right of McCain, Limbaugh assured it a permanent minority status. As Mc-Cain proved, even within the Republican Party there is strong opposition to Limbaugh's far-right-wing rhetoric and ideas.

LIMBAUGH'S PARTISAN REASONING

Partisanship is the foundation of Limbaugh's show. He declared in 2009 that in the battle of left and right, "the only thing that matters is beating them."[124] Limbaugh was willing to invent any fact necessary to prop up Republicans. Trying to defend George W. Bush's 34 percent approval rating in February 2006, he claimed it was a "bugged poll" that couldn't be true: "This is not representative of the—of the population of the country in any way, shape, manner, or form. Nor is the fact that Bush has 34 percent. . . . You just know that's not possible. It simply isn't possible."[125] There was nothing inaccurate about the poll. Only a few months later, when poll after poll showed low support for Bush, Limbaugh touted the "modest improvement" in his poll numbers up to 36 percent, and declared, "If you went back and looked at several other second-term presidents at this time in their terms, you'd find almost parallel poll results. We know that Bill Clinton was down in the 20s at one point."[126] Clinton's approval ratings never dropped below 50 percent in his second term.[127] To Limbaugh, polls that show people disagreeing with his doctrinaire conservative views are somehow "fixed," while those that agree with him (an increasingly rare commodity) are touted as the truth.

While he denounces every poll showing support for Obama as manipulated by the government, Limbaugh embraces every negative poll as a sign of America's unique hatred for Obama: "Just 25 percent of voters now say the country is headed in the right direction. I don't ever remember it being 25 percent at any time in my illustrious life."[128] Limbaugh has a short memory. While the "right track" ratings have been low under the Obama administration, due to the Bush recession and the conservative resistance to Obama's reform efforts, they can't compare to the low ratings under George W. Bush. The "right direction" rating was under 25 percent for the last eighteen months of the Bush era, from April 2007 to November 2008 (when it hit 11 percent), according to the NBC News/*Wall Street Journal* poll.[129]

In Limbaugh's partisan world, inconvenient facts are quickly tossed down the memory hole. He falsely claimed that "not one Republican voted for the TARP bailout."[130] In reality, thirty-four Republicans in the Senate (an overwhelming majority) voted for the TARP legislation in 2008, and ninety-one House Republicans voted for it, while George W. Bush was the one who proposed it and signed it into law.[131]

Partisan hypocrisy is common on Limbaugh's show. In 2004, when false rumors hit the Internet about John Kerry having an affair, Limbaugh was their biggest promoter in the mass media. On February 12, 2004, Limbaugh discussed the rumors and declared, "This is sort of like the Lewinsky situation. . . . If Kerry denies this, that's not going to be good enough."[132] On February 16, 2004, Limbaugh said about Kerry: "I mean his horndog reputation is apparently well known inside the Beltway. But it's not a big deal to people there. And I warned you people last week when this all hit that it wasn't going to be in the press and that they're going to do everything they could not to make anything of it."[133] *Wall Street Journal* national political editor John Harwood noted, "This is one issue on which Rush Limbaugh is a big, fat idiot. He's exactly wrong on that. . . . what could the press look into? There's nothing—there's nothing to look into. Nobody has alleged anything."[134]

Yet Limbaugh continued to push the false rumors for months, doing his Clinton imitation to advise Kerry, "John, whatever you do, keep that babe in Africa. Don't let her come back here. I've been there, too, and this is not a good thing. What was her name? Alex? Yeah."[135]

Limbaugh's position was very different four years later when rumors about John McCain having an affair with a lobbyist hit *The New York Times.* The McCain rumors were far more substantial than Kerry's: McCain's former campaign manager revealed that he and other aides were concerned that McCain might be having an affair, a fact that in itself was newsworthy since it showed how close McCain was to the lobbyist. But this time, Limbaugh denounced the slightest hint of an affair, even though *The New York Times* didn't even allege there was one: "There's no substance to it; there's no proof; there's no pictures," and he added, "There is evidence every day of how Republicans get treated and conservatives get treated in *The New York Times* or elsewhere in the drive-by media, and yet people are shocked, and people are stunned."[136]

With the election of a Democrat, Limbaugh went back to his earlier stand in favor of sexual innuendo. When Barack Obama went to watch his daughter play soccer in 2010, Limbaugh immediately hinted at a "Clinton-esque" conspiracy to conceal a sexual affair: "Nobody knows where he really went. . . . What was he doing out there? What was he doing? And, of course, the media, this breaks with decades of tradition, but they are not offended by this as they would be. I don't know if Michelle knows where he went. Nobody knows. He went to a soccer game that wasn't played."[137] As ABC News reporter Jake Tapper tweeted, "Don't know genesis of latest insane conspiracy theory, but yes: many ppl saw POTUS at daughter's soccer game at ft reno park soccer field."[138] Limbaugh never corrected his error, and never apologized for suggesting that Obama was cheating on his wife.

The Kerry, Obama, and McCain "affairs" showed Limbaugh's double standard when it comes to politics. A nonexistent Democratic affair was worthy of spreading false rumors. A nonexistent Republican affair was denounced as liberal media bias.

Limbaugh's Partisanship at War

Limbaugh, who had refused to criticize George W. Bush during all the years of mismanaging the war in Afghanistan, suddenly became very interested in the conflict after a leaked report came forth that military leaders might ask Obama to expand the military commitment in Afghanistan. After just a few weeks, as the Obama administration deliberated about its policy in Afghanistan, Limbaugh complained that "all this dithering goes on" about sending additional troops to Afghanistan beyond the increase Obama made: "These incompetent boobs and these competent fascists are destroying the United States of America."[139] It's a strange double standard: For seven years, the Bush administration kept a minimal force in Afghanistan, failed to find Osama bin Laden, and then was distracted by a war in Iraq, all without a peep of critique from the radio host. Now that a Democratic president is in office and has finally made Afghanistan a top priority, Limbaugh complains about waiting a few weeks to approve a massive increase in forces. How can he denounce Obama's actions as inadequate when the president has done far more in one year than George W. Bush ever committed to the war in Af-

ghanistan? Limbaugh quickly forgets the political past, consigning his relentless defense of George W. Bush's incompetence at fighting a war to the
dustbin of history.

It's not just the hypocrisy but the vehemence of it that's so startling. Limbaugh doesn't really have a foreign policy. His foreign policy is strictly defined by opposing Democratic presidents and supporting Republican ones.

LIMBAUGH LOSING IN THE POLLS

According to a Gallup Poll, from 2001 to 2009 the Republican Party faced
dramatic declines in party identification by Americans. Among those who
considered themselves conservative, the Republican Party membership
stayed about the same, dropping from 66 percent to 65 percent. But among
moderates, Republicans dropped by a quarter, from 37 to 28 percent, and
among liberals, GOP identification was cut in half, from 17 to 9 percent.[140]
Limbaugh's Republican Party has become more ideologically pure, following his demands, but in doing so it may have established for itself a permanent minority status in America.

A March 2009 CBS poll put Limbaugh's favorable rating at 19 percent.[141] A May 2009 CNN poll found that Limbaugh was less popular than
even Dick Cheney, with a favorable rating of 30 percent and an unfavorable
rating of 53 percent. By contrast, Colin Powell had a 70 percent favorable
rating. Even among Republicans, Powell was more popular (64 percent)
than Limbaugh (62 percent).[142] Limbaugh explained away the poll by claiming, "I have been evil incarnate for a long time."[143] To the contrary, he has
received positive coverage from most conservatives and Republicans. A person would look in vain for any negative or even balanced coverage of Limbaugh on Fox News, where he often makes appearances if he's assured of a
warm welcome. The fact that polls show overwhelming hatred of Limbaugh
indicates how his views represent only a small minority of Americans.

Even in Arkansas, where McCain beat Obama by twenty percentage
points in 2008 and less than half of the people believe Obama was born in
the United States, only 35 percent of people in a 2009 poll had a favorable
view of Limbaugh, compared to 44 percent unfavorable.[144]

A June 2009 NBC/*Wall Street Journal* poll showed that many Americans thoroughly hate Rush Limbaugh. Just 8 percent of Americans have a strongly positive view of him, compared to 37 percent who have a strongly negative view.[145] Still, that didn't stop Limbaugh from living under the delusion that he is more popular than Obama: "I'll take my ratings over Obama's any day of the week, folks. Mine are way up, his are way down."[146]

An October 2009 CNN poll found that even after George W. Bush had been gone from office for more than ten months, public opinion of the Republican Party was at its lowest level in more than ten years. Thirty-six percent of Americans viewed the Republican Party favorably, and 54 percent negatively. That -18 rating was compared to a +12 rating for the Democratic Party.[147]

Although many factors aided in the decline and fall of the Republican Party, Rush Limbaugh made a strong contribution. By pushing the Republican Party far to the right, he helped make sure that it would be unpopular. Amazingly, at the same time that these polls were being conducted, Limbaugh was celebrating his influence on the Republican Party: "Conservatism is in the ascendancy."[148] Limbaugh believes in his mythology that if Republicans stand up for conservative values, they will become as popular as Ronald Reagan. It takes a remarkable kind of ideological commitment for him to cry out for ideological purity at a moment when the Republican Party is swinging simultaneously far to the right and far down in popularity.

THE DECLINE OF THE GOP

Rush Limbaugh swept into talk radio thanks to the popularity of Ronald Reagan, and has helped make the Republican Party the party of right-wing talk radio. But while his reign over talk radio has grown, the Republican Party has fallen in popularity, shifting from a national party to a regional, ideological faction presided over by Limbaugh; with the exception of the 1994 elections, when the right took advantage of a Democratic Party full of disarray and corruption, the conservative movement has continued to fade in public support. Even the Republican rebound in 2010 due to the Bush recession and dislike of incumbents still leaves the Republican Party below its past power.

As Limbaugh drives the party further from majority status, though, he does all he can to keep ideological control. When conservative Dough Hoffman lost the 2009 race for Congress in New York's heavily Republican twenty-third District, Limbaugh celebrated because a moderate Republican had been destroyed: "The real victory was making sure that a Republican-in-name-only did not win." Though Limbaugh declared in 2009, "Barack Obama may be destroying the Democrat [sic] Party," it's Limbaugh who is destroying the Republican Party, turning it into a far-right party with no hope of majority status in the foreseeable future. New York Times columnist David Brooks noted, "Over the years, I have asked many politicians what happens when Limbaugh and his colleagues attack. The story is always the same. Hundreds of calls come in. The receptionists are miserable. But the numbers back home do not move. There is no effect on the favorability rating or the reelection prospects. In the media world, he is a giant. In the real world, he's not." Brooks added, "Just months after the election and the humiliation, everyone is again convinced that Limbaugh, Beck, Hannity, and the rest possess real power. And the saddest thing is that even Republican politicians come to believe it. They mistake media for reality. They pre-emptively surrender to armies that don't exist. They pay more attention to Rush's imaginary millions than to the real voters down the street. The Republican Party is unpopular because it's more interested in pleasing Rush's ghosts than actual people. The party is leaderless right now because nobody has the guts to step outside the rigid parameters enforced by the radio jocks and create a new party identity. The party is losing because it has adopted a radio entertainer's niche-building strategy, while abandoning the politician's coalition-building strategy."[149]

Limbaugh responded that Brooks was "JEALOUS" and added, "How many Americans know who David Brooks is?"[150]

Limbaugh succeeds by attracting a small, loyal core of conservative listeners, but imagines that his Dittoheads represent the entire country. As conservative talk show host Michael Medved wrote, "A radio show (locally or nationally) that draws just 5 percent of the available audience can achieve notable success in ratings and revenue, but a conservatism that connects with only a disgruntled, paranoid 5 percent of the public will wither and die." He continued, "Talk radio can't afford long-term marginalization as a sulking, sniping, angry irrelevancy."[151] Actually, it can. In fact, talk radio can afford marginalization from the mainstream of society and make a very good living at it. The era when almost everyone watched the three major network newscasts is gone. Limbaugh can make vast sums of money and wield enormous influence with his audience of 5 percent of the American public.

THE CONSERVATIVE ARGUMENT AGAINST LIMBAUGH

Although liberals hate Limbaugh, many conservatives and Republicans also dislike what he's done to American politics. Reihan Salam, coauthor of *Grand New Party: How Republicans Can Win the Working Class and Save the American Dream,* argued: "As the Republican tent shrinks, Rush Limbaugh, arguably the most successful and influential radio host in American history, has emerged as its most prominent voice. No elected Republican— not John McCain, not Arnold Schwarzenegger, not Bobby Jindal—commands the loyalty of as many grassroots conservatives." Salam noted that Limbaugh "seems increasingly intolerant of even the slightest dissent" and added, "Limbaugh himself . . . uses his obvious talent and cutting wit to do little more than ridicule his political opponents. True believers have their place. But right now, Republicans are in desperate need of evangelizers. And if Limbaugh really does manage to drive them out of his party, he'll find his merry band of Dittoheads age and shrink into oblivion."[152]

As conservative columnist Rod Dreher has said, "Anybody who challenges Limbavian orthodoxy is, ipso facto, the Enemy. If you suggest reform, even from the Right, you are a useful idiot for the Media, which are the Enemy, and can never be anything but the Enemy. Limbaughism sounds a lot like Leninism."[153]

Former George W. Bush speechwriter David Frum wrote a cover story in 2009 for *Newsweek,* "Why Rush Is Wrong." Frum doesn't disagree with Limbaugh's viewpoint but with his rhetoric: "I'm a pretty conservative guy. On most issues, I doubt Limbaugh and I even disagree very much. But the issues on which we do disagree are maybe the most important to the future of the conservative movement and the Republican Party: Should conservatives be trying to provoke or persuade? To narrow our coalition or enlarge it? To enflame or govern? And finally (and above all): to profit—or to serve?"[154]

According to Frum, "From a political point of view, Limbaugh is kryptonite, weakening the GOP nationally. No Republican official will say that;

Limbaugh demands absolute deference from the conservative world, and he generally gets it. When offended, he can extract apologies from Republican members of Congress, even the chairman of the Republican National Committee. And Rush is very easily offended." Frum warned about "the outlook Rush Limbaugh has taught his fans and followers: we want to transform the party of Lincoln, Eisenhower, and Reagan into a party of unanimous dittoheads—and we don't care how much the party has to shrink to do it. That's not the language of politics. It's the language of a cult."[155]

In the cult of Limbaugh, Frum is a heretic. But his critique of a conservative movement led by an egomaniac is right on target.

Among intellectuals on the right, Limbaugh is regarded with derision. John Derbyshire, a contributing editor for *National Review,* called Limbaugh's show "Happy Meal conservatism: cheap, childish, familiar." According to Derbyshire, "Conservatives have never had, and never should have, a problem with elitism. Why have we allowed carny barkers to run away with the Right?"[156] Jeffrey Hart, another *National Review* writer, noted: "Revolt against the masses? Limbaugh is the masses."[157]

Limbaugh's failure to critique Republican politicians offends real conservatives. Derbyshire wrote, "At the very least, by yoking themselves to the clueless George W. Bush and his free-spending administration, they helped create the great debt bubble that has now burst so spectacularly. The big names, too, were all uncritical of the decade-long (at least) efforts to 'build democracy' in no-account nations with politically primitive populations. . . . Much as their blind loyalty discredited the Right, perhaps the worst effect of Limbaugh et al. has been their draining away of political energy from what might have been a much more worthwhile project: the fostering of a middlebrow conservatism."[158]

Judge Richard Posner, one of the leading conservative law-and-economics thinkers, has lamented the "intellectual deterioration of the once-vital conservative movement in the United States," writing, "The policies of the new conservatism are powered largely by emotion and religion and have for the most part weak intellectual groundings." He argued that "the conservative movement is at its lowest ebb since 1964."[159] Posner said about Limbaugh: "I've never listened to his program, but I have read newspaper articles that quote him, and I disagree with many of his views and I don't like the manner in which he expresses them."[160]

Limbaugh has become the best barometer of how badly the conservative movement is failing. Conservative David Frum wrote, "The worse conservatives do, the more important Rush becomes as leader of the ardent remnant. The better conservatives succeed, the more we become a broad national governing coalition, the more Rush will be sidelined."[161] Limbaugh reigns triumphant precisely when conservatives and the Republican Party are marginalized and defeated.

Mark Helprin, a senior fellow at the conservative Claremont Institute, criticized "talk-radio hosts whose major talent is that, like hairdressers, they can talk all day long to one client after another as they snip," and added, "The depth of their thought is truly Oprah-like."[162] Conservative pundit Fred Barnes noted, "When the GOP rose in the late 1970s, it had Ronald Reagan. Now the loudest Republican voice belongs to Rush Limbaugh."[163]

Even some fans of Limbaugh can admit his intellectual failings. Conservative philosophy professor John Mark Reynolds noted, "Rush is a great, great entertainer. He is the best at a certain kind of talk radio ever, but he is a shallow thinker who often fails to practice what he preaches. As such he is a bad public face for the conservative movement."[164] Republican strategist Michelle Laxalt said: "I couldn't disagree more with Rush Limbaugh, excuse me very much, I don't think he has been elected even dogcatcher as yet and as a Republican, I don't want him as part of my party."[165] Limbaugh is an embarrassment to the conservative movement.

The cult of Limbaugh revolves around his personality. But it is also driven by ideology. Limbaugh fills a need among his conservative listeners, a voice of unrelenting partisanship and uncompromising certainty.

Former Republican congressman and MSNBC morning show host Joe Scarborough worried that voters would hear Limbaugh cheering America's failure to get the 2016 Olympics and think that "the Republicans have gone off the deep-end."[166] Limbaugh responded by calling him "PMSNBC Scarborough doing his best impression of a neutered chickified moderate."[167] Scarborough answered Limbaugh by saying, "There are a lot of people on the right that in fact did put their testicles in a blind trust for the past eight years and stopped being conservative and started being apologists."[168] Scarborough isn't a moderate. He's a conservative Republican who objects to hypocrites such as Limbaugh controlling the Republican Party.

Back in 2007, Glenn Beck offered this criticism of Limbaugh: "I truly believe it's going to be the death of us. It's going to be the death of our industry, and the death of our country, if we don't stop dividing ourselves like this. It's not right."[169] But Beck learned how profitable Limbaugh's divisive rhetoric could be, as he and other right-wingers have imitated his hateful rhetoric, spawning a new conservative movement based on anger and hate that has seized control of the Republican Party.

CONCLUSION

RUSH LIMBAUGH HAS BECOME the symbol of what's wrong with the Republican Party and the conservative movement. Howard Dean noted during the 2004 primaries, "We are taking our country back piece by piece from the Rush Limbaughs. You have the power to take back our country so that the flag no longer represents solely Rush Limbaugh."[1] In 2009 Limbaugh declared, "I must present a problem, must present an obstacle. If I had no impact, if I had no influence, if I was such an extremist appealing to such a small number of people, why, what they'd be doing is laughing, or ignoring."[2]

Limbaugh's influence is powerful. *Chicago Tribune* columnist Clarence Page asked, "Does anybody really take Rush seriously?"[3] Yes, they do. Limbaugh mobilizes and inspires the lunatic fringe of the far right. However, his influence extends far beyond the hard-core conservatives; he popularizes right-wing ideas to a mass audience of mainstream Republicans and independents. Limbaugh pushes the Republican Party—and American politics—far to the right.

The radio host is right: He has a powerful impact on America and a tremendous influence on politics. If he were a random blogger spewing out bigotry and idiocy, he wouldn't be worth a second glance. He would be dismissed as just another crackpot. Limbaugh isn't a serious intellectual presenting powerful arguments that liberals need to answer; he isn't an investigative reporter uncovering inconvenient facts; he isn't an incisive commentator offering sharp analysis while skewering liberal sacred cows. The primary reason to pay attention to Limbaugh is because so many other people do.

Liberating political debate from the clutches of journalism has been one of Limbaugh's greatest accomplishments, and perhaps the most destructive to the intellectual climate in America. He has abandoned all journalistic standards of accuracy, objectivity, fact-checking, and telling both sides of the story. By using the label "entertainment," Rush can talk about politics with the same kind of standards that the *National Enquirer* applies to celebrities. His greatest talent is to take crazy ideas and make them sound so reasonable that no one could imagine that a contrary view exists.

Limbaugh told *Talkers magazine,* "I never debate. That's not what I do."[4] As often happens when he encounters an opposing view, he accuses his enemies of relying on faith and feelings: "I hate people who feel rather than think. Most people feel they don't matter. When they are told they can save the planet, well, that gives their lives meaning."[5] But Limbaugh has the same dependence on feelings that he projects to his enemies. The difference is that Limbaugh has a visceral reaction against the idea of saving the planet; he gets his meaning in life from opposing liberalism.

LIMBAUGH, THE LEADER OF CONSERVATIVES

Limbaugh is not some random guy who happens to express a political view every now and then; he's a leader, some would say *the* leader, of the conservative movement in America, and his views are a powerful force in American politics. He deserves scrutiny because of his power and influence, and also because he scrutinizes liberals so intensely. If any driving force in the Democrat Party had made the kinds of errors, lies, and exaggerations Limbaugh conducts on a regular basis, Limbaugh would delight in exposing every single misstep.

Limbaugh lies without restraint, knowing that few of his listeners will ever hear the truth. When he speaks some falsehood, however, it's not necessarily an intentional lie being spoken. Instead, his lies often reflect the worldview of a man who carefully edits reality in his head. Limbaugh reads widely but remembers the facts very selectively. If something doesn't accord with the way he thinks things ought to be, Limbaugh simply ignores it. It disappears from his reality, and therefore it doesn't exist for his followers, either.

Conservative talk show host Hugh Hewitt has argued, "The most trusted journalist in America—it might shock you—is Rush Limbaugh. He has the highest sustained audience."[6] Hewitt is right: Limbaugh is trusted far more than any other media figure. His audience of 20 million per week exceeds that of anyone else in the media. And while many people watch, read, and listen to the mainstream press with a skeptical or distrustful viewpoint, most of his audience is fully devoted to him and trusts him to be right. This trust gives Limbaugh a license to lie, and he uses it often. He knows his audience will believe anything he says.

Limbaugh also has the benefit of having employees who can help him correct some of his particularly dumb mistakes. When he accidentally claimed that torture had prevented a "nuclear" attack on Los Angeles, his staff quickly intervened and informed him about it, allowing Limbaugh to correct himself on the air a few minutes later.[7] But Limbaugh never corrected his error in falsely claiming that torture had stopped any kind of terrorist attack on Los Angeles.

Why does Rush lie so much, when it is so easy to refute what he says? One reason is simple laziness. After two decades as king of the right-wing hill, Limbaugh doesn't have to worry about anything he says. To his audience, it doesn't matter whether he's right or not. In fact, the lies are much more entertaining than the truth.

But the deeper reason for Limbaugh's lies is psychological. After years of listening to his Dittoheads enthusiastically praise him (and to his own endless praise of himself), Limbaugh lives in a world largely free from any challenge. In the realm of this groupthink, dissent disappears and Limbaugh loses any reason to maintain accuracy. Considering that his most outrageous lies also generate the biggest positive response from his conservative listeners, he is constantly being pushed to exaggerate every point he makes.

It's impossible to say whether Limbaugh knows he is lying or simply makes these errors out of indifference to the truth. He suffers from the delusions of his own megalomania, fed by years of praise from adoring fans. Limbaugh has said, "I'm an expert in everything."[8]

Does Limbaugh actually believe all of the idiotic and loony things that he says? Apart from his jokes, does he really think all of his conspiracy theories are real? There is some evidence that Limbaugh is doing this all as a game. As he admitted, "I am doing my show for ratings. I want the largest audience I can get because that's how I can charge the highest advertising rates. Which means what else do I want? Money."[9]

Steve Cameron, a sports journalist who has known Limbaugh distantly for more than thirty years since his days with the Kansas City Royals, reported on one incident: "I've been at Stroud's chicken palace when Rush—now the multimillionaire—has filled the place with smoke and confessed that he loves his critics because they fill his pockets, that his journey to the far right was an accident that kept on making him richer and . . . that if some liberal-leaning radio network offered him twice the money to claim he went through a 'St. Paul moment,' he'd change politics for profit."[10]

Certainly, if Limbaugh was looking to get rich, he picked the correct ideological path. But Limbaugh is already rich beyond belief and has an iron-clad eight-year contract. There's nothing about the money that forces him to be dishonest or to make bigoted comments. In the end, Limbaugh does seem to be sincere, and to believe passionately that he is always right.

The accusation of lying always offends Limbaugh: "The running criticism of old El Rushbo out there from the White House on down to State-Run Media is that I lie. I make it up."[11] That criticism of Limbaugh as a liar is so prevalent because he is a liar. He does make it up. As Limbaugh has put it, "You know, hearing somebody lie to you repeatedly is a grating thing."[12] But Limbaugh's followers look the other way and refuse to confront the overwhelming evidence of his misrepresentations.

What makes Limbaugh so appealing to his loyal listeners is his consistency. Every day, they hear the same thing from him, often repeatedly. It's the force of repetition that leads to Limbaugh's success. What Limbaugh does is translate current events according to conservative dogma. He explains to his listeners how a true conservative should think about every new issue that pops up, and he provides them with a bulwark of interpretations and catchphrases to defend their ideas against the onslaught of reality intruding in from the invariably "liberal" media. Limbaugh is the drill sergeant of the conservative movement, keeping the troops in line and making sure that they do not stray.

"WITH TALENT ON LOAN FROM GOD"

Limbaugh is famous as an egomaniac who proclaims his greatness at every turn. "I'm totally concerned with me," he told *The New York Times* in 1993.[13] A full-size oil portrait of himself hangs on the wall of the main staircase in his enormous mansion.[14] Tom Shales noted in *The Washington Post* about Limbaugh's television show, "He demands unconditional approval, and his TV program is a relentless orgy of bombastic self-promotion."[15]

Oblivious to his projection, Limbaugh repeatedly denounces Barack Obama as "an arrogant little narcissist"[16] and has claimed, "Obama's got a messianic complex,"[17] and, "We've got a two-year-old man-child with a Mars-size ego."[18]

But such is the extent of Limbaugh's egomania that he believes that he is talking with God on a daily basis. He wrote to his friend Mark Levin, "I have incredible faith. I don't go to church but communicate with God so many times a day I can't count it."[19] With his direct pipeline to God, Limbaugh doesn't need a church, and he certainly doesn't want to hear anyone else's opinions. And like the followers of a cult, his Dittoheads need no explanations nor evidence from their leader; only obedient nodding is necessary. *The Rush Limbaugh Show* is a cocoon of conservatism where he and his listeners can be protected from liberal ideas.

Limbaugh loves to whine about his critics: "After twenty years of these types of attacks—me being taken out of context and every one of them being shown to be wrong, every one of these attacks being shown to be fallacious."[20] In reality, with the exception of two obscure quotes about race, almost none of the criticism of Limbaugh has been taken out of context or shown to be wrong. It's Limbaugh, not his critics, who stands guilty of lies, smears, and vile attacks.

For more than two decades, Limbaugh's voice of hatred toward everything liberal has resonated across America. Limbaugh uses his power to misinform his listeners, smear his enemies, and undermine reasonable debate. His bigotry and ignorance are revealed on a daily basis during his show, yet he remains more popular than ever. Limbaugh's vast, adoring audience for his conspiracy theories and hateful campaigns are an indictment of American democracy itself.

NOTES

INTRODUCTION

In the following pages, *RLS* is used for *The Rush Limbaugh Show*, MMA for Media Matters for America, and FAIR for Fairness and Accuracy in Reporting.

1. *60 Minutes/Vanity Fair* poll, November 29, 2009, http://www.cbsnews.com/stories/2009/11/24/60minutes/main5761182_page7.shtml?tag=contentMain;contentBody.

2. *RLS*, July 20, 2009, http://www.rushlimbaugh.com/home/daily/site_072009/content/01125116.guest.html.

3. *RLS*, November 23, 2009, http://www.rushlimbaugh.com/home/daily/site_112309/content/01125106.guest.html.

4. *RLS*, July 16, 2009, http://www.rushlimbaugh.com/home/daily/site_071609/content/01125108.guest.html.

5. Evan Thomas, "'I Am Addicted to Prescription Pain Medication,'" *Newsweek*, October 20, 2003.

6. "Rush Limbaugh: Playboy Interview," *Playboy*, December 1993, http://www.playboy.com/articles/rush-limbaugh-interview/index.html.

7. *Today* show, NBC, October 12, 2009, http://www.rushlimbaugh.com/home/daily/site_101209/content/01125106.guest.html.

8. *RLS*, December 7, 2009, http://www.rushlimbaugh.com/home/daily/site_120709/content/01125109.guest.html.

9. *Hannity & Colmes,* Fox News Channel, October 19, 2005, http://www.foxnews
   .com/story/0,2933,172675,00.html.

10. Rush Limbaugh, *The Way Things Ought to Be* (New York: Pocket Books,
    1992), 20.

11. Paul Colford, *The Rush Limbaugh Story: Talent on Loan from God* (New York:
    St. Martin's Press, 1993) 24.

12. Ibid., 22.

13. Ibid., 26.

14. Ibid., 30, 36.

15. Ibid., 38, 49.

16. *RLS,* May 10, 1995, cited in Al Franken, *Rush Limbaugh Is a Big, Fat Idiot and
    Other Observations* (New York: Delacorte Press, 1996), 25.

17. Colford, *The Rush Limbaugh Story,* 51.

18. Ibid., 57.

19. "Rush Limbaugh: Playboy Interview."

20. Colford, *The Rush Limbaugh Story,* 58.

21. *RLS,* November 11, 2009, http://www.rushlimbaugh.com/home/daily/site_
    111109/content/01125106.guest.html.

22. Zev Chafets, "Late Period Limbaugh," *The New York Times Magazine,* July 6,
    2008, http://www.nytimes.com/2008/07/06/magazine/06Limbaugh-t.html?_r=1
    &hp=&pagewanted=print.

23. Colford, *The Rush Limbaugh Story,* 119.

24. Ibid., 131.

25. Joseph N. Cappella, Joseph Turow, and Kathleen Hall Jamieson, "Call-In Political
    Talk Radio: Background, Content, Audiences, Portrayal in Mainstream Media,"
    Annenberg Public Policy Center, August 7, 1996, http://www.annenbergpublic
    policycenter.org/Downloads/Political_Communication/Political_Talk_Radio/
    1996_03_political_talk_radio_rpt.PDF, 6.

26. Mary Strom Larson, "Rush Limbaugh—Broadcast Demagogue," *Journal of
    Radio Studies,* 1997, 4: 189; Colford, *The Rush Limbaugh Story,* 94.

27. Cappella, Turow, and Jamieson, "Call-In Political Talk Radio," 12.

28. Paul Farhi, "Limbaugh's Audience Size? It's Largely Up in the Air," *Washington
    Post,* March 7, 2009.

29. "Rush Ratings Through the Roof: Memo to Rush from EIB Ratings Analysis
    Unit," March 26, 2009, http://www.rushlimbaugh.com/home/daily/site_032609/
    content/01125106.guest.html.

30. Brian Maloney, "Rush Who?" *RadioEqualizer,* September 14, 2009, http://radio
    equalizer.blogspot.com/2009/09/state-run-media-sidestep-limbaugh.html.

31. Paul Farhi, "Rush Limbaugh Signs $400 Million Radio Deal," *The Washington
    Post,* July 3, 2008, http://www.washingtonpost.com/wp-dyn/content/article/2008/
    07/02/AR2008070202063.html.

32. Ibid.

33. Zev Chafets, "Late Period Limbaugh," *The New York Times Magazine,* July 6,
    2008, http://www.nytimes.com/2008/07/06/magazine/06Limbaugh-t.html?_r=
    1&hp=&pagewanted=print.

34. Julie Limbaugh, "Rusty and Me," Salon.com, April 1, 2009, http://www.salon
    .com/news/feature/2009/03/01/limbaugh/print.html.

35. *Talkers magazine* award, June 6, 2009, http://www.rushlimbaugh.com/home/
    daily/site_060909/content/01125106.guest.html.

36. *RLS,* June 10, 2009, http://www.rushlimbaugh.com/home/daily/site_061009/
    content/01125114.guest.html.

37. David Hinckley, "Rush's Star: Advertising," *New York Daily News,* April 8,
    2008.

38. Rush Limbaugh, interview with Pat Sajak, CNN, May 3, 2001, http://edition
    .cnn.com/TRANSCRIPTS/0105/03/lkl.00.html.

39. ". . . and the rest of the 2009 Most Searched goes to . . . ," December 22, 2009,
    http://www.bing.com/community/blogs/search/archive/2009/12/22/and-the-rest-
    of-the-2009-most-searched-goes-to.aspx/

40. Katy Bachman, "Radio Personality of the Decade: Rush Limbaugh," *AdWeek-
    Media,* Best of the 2000s, http://www.bestofthe2000s.com/radio-personality-of-
    the-decade.html.

41. James Bowman, "Rush: The Leader of the Opposition," *National Review,* Sep-
    tember 6, 1993, http://article.nationalreview.com/269545/rush-the-leader-of-
    the-opposition/james-bowman.

CHAPTER 1: RUSH LIMBAUGH'S RACISM

1. Ben Armbruster, "Black NFL Players 'Wouldn't Play' For Limbaugh's Team:
   'He's A Jerk,'" *Think Progress,* October 10, 2009, http://www.thinkprogress.
   org//143199/.

2. "You Know Who Deserves a Posthumous Medal of Honor? James Earl Ray Is
   a Lie," Smash Mouth Politics. http://maaadddog.wordpress.com/you-know-

who-deserves-a-posthumous-medal-of-honor-james-earl-ray-is-a-damnable-lie
-made-up-by-liberals.

3. John K. Wilson, "Limbaugh's Fake Outrage at Fake Quotes," DailyKos.com, October 16, 2009, http://www.dailykos.com/story/2009/10/16/793990/-Lim baughs-Fake-Outrage-at-Fake-Quotes.

4. *RLS,* October 13, 2009, http://www.rushlimbaugh.com/home/daily/site_101309/ content/01125108.guest.html.

5. Ibid.

6. Wilson, "Limbaugh's Fake Outrage at Fake Quotes," http://www.dailykos.com/ story/2009/10/16/793990/-Limbaughs-Fake-Outrage-at-Fake-Quotes.

7. *O'Reilly Factor,* October 15, 2009.

8. *RLS,* October 15, 2009, http://www.rushlimbaugh.com/home/daily/site_101509/ content/01125106.guest.html.

9. Dave Zirin, "The NFL Must Flush Rush," *The Nation,* October 9, 2009, http:// www.thenation.com/doc/20091026/zirin.

10. John McWhorter, "Within Bounds," *The New York Times,* October 4, 2003, http://www.nytimes.com/2003/10/04/opinion/04MCWH.html.

11. Richard Sandomir, "Limbaugh Resigns From ESPN's N.F.L. Show," *The New York Times,* October 2, 2003, http://www.nytimes.com/2003/10/02/sports/ football-limbaugh-resigns-from-espn-s-nfl-show.html.

12. Thomas George, "INSIDE THE N.F.L.; The Pushing and Pulling Of Black Quarterbacks," *The New York Times,* October 3, 2003, http://www.nytimes .com/2003/10/03/sports/inside-the-nfl-the-pushing-and-pulling-of-black-quarter backs.html.

13. Ron Reid, "ESPN Crew Lashes Out at Limbaugh," *Philadelphia Inquirer,* October 6, 2003.

14. David Niven, "Race, Quarterbacks, and the Media: Testing the Rush Limbaugh Hypothesis," *Journal of Black Studies* 2005, 35(5):684–694.

15. *RLS,* October 12, 2009, http://www.rushlimbaugh.com/home/daily/site_101209/ content/01125123.guest.html.

16. *RLS,* February 5, 2007, http://www.rushlimbaugh.com/home/daily/site_020507/ content/0205078.guest.html.

17. Ibid.

18. "Rex Grossman," http://www.nfl.com/players/rexgrossman/careerstats?id= GRO597298.

19. "Donovan McNabb," http://www.nfl.com/players/donovanmcnabb/careerstats ?id=MCN017517.

20. In addition, McNabb had 3,109 career rushing yards (which aren't counted in passer ratings), 3,029 more than Grossman. (See http://www.nfl.com/players/donovanmcnabb/careerstats?id=MCN017517.) Grossman had nineteen fumbles in 1,013 passing attempts and rushes (1.9 percent), while McNabb had seventy-three fumbles in 4,839 passes and rushes (1.5 percent). In fifteen playoff games, McNabb had an average passer rating of 80.8, and 409 rushing yards. See http://www.pro-football-reference.com/players/M/McNaDo00_playoffs.htm. By comparison, Grossman had a passer rating of 67.3 and two rushing yards in four playoff games. See http://www.pro-football-reference.com/players/G/GrosRe00_playoffs.htm.

21. *RLS,* February 13, 2007, http://www.rushlimbaugh.com/home/daily/site_021307/content/01125104.guest.html.

22. *RLS,* October 28, 2009, http://www.rushlimbaugh.com/home/daily/site_102809/content/01125114.guest.html.

23. Ibid.

24. Rep. Steve King, October 28, 2009 House Judiciary Committee hearing, http://www.rushlimbaugh.com/home/daily/site_102809/content/01125114.guest.html.

25. Ibid.

26. *RLS,* October 30, 2009, http://www.rushlimbaugh.com/home/daily/site_103009/content/01125117.guest.html.

27. *RLS,* October 15, 2009, http://www.rushlimbaugh.com/home/daily/site_101509/content/01125106.guest.html.

28. *Today* show, NBC, October 11, 2000.

29. Rush Limbaugh, *See, I Told You So* (New York: Pocket Books, 1993) 273.

30. Charles Barkley, *Tonight Show,* NBC, April 17, 2009, quoted by Daily Kos, http://www.dailykos.com/story/2009/4/20/722399/-Charles-Barkley-Dunks-on-Limbaugh,-Hannity,-and-Glenn-Beck.

31. *RLS,* January 19, 2007, http://www.rushlimbaugh.com/home/estack_12_13_06/the_classless_nfl_culture_.guest.html.

32. *RLS,* December 8, 2004, quoted by MMA, http://mediamatters.org/research/200412100008.

33. *RLS,* November 22, 2004, quoted by MMA, http://mediamatters.org/research/200411230007.

34. Paul Colford, *The Rush Limbaugh Story: Talent on Loan from God* (New York: St. Martin's Press, 1993), 225.

35. *See, I Told You So,* 268.

36. William Raspberry, "Rush to Judgment," *The Washington Post,* February 1, 1993.

37. William Raspberry, "Rush to Judgment (Cont'd)," *The Washington Post*, February 12, 1993.

38. Howard Kurtz, "Carl Rowan's Labors of Hate," *The Washington Post*, November 25, 1996.

39. *RLS*, April 20, 2009, http://www.rushlimbaugh.com/home/daily/site_042009/content/01125108.guest.html.

40. Timothy Egan, "Fears of a Clown," *The New York Times*, March 4, 2009, http://egan.blogs.nytimes.com/2009/03/04/fears-of-a-clown/.

41. Jeff Cohen and Steve Rendall, "Limbaugh: A Color Man Who Has a Problem With Color?" FAIR, June 7, 2000, http://www.fair.org/index.php?page=2549.

42. "Bone Voyage," Snopes, http://www.snopes.com/politics/quotes/limbaugh.asp.

43. Erin Steuter and Deborah Wills, *At War with Metaphor* (Lanham, MD: Lexington Books, 2008), 134.

44. *RLS*, September 29, 2004, quoted by MMA, http://mediamatters.org/research/200409300008.

45. Cohen and Rendall, "Limbaugh," http://www.fair.org/index.php?page=2549.

46. Joshua Hammer, "Welcome to Rush's World," *Newsweek*, September 28, 1992.

47. Cohen and Rendall, "Limbaugh," http://www.fair.org/index.php?page=2549.

48. *RLS*, July 28, 2009, http://www.rushlimbaugh.com/home/daily/site_072809/content/01125112.guest.html.

49. "NAACP Centennial Celebration," February 12, 2009, http://www.naacp.org/about/history.

50. *RLS*, June 6, 2007, quoted by MMA, http://mediamatters.org/research/200706070003.

51. *RLS*, March 21, 2008, http://www.rushlimbaugh.com/home/daily/site_032108/content/01125106.guest.html.

52. Cohen and Rendall, "Limbaugh," http://www.fair.org/index.php?page=2549.

53. David Brock, *Blinded by the Right: The Conscience of an Ex-Conservative* (New York: Crown, 2002). David Neiwert, *The Eliminationists: How Hate Talk Radicalized the American Right* (Sausalito, CA: Polipoint Press, 2009), 276.

54. *The Eliminationists*, 72.

55. Rush Limbaugh TV show, May 24, 1994; transcript archived on Nexis; http://www.fair.org/index.php?page=3928.

56. *RLS*, August 23, 2006, http://www.rushlimbaugh.com/home/estack_12_13_06/New_Survivor_Season__A_War_of_the_Races.guest.html.

57. *RLS,* February 1, 2007, at MMA, http://mediamatters.org/mobile/research/200702060001.

58. Rush Limbaugh, *The Way Things Ought to Be* (New York: Pocket Books, 1992), 117.

59. Rush Limbaugh, Conservative Political Action Conference Speech, Washington, DC, February 28, 2009, http://www.rushlimbaugh.com/home/daily/site_030209/content/01125106.guest.html.

60. *Today* show, NBC, October 11, 2000.

61. Nigel Farndale, "The Man Who's Always Right," *Sunday Telegraph* (London), November 2, 2008.

62. *RLS,* August 28, 2009, http://www.rushlimbaugh.com/home/daily/site_082809/content/01125107.guest.html.

63. Ibid.

64. Renee Graham, "Limbaugh's Attack of Kerry Is a Bad Rap," *Boston Globe,* April 13, 2004.

65. *RLS,* November 16, 2009, http://www.rushlimbaugh.com/home/daily/site_111609/content/01125107.guest.html.

66. David Paul Kuhn, "Exit Polls: How Obama Won," Politico.com, November 5, 2008, http://www.politico.com/news/stories/1108/15297.html.

67. *RLS,* February 7, 2008, http://www.rushlimbaugh.com/home/daily/site_020708/content/01125112.guest.html; *RLS,* April 22, 2008, http://www.rushlimbaugh.com/home/daily/site_042208/content/01125115.guest.html; *RLS,* November 9, 2007, http://www.rushlimbaugh.com/home/daily/site_110907/content/01125111.guest.html; *RLS,* October 15, 2007, http://www.rushlimbaugh.com/home/daily/site_101507/content/01125109.guest.html.

68. ABC News, "Election 2008 Exit Polls," http://abcnews.go.com/PollingUnit/Exit Polls/.

69. *RLS,* June 4, 2009, http://www.rushlimbaugh.com/home/daily/site_060409/content/01125110.guest.html.

70. *RLS,* June 3, 2009, http://www.rushlimbaugh.com/home/daily/site_060309/content/01125111.guest.html.

71. *RLS,* January 12, 2007, quoted by MMA, http://mediamatters.org/research/200701120014.

72. *RLS,* October 15, 2009, http://www.rushlimbaugh.com/home/daily/site_101509/content/01125108.guest.html.

73. *RLS,* August 22, 2007, http://www.rushlimbaugh.com/home/daily/site_082207/content/01125110.guest.html.

74. Ibid.

75. Limbaugh, *The Way Things Ought to Be*, 48.

76. Nigel Farndale, "The Man Who's Always Right."

77. Joshua Hammer, "Welcome to Rush's World," *Newsweek*, September 28, 1992.

78. *RLS*, February 14, 2006.

79. *RLS*, February 20, 2006, quoted by MMA, http://mediamatters.org/research/200602220006.

80. *RLS*, May 29, 2009, http://www.rushlimbaugh.com/home/daily/site_052909/content/01125106.guest.html.

81. Limbaugh, *The Way Things Ought to Be*, 207.

82. *RLS*, March 6, 2008, http://politicalticker.blogs.cnn.com/2008/03/06/limbaugh-so-called-dream-ticket-doesnt-have-a-prayer/?eref=ib_politicalticker.

83. Steve Rendall, "Listening to Limbaugh," FAIR, April 1, 2009, http://www.fair.org/blog/2009/04/01/listening-to-limbaugh/.

84. Andrew Klavan, "Take the Limbaugh Challenge," *Los Angeles Times*, March 29, 2009, http://www.latimes.com/news/opinion/commentary/la-oe-klavan29-2009mar29,0,5456892.story.

85. *RLS*, August 17, 2009, http://www.rushlimbaugh.com/home/daily/site_081709/content/01125106.guest.html.

86. CNN, *Anderson Cooper 360*, August 31, 2004, http://mediamatters.org/research/200409010003.

87. Rush Limbaugh, interview, *Sean Hannity Show*, Fox News Channel, January 19, 2009, http://www.rushlimbaugh.com/home/daily/site_012209/content/01125106.guest.html.

88. Ibid.

89. *RLS*, February 7, 2006, quoted by MMA, http://mediamatters.org/research/200602090012.

90. *RLS*, December 11, 2006, quoted in "Republicans seek to quell 'Obama-mania,' " *National Post*, December 13, 2006.

91. *RLS*, January 24, 2007, quoted by MMA, http://mediamatters.org/research/200701240010.

92. "Limbaugh: Obama Should 'Renounce' His Race and Just 'Become White.' " ThinkProgress.org, February 14, 2007, http://thinkprogress.org/2007/02/14/limbaugh-obama-white.

93. *RLS*, March 21, 2008.

94. *RLS*, September 29, 2008; *RLS*, Jan. 16, 2007, quoted by MMA http://mediamatters.org/items/200701170010?f=s_search; *RLS*, August 20, 2008.

95. *RLS,* February 23, 2010, http://www.rushlimbaugh.com/home/daily/site_022310/content/01125104.guest.html.

96. *RLS,* September 22, 2008.

97. Campbell Brown, "So What If Obama Were a Muslim or an Arab?" CNN .com, October 13, 2008, http://www.cnn.com/2008/POLITICS/10/13/campbell.brown.obama/index.html.

98. Princeton Survey Research Associates, "National Annenberg Election Survey, November 5–18, 2008, http://www.factcheck.org/UploadedFiles/Disinformed_Electorate_Data.pdf.

99. *RLS,* September 22, 2008, quoted by MMA, http://mediamatters.org/research/200809220015.

100. *The O'Reilly Factor,* Fox News, February 29, 2009, http://www.foxnews.com/story/0,2933,334669,00.html.

101. *RLS,* December 22, 2004, http://mediamatters.org/research/200501120011.

102. Ibid.

103. Rush Limbaugh, interview, *Sean Hannity Show*, Fox News Channel, January 19, 2009, http://www.rushlimbaugh.com/home/daily/site_012209/content/01125106.guest.html.

104. *RLS,* May 14, 2008, http://www.rushlimbaugh.com/home/daily/site_051408/content/01125110.guest.html.

105. Rush Limbaugh, Conservative Political Action Conference Speech, Washington, DC, February 28, 2009, http://www.rushlimbaugh.com/home/daily/site_030209/content/01125106.guest.html.

106. *RLS,* May 26, 2009, http://www.rushlimbaugh.com/home/daily/site_052609/content/01125106.guest.html; *RLS,* August 4, 2009, http://www.rushlimbaugh.com/home/daily/site_080409/content/01125108.guest.html.

107. *Hannity,* Fox News Channel, January 21, 2009.

108. *RLS,* March 19, 2007, quoted by MMA, http://mediamatters.org/mmtv/200703200012.

109. *RLS,* September, 18, 2008.

110. *RLS,* August 24, 2009, quoted by MMA, http://mediamatters.org/mmtv/200908240028;   http://www.rushlimbaugh.com/home/daily/site_082709/content/01125109.guest.html.

111. Cohen and Rendall, "Limbaugh," http://www.fair.org/index.php?page=2549.

112. *RLS,* February 22, 2010, http://www.rushlimbaugh.com/home/daily/site_022210/content/01125108.guest.html.

113. "Rush Interview," Human Events Online, July 28, 2008, http://www.human events.com/article.php?id=27717.

114. *RLS,* May 28, 2008, http://www.rushlimbaugh.com/home/daily/site_052708/content/01125108.guest.html.

115. Limbaugh, interview with Gretchen Carlson, *Fox & Friends,* Fox News Channel, January 29, 2010, http://www.rushlimbaugh.com/home/daily/site_020310/content/01125120.guest.html.

116. Emails to the author, February 3, 2010.

117. *RLS,* February 10, 2010, http://www.rushlimbaugh.com/home/daily/site_021010/content/01125113.guest.html.

118. *RLS,* August 19, 2008, http://www.rushlimbaugh.com/home/daily/site_081908/content/01125117.guest.html.

119. *RLS,* January 5, 2009, http://www.rushlimbaugh.com/home/daily/site_010509/content/01125107.guest.html.

120. *RLS,* October 12, 2009, http://www.rushlimbaugh.com/home/daily/site_101209/content/01125115.guest.html.

121. Greg Sargent, "Rush Limbaugh's Lovely 'Racially Charged' Songs about Sharpton and Obama," Talking Points Memo, April 27, 2007, http://www.talkingpointsmemo.com/horsesmouth/2007/04/rush_limbaugh_p.php.

122. Jake Tapper, "Is Obama Offended by 'Barack the Magic Negro'?" ABCNews.com, May 5, 2007, http://blogs.abcnews.com/politicalpunch/2007/05/is_obama_offend.html.

123. John Nichols, "Puff Goes the GOP's Credibility," *Nation,* December 29, 2008, http://www.thenation.com/blogs/state_of_change/392189/puff_goes_the_gop_s_credibility.

124. *RLS,* January 14, 2008, http://www.rushlimbaugh.com/home/daily/site_011408/content/01125106.guest.html.

125. *RLS,* July 27, 2009, http://mediamatters.org/mmtv/200907270033.

126. *RLS,* May 13, 2010, http://www.rushlimbaugh.com/home/daily/site_051310/content/01125109.guest.html.

127. *RLS,* April 13, 2009, http://www.rushlimbaugh.com/home/daily/site_041309/content/01125106.guest.html.

128. *RLS,* July 22, 2009, http://www.rushlimbaugh.com/home/daily/site_072209/content/01125117.guest.html.

129. *RLS,* September 17, 2009, http://www.rushlimbaugh.com/home/daily/site_091709/content/01125113.guest.html.

130. Melissa Harris-Lacewell, "Rush and Reparations," TheNation.com, May 12, 2009, http://www.thenation.com/blogs/notion/435392/rush_and_reparations.

131. *Colbert Report,* Comedy Central, September 24, 2009.

132. *RLS,* May 29, 2009, http://www.rushlimbaugh.com/home/daily/site_052909/content/01125106.guest.html.

133. *RLS,* June 11, 2009, http://www.rushlimbaugh.com/home/daily/site_061109/content/01125106.guest.html.

134. *RLS,* August 12, 2009, http://www.rushlimbaugh.com/home/daily/site_081209/content/01125106.guest.html.

135. William F. Buckley, "In Search of Anti-Semitism," *National Review,* December 30, 1991.

136. *RLS,* January 20, 2010, http://www.rushlimbaugh.com/home/daily/site_012010/content/01125104.guest.html.

137. Anti-Defamation League, "ADL: Rush Limbaugh Reaches New Low With 'Borderline Anti-Semitic' Remarks About Jews," January 21, 2010, http://www.adl.org/PresRele/ASUS_12/5695_12.htm.

138. *RLS,* January 22, 2010, http://www.rushlimbaugh.com/home/daily/site_012210/content/01125108.guest.html.

139. *RLS,* May 29, 2009, http://www.rushlimbaugh.com/home/daily/site_052909/content/01125106.guest.html.

140. Chris Strohm, "Powell Says Shrinking GOP Should Return to the Center," *CongressDaily,* May 5, 2009, http://www.nationaljournal.com/congressdaily/print_friendly.php?ID=cda_20090505_8843.

141. Ibid.

142. Jonathan Martin, "Limbaugh: Where Are All the Inexperienced, White Liberals Powell Has Endorsed?" Politico.com, October 19, 2008, http://www.politico.com/blogs/jonathanmartin/1008/Limbaugh_Where_are_the_inexperienced_white_liberals_Powell_has_endorsed.html.

143. CNN, July 5, 2009, http://thinkprogress.org/2009/07/05/powell-limbaugh-sotomayor-nonsense.

144. *Evans & Novak,* CNN, November 15, 1997.

145. *RLS,* March 20, 2009, http://www.rushlimbaugh.com/home/daily/site_032009/content/01125106.guest.html.

146. *RLS,* July 27, 2009, http://www.rushlimbaugh.com/home/daily/site_072709/content/01125108.guest.html.

147. *On the Record* with Greta Van Susteren, Fox News Channel, July 23, 2009, http://www.rushlimbaugh.com/home/daily/site_073009/content/01125110.guest.html.

148. *RLS,* June 29, 2009, http://www.rushlimbaugh.com/home/daily/site_062909/content/01125110.guest.html.

149. Richard Cohen, "Obama's Identity Crisis," *Washington Post,* October 19, 2009, http://www.washingtonpost.com/wp-dyn/content/article/2009/10/19/AR2009101902509.html.

150. *RLS,* July 27, 2009, http://www.rushlimbaugh.com/home/daily/site_072709/content/01125108.guest.html.

151. *RLS,* October 24, 2008. More examples of Limbaugh's language: "Obama was taught by angry people" (*RLS,* June 2, 2009); "This is a very arrogant, radical guy who is angry. No one is going to be able to convince me otherwise. I mean, he doesn't show it, but sometimes I think I notice it. I think it flares sometimes. Not the anger, but the—he reveals that he has a bunch of chips on his shoulder" (*RLS,* March 30, 2009); "I know I'm right about him being an angry guy" (*RLS,* June 5, 2009). Limbaugh explicitly tied the anger of Obama and his wife to race: "He's got anger about race in this country, and so does she" (RLS, May 28, 2009), and repeatedly pushed the racial stereotype of Obama as the angry black man: "He's an angry black guy. I do believe that about the president. I do believe he's angry. I think his wife is angry. All liberals are enraged all the time anyway. They're always mad. But if he's not mad, if he's not angry, why does he run around apologizing for the country all over the place?" (*RLS,* July 27, 2009, http://www.rushlimbaugh.com/home/daily/site_072709/content/01125108.guest.html).

152. *RLS,* July 27, 2009, http://www.rushlimbaugh.com/home/daily/site_072709/content/01125108.guest.html.

153. *RLS,* June 24, 2009, http://www.rushlimbaugh.com/home/daily/site_062409/content/01125110.guest.html.

154. Rush Limbaugh, "Obama Is Stoking Racial Antagonism," *Wall Street Journal,* September 19, 2008, http://online.wsj.com/article/SB122178554189155003.html.

155. *RLS,* September 22, 2008, http://www.rushlimbaugh.com/home/daily/site_092208/content/01125113.html.LogIn.html.

156. Limbaugh, "Obama Is Stoking Racial Antagonism."

157. *RLS,* September 18, 2008, http://www.rushlimbaugh.com/home/daily/site_091808/content/01125114.guest.html.

158. Limbaugh, "Obama Is Stoking Racial Antagonism."

159. *RLS,* September 18, 2008, http://www.rushlimbaugh.com/home/daily/site_091808/content/01125114.guest.html.

160. FAIR, "The Way Things Aren't," Extra, July-August 1994, http://www.fair.org/index.php?page=1895.

161. *RLS,* March 2, 1998, quoted in Norman Solomon, "And Now, the P.U.-litzer

Prizes for 1998," December 17, 1998, http://www.fair.org/index.php?page=2326.

162. *RLS*, March 26, 2004, quoted by MMA, http://mediamatters.org/research/200405020008.

163. *RLS*, April 1, 2005, quoted by MMA, http://mediamatters.org/mmtv/200504040001.

164. *RLS*, March 27, 2006, quoted by MMA, http://mediamatters.org/research/200603280009.

165. *RLS*, May 5, 2008, http://www.rushlimbaugh.com/home/daily/site_050508/content/01125106.guest.html.

166. *RLS*, March 27, 2007, quoted by MMA, http://mediamatters.org/research/200703280008.

167. *RLS*, May 27, 2009, http://www.rushlimbaugh.com/home/daily/site_052709/content/01125107.guest.html.

168. *RLS*, June 3, 2009, http://www.rushlimbaugh.com/home/daily/site_060309/content/01125111.guest.html.

169. Brock, *Blinded by the Right*, 275.

170. *RLS*, May 28, 2009, http://www.rushlimbaugh.com/home/daily/site_052809/content/01125112.guest.html.

171. *RLS*, May 28, 2009, http://www.rushlimbaugh.com/home/daily/site_052809/content/01125108.guest.html.

172. *RLS*, June 29, 2009, http://www.rushlimbaugh.com/home/daily/site_062909/content/01125109.guest.html.

173. "Rush Interviewed by Sean Hannity, Part One," Fox News Channel, Recorded: June 2, 2009, http://www.rushlimbaugh.com/home/daily/site_060409/content/01125106.guest.html.

174. *RLS*, May 29, 2009, http://www.rushlimbaugh.com/home/daily/site_052909/content/01125106.guest.html.

175. *RLS*, June 3, 2009, http://www.rushlimbaugh.com/home/daily/site_060309/content/01125111.guest.html.

176. *RLS*, June 1, 2009, http://www.rushlimbaugh.com/home/daily/site_060109/content/01125107.guest.html.

177. *RLS*, July 13, 2009, http://www.rushlimbaugh.com/home/daily/site_071309/content/01125110.guest.html.

178. *RLS*, May 26, 2009, http://www.rushlimbaugh.com/home/daily/site_052609/content/01125106.guest.html.

179. "How Many Sotomayor Opinions Were Overturned?" FactCheck.org, May 29, 2009, http://www.newsweek.com/id/199955.

180. *RLS,* July 13, 2009, http://www.rushlimbaugh.com/home/daily/site_071309/content/01125111.guest.html.

181. *RLS,* May 28, 2009, http://www.rushlimbaugh.com/home/daily/site_052809/content/01125108.guest.html.

182. Rush Limbaugh, "Introduction," in Mark Levin, *Men in Black* (Washington, DC: Regnery Publishing, 2005), xi.

183. *RLS,* May 26, 2009, http://www.rushlimbaugh.com/home/daily/site_052609/content/01125106.guest.html.

184. "Rush Interviewed by Sean Hannity, Part One," Fox News Channel, Recorded: June 2, 2009, http://www.rushlimbaugh.com/home/daily/site_060409/content/01125106.guest.html.

185. *RLS,* June 29, 2009, http://www.rushlimbaugh.com/home/daily/site_062909/content/01125110.guest.html.

186. "United States Congress Quick Facts," http://www.thisnation.com/congress-facts.html.

187. *RLS,* October 1, 2009, http://www.rushlimbaugh.com/home/daily/site_100109/content/01125113.guest.html.

188. *RLS,* September 15, 2009, http://www.rushlimbaugh.com/home/daily/site_091509/content/01125106.guest.html.

189. *Colbert Report,* Comedy Central, September 24, 2009.

190. *RLS,* September 16, 2009, http://www.rushlimbaugh.com/home/daily/site_091609/content/01125107.guest.html.

191. *RLS,* August 25, 2009, http://www.rushlimbaugh.com/home/daily/site_082509/content/01125109.guest.html.

CHAPTER 2: BITCHES, BUTT BOYS, AND FEMINAZIS: LIMBAUGH'S SEXISM AND HOMOPHOBIA

1. Rush Limbaugh, *See, I Told You So* (New York: Pocket Books, 1993) 222.

2. Paul Colford, *The Rush Limbaugh Story: Talent on Loan from God* (New York: St. Martin's Press, 1993), 66.

3. *RLS,* June 11, 2009, http://www.rushlimbaugh.com/home/daily/site_061109/content/01125106.guest.html.

4. *RLS,* May 27, 2009.

5. *RLS,* January 26, 2009, http://www.rushlimbaugh.com/home/daily/site_012609/content/01125106.guest.html.

6. FAIR, *The Way Things Aren't: Rush Limbaugh's Reign of Error* (New York: New Press, 1995), 109.

7. *RLS,* April 9, 2009, http://www.rushlimbaugh.com/home/daily/site_040909/content/01125106.guest.html.

8. *All Things Considered,* NPR, January 25, 2007.

9. *RLS,* March 3, 2006, quoted by MMA, http://mediamatters.org/research/200603070003.

10. *RLS,* April 15, 2004, quoted by MMA, http://mediamatters.org/research/200405020008.

11. *RLS,* August 12, 2009, http://www.rushlimbaugh.com/home/daily/site_081209/content/01125113.guest.html.

12. *RLS,* March 31, 2008, http://www.rushlimbaugh.com/home/daily/site_033108/content/01125114.guest.html.

13. *RLS,* December 17, 2007, http://www.rushlimbaugh.com/home/daily/site_121707/content/01125114.guest.html.

14. *RLS,* December 17, 2007, http://www.rushlimbaugh.com/home/daily/site_121707/content/01125114.guest.html.

15. *Hannity and Colmes,* Fox News Channel, October 18, 2005.

16. *RLS,* May 12, 2005, http://mediamatters.org/research/200506080002.

17. *Glenn Beck Program,* Fox News Channel, May 21, 2009, http://www.rushlimbaugh.com/home/daily/site_052109/content/01125116.guest.html.

18. *RLS,* March 27, 2009, http://www.rushlimbaugh.com/home/daily/site_032709/content/01125107.guest.html.

19. *RLS,* June 7, 2005.

20. *RLS,* June 21, 2005, quoted by MMA, http://mediamatters.org/research/200506230004.

21. *RLS,* January 7, 2008, quoted by MMA, http://mediamatters.org/research/200801080008.

22. *Today* show, NBC, October 11, 2000, http://mediamatters.org/mobile/research/200712070003.

23. *RLS,* February 14, 2008, quoted by MMA, http://mediamatters.org/research/200802150004.

24. *RLS,* August 26, 2009, http://www.rushlimbaugh.com/home/daily/site_082609/content/01125110.guest.html; *Today* show, NBC, October 13, 2009, http://www.rushlimbaugh.com/home/daily/site_101209/content/01125122.guest.html.

25. *RLS*, January 5, 2007, http://www.rushlimbaugh.com/home/daily/site_010507/content/america_s_anchorman.guest.html.

26. Naftali Bendavid, *The Thumpin': How Rahm Emanuel and the Democrats Learned to Be Ruthless and Ended the Republican Revolution* (New York: Doubleday, 2007) 206–207.

27. *RLS*, January 5, 2007, http://www.rushlimbaugh.com/home/daily/site_010507/content/america_s_anchorman.guest.html.

28. Ibid.

29. Ibid.

30. *RLS*, May 11, 2009, http://www.rushlimbaugh.com/home/daily/site_051109/content/01125108.guest.html.

31. *RLS*, September 17, 2009, http://www.rushlimbaugh.com/home/daily/site_091709/content/01125115.guest.html; 3/27/09.

32. *RLS*, March 4, 2010, http://www.rushlimbaugh.com/home/daily/site_030410/content/01125107.guest.html.

33. *RLS*, May 22, 2009.

34. Laurie Kellman, "Rush Rallies Freshmen to Fight On," *Washington Times,* December 11, 1994.

35. *RLS*, May 8, 2007, quoted by MMA, http://mediamatters.org/research/200706130010.

36. *RLS*, June 4, 2007, quoted by MMA, http://mediamatters.org/research/200706130010.

37. *RLS*, June 29, 2009, http://www.rushlimbaugh.com/home/daily/site_062909/content/01125108.guest.html.

38. *RLS*, June 30, 2009, http://www.rushlimbaugh.com/home/daily/site_063009/content/01125107.guest.html.

39. *RLS*, April 2, 2009.

40. *RLS*, April 30, 2009.

41. *RLS*, April 21, 2009.

42. Nigel Farndale, "The Man Who's Always Right," *Sunday Telegraph* (London), November 2, 2008.

43. *RLS*, August 29, 2008, http://www.rushlimbaugh.com/home/daily/site_082908/content/01125106.guest.html.

44. *RLS*, September 2, 2008, http://www.rushlimbaugh.com/home/daily/site_090208/content/01125106.guest.html.

45. *RLS*, February 28, 2008, http://www.rushlimbaugh.com/home/daily/site_022808/content/01125113.guest.html.

46. Colford, *The Rush Limbaugh Story,* 70.

47. *RLS,* September 18, 2009, http://www.rushlimbaugh.com/home/daily/site_091809/content/01125107.guest.html.

48. *RLS,* December 2, 2006.

49. Limbaugh, *The Way Things Ought to Be,* 53.

50. *RLS,* March 24, 2010, http://www.rushlimbaugh.com/home/daily/site_032410/content/01125115.guest.

51. "Rush Limbaugh: Playboy Interview," *Playboy,* December 1993, http://www.playboy.com/articles/rush-limbaugh-interview/index.html.

52. FAIR, "The Way Things Aren't," Extra! July/August 1994.

53. *RLS,* April 26, 2004.

54. *RLS,* January 10, 2006.

55. Colford, *The Rush Limbaugh Story,* 133.

56. Maureen Dowd, "At Dinner With: Rush Limbaugh; A Shy, Sensitive Guy Trying to Get By in Lib City," *New York Times,* March 24, 1993.

57. Ibid.

58. Rush Limbaugh Interview With Barbara Walters, *20/20,* ABC, August 16, 1994.

59. Limbaugh, *The Way Things Ought to Be,* 145.

60. Gabriel Winant, "Rush Limbaugh's Race to the Bottom," Salon.com, May 21, 2009, http://www.salon.com/news/feature/2009/05/21/limbaugh_obsession.

61. *RLS,* January 13, 2006, quoted by MMA, http://mediamatters.org/research/200601190007.

62. Rush Limbaugh TV show, February 23, 1994; FAIR, *The Way Things Aren't,* 56.

63. *RLS,* April 8, 2010, http://www.rushlimbaugh.com/home/daily/site_040810/content/01125111.guest.html.

64. *RLS,* June 16, 2009, http://www.rushlimbaugh.com/home/daily/site_061609/content/01125107.guest.html.

65. *RLS,* September 2, 2008, http://www.rushlimbaugh.com/home/daily/site_090208/content/01125106.guest.html.

66. *RLS,* June 12, 2009, http://www.rushlimbaugh.com/home/daily/site_061209/content/01125112.guest.html.

67. CNN.com, "Chelsea Clinton's Boyfriend Is a White House Intern," September 8, 2000, http://archives.cnn.com/2000/fyi/real.life/09/07/chelsea.boyfriend.

68. Rush Limbaugh TV show, November 6, 1992.

69. Ryan Larsen, "Franken's Rush/Chelsea Lie," Lying Liar, August 30, 2007, http://lyingliar.com/?p=17; a slightly different version told by Molly Ivins and widely

repeated claims that Limbaugh put up a picture of the Clintons' cat, Socks, and then asked: "Did you know there's a White House dog?" This appears to be inaccurate; there was no discussion in any transcripts of Socks the cat and the dog. See Molly Ivins, "Lyin' Bully," *Mother Jones,* May 1995, http://www.motherjones.com/politics/1995/05/lyin-bully.

70. Rush Limbaugh TV show, November 6, 1992.

71. Peter Johnson, "Rush Limbaugh's Right of way," *USA Today,* October 28, 1992.

72. Colford, *The Rush Limbaugh Story,* 103.

73. *RLS,* February 25, 2010, http://www.rushlimbaugh.com/home/daily/site_022510/content/01125106.guest.html.

74. *RLS,* September 2, 2008, http://www.rushlimbaugh.com/home/daily/site_090208/content/01125106.guest.html.

75. *RLS,* November 11, 2009, http://www.rushlimbaugh.com/home/daily/site_111109/content/01125107.guest.html.

76. "Chelsea Clinton Speaks about Sept. 11 Terror Attacks," *St. Petersburg Times,* November 11, 2001, http://www.sptimes.com/News/111101/Worldandnation/Chelsea_Clinton_speak.shtml.

77. *RLS,* March 26, 2008, http://www.rushlimbaugh.com/home/daily/site_032608/content/01125114.guest.html.

78. Limbaugh, *See, I Told You So,* 232.

79. Rush Limbaugh TV show, February 2, 1994; FAIR, *The Way Things Aren't,* 52.

80. FAIR, *The Way Things Aren't,* 32.

81. "Jargon of the Rush Limbaugh Show," Wikipedia, http://en.wikipedia.org/wiki/Jargon_of_The_Rush_Limbaugh_Show.

82. FAIR, *The Way Things Aren't,* 56.

83. *RLS,* April 15, 2004.

84. "Limbaugh Holds Onto His Niche—Conservative Men," Pew Research Center for the People & the Press, February 3, 2009, http://pewresearch.org/pubs/1102/limbaugh-audience-conservative-men.

85. Limbaugh, *See, I Told You So,* 224.

86. Rush Limbaugh TV show, February 23, 1994; FAIR, *The Way Things Aren't,* 57.

87. *RLS,* December 10, 2007, quoted by MMA, http://mediamatters.org/research/200712120007.

88. *RLS,* March 13, 2006, quoted by MMA, http://mediamatters.org/research/200603140014.

89. *RLS,* February 1, 2006, quoted by MMA, http://mediamatters.org/research/200602020007.

90. Limbaugh, *The Way Things Ought to Be,* 185

91. Limbaugh, *The Way Things Ought to Be,* 301.

92. *RLS,* May 12, 2005, quoted by MMA, http://mediamatters.org/research/200506080002.

93. "Rush Limbaugh: Playboy Interview."

94. Rush Limbaugh, Interview With Barbara Walters, *20/20,* ABC, August 16, 1994.

95. Limbaugh, *See, I Told You So,* 224.

96. Colford, *The Rush Limbaugh Story,* 155.

97. Ibid.

98. *RLS,* April 27, 1995, quoted by Mother Jones, July/August 1995, 6.

99. *RLS,* May 27, 2004, quoted by MMA, http://mediamatters.org/research/200506240002.

100. *RLS,* April 26, 2004, quoted by MMA, http://mediamatters.org/research/200506240002.

101. Limbaugh, *The Way Things Ought to Be,* 56.

102. Ibid, 204.

103. Limbaugh, *The Way Things Ought to Be,* 204.

104. *RLS,* May 21, 2007, quoted by MMA, http://mediamatters.org/research/200705230007.

105. Debra Dickerson, "Michelle Obama's Sacrifice," Salon.com, May 21, 2007, http://www.salon.com/opinion/feature/2007/05/21/michelle_obama.

106. *RLS,* April 5, 2010, http://www.rushlimbaugh.com/home/daily/site_040510/content/01125104.guest.html.

107. *RLS,* April 7, 2009, http://www.rushlimbaugh.com/home/daily/site_040709/content/01125112.guest.html.

108. Colford, *The Rush Limbaugh Story,* 101.

109. *RLS,* February 14, 2006, quoted by MMA, http://mediamatters.org/research/200602160006.

110. *RLS,* July 13, 2009, http://www.rushlimbaugh.com/home/daily/site_071309/content/01125107.guest.html.

111. Colford, *The Rush Limbaugh Story,* 173.

112. Limbaugh, *The Way Things Ought to Be,* 194.

113. Ibid, 53.

114. *RLS,* July 13, 2009, http://www.rushlimbaugh.com/home/daily/site_071309/
content/01125107.guest.html.

115. *RLS,* August 18, 2009, http://www.rushlimbaugh.com/home/daily/site_081909/
content/01125113.guest.html.

116. FAIR, *The Way Things Aren't: Rush Limbaugh's Reign of Error,* 32–33.

117. Limbaugh, *See, I Told You So,* 217.

118. David Remnick, "Day of the Dittohead," *Washington Post,* February 20,
1994.

119. *RLS,* February 23, 1995.

120. Lewis Grossberger, "The Rush Hours," *The New York Times Magazine,*
December 16, 1990, http://www.nytimes.com/1990/12/16/magazine/the-rush-
hours.html.

121. "Rush Limbaugh: Playboy Interview."

122. Colford, *The Rush Limbaugh Story,* 121.

123. Brock, *Blinded by the Right,* 275.

124. Limbaugh, *The Way Things Ought to Be,* 131.

125. Ibid.

126. Gabriel Winant, "Rush Limbaugh's Race to the Bottom," Salon.com, May 21,
2009, http://www.salon.com/news/feature/2009/05/21/limbaugh_obsession/
index.html?source=rss&aim=/news/feature.

127. *RLS,* March 12, 2009, quoted by MMA, http://mediamatters.org/mmtv/
200903120015.

128. *RLS,* November 6, 2008, http://www.rushlimbaugh.com/home/daily/site_
110608/content/01125110.guest.html.

129. Winant, "Rush Limbaugh's Race to the Bottom."

130. Brock, *Blinded by the Right,* 273.

131. *RLS,* April 15, 2004, quoted by MMA, http://mediamatters.org/mmtv/
200508260005.

132. *RLS,* February 14, 2008, quoted by MMA, http://mediamatters.org/research/
200802150004.

133. *RLS,* December 10, 2007, http://www.rushlimbaugh.com/home/daily/site_
121007/content/01125108.guest.html.

134. Rush Limbaugh, Conservative Political Action Conference Speech, Washington, DC, February 28, 2009, http://www.rushlimbaugh.com/home/daily/site_
030209/content/01125106.guest.html.

135. *RLS,* November 17, 2009, http://www.rushlimbaugh.com/home/daily/site_111709/content/01125109.guest.html.

136. *RLS,* March 4, 2009, http://www.rushlimbaugh.com/home/daily/site_030409/content/01125106.guest.html.

137. *RLS,* July 16, 2004, quoted by MMA, http://mediamatters.org/research/200407190005.

138. *RLS,* March 16, 2004.

139. *RLS,* March 26, 2004.

140. *RLS,* July 17, 2007, quoted by MMA, http://mediamatters.org/research/200707190001.

141. Joan Walsh, "The Salon Interview: Elizabeth Edwards," Salon.com, July 17, 2007, http://www.salon.com/news/feature/2007/07/17/elizabeth_edwards.

142. *RLS,* March 8, 2007, http://www.rushlimbaugh.com/home/daily/site_030907/content/john_edwards_touted_as_first_female_president.guest.html.

143. *RLS,* April 5, 2010, http://www.rushlimbaugh.com/home/daily/site_040510/content/01125115.guest.html.

144. *RLS,* August 12, 2008, http://www.rushlimbaugh.com/home/daily/site_081208/content/01125114.guest.html.

145. *RLS,* February 21, 2006, quoted by MMA, http://mediamatters.org/clips/200602230001.

146. *RLS,* October 6, 2009, http://www.rushlimbaugh.com/home/daily/site_100609/content/01125106.guest.html.

147. *RLS,* October 5, 2009, http://www.rushlimbaugh.com/home/daily/site_100509/content/01125106.guest.html.

148. *RLS,* July 15, 2009, http://www.rushlimbaugh.com/home/daily/site_071509/content/01125106.guest.html.

149. *RLS,* February 21, 2006, quoted by MMA, http://mediamatters.org/clips/200602230001.

150. *RLS,* August 25, 2009, quoted by MMA, http://mediamatters.org/mmtv/200908250038.

151. *RLS,* August 26, 2009, http://www.rushlimbaugh.com/home/daily/site_082609/content/01125104.guest.html.

152. *RLS,* September 2, 2004, quoted by MMA, http://mediamatters.org/research/200409030001.

153. Brock, *Blinded by the Right,* 275.

154. Kurt Andersen, "Radio: Big Mouths," *Time* magazine, November 1, 1993, http://www.time.com/time/magazine/article/0,9171,979470-7,00.html.

155. *RLS,* October 8, 2009, http://www.rushlimbaugh.com/home/daily/site_100809/content/01125108.guest.html.

156. *RLS,* October 2, 2006.

157. *RLS,* March 18, 2009.

158. *RLS,* August 19, 2009, http://www.rushlimbaugh.com/home/daily/site_081909/content/01125106.guest.html.

159. *RLS,* August 20, 2009, http://www.rushlimbaugh.com/home/daily/site_082009/content/01125104.guest.html.

160. *RLS,* November 8, 2005, quoted by MMA, http://mediamatters.org/research/200511100009.

161. *RLS,* May 12, 2004, http://cloudfront.mediamatters.org/static/pdf/limbaugh-20040512.pdf.

162. Limbaugh, *The Way Things Ought to Be,* 193.

163. *RLS,* December 11, 2009, http://www.rushlimbaugh.com/home/daily/site_121109/content/01125112.guest.html.

164. *RLS,* December 9, 2009, http://www.rushlimbaugh.com/home/daily/site_120909/content/01125114.guest.html.

165. *RLS,* November 5, 2004, quoted by MMA, http://mediamatters.org/research/200411090003.

166. *RLS,* November 5, 2004, quoted by MMA, http://mediamatters.org/research/200411090003.

167. Colford, *The Rush Limbaugh Story,* 121.

CHAPTER 3: BASHING OBAMA: WHY LIMBAUGH HATES THE PRESIDENT

1. *RLS,* October 7, 2009, http://www.rushlimbaugh.com/home/daily/site_100709/content/01125106.guest.html.

2. Amanda Carpenter, "Hot Button," *Washington Times,* April 16, 2009, http://www.washingtontimes.com/news/2009/apr/16/hot-button-4345751.

3. *RLS,* December 14, 2006, http://www.rushlimbaugh.com/home/daily/site_121406/content/truth_detector.guest.html.

4. "Rush Interview," Human Events Online, July 28, 2008, http://www.humanevents.com/article.php?id=27717.

5. *RLS,* April 20, 2007, http://www.rushlimbaugh.com/home/daily/site_042007/content/01125106.guest.html.

6. Rush Limbaugh, interview by Laura Ingraham, *O'Reilly Factor,* Fox News Channel, February 29, 2008, http://www.rushlimbaugh.com/home/daily/site_030308/content/01125106.guest.html.

7. David Plouffe, *The Audacity to Win: The Inside Story and Lessons of Barack Obama's Historic Victory* (Viking: New York, 2009).

8. John K. Wilson, "The Limbaugh Effect (and Racism) in NC and Indiana," *DailyKos,* May 6, 2008, http://www.dailykos.com/story/2008/5/6/510324/-The-Limbaugh-Effect-%28and-Racism%29-in-NC-and-Indiana.

9. John K. Wilson, "Racist Democrats, Not Republicans, Created Clinton Victory in Pennsylvania," *DailyKos,* April 22, 2008, http://www.dailykos.com/story/2008/4/22/501227/-Racist-Democrats,-Not-Republicans,-Created-Clinton-Victory-in-Pennsylvania.

10. John K. Wilson, "The Limbaugh Effect in Mississippi, Texas, and Ohio," *DailyKos,* March 12, 2008, http://www.dailykos.com/story/2008/3/12/34934/1285/66/474867.

11. *RLS,* February 13, 2008, http://www.rushlimbaugh.com/home/daily/site_021308/content/01125109.guest.html.

12. *RLS,* April 23, 2008, http://www.rushlimbaugh.com/home/daily/site_042308/content/01125112.guest.html.

13. Joey Bunch, "Limbaugh 'Dreams' of—Doesn't Advocate—Denver Riot," *Denver Post,* April 24, 2008, http://www.denverpost.com/breakingnews/ci_9043850.

14. *RLS,* March 27, 2008, http://www.rushlimbaugh.com/home/daily/site_032708/content/01125113.guest.html.

15. Nigel Farndale, "The Man Who's Always Right," *Sunday Telegraph* (London), November 2, 2008, http://www.telegraph.co.uk/news/worldnews/northamerica/usa/barackobama/4343753/Rush-Limbaugh-the-Right-wing-talk-show-host-Barack-Obama-has-told-Republicans-to-ignore.html.

16. *RLS,* January 15, 2008, http://www.rushlimbaugh.com/home/daily/site_011508/content/01125107.guest.html.

17. *RLS,* March 25, 2008, http://www.rushlimbaugh.com/home/daily/site_032508/content/01125110.guest.html.

18. Justin Bank, "Specter's Statistic on the Switch," Fact Check, April 29, 2009, http://www.factcheck.org/2009/04/specters-statistic-on-the-switch.

19. *RLS,* April 1, 2009, http://www.rushlimbaugh.com/home/daily/site_040109/content/01125113.guest.html.

20. *RLS,* May 18, 2008, http://www.rushlimbaugh.com/home/daily/site_051809/content/01125106.guest.html.

21. *RLS,* February 14, 2008, quoted by MMA, http://mediamatters.org/research/ 200802210011.

22. *RLS,* October 2, 2008, http://www.rushlimbaugh.com/home/daily/site_100208/ content/01125109.guest.html.

23. *RLS,* October 6, 2008, quoted by MMA, http://mediamatters.org/research/ 200810060020.

24. *RLS,* May 14, 2009, http://www.rushlimbaugh.com/home/daily/site_100208/ content/01125109.guest.html.

25. *RLS,* May 21, 2009, http://www.rushlimbaugh.com/home/daily/site_052109/ content/01125110.guest.html.

26. *RLS,* December 11, 2008, http://www.rushlimbaugh.com/home/daily/site_121108/ content/01125111.guest.html.

27. *RLS,* October 10, 2008, http://www.rushlimbaugh.com/home/daily/site_101008/ content/01125107.guest.html.

28. *RLS,* April 2, 2010, http://www.rushlimbaugh.com/home/daily/site_040210/ content/01125106.guest.html.

29. *RLS,* June 2, 2009, quoted by MMA, http://mediamatters.org/research/ 200909030032.

30. James Rainey, "A Rush to Judgment . . . and Proud of It," *Los Angeles Times,* January 21, 2009.

31. *RLS,* September 30, 2009, http://www.rushlimbaugh.com/home/daily/site_ 093009/content/01125111.guest.html.

32. *RLS,* January 29, 2010, http://www.rushlimbaugh.com/home/daily/site_ 012910/content/01125108.guest.html.

33. Richard Roeper, "Obama's Rep for Speaking Skills Dealt Setback," *Chicago Sun-Times,* March 26, 2009, http://www.suntimes.com/news/roeper/1496820, CST-NWS-roep26.article.

34. Michelle Malkin, "Fun with TOTUS (Teleprompter of the United States)," March 23, 2009, http://michellemalkin.com/2009/03/23/fun-with-totus-tele prompter-of-the-united-states/.

35. *RLS,* March 20, 2009, http://www.rushlimbaugh.com/home/daily/site_032009/ content/01125106.guest.html.

36. *RLS,* August 13, 2009, http://www.rushlimbaugh.com/home/daily/site_081309/ content/01125109.guest.html.

37. "All the President's Pressers," Journalism.org, October 16, 2006, http://www .journalism.org/node/2409.

38. Mortimer Zuckerman, "Obama's Big Swoon," *US News & World Report,* February 2010, 84.

39. *RLS*, February 12, 2008, quoted by MMA, http://mediamatters.org/research/
    200802120012.

40. *RLS*, March 18, 2009, http://www.rushlimbaugh.com/home/daily/site_031809/
    content/01125107.guest.html.

41. "Conservative Media Run with Dubious SkyNews Claim of Obama 'Tele-
    prompt Blunder,'" MMA, March 25, 2009, http://mediamatters.org/research/
    200903250039.

42. Rush Limbaugh, Conservative Political Action Conference Speech, Washington,
    DC, February 28, 2009, http://www.rushlimbaugh.com/home/daily/site_030209/
    content/01125106.guest.html.

43. *RLS*, January 16, 2009, http://www.rushlimbaugh.com/home/daily/site_011609/
    content/01125113.guest.html.

44. *RLS*, February 13, 2009, http://www.rushlimbaugh.com/home/daily/site_021309/
    content/01125114.guest.html.

45. *RLS*, March 5, 2009, http://www.msnbc.msn.com/id/29530231/.

46. Manu Raju, "Trapped Between Rush and Hard Place," *Politico*, March 5, 2009,
    http://www.politico.com/news/stories/0309/19641.html.

47. *RLS*, February 13, 2009, http://www.rushlimbaugh.com/home/daily/site_
    021309/content/01125114.guest.html.

48. Ibid.

49. *RLS*, February 13, 2009, http://www.rushlimbaugh.com/home/daily/site_021309/
    content/01125114.guest.html.

50. *RLS*, October 20, 2009, http://www.rushlimbaugh.com/home/daily/site_102009/
    content/01125113.guest.html.

51. *RLS*, June 24, 2009, http://www.rushlimbaugh.com/home/daily/site_062409/
    content/01125116.guest.html.

52. Dan Gilgoff, "Exclusive: Pat Robertson Says Obama 'Showing Partisanship,'
    Denounces Rush Limbaugh's 'I Hope He Fails' Remark," God & Country blog,
    US News & World Report, February 17, 2009, http://www.usnews.com/blogs/
    god-and-country/2009/2/17/exclusive-pat-robertson-says-obama-showing-
    partisanship-denounces-rush-limbaughs-i-hope-he-fails-remark.html.

53. *RLS*, May 28, 2009, http://www.rushlimbaugh.com/home/daily/site_052809/
    content/01125107.guest.html.

54. *Today* show, NBC, October 12, 2009, http://www.rushlimbaugh.com/home/
    daily/site_101209/content/01125106.guest.html.

55. David Frum, "Why Rush Is Wrong," *Newsweek,* March 16, 2009, http://www
    .newsweek.com/id/188279.

56. Rush Limbaugh, *See, I Told You So* (New York: Pocket Books, 1993), 344.

57. Johanna Neuman, "Obama and Limbaugh, the Last Laugh," *Los Angeles Times* blog, January 26, 2009, http://latimesblogs.latimes.com/washington/2009/01/obama-and-limba.html.

58. Jonathan Martin, "Rush Job: Inside Dems' Limbaugh Plan," Politico.com, March 4, 2009.

59. Sean Lengell, "Emanuel: GOP relies on Limbaugh," *Washington Times,* March 2, 2009, http://www.washingtontimes.com/news/2009/mar/02/emanuel-says-gop-relies-on-limbaugh.

60. "Rush Interviewed by Sean Hannity, Part Two," Fox News Channel, Recorded: June 3, 2009, http://www.rushlimbaugh.com/home/daily/site_060509/content/01125106.guest.html.

61. *Countdown with Keith Olbermann,* MSNBC, March 4, 2009.

62. "NY Post Retracts Its Smear against Michelle Obama," *DailyKos,* October 21, 2008, http://www.dailykos.com/story/2008/10/21/637523/-NY-Post-retracts-its-smear-against-Michelle-Obama; RLS, October 17, 2008, http://www.rushlimbaugh.com/home/daily/site_101708/content/01125114.guest.html.

63. *RLS,* October 30, 2008, http://www.rushlimbaugh.com/home/daily/site_103008/content/01125107.guest.html.

64. *RLS,* June 15, 2008, http://transcripts.cnn.com/TRANSCRIPTS/0806/15/rs.01.html.

65. *RLS,* April 16, 2009; May 14, 2009; May 21, 2009.

66. *RLS,* August 20, 2009, http://www.rushlimbaugh.com/home/daily/site_082009/content/01125109.guest.html.

67. *RLS,* October 1, 2009, http://www.rushlimbaugh.com/home/daily/site_100109/content/01125106.guest.html.

68. Michelle Obama, "Remarks By the First Lady at Mayor Daley's Welcome Reception," Copenhagen, Denmark, September 30, 2009, www.whitehouse.gov/the_press_office/Remarks-by-the-first-Lady-at-Mayor-Daleys-welcome-reception-in-Copenhagen-Denmark.

69. *RLS,* April 21, 2009, http://www.rushlimbaugh.com/home/daily/site_042109/content/01125107.guest.html.

70. *RLS,* May 4, 2009.

71. Rush Limbaugh, Conservative Political Action Conference Speech, Washington, DC, February 28, 2009, http://www.rushlimbaugh.com/home/daily/site_030209/content/01125106.guest.html.

72. John K. Wilson, "Another Phony 'Scandal' About Obama," ObamaPolitics.com, January 19, 2008, http://obamapolitics.com/node/45.

73. *RLS,* October 23, 2009, http://www.rushlimbaugh.com/home/daily/site_102309/content/01125107.guest.html.

74. Matthew Avitabile, "Obama College Thesis: 'Constitution Is Inherently Flawed,'" Jumping In Pools, August 25, 2009, http://jumpinginpools.blogspot.com/2009/08/obama-college-thesis-constitution-is.html.

75. Kyle Drennen, "Fox News Misreported Robert Gibbs Press Gaggle Comments," NewsBusters, November 4, 2009, http://newsbusters.org/blogs/kyle-drennen/2009/11/04/fox-news-misreported-robert-gibbs-press-gaggle-comments.

76. *RLS,* November 4, 2009, http://www.rushlimbaugh.com/home/daily/site_110409/content/01125109.guest.html.

77. *RLS,* August 25, 2009, http://www.rushlimbaugh.com/home/daily/site_082509/content/01125106.guest.html.

78. *RLS,* October 2, 2008, http://www.rushlimbaugh.com/home/daily/site_100208/content/01125109.guest.html.

79. "Editorial Board with Sen. Obama," Military Times, July 7, 2008, militarytimes.com/projects/07072008_obama_interview_main; Barack Obama, "American Legion Conference Remarks," Springfield, Illinois, obamaspeeches.com/025-American-Legion-Conference-Obama-speech.htm; "NRO's Pollowitz falsely claimed Palin visited troops in Kuwait 'a year before' Obama 'felt the need to go,'" MMA, August 30, 2008, http://mediamatters.org/research/200808300007.

80. http://obama.3cdn.net/4318d63a632c966be0_pq86mvri6.pdf.

81. *RLS,* October 2, 2008, quoted by MMA, http://mediamatters.org/research/200810060020.

82. *RLS,* July 2, 2008, http://www.rushlimbaugh.com/home/daily/site_070208/content/01125106.guest.html.

83. "Obama Responds to Attacks on His Patriotism," CNN.com, June 30, 2008, http://edition.cnn.com/2008/POLITICS/06/30/campaign.wrap/?iref=mpstoryview.

84. *RLS,* July 2, 2008, quoted by MMA, http://mediamatters.org/research/200807030005.

85. Barack Obama, May 12, 2008, Charleston, West Virginia, http://www.barackobama.com/2008/05/12/in_charleston_obama_vows_to_ke.php.

86. *RLS,* August 25, 2009, http://www.rushlimbaugh.com/home/daily/site_082509/content/01125111.guest.html.

87. *RLS,* July 21, 2008, quoted by MMA, http://mediamatters.org/research/200807220007.

88. *RLS*, July 28, 2004, quoted by MMA, http://mediamatters.org/research/200407300001.

89. *RLS*, March 26, 2009, http://rushlimbaugh.com/home/daily/site_032609/content/01125111.guest.html.

90. *RLS*, June 4, 2009, http://www.rushlimbaugh.com/home/daily/site_060409/content/01125106.guest.html.

91. *RLS*, June 2, 2009, http://www.rushlimbaugh.com/home/daily/site_060209/content/01125113.guest.html.

92. *RLS*, August 25, 2009, http://www.rushlimbaugh.com/home/daily/site_082509/content/01125106.guest.html.

93. *RLS*, April 5, 2010, http://www.rushlimbaugh.com/home/daily/site_040510/content/01125106.guest.html.

94. *RLS*, September 25, 2009, http://www.rushlimbaugh.com/home/daily/site_092509/content/01125107.guest.html.

95. *RLS*, August 6, 2009, http://www.rushlimbaugh.com/home/daily/site_080609/content/01125106.guest.html.

96. *RLS*, August 13, 2009, http://www.rushlimbaugh.com/home/daily/site_081309/content/01125110.guest.html.

97. *RLS*, August 17, 2009, http://www.rushlimbaugh.com/home/daily/site_081709/content/01125108.guest.html.

98. *RLS*, August 6, 2009, http://www.rushlimbaugh.com/home/daily/site_080609/content/01125106.guest.html.

99. Ibid.

100. Ibid; RLS, August 6, 2009, http://www.rushlimbaugh.com/home/daily/site_080609/content/01125109.guest.html.

101. *RLS*, August 19, 2009, http://www.rushlimbaugh.com/home/daily/site_081909/content/01125109.guest.html.

102. Ibid.

103. David Weigel, "Anti-Defamation League Condemns Limbaugh: 'Deeply Offensive,'" *Washington Independent,* August 7, 2009, http://washingtonindependent.com/54299/anti-defamation-league-condemns-limbaugh-deeply-offensive.

104. Glenn Greenwald, "Reactions to Rush Limbaugh's Obama/Hitler comparison," Salon.com, August 7, 2009, http://www.salon.com/opinion/greenwald/2009/08/07/limbaugh/index.html?source=rss&aim=/opinion/greenwald.

105. Jake Tapper, "Jewish Groups Assail Nazi Comparisons Made By Conservatives in Health Care Debate," ABCNews.com, August 7, 2009, http://blogs.abcnews.com/politicalpunch/2009/08/jewish-groups-assail-nazi-comparisons-made-by-conservatives-in-health-care-debate.html.

106. *Meet the Press*, NBC, August 9, 2009, quoted by MMA, http://mediamatters
     .org/mmtv/200908090008?lid=1056911&rid=33004982.

107. *RLS*, August 7, 2009, http://www.rushlimbaugh.com/home/daily/site_080709/
     content/01125107.guest.html.

108. *RLS*, August 10, 2009, http://www.rushlimbaugh.com/home/daily/site_081009/
     content/01125106.guest.html.

109. "AstroTurf Chairman Is Offended Pelosi Is Using His Product to Insult Health
     Care Protestors," FoxNews.com, August 7, 2009, www.foxnews.com/story/0,
     2933,537984,00.html.

110. *RLS*, June 26, 2009, http://www.rushlimbaugh.com/home/daily/site_062609/
     content/01125112.guest.html; RLS, February 15, 2010, http://www.rush
     limbaugh.com/home/daily/site_021510/content/01125109.guest.html.

111. "No Black Cars Allow in America," *The Stormtrooper*, April 1, 2009, http://
     www.nsm88.org/stormtrooper/ST%2029.pdf, 7.

112. *RLS*, March 30, 2009, http://www.rushlimbaugh.com/home/daily/site_033009/
     content/01125107.guest.html.

113. *RLS*, July 1, 2009, http://www.rushlimbaugh.com/home/daily/site_070109/
     content/01125111.guest.html.

114. *RLS*, February 15, 2010, http://www.rushlimbaugh.com/home/daily/site_021510/
     content/01125111.guest.html.

115. *RLS*, September 18, 2009, http://www.rushlimbaugh.com/home/daily/site_
     091808/content/01125114.guest.html.

116. *RLS*, August 10, 2009, http://www.rushlimbaugh.com/home/daily/site_081009/
     content/01125106.guest.html.

117. *RLS*, August 7, 2009, http://www.rushlimbaugh.com/home/daily/site_080709/
     content/01125106.guest.html.

118. *RLS*, March 12, 2009, quoted by MMA, http://mediamatters.org/countyfair/
     200903120010.

119. *RLS*, May 6, 2009.

120. *RLS*, August 6, 2009, http://www.rushlimbaugh.com/home/daily/site_080609/
     content/01125106.guest.html.

121. *RLS*, June 10, 2008, http://www.rushlimbaugh.com/home/daily/site_061008/
     content/01125104.guest.html.

122. *RLS*, June 18, 2009, http://www.rushlimbaugh.com/home/daily/site_061809/
     content/01125106.guest.html.

123. *RLS*, July 15, 2009, http://www.rushlimbaugh.com/home/daily/site_071509/
     content/01125112.guest.html.

124. *RLS,* September 29, 2009, http://www.rushlimbaugh.com/home/daily/site_092909/content/01125104.guest.html.

125. *RLS,* April 2, 2010, http://www.rushlimbaugh.com/home/daily/site_040210/content/01125110.guest.html.

126. See, for example, *RLS,* February 11, 2010, http://www.rushlimbaugh.com/home/daily/site_021110/content/01125116.guest.html; *RLS,* July 22, 2009, http://www.rushlimbaugh.com/home/daily/site_072209/content/01125104.guest.html; *RLS,* December 5, 2008, http://www.rushlimbaugh.com/home/daily/site_120508/content/01125112.guest.html.

127. Daniel De Groot, "Dear Rush: 'Capitalism' Is a Marxist/Socialist Term Too," April 2, 2010, Open Left, http://www.openleft.com/diary/18121/dear-rush-capitalism-is-a-marxistsocialist-term-too.

128. *RLS,* April 21, 2009, http://www.rushlimbaugh.com/home/daily/site_042109/content/01125115.guest.html.

129. *RLS,* July 14, 2009, http://www.rushlimbaugh.com/home/daily/site_071409/content/01125106.guest.html.

130. *RLS,* July 3, 2009, http://www.rushlimbaugh.com/home/daily/site_070309/content/01125108.guest.html.

131. *RLS,* April 1, 2009, http://www.rushlimbaugh.com/home/daily/site_040109/content/01125110.guest.html.

132. *RLS,* March 31, 2009, http://www.rushlimbaugh.com/home/daily/site_033109/content/01125106.guest.html.

133. *RLS,* May 22, 2009, http://www.rushlimbaugh.com/home/daily/site_052209/content/01125104.guest.html.

134. *RLS,* May 21, 2009, http://www.rushlimbaugh.com/home/daily/site_052109/content/01125107.guest.html.

135. "Obama National Archives Speech," May 21, 2009, http://www.huffingtonpost.com/2009/05/21/obama-national-archives-s_n_206189.html.

136. *RLS,* May 22, 2009, http://www.rushlimbaugh.com/home/daily/site_052209/content/01125104.guest.html.

137. Rush Limbaugh, CPAC, March 3, 2009, http://acu.libsyn.com/index.php?post_id=440648.

138. *RLS,* March 26, 2009, http://www.rushlimbaugh.com/home/daily/site_061609/content/01125106.guest.html.

139. *RLS,* June 16, 2009, http://www.rushlimbaugh.com/home/daily/site_061609/content/01125106.guest.html.

140. *RLS,* September 25, 2009, http://www.rushlimbaugh.com/home/daily/site_092509/content/01125107.guest.html.

141. *RLS,* February 17, 2009, http://www.rushlimbaugh.com/home/daily/site_ 021709/content/01125108.guest.html.

142. *RLS,* July 27, 2009, http://www.rushlimbaugh.com/home/daily/site_072709/ content/01125106.guest.html.

143. Ryan Powers, "Limbaugh: I Fear Obama's Repeal of Bush-Era Secrecy Rules 'Makes It Easier' to Hold Bush to Account," *Think Progress,* January 21, 2009, http://thinkprogress.org/2009/01/21/limbaugh-foia-bush/.

144. *RLS,* July 2, 2009, http://www.rushlimbaugh.com/home/daily/site_070209/ content/01125106.guest.html.

145. http://www.huffingtonpost.com/2009/03/24/limbaugh-confuses-obama-w_n_ 178660.html.

146. *RLS,* April 30, 2009.

147. *RLS,* June 26, 2009, http://www.rushlimbaugh.com/home/daily/site_062609/ content/01125106.guest.html.

148. *RLS,* July 13, 2009.

149. *RLS,* June 26, 2009, http://www.rushlimbaugh.com/home/daily/site_062609/ content/01125107.guest.html.

150. *RLS,* March 31, 2009.

151. *RLS,* July 27, 2009, http://www.rushlimbaugh.com/home/daily/site_072709/ content/01125114.guest.html.

152. *RLS,* March 9, 2010, quoted by MMA, http://mediamatters.org/mmtv/ 201003090035?lid=1102212&rid=43354628.

153. *RLS,* August 7, 2009, http://www.rushlimbaugh.com/home/daily/site_080709/ content/01125112.guest.html.

154. *RLS,* May 6, 2009.

155. *RLS,* May 12, 2009, http://www.rushlimbaugh.com/home/daily/site_062609/ content/01125113.guest.html.

156. *RLS,* June 30, 2009, http://www.rushlimbaugh.com/home/daily/site_063009/ content/01125109.guest.html.

157. *RLS,* June 29, 2009, http://www.rushlimbaugh.com/home/daily/site_062909/ content/01125111.guest.html.

158. *RLS,* June 5, 2009.

159. *RLS,* August 4, 2009, http://www.rushlimbaugh.com/home/daily/site_080409/ content/01125114.guest.html.

160. *RLS,* June 2, 2009.

161. *RLS,* July 24, 2009, http://www.rushlimbaugh.com/home/daily/site_072409/ content/01125108.guest.html.

162. *RLS,* June 29, 2009, http://www.rushlimbaugh.com/home/daily/site_062909/content/01125111.guest.html.

163. *RLS,* July 2, 2009.

164. *RLS,* June 30, 2009, http://www.rushlimbaugh.com/home/daily/site_063009/content/01125109.guest.html.

165. *RLS,* July 3, 2009, http://www.rushlimbaugh.com/home/daily/site_070209/content/01125118.guest.html.

166. *RLS,* October 22, 2009, http://www.rushlimbaugh.com/home/daily/site_102209/content/01125110.guest.html.

167. *RLS,* April 19, 2010, http://www.rushlimbaugh.com/home/daily/site_041910/content/01125107.guest.html.

168. *RLS,* April 20, 2010, http://www.rushlimbaugh.com/home/daily/site_042010/content/01125106.guest.html.

169. Peter Hamby, "Google Backs Up DNC after GOP Claims of Goldman Conspiracy," CNN.com, April 21, 2010, http://politicalticker.blogs.cnn.com/2010/04/21/google-backs-up-dnc-after-gop-claims-of-goldman-conspiracy/?fbid=gaRrGL3tQjq.

170. *RLS,* March 25, 2010, http://www.rushlimbaugh.com/home/daily/site_032510/content/01125106.guest.html.

171. *RLS,* July 16, 2009, http://www.rushlimbaugh.com/home/daily/site_071609/content/01125115.guest.html.

172. *RLS,* August 25, 2009, http://www.rushlimbaugh.com/home/daily/site_082509/content/01125109.guest.html.

173. "Rush Interviewed by Sean Hannity, Part Two," Fox News Channel, Recorded: June 3, 2009, http://www.rushlimbaugh.com/home/daily/site_060509/content/01125106.guest.html.

174. Ibid.

CHAPTER 4: THE LIMBAUGH CONSPIRACIES: KILLER CLINTONS, TREASONOUS DEMOCRATS, AND THE BIRTHERS

1. FAIR, "Koppel Covers for Limbaugh's Rumor Mongering," Extra! July/August 1994, http://www.fair.org/index.php?page=1236.

2. Ibid.

3. Rush Limbaugh TV show, January 12, 1994.

4. *RLS,* January 27, 1994.

5. FAIR, *The Way Things Aren't: Rush Limbaugh's Reign of Error,* 99.

6. FAIR, Extra!, "Koppel Covers for Limbaugh's Rumor-Mongering," http://www.fair.org/index.php?page=1236.

7. *RLS,* April 13, 2004, quoted by MMA, http://mediamatters.org/research/200405020008#20050921.

8. *RLS,* April 15, 2004, quoted by MMA, http://mediamatters.org/research/200406280004.

9. *RLS,* July 20, 2004, quoted by MMA, http://mediamatters.org/research/200407230001#20050921.

10. *RLS,* September 19, 2005, quoted by MMA, http://mediamatters.org/research/200509210002.

11. *RLS,* September 20, 2005, quoted by MMA, http://mediamatters.org/research/200509210002.

12. *RLS,* November 13, 2007, quoted by MMA, http://mediamatters.org/research/200711140013.

13. *RLS,* July 8, 2008, http://www.rushlimbaugh.com/home/daily/site_070808/content/01125008.guest.html.

14. *RLS,* January 5, 2009, http://www.rushlimbaugh.com/home/daily/site_010509/content/01125106.guest.html.

15. *RLS,* July 16, 2009, http://www.rushlimbaugh.com/home/daily/site_071609/content/01125108.guest.html.

16. *RLS,* October 3, 2006, quoted by MMA, http://mediamatters.org/research/200610040010.

17. *RLS,* October 3, 2006, quoted by MMA, http://mediamatters.org/print/research/200610040013.

18. *RLS,* October 2, 2006, quoted by MMA, http://mediamatters.org/research/200610020013?src=newsbox-www.crooksandliars.com.

19. *RLS,* October 2, 2006, quoted by MMA, http://mediamatters.org/research/200610020013.

20. *RLS,* October 3, 2006, quoted by MMA, http://mediamatters.org/research/200610040013.

21. Anne Kornblut and Katharine Seelye, "Papers Know of Foley E-Mail But Did Not Publish Stories," *The New York Times,* October 3, 2006, http://www.nytimes.com/2006/10/03/washington/03media.html?_r=1&pagewanted=print&oref=slogin.

22. *RLS,* February 13, 2009.

23. *RLS,* November 19, 2009, http://www.rushlimbaugh.com/home/daily/site_111909/content/01125106.guest.html.

24. Frank Newport, "Response to Rush Limbaugh's Claim," Gallup.com, November 19, 2009, http://pollingmatters.gallup.com/2009/11/response-to-rush-limbaughs-claim.html.

25. *RLS,* March 24, 2010, http://www.rushlimbaugh.com/home/daily/site_032410/content/01125114.guest.html.

26. *RLS,* May 19, 2009.

27. Ibid.

28. *RLS,* February 16, 2010, http://www.rushlimbaugh.com/home/daily/site_021610/content/01125114.guest.html.

29. *RLS,* August 14, 2009, http://www.rushlimbaugh.com/home/daily/site_081409/content/01125106.guest.html.

30. *RLS,* October 7, 2009, http://www.rushlimbaugh.com/home/daily/site_100709/content/01125107.guest.html.

31. *RLS,* June 29, 2009, http://www.rushlimbaugh.com/home/daily/site_062909/content/01125106.guest.html.

32. *RLS,* June 29, 2009, http://www.rushlimbaugh.com/home/daily/site_062909/content/01125106.guest.html.

33. "American Clean Energy and Security Act of 2009," H.R. 2454, May 15, 2009, http://frwebgate.access.gpo.gov/cgi-bin/getdoc.cgi?dbname=111_cong_bills&docid=f:h2454ih.txt.pdf.

34. *RLS,* October 5, 2009, http://www.rushlimbaugh.com/home/daily/site_100509/content/01125104.guest.html.

35. *RLS,* March 26, 2009, quoted by MMA, http://mediamatters.org/limbaughwire/2009/03/26#0015.

36. *RLS,* April 8, 2009, quoted by MMA, http://mediamatters.org/limbaughwire/2009/04/08#0021.

37. Ibid.

38. *RLS,* December 1, 2009, http://www.rushlimbaugh.com/home/daily/site_120109/content/01125107.guest.html.

39. *RLS,* June 1, 2009, http://www.rushlimbaugh.com/home/daily/site_060109/content/01125106.guest.html.

40. Rush Limbaugh, Conservative Political Action Conference Speech, Washington, DC, February 28, 2009, http://www.rushlimbaugh.com/home/daily/site_030209/content/01125106.guest.html.

41. *RLS,* May 6, 2009, quoted by MMA, http://mediamatters.org/limbaughwire/
    2009/05/06.

42. *RLS,* October 2, 2009, http://www.rushlimbaugh.com/home/daily/site_100209/
    content/01125106.guest.html.

43. *RLS,* April 9, 2009, http://www.rushlimbaugh.com/home/daily/site_040909/
    content/01125108.guest.html.

44. *RLS,* November 6, 2008, http://www.rushlimbaugh.com/home/daily/site_110608/
    content/01125107.guest.html.

45. *RLS,* December 3, 2009, http://www.rushlimbaugh.com/home/daily/site_120309/
    content/01125104.guest.html.

46. *RLS,* October 20, 2009, http://www.rushlimbaugh.com/home/daily/site_102009/
    content/01125107.guest.html.

47. *RLS,* August 25, 2009, http://www.rushlimbaugh.com/home/daily/site_082509/
    content/01125109.guest.html.

48. *RLS,* October 22, 2009, http://www.rushlimbaugh.com/home/daily/site_102209/
    content/01125112.guest.html.

49. Facts on File, *Watergate and the White House,* Vol. 1, 96–97, http://web.archive
    .org/web/20030621235432/www.artsci.wustl.edu/~polisci/calvert/PolSci3103/
    watergate/enemy.htm.

50. Ibid.

51. *RLS,* July 21, 2009, http://www.rushlimbaugh.com/home/daily/site_072109/
    content/01125108.guest.html.

52. *RLS,* September 17, 2008, http://www.rushlimbaugh.com/home/daily/site_
    060109/content/01125106.guest.html.

53. *RLS,* June 25, 2009, http://www.rushlimbaugh.com/home/daily/site_062509/
    content/01125106.guest.html.

54. *RLS,* May 19, 2009.

55. *RLS,* March 10, 2009.

56. *RLS,* April 16, 2009.

57. *RLS,* April 15, 2010, http://www.rushlimbaugh.com/home/daily/site_041510/
    content/01125107.guest.html.

58. Peter Hart, "In Discussion of Mine Disaster Coverage, Only Imaginary Unions
    Allowed," FAIR blog, April 16, 2010, http://www.fair.org/blog/2010/04/16/in-
    discussion-of-mine-disaster-coverage-only-imaginary-unions-allowed.

59. *RLS,* May 5, 2009.

60. Ibid.

61. *RLS,* January 27, 2009.

62. *RLS,* November 6, 2008, http://www.rushlimbaugh.com/home/daily/site_110608/content/01125107.guest.html.

63. *RLS,* March 11, 2009, quoted by MMA, http://mediamatters.org/items/200903110021?f=s_search.

64. *RLS,* June 17, 2009, http://www.rushlimbaugh.com/home/daily/site_061709/content/01125111.guest.html.

65. "Myths and Falsehoods About the Purported Link Between Affordable Housing Initiatives and the Financial Crisis," MMA, October 10, 2008, http://media matters.org/research/200810100022?lid=1044534&rid=29936809.

66. Ibid.

67. *RLS,* October 14, 2008; John Amato, "Rush Limbaugh Says Angry Blacks Are in 30 Year Plot to Train Black Children as Militants," Crooks and Liars, October 14, 2008, http://crooksandliars.com/john-amato/rush-limbaugh-says-blacks-are-angry-and.

68. *RLS,* August 21, 2009, http://www.rushlimbaugh.com/home/daily/site_082109/content/01125112.guest.html.

69. *RLS,* October 2, 2009, http://www.rushlimbaugh.com/home/daily/site_100209/content/01125108.guest.html.

70. Tom Jensen, "ACORN," Public Policy Polling, November 19, 2009, http://publicpolicypolling.blogspot.com/2009/11/acorn.html.

71. *RLS,* November 2, 2009, http://www.rushlimbaugh.com/home/daily/site_110209/content/01125112.guest.html.

72. "Barack Obama's Birth Certificate Revealed Here," LATimes.com, June 16, 2008, http://latimesblogs.latimes.com/washington/2008/06/obama-birth.html.

73. *RLS,* October 23, 2008, http://www.rushlimbaugh.com/home/daily/site_102308/content/01125106.guest.html.

74. *RLS,* June 10, 2009, http://www.rushlimbaugh.com/home/daily/site_061009/content/01125110.guest.html.

75. *RLS,* June 10, 2009, http://www.rushlimbaugh.com/home/daily/site_061009/content/01125113.guest.html.

76. *RLS,* April 8, 2009, http://www.rushlimbaugh.com/home/daily/site_040809/content/01125107.guest.html.

77. *RLS,* June 30, 2009, http://www.rushlimbaugh.com/home/daily/site_063009/content/01125107.guest.html.

78. *RLS,* July 20, 2009, http://www.rushlimbaugh.com/home/daily/site_072009/content/01125104.guest.html.

79. *RLS,* July 24, 2009, http://www.rushlimbaugh.com/home/daily/site_072409/content/01125114.guest.html.

80. *RLS,* July 31, 2009, http://www.rushlimbaugh.com/home/daily/site_073109/content/01125104.guest.html.

81. *RLS,* July 20, 2009, http://www.rushlimbaugh.com/home/daily/site_072009/content/01125113.guest.html.

82. *RLS,* July 31, 2009, http://www.rushlimbaugh.com/home/daily/site_073109/content/01125104.guest.html.

83. *RLS,* August 20, 2009, http://www.rushlimbaugh.com/home/daily/site_082009/content/01125104.guest.html.

84. "Obama Not Faring Well in Arkansas," Public Policy Polling, August 25, 2009, http://www.publicpolicypolling.com/pdf/surveys/2009_Archives/PPP_Release_AR_825.pdf.

85. *RLS,* April 21, 2010, http://www.rushlimbaugh.com/home/daily/site_042110/content/01125104.guest.html.

86. David Weigel, "'Birther' Movement Dogs Republicans," *Washington Independent,* July 17, 2009, http://washingtonindependent.com/5w1489/birther-movement-picks-up-steam.

87. *RLS,* March 16, 2010, http://www.rushlimbaugh.com/home/daily/site_031610/content/01125111.guest.html.

88. *RLS,* April 20, 2010, http://www.rushlimbaugh.com/home/daily/site_042010/content/01125106.guest.html.

89. *RLS,* March 16, 2010, http://www.rushlimbaugh.com/home/daily/site_031610/content/01125111.guest.html.

90. *RLS,* March 16, 2010, http://www.rushlimbaugh.com/home/daily/site_031610/content/01125111.guest.html.

91. Rush Limbaugh, interview with Greta van Susteren, *On the Record with Greta Van Susteren,* Fox News Channel, July 23, 2009, http://www.rushlimbaugh.com/home/daily/site_072409/content/01125106.guest.html.

92. *RLS,* August 27, 2009, http://www.rushlimbaugh.com/home/daily/site_082709/content/01125106.guest.html.

93. *RLS,* August 14, 2009, http://www.rushlimbaugh.com/home/daily/site_081409/content/01125108.guest.html.

94. *RLS,* June 1, 2009, http://www.rushlimbaugh.com/home/daily/site_060109/content/01125109.guest.html.

95. *RLS,* April 22, 2010, http://www.rushlimbaugh.com/home/daily/site_042210/content/01125106.guest.html.

96. *RLS,* April 26, 2010, http://www.rushlimbaugh.com/home/daily/site_042610/content/01125104.guest.html.

97. Interview with Greta van Susteren, *On the Record with Greta van Susteren,* July 23, 2009.

98. Ibid.

99. *RLS,* February 8, 2010, http://www.rushlimbaugh.com/home/daily/site_020810/content/01125104.guest.html.

100. *RLS,* March 17, 2010, http://www.rushlimbaugh.com/home/daily/site_031710/content/01125104.guest.html.

101. *RLS,* July 24, 2009, http://www.rushlimbaugh.com/home/daily/site_072409/content/01125111.guest.html.

CHAPTER 5: LIMBAUGHNOMICS: THE STRANGE ECONOMIC IDEAS OF RUSH

1. *RLS,* July 13, 2009, http://www.rushlimbaugh.com/home/daily/site_071309/content/01125106.guest.html.

2. Rush Limbaugh, interview with Greta van Susteren, *On the Record with Greta van Susteren,* Fox News Channel, July 23, 2009, http://www.rushlimbaugh.com/home/daily/site_072409/content/01125106.guest.html.

3. *RLS,* June 1, 2009, http://www.rushlimbaugh.com/home/daily/site_060109/content/01125106.guest.html.

4. *RLS,* June 26, 2009, http://www.rushlimbaugh.com/home/daily/site_062609/content/01125106.guest.html.

5. Dean Baker, "Are We Better Off Because of the Stimulus?" *New Republic,* July 31, 2009, http://blogs.tnr.com/tnr/blogs/the_plank/archive/2009/07/31/are-we-better-off-because-of-the-stimulus.aspx.

6. Niall Ferguson, "A Runaway Deficit May Soon Test Obama's Luck," *Financial Times,* August 10, 2009, http://www.niallferguson.com/site/FERG/Templates/ArticleItem.aspx?pageid=211.

7. *RLS,* July 31, 2009, http://www.rushlimbaugh.com/home/daily/site_073109/content/01125107.guest.html.

8. *RLS,* July 13, 2009, http://www.rushlimbaugh.com/home/daily/site_071309/content/01125109.guest.html.

9. *RLS,* July 3, 2009, http://www.rushlimbaugh.com/home/daily/site_070209/content/01125107.guest.html.

10. *RLS,* July 15, 2009, http://www.rushlimbaugh.com/home/daily/site_071509/content/01125108.guest.html.

11. *RLS,* July 14, 2009, http://www.rushlimbaugh.com/home/daily/site_071409/content/01125109.guest.html.

12. *RLS,* April 8, 2010, http://www.rushlimbaugh.com/home/daily/site_040810/content/01125106.guest.html.

13. Michael Medved, "Why Didn't Obama Wreck the Economy When He Had the Chance?" TownHall.com, March 17, 2010, http://townhall.com/columnists/MichaelMedved/2010/03/17/why_didnt_obama_wreck_the_economy_when_he_had_the_chance?page=full&comments=true.

14. *The Beemer Report,* March 24, 2010, http://beemerreport.com/newssingle.php?id=12.

15. *RLS,* November 6, 2008, http://www.rushlimbaugh.com/home/daily/site_110608/content/01125107.guest.html.

16. *RLS,* November 11, 2008, quoted by MMA, http://mediamatters.org/research/200811120011.

17. *RLS,* January 27, 2009.

18. Rush Limbaugh, Conservative Political Action Conference Speech, Washington, DC, February 28, 2009, http://www.rushlimbaugh.com/home/daily/site_030209/content/01125106.guest.html.

19. *RLS,* February 19, 2009, http://www.rushlimbaugh.com/home/daily/site_021909/content/01125109.guest.html.

20. *RLS,* January 29, 2009, http://www.rushlimbaugh.com/home/daily/site_012609/content/01125108.guest.html.

21. *RLS,* January 21, 2009, quoted by MMA, http://mediamatters.org/research/200901220007.

22. Rush Limbaugh, "America's Paul Revere," *Limbaugh Letter,* July 2009, 3.

23. *RLS,* November 10, 2009, http://www.rushlimbaugh.com/home/daily/site_111009/content/01125110.guest.html.

24. *RLS,* August 7, 2009, http://www.rushlimbaugh.com/home/daily/site_080709/content/01125104.guest.html.

25. http://www.blogmybrain.com/stock_apps/graphical_economy/Employment%20vs.%20Unemployment/n00/00r/a.

26. *RLS,* July 3, 2009, http://www.rushlimbaugh.com/home/daily/site_070209/content/01125107.guest.html.

27. *RLS,* July 31, 2009, http://www.rushlimbaugh.com/home/daily/site_073109/content/01125106.guest.html.

28. Bureau of Economic Analysis, "Gross Domestic Product: First Quarter 2010 (Third Estimate)," June 25, 2010, http://www.bea.gov/newsreleases/national/gdp/gdpnewsrelease.htm.

29. *RLS,* July 31, 2009, http://www.rushlimbaugh.com/home/daily/site_073109/content/01125106.guest.html.

30. *RLS,* September 30, 2009, http://www.rushlimbaugh.com/home/daily/site_ 093009/content/01125104.guest.html.

31. *RLS,* October 1, 2009, http://www.rushlimbaugh.com/home/daily/site_100109/ content/01125112.guest.html.

32. Christopher Flavelle and Jeff Larson, "Stimulus: How Fast We're Spending Nearly $800 Billion," ProPublica, http://projects.propublica.org/tables/stimulus-spending-progress.

33. *RLS,* December 3, 2009, http://www.rushlimbaugh.com/home/daily/site_ 120309/content/01125104.guest.html.

34. Jeannine Aversa and Christopher Rugaber, "Unemployment Rate Falls to 10%, UK Jobs Lost in November," December 4, 2009, http://www.huffingtonpost.com/2009/12/04/unemployment-rate-falls-t_0_n_379919.html.

35. Interview with Dick Cheney, *RLS,* January 30, 2008.

36. *RLS,* January 23, 2008, http://www.rushlimbaugh.com/home/daily/site_012308/ content/01125109.guest.html.

37. Campbell Brown, "Commentary: A Challenge to Rush Limbaugh," CNN.com, January 30, 2009.

38. Rush Limbaugh, Conservative Political Action Conference Speech, Washington, DC, February 28, 2009, http://www.rushlimbaugh.com/home/daily/site_030209/ content/01125106.guest.html.

39. Bernard Sherman, "Reaganomics," May 2006, http://www.bsherman.net/rush more.html.

40. Rush Limbaugh, *The Way Things Ought to Be* (New York: Pocket Books, 1992), 71.

41. *RLS,* October 1, 2009, http://www.rushlimbaugh.com/home/daily/site_100109/ content/01125116.guest.html.

42. *RLS,* October 6, 2009, http://www.rushlimbaugh.com/home/daily/site_100609/ content/01125110.guest.html.

43. *RLS,* October 7, 2009, http://www.rushlimbaugh.com/home/daily/site_100709/ content/01125109.guest.html.

44. Tom Blumer, "Record Teen Unemployment," *News Busters,* October 5, 2009, http://newsbusters.org/blogs/tom-blumer/2009/10/05/record-teen-unemploy-ment-only-wsj-seriously-looks-minimum-wage-hikes-cau.

45. *RLS,* August 3, 2009, http://www.rushlimbaugh.com/home/daily/site_080309/ content/01125107.guest.html.

46. Office of Management and Budget, "President's Budget 2011: Historical Tables," http://www.whitehouse.gov/omb/budget/Historicals/.

47. Ibid.

48. Ibid.

49. *RLS*, August 27, 2009, http://www.rushlimbaugh.com/home/daily/site_082709/content/01125106.guest.html.

50. Rush Limbaugh, *See, I Told You So* (New York: Pocket Books, 1993) 126.

51. http://www.census.gov/hhes/www/poverty/histpov/hstpov2.xls.

52. Al Franken, *Rush Limbaugh Is a Big, Fat Idiot and Other Observations* (New York: Delacorte Press, 1996), 127–8.

53. Limbaugh, *See, I Told You So,* 333.

54. Ibid., xvii.

55. Ibid., 137.

56. Ibid., 340.

57. "Rush Limbaugh: Playboy Interview," *Playboy,* http://www.playboy.com/articles/rush-limbaugh-interview/index.html.

58. "Graphical Economy," Blog My Brain http://www.blogmybrain.com/stock_apps/graphical_economy/Employment%20vs.%20Unemployment/n00/00r/a.

59. Bureau of Labor Statistics, "Consumer Price Index," ftp://ftp.bls.gov/pub/special.requests/cpi/cpiai.txt.

60. Office of Management and Budget, "Historical Tables," Fiscal Year 2011, p. 22, www.whitehouse.gov/omb/budget/fy2011/assets/hist.pdf.

61. "Presidential Approval Ratings—Bill Clinton," Gallup Poll, http://www.gallup.com/poll/116584/Presidential-Approval-Ratings-Bill-Clinton.aspx.

62. "Rush Limbaugh: Playboy Interview," *Playboy,* December 1993, http://www.playboy.com/articles/rush-limbaugh-interview/index.html.

63. *RLS*, January 24, 2005, quoted by MMA, http://mediamatters.org/research/200501270006.

64. *RLS*, June 18, 2009, http://www.rushlimbaugh.com/home/daily/site_061809/content/01125106.guest.html.

65. *RLS,* December 22, 2009, http://www.rushlimbaugh.com/home/daily/site_122109/content/01125106.guest.html.

66. Office of Management and Budget, "Historical Tables: Budget of the US Government, Fiscal Year 2010," http://www.whitehouse.gov/omb/budget/fy2010/assets/hist.pdf; "Final Estimate for U.S. Budget Deficit: $1.4 trillion," Reuters, October 7, 2009, http://www.reuters.com/article/idUSTRE5966HC20091007.

67. Bruce Bartlett, "Why the Economy Needs Spending, Not Tax Cuts," Capital Gains and Games, October 24, 2009, http://capitalgainsandgames.com/blog/bruce-bartlett/1200/why-economy-needs-spending-not-tax-cuts.

68. *RLS*, June 8, 2009, http://www.rushlimbaugh.com/home/daily/site_060809/content/01125106.guest.html.

69. *RLS*, December 3, 2009, http://www.rushlimbaugh.com/home/daily/site_120309/content/01125106.guest.html.

70. Rush Limbaugh, "America's Paul Revere," *Limbaugh Letter,* July 2009, 3.

71. *RLS*, May 12, 2008, http://www.rushlimbaugh.com/home/daily/site_051208/content/01125106.guest.html.

72. *RLS*, May 12, 2008, quoted by MMA, http://mediamatters.org/research/200805130006; http://www.eia.doe.gov/emeu/steo/pub/fsheets/real_prices.html.

73. *RLS*, February 17, 2010, http://www.rushlimbaugh.com/home/daily/site_021710/content/01125106.guest.html.

74. Bureau of Labor Statistics, "Labor Force Statistics from the Current Population Survey," http://data.bls.gov/PDQ/servlet/SurveyOutputServlet?data_tool=latest_numbers&series_id=LNS14000000.

75. *RLS*, July 15, 2009, http://www.rushlimbaugh.com/home/daily/site_071509/content/01125111.guest.html.

76. *RLS*, July 1, 2009, http://www.rushlimbaugh.com/home/daily/site_070109/content/01125109.guest.html.

77. *RLS*, July 3, 2009, http://www.rushlimbaugh.com/home/daily/site_070309/content/01125108.guest.html.

78. *RLS*, January 15, 2009, http://www.rushlimbaugh.com/home/daily/site_011509/content/01125112.guest.html.

79. Ibid.

80. *RLS*, February 20, 2009, http://www.rushlimbaugh.com/home/daily/site_022009/content/01125107.guest.html.

81. *RLS*, April 2, 2009, http://www.rushlimbaugh.com/home/daily/site_040209/content/01125106.guest.html.

82. *RLS*, April 7, 2009 quoted by MMA, mediamatters.org/limbaughwire/2009/04/07.

83. *RLS*, May 28, 2009, http://www.rushlimbaugh.com/home/daily/site_052809/content/01125106.guest.html.

84. *RLS*, July 27, 2009, http://www.rushlimbaugh.com/home/daily/site_072709/content/01125115.guest.html.

85. "The Economy Under Past Presidents," *Philadelphia Inquirer,* http://www
    .philly.com/inquirer/online_extras/34212684.html.

86. *RLS,* February 4, 2010, http://www.rushlimbaugh.com/home/daily/site_
    020410/content/01125106.guest.html.

87. *RLS,* May 7, 2010, http://www.rushlimbaugh.com/home/daily/site_050710/
    content/01125107.guest.html.

88. *RLS,* February 5, 2010, http://www.rushlimbaugh.com/home/daily/site_020510/
    content/01125113.guest.html.

89. *RLS,* June 30, 2009, http://www.rushlimbaugh.com/home/daily/site_063009/
    content/01125106.guest.html.

90. S. Mitra Kalita, "Americans see 18% of Wealth Vanish," *The Wall Street Journal,*
    March 13, 2009, http://online.wsj.com/article/SB123687371369308675.html.

91. *RLS,* June 16, 2009, http://www.rushlimbaugh.com/home/daily/site_061609/
    content/01125113.guest.html.

92. *RLS,* June 16, 2009, http://www.rushlimbaugh.com/home/daily/site_061609/
    content/01125113.guest.html.

93. *RLS,* June 24, 2009, http://www.rushlimbaugh.com/home/daily/site_062409/
    content/01125110.guest.html.

94. *RLS,* May 29, 2009, http://www.rushlimbaugh.com/home/daily/site_052909/
    content/01125106.guest.html.

95. Rush Limbaugh, interview with Greta van Susteren, *On the Record with
    Greta van Susteren,* Fox News Channel, July 24, 2009, http://www.rush
    limbaugh.com/home/daily/site_072409/content/01125121.guest.html.

96. Ben Steverman, "Rare Optimism from Caterpillar's CEO," *Business Week,*
    July 21, 2009, http://www.businessweek.com/investing/insights/blog/archives/
    2009/07/rare_optimism_f.html.

97. *RLS,* January 8, 2009, http://www.rushlimbaugh.com/home/daily/site_010809/
    content/01125106.guest.html.

98. *RLS,* January 26, 2009, http://www.rushlimbaugh.com/home/daily/site_012609/
    content/01125108.guest.html.

99. *RLS,* November 20, 2008, http://mediamatters.org/research/200901280001.

100. Jim Jubak, "Will US Repeat Mistakes of 1937?" *MSN Money,* September 22,
    2009, http://articles.moneycentral.msn.com/Investing/JubaksJournal/will-us-
    repeat-mistakes-of-1937.aspx.

101. *RLS,* July 3, 2009, http://www.rushlimbaugh.com/home/daily/site_070209/
    content/01125107.guest.html.

102. *RLS,* July 3, 2009, http://www.rushlimbaugh.com/home/daily/site_070309/content/01125108.guest.html.

CHAPTER 6: "TRUTHINESS" ON PARADE: LIMBAUGH'S LIES, ERRORS, AND DISTORTIONS

1. Nathan Rabin, "Interview with Stephen Colbert," *Onion AV Club,* January 25, 2006, http://www.avclub.com/articles/stephen-colbert,13970/.
2. *RLS,* November 24, 2009, http://www.rushlimbaugh.com/home/daily/site_112409/content/01125108.guest.html.
3. *RLS,* November 24, 2009, http://www.rushlimbaugh.com/home/daily/site_112409/content/01125109.guest.html.
4. *RLS,* September 29, 2009, http://www.rushlimbaugh.com/home/daily/site_092909/content/01125111.guest.html.
5. *Today* show, NBC, October 12, 2009, http://www.rushlimbaugh.com/home/daily/site_101209/content/01125106.guest.html.
6. *RLS,* February 15, 2005, quoted by MMA, http://mediamatters.org/research/200502180006.
7. *RLS,* September 21, 2009, http://www.rushlimbaugh.com/home/daily/site_092109/content/01125111.guest.html.
8. Rush Limbaugh, *See, I Told You So* (New York: Pocket Books, 1993), 320–321.
9. *RLS,* March 24, 2009, http://www.rushlimbaugh.com/home/daily/site_032409/content/01125109.guest.html.
10. James Rainey, "A Rush to Judgment . . . and Proud of It," *Los Angeles Times,* January 21, 2009.
11. *RLS,* July 16, 2009, http://www.rushlimbaugh.com/home/daily/site_071609/content/01125112.guest.html.
12. Rainey, "A Rush to Judgment."
13. Nigel Farndale, "The Man Who's Always Right," *Sunday Telegraph* (London), November 2, 2008.
14. *RLS,* August 19, 2009, http://www.rushlimbaugh.com/home/daily/site_081909/content/01125106.guest.html.
15. Tommy Stevenson, "Bachus Discusses Social Security, Health Care," *Tuscaloosa News,* August 18, 2009, http://www.tuscaloosanews.com/article/20090818/NEWS/908189977/1007?Title=Bachus-Discusses-Social-Security-Health-Care.
16. Publisher description, *The Way Things Ought To Be,* 1992, http://www.amazon.com/exec/obidos/ASIN/067175145X/ref=nosim/librarythin08-20.

17. *RLS*, March 4, 2009, http://www.rushlimbaugh.com/home/daily/site_030409/ content/01125111.guest.html.

18. *RLS*, August 14, 2009, http://www.rushlimbaugh.com/home/daily/site_081409/ content/01125109.guest.html.

19. Ibid.

20. *RLS*, July 19, 2010, http://webtest1.rushlimbaugh.com/home/daily/site_071910/ content/01125100.guest.htm.

21. FAIR, "The Way Things Aren't: Rush Limbaugh Debates Reality," Extra! July/ August 1994, http://www.fair.org/index.php?page=1895.

22. "Limbaugh Responds to FAIR: Responding to FAIR's charges printed by major print media outlets," FAIR, June 28, 1994, http://www.fair.org/index.php?page= 1906.

23. FAIR, "The Way Things Aren't."

24. "Limbaugh Responds to FAIR."

25. "FAIR's Reply to Limbaugh's Non-Response," October 17, 1994, http://www .fair.org/index.php?page=18.

26. FAIR, "The Way Things Aren't."

27. Ibid.

28. "Limbaugh Responds to FAIR."

29. FAIR, "The Way Things Aren't."

30. Ibid.

31. "Limbaugh Responds to FAIR."

32. FAIR, "The Way Things Aren't."

33. Ibid.

34. "Limbaugh Responds to FAIR."

35. FAIR, "The Way Things Aren't."

36. "FAIR's Reply to Limbaugh's Non-Response."

37. FAIR, "The Way Things Aren't."

38. Ibid.

39. "Limbaugh Responds to FAIR." "FAIR's Reply to Limbaugh's Non-Response."

40. FAIR, "The Way Things Aren't."

41. Ibid.

42. "Limbaugh Responds to FAIR."

43. "FAIR's Reply to Limbaugh's Non-Response."

44. FAIR, "The Way Things Aren't."

45. Ibid.

46. *RLS,* July 5, 1994; "FAIR's Reply to Limbaugh's Non-Response."

47. "FAIR's Reply to Limbaugh's Non-Response."

48. FAIR, "The Way Things Aren't." Limbaugh, *See, I Told You So,* 304.

49. FAIR, "The Way Things Aren't."

50. "Limbaugh Responds to FAIR."

51. FAIR, "The Way Things Aren't."

52. Ibid.

53. "Limbaugh Responds to FAIR."

54. FAIR, "The Way Things Aren't."

55. Ibid.

56. "Limbaugh Responds to FAIR."

57. "FAIR's Reply to Limbaugh's Non-Response."

58. FAIR, "The Way Things Aren't."

59. Ibid.

60. "Limbaugh Responds to FAIR."

61. FAIR, "The Way Things Aren't."

62. Ibid.

63. "FAIR's Reply to Limbaugh's Non-Response."

64. Rush Limbaugh TV show, April 27, 1994; FAIR, "The Way Things Aren't."

65. "Limbaugh Responds to FAIR."

66. "FAIR's Reply to Limbaugh's Non-Response."

67. FAIR, "The Way Things Aren't."

68. "Limbaugh Responds to FAIR."

69. "FAIR's Reply to Limbaugh's Non-Response."

70. FAIR, "The Way Things Aren't."

71. Ibid.

72. "Limbaugh Responds to FAIR."

73. "FAIR's Reply to Limbaugh's Non-Response."

74. FAIR, "The Way Things Aren't."

75. "Limbaugh Responds to FAIR."

76. Ibid.

77. FAIR, "The Way Things Aren't."

78. "Limbaugh Responds to FAIR."

79. "FAIR's Reply to Limbaugh's Non-Response."

80. FAIR, "The Way Things Aren't."

81. "Limbaugh Responds to FAIR."

82. FAIR, "The Way Things Aren't."

83. Ibid.

84. "Limbaugh Responds to FAIR."

85. "FAIR's Reply to Limbaugh's Non-Response."

86. *RLS,* April 29, 1994; FAIR, *The Way Things Aren't,* 61.

87. "Limbaugh Responds to FAIR."

88. *RLS,* June 12, 2009, http://www.rushlimbaugh.com/home/daily/site_061209/content/01125106.guest.html.

89. "Limbaugh Responds to FAIR."

90. "FAIR's Reply to Limbaugh's Non-Response."

91. Ibid.

92. Ibid.

93. FAIR, *The Way Things Aren't,* 40.

94. FAIR, *The Way Things Aren't,* 39.

95. Ibid.

96. Limbaugh, *See, I Told You So,* 76; FAIR, *The Way Things Aren't,* 79.

97. Massachusetts School Law of 1647, http://www.extremeintellect.com/08EDUCATION/masslaw1647.htm.

98. Rush Limbaugh TV show, May 13, 1994.

99. *RLS,* November 11, 2009, http://www.rushlimbaugh.com/home/daily/site_111109/content/01125104.guest.html.

100. *RLS,* May 7, 2010, http://www.rushlimbaugh.com/home/daily/site_050710/content/01125104.guest.html.

101. FAIR, "Yet More Limbecile Statements," *Extra!* Update, June 1995, http://www.fair.org/index.php?page=1305.

102. *RLS,* April 5, 1995, quoted in FAIR, "Yet More Limbecile Statements," *Extra!* Update, June 1995, http://www.fair.org/index.php?page=1305.

103. Ann Coulter, *Slander: Liberal Lies About the American Right* (New York: Crown, 2002), 24–25.

104. Coulter, *Slander,* 32.

105. Steve Rendall, "Ann Slanders," Extra! November/December 2002, FAIR, http://www.fair.org/index.php?page=1124.

106. WLS-AM, March 6, 2009.

107. *RLS,* April 27, 1995, quoted in FAIR, "Yet More Limbecile Statements," Extra! Update, June 1995, http://www.fair.org/index.php?page=1305.

108. Ibid.

109. FAIR, "The Way Things Aren't."

110. Rush Limbaugh, "Introduction," Mark Levin's *Men in Black,* x.

111. Ibid., p. xi.

112. Limbaugh, *The Way Things Ought to Be,* xiv.

113. *RLS,* July 23, 2009, http://www.rushlimbaugh.com/home/daily/site_072309/content/01125106.guest.html.

114. Ibid.

115. Rush Limbaugh, Conservative Political Action Conference Speech, Washington, DC, February 28, 2009, http://www.rushlimbaugh.com/home/daily/site_030209/content/01125106.guest.html.

116. *RLS,* March 2, 2009, http://www.rushlimbaugh.com/home/daily/site_091009/content/01125110.guest.html.

117. *RLS,* October 12, 2009, http://www.rushlimbaugh.com/home/daily/site_101209/content/01125115.guest.html.

118. U.S. Constitution, http://www.archives.gov/exhibits/charters/constitution_transcript.html.

119. "Thomas Jefferson's Draft of the Declaration of Independence," http://www.vindicatingthefounders.com/library/jeffersons-draft.html.

120. *RLS,* April 15, 2010, http://www.rushlimbaugh.com/home/daily/site_041510/content/01125111.guest.html.

121. "Abolitionism," Wikipedia, http://en.wikipedia.org/wiki/Abolitionism.

122. *RLS,* October 27, 2008, http://www.rushlimbaugh.com/home/daily/site_102708/content/01125107.guest.html.

123. "Limbaugh Smears Obama with Misrepresentation of Comments on Constitution," MMA, October 28, 2008, http://mediamatters.org/mobile/research/200810280007.

124. Ibid.

125. *RLS,* May 27, 2009, http://www.rushlimbaugh.com/home/daily/site_052709/content/01125109.guest.html.

126. *RLS,* January 15, 2010, http://www.rushlimbaugh.com/home/daily/site_011510/content/01125111.guest.html.

127. *RLS,* January 22, 2010, http://www.rushlimbaugh.com/home/daily/site_012210/content/01125109.guest.html.

128. *RLS,* August 19, 1994; FAIR, *The Way Things Aren't,* 36.

129. Limbaugh, *The Way Things Ought to Be,* 281.

130. Rush Limbaugh, Conservative Political Action Conference Speech.

131. *RLS,* April 8, 2009, http://www.rushlimbaugh.com/home/daily/site_040809/content/01125110.guest.html.

132. "Rush Limbaugh Incorrect about Washington's Religious Views," Politifact .com, April 10, 2009, http://www.politifact.com/truth-o-meter/statements/2009/apr/10/rush-limbaugh/Rush-limbaugh-washington-religion/.

133. *RLS,* March 1, 2010, http://www.rushlimbaugh.com/home/daily/site_030110/content/01125110.guest.html.

134. *RLS,* March 24, 2010, http://www.rushlimbaugh.com/home/daily/site_032410/content/01125116.guest.html.

135. *RLS,* October 23, 2006, quoted by MMA, http://mediamatters.org/research/200610240001.

136. "Limbaugh: Ditto Cam Footage Altered," DailyKos.com, October 30, 2006, http://www.dailykos.com/story/2006/10/30/112420/96.

137. William Saletan, "Limbaugh Outfoxed," *The Washington Post,* October 29, 2006; http://www.rushlimbaugh.com/home/estack_12_13_06/Rush_Speeches___Public_Appearances/Rush_Limbaugh_Speech_at_the_Warner_Theatre.LogIn.html.

138. *RLS,* October 24, 2006, quoted by MMA, http://mediamatters.org/mobile/research/200610250005.

139. *CBS Evening News,* CBS, October 26, 2006, http://mediamatters.org/research/200610270019.

140. *RLS,* October 26, 2006.

141. *RLS,* October 27, 2006, http://www.rushlimbaugh.com/home/eibessential3/mjf0/recap.guest.html.

142. Tim Molloy, "Michael J. Fox: Mockery from Rush Limbaugh Was a 'Great Favor,' " *Seattle Post-Intelligencer,* May 7, 2009, http://www.seattlepi.com/tvguide/405976_tvgif7.html?source=rss.

143. "The Limbaugh Museum of Broadcasting," http://downloadpremiereradio.net/guest/rushlimb/LimbaughMuseum/Iphone2/PRELOAD_Outside.html.

144. Arian Campo-Flores and Evan Thomas, "Rehabbing Rush," *Newsweek,* May 8, 2006.

145. Evan Thomas, "True Confessions," *Newsweek,* October 20, 2003, http://www
    .newsweek.com/id/61855.

146. Evan Thomas, "'I am Addicted to Prescription Pain Medication,'" *Newsweek,*
    October 20, 2003; http://www.observer.com/node/48189.

147. Brian Ross, "Money Charges Eyed Against Limbaugh," ABCNews.com, No-
    vember 18, 2003, http://abcnews.go.com/WNT/story?id=131452&page=1.

148. Jim Rutenberg, "Lawyer Accuses Housekeeper of Blackmailing Limbaugh,"
    New York Times, December 23, 2003, http://www.nytimes.com/2003/12/23/
    us/lawyer-accuses-housekeeper-of-blackmailing-limbaugh.html.

149. Bill Hutchinson, "Rush's Maid Tattled After Payoff—Lawyer," *New York
    Daily News,* December 23, 2003.

150. Jarrett Murphy, "Rush Limbaugh Arrested on Drug Charges," CBSNews.com,
    April   28,   2006,   http://www.cbsnews.com/stories/2006/04/28/national/
    main1561324.shtml.

151. Peter Whoriskey, "Rush Limbaugh Turns Himself In on Fraud Charge in Rx
    Drug Probe," *Washington Post,* April 29, 2006.

152. Hendrik Hertzberg, "Rush in Rehab," *New Yorker,* October 27, 2003.

153. Letter from Barry Krischer to Roy Black, December 15, 2003, http://www
    .thesmokinggun.com/archive/rushletters3.html.

154. Campo-Flores and Thomas, "Rehabbing Rush."

155. Ibid.

156. Nigel Farndale, "The Man Who's Always Right," *Sunday Telegraph* (London),
    November 2, 2008.

157. Jacques Steinberg, "Limbaugh Signs On Again, Sharing Life's Tough Lessons,"
    New York Times, November 18, 2003, http://www.nytimes.com/2003/11/18/arts/
    limbaugh-signs-on-again-sharing-life-s-tough-lessons.html?pagewanted=1.

158. *RLS,* May 5, 2006, quoted by MMA, http://mediamatters.org/research/
    200605080015.

159. Ibid.

160. *RLS,* May 1, 2006, quoted by MMA, http://mediamatters.org/research/
    200605010012.

161. Associated Press, "Limbaugh Reaches Settlement in Drugs Case," MSNBC.com,
    April 29, 2006, http://www.msnbc.msn.com/id/12536446/.

162. Campo-Flores and Thomas, "Rehabbing Rush."

163. Ibid.

164. *RLS,* May 1, 2006, quoted by MMA, http://mediamatters.org/research/
    200605010012.

165. *Good Morning America,* ABC, October 13, 2003.

166. Limbaugh, *The Way Things Ought to Be,* 52.

167. Ibid., 54.

168. Ibid., 55.

169. Ibid., 57.

170. Ibid., 114.

171. Rush Limbaugh TV show, December 9, 1993, http://www.fair.org/index.php?page=1159.

172. Laurie Kellman, "Rush Rallies Freshmen to Fight On," *Washington Times,* December 11, 1994.

173. Rush Limbaugh TV show, October 5, 1995, quoted by FAIR, http://www.fair.org/index.php?page=1159.

174. *RLS,* August 18, 2003, quoted by FAIR, http://www.fair.org/index.php?page=1159.

175. "Rush Limbaugh: Playboy Interview," *Playboy,* December 1993, http://www.playboy.com/articles/rush-limbaugh-interview/index.html.

176. Rush Limbaugh TV show, December 9, 1993, quoted by FAIR, http://www.fair.org/index.php?page=1159.

177. Jarrett Murphy, "Rush Limbaugh Detained With Viagra," CBSNews.com, June 27, 2006, http://www.cbsnews.com/stories/2006/06/27/national/main1753947.shtml.

178. *RLS,* April 7, 2003, quoted by FAIR, http://www.fair.org/blog/2009/04/01/listening-to-limbaugh/; Steve Rendall, "Listening to Limbaugh," FAIR, April 1, 2009, http://www.fair.org/blog/2009/04/01/listening-to-limbaugh.

179. *RLS,* June 22, 2006, quoted by MMA, http://mediamatters.org/research/200606230008.

180. *RLS,* July 14, 2009, http://www.rushlimbaugh.com/home/daily/site_071409/content/01125109.guest.html.

181. *RLS,* May 26, 2009.

182. *RLS,* June 20, 2005, quoted by MMA, http://mediamatters.org/research/200506210007.

183. "The Secret Downing Street Memo," *Sunday Times* (London), May 1, 2005, http://www.timesonline.co.uk/tol/news/uk/article387374.ece.

184. *RLS,* August 24, 2005, quoted by MMA, http://mediamatters.org/research/200508260004.

185. *Face the Nation,* CBS, March 16, 2003.

186. *Meet the Press,* NBC, September 14, 2003.

187. Donald Rumsfeld, Aviano Air Base, Italy, February 7, 2003.

188. *RLS*, June 17, 2004, quoted by MMA, http://mediamatters.org/research/200406210002.

189. "Limbaugh Lied about 9-11 Commission Report, Atta Meeting in Prague," June 21, 2004, quoted by MMA, http://mediamatters.org/research/200406210002.

190. *RLS*, November 8, 2004, quoted by MMA, http://mediamatters.org/research/200411100008.

191. *RLS*, August 7, 2002, http://www.wnd.com/news/article.asp?ARTICLE_ID=28545.

192. *RLS*, September 29, 2009, http://www.rushlimbaugh.com/home/daily/site_092909/content/01125106.guest.html.

193. "Rush 24/7 Adopt-A-Soldier Program," http://www.rushlimbaugh.com/home/rush_24_7_adopt_a_soldier.guest.html.

194. "House Resolution Supporting Limbaugh," October 1, 2007, http://think progress.org/limbaugh-resolution/.

195. *RLS*, September 26, 2007, quoted by MMA, http://mediamatters.org/research/200709270010.

196. Limbaugh, *See, I Told You So*, 286.

197. *RLS*, April 29, 2004, quoted by MMA, http://mediamatters.org/research/200405030001.

198. "Limbaugh Lied," April 30, 2004.

199. Ibid.

200. Limbaugh, *See, I Told You So*, 287.

201. Ibid., 288.

CHAPTER 7: HOT AIR AND GLOBAL WARMING

1. *RLS*, May 11, 2009.

2. Steve Forbes, "Empowerer of the Modern Conservative Movement," Human Events Online, July 31, 2008.

3. Frank Newport, "Americans' Global Warming Concerns Continue to Drop," Gallup Poll, March 11, 2010, http://www.gallup.com/poll/126560/Americans-Global-Warming-Concerns-Continue-Drop.aspx.

4. *RLS*, February 4, 1992.

5. FAIR, "The Way Things Aren't: Rush Limbaugh Debates Reality," *Extra!* July/August 1994, FAIR, http://www.fair.org/index.php?page=1895.

6. Ibid.

7. Environmental Defense Fund, "The Way Things Really Are: Debunking Rush Limbaugh on the Environment," 1994, http://www.bestofmaui.com/rush.html.

8. FAIR, "The Way Things Aren't."

9. Ibid.

10. Ibid.

11. Environmental Defense Fund, "The Way Things Really Are."

12. *RLS,* August 10, 2005, quoted by MMA, http://mediamatters.org/research/200508160007.

13. *Nightline,* ABC, February 4, 1992.

14. *The Edge with Paula Zahn,* Fox News Channel, November 1, 2000.

15. *RLS,* November 23, 2009, http://www.rushlimbaugh.com/home/daily/site_112309/content/01125106.guest.html.

16. Rush Limbaugh, *The Way Things Ought to Be* (New York: Pocket Books, 1992), 156.

17. Ibid., 165.

18. *RLS,* April 29, 2010, http://www.rushlimbaugh.com/home/daily/site_042910/content/01125113.guest.html.

19. *RLS,* May 4, 2010, http://www.rushlimbaugh.com/home/daily/site_050410/content/01125109.guest.html.

20. *Hardball* with Chris Matthews, MSNBC, May 3, 2010, quoted by *RLS,* May 4, 2010, http://www.rushlimbaugh.com/home/daily/site_050410/content/01125109.guest.html.

21. *RLS,* April 29, 2010, http://www.rushlimbaugh.com/home/daily/site_042910/content/01125113.guest.html.

22. *RLS,* May 3, 2010, http://www.rushlimbaugh.com/home/daily/site_050310/content/01125112.guest.html.

23. *RLS,* March 31, 2009.

24. Rush Limbaugh, *See, I Told You So* (New York: Pocket Books, 1993), 194.

25. *RLS,* August 3, 2005, quoted by MMA, http://mediamatters.org/research/200508090007.

26. Columbia Accident Investigation Board, *Report,* Vol. IV, October 2003, http://www.nasa.gov/columbia/caib/PDFS/VOL4/F01.PDF.

27. *RLS*, November 13, 2009, http://www.rushlimbaugh.com/home/daily/site_113009/content/01125109.guest.html.

28. *RLS*, April 14, 2009.

29. Roy W. Spencer, "Re: Global Warming Study Hoax," November 8, 2007, http://www.desmogblog.com/rush-limbaugh-falls-for-global-warming-hoax.

30. Nigel Farndale, "The Man Who's Always Right," *Sunday Telegraph* (London), November 2, 2008.

31. Ibid.

32. Al Franken, *Rush Limbaugh Is a Big, Fat Idiot and Other Observations* (New York: Delacorte Press, 1996), 197.

33. *RLS*, August 20, 2009, http://www.rushlimbaugh.com/home/daily/site_082009/content/01125104.guest.html.

34. *RLS*, October 21, 2009, http://www.rushlimbaugh.com/home/daily/site_102109/content/01125115.guest.html.

35. "Global Land+Ocean Surface Temperature Anomaly," http://data.giss.nasa.gov/gistemp/graphs/Fig.A2.txt.

36. *RLS*, September 21, 2005.

37. "Selectively Quoting from Telegraph Article, Limbaugh Again Misled on Global Warming," September 23, 2005, MMA, http://mediamatters.org/research/200509230005.

38. *RLS*, May 22, 2006, quoted by MMA, http://mediamatters.org/research/20065230011.

39. *RLS*, April 8, 2009, quoted by MMA, http://mediamatters.org/limbaughwire/2009/04/08.

40. *RLS*, June 24, 2009, http://www.rushlimbaugh.com/home/daily/site_062409/content/01125110.guest.html.

41. *RLS*, June 29, 2009, http://www.rushlimbaugh.com/home/daily/site_062909/content/01125106.guest.html.

42. *RLS*, February 2, 2010, http://www.rushlimbaugh.com/home/daily/site_020210/content/01125104.guest.html.

43. *Nightline*, ABC, February 4, 1992, http://www.rushlimbaugh.com/home/daily/site_073008/content/01125111.guest.html.

44. Limbaugh, *See, I Told You So*, 180.

45. Environmental Defense Fund, "The Way Things Really Are."

46. *RLS*, June 26, 2009, http://www.rushlimbaugh.com/home/daily/site_062609/content/01125106.guest.html.

47. *RLS,* June 29, 2009, http://www.rushlimbaugh.com/home/daily/site_062909/content/01125113.guest.html.

48. *RLS,* August 21, 2009, http://www.rushlimbaugh.com/home/daily/site_082109/content/01125104.guest.html.

49. Gavin Schmidt and Michael Mann, "Lindzen in Newsweek," Real Climate, April 17, 2007, http://www.realclimate.org/index.php/archives/2007/04/lindzen-in-newsweek/.

50. Sokolov, A.P., P.H. Stone, C.E. Forest, R.G. Prinn, M.C. Sarofim, M. Webster, S. Paltsev, C.A. Schlosser, D. Kicklighter, S. Dutkiewicz, J. Reilly, C. Wang, B. Felzer, J. Melillo, H.D. Jacoby, "Probabilistic Forecast for 21st Century Climate Based on Uncertainties in Emissions (without Policy) and Climate Parameters," *Report 169,* January 2009, http://globalchange.mit.edu/pubs/abstract.php?publication_id=990.

51. *RLS,* February 15, 2010, http://www.rushlimbaugh.com/home/daily/site_021510/content/01125110.guest.html.

52. *RLS,* November 30, 2009, http://www.rushlimbaugh.com/home/daily/site_113009/content/01125113.guest.html.

53. *RLS,* May 6, 2009.

54. *RLS,* April 8, 2009.

55. *RLS,* March 24, 2009.

56. "Municipal Waste Per Capita (Most Recent) by Country," NationMaster.com, http://www.nationmaster.com/graph/env_pol_mun_was_per_cap-pollution-municipal-waste-per-capita; "Carbon Dioxide Per Capita (Most Recent) by Country," NationMaster.com, http://www.nationmaster.com/graph/env_pol_car_dio_per_cap-pollution-carbon-dioxide-per-capita.

57. "2008 Environmental Performance Index," http://epi.yale.edu/CountryScores.

58. Limbaugh, *The Way Things Ought to Be,* 442.

59. *RLS,* August 5, 2008, http://www.rushlimbaugh.com/home/daily/site_080508/content/01125115.html.LogIn.html.

60. Elizabeth Weise, "Damage of Exxon Valdez Endures," *USA Today,* January 31, 2007, http://www.usatoday.com/news/nation/2007-01-31-exxon-alaska_x.htm.

61. "Limbaugh: 'Nature cleaned up itself' after Exxon Valdez oil spill," August 8, 2008, quoted by MMA, http://mediamatters.org/research/200808080006.

62. *RLS,* December 9, 2005, quoted by MMA, http://mediamatters.org/research/200512190008.

63. *RLS,* May 6, 2009.

64. Limbaugh, *The Way Things Ought to Be,* 153.

65. *RLS*, February 2, 2010, http://www.rushlimbaugh.com/home/daily/site_020210/content/01125104.guest.html.

66. Limbaugh, *The Way Things Ought to Be,* 155.

67. Farndale, "The Man Who's Always Right."

68. *RLS*, November 23, 2009, http://www.rushlimbaugh.com/home/daily/site_112309/content/01125106.guest.html.

69. *RLS,* November 24, 2009, http://www.rushlimbaugh.com/home/daily/site_112409/content/01125112.guest.html.

70. Limbaugh, *See, I Told You So,* 203.

71. *RLS*, June 26, 2009, http://www.rushlimbaugh.com/home/daily/site_062609/content/01125106.guest.html; "Polpourri: Rush Limbaugh's Mention of Ehlers on Cap and Trade Bill Jammed the Congressman's Phones," *Grand Rapids Press,* June 27, 2009, http://blog.mlive.com/talkingpolitics/2009/06/polpourri_rush_limbaughs_menti.html.

72. "Energy Bill and Existing Homes," FactCheck.org, July 20, 2009, http://www.factcheck.org/2009/07/energy-bill-and-existing-homes.

73. Ibid.

74. *RLS*, June 30, 2009, http://www.rushlimbaugh.com/home/daily/site_063009/content/01125111.guest.html.

75. *RLS*, October 9, 2009, http://www.rushlimbaugh.com/home/daily/site_100909/content/01125104.guest.html.

76. Betsy Schiffman, "Why Your Electricity Bills are Soaring," Forbes.com, 2004, http://moneycentral.msn.com/content/SavingandDebt/P87298.asp.

77. "Climate Bill Cuts Electricity Bills," National Resources Defense Council, http://switchboard.nrdc.org/blogs/paltman/media/HR%202454%20Average%20Household%20Savings%20by%20State.pdf.

78. Justin Rood, "Update: Inhofe Tipped to UN 'Brainwashing' by Former Limbaugh Producer," Talking Points Memo, November 17, 2006, http://tpmmuckraker.talkingpointsmemo.com/archives/002010.php.

79. David Frum, "Why Rush Is Wrong," *Newsweek,* March 16, 2009, http://www.newsweek.com/id/188279.

80. *RLS*, November 30, 2009, http://www.rushlimbaugh.com/home/daily/site_113009/content/01125110.guest.html.

81. *RLS*, February 12, 2010, http://www.rushlimbaugh.com/home/daily/site_021210/content/01125107.guest.html.

82. *RLS*, November 24, 2009, http://www.rushlimbaugh.com/home/daily/site_112409/content/01125112.guest.html.

83. Thomas Friedman, *Hot, Flat, and Crowded* (New York: Farrar, Straus and Giroux, 2008), 138.

84. *RLS*, March 27, 2009.

CHAPTER 8: DEATH PANELS AND PROHIBITED POPCORN: LIMBAUGH'S LIES ON HEALTH CARE

1. David Brock, *Blinded by the Right: The Conscience of an Ex-Conservative* (New York: Crown, 2002) 285.

2. Stephen Talbot, "Wizard of Ooze," *Mother Jones*, May/June 1995, http://mother jones.com/politics/1995/05/wizard-ooze.

3. Brock, *Blinded by the Right*, 284.

4. *RLS*, June 25, 2009, http://www.rushlimbaugh.com/home/daily/site_062509/content/01125108.guest.html.

5. *RLS*, August 10, 2009, http://www.rushlimbaugh.com/home/daily/site_081009/content/01125106.guest.html.

6. See Alan Caruba, "Page after Page of Reasons to Hate Obamacare," *Canada Free Press*, July 26, 2009, http://canadafreepress.com/index.php/article/13158.

7. *RLS*, August 10, 2009, http://www.rushlimbaugh.com/home/daily/site_081009/content/01125108.guest.html.

8. *RLS*, August 4, 2009, http://www.rushlimbaugh.com/home/daily/site_080409/content/01125111.guest.html.

9. *RLS*, August 10, 2009, http://www.rushlimbaugh.com/home/daily/site_081009/content/01125114.guest.html; H.R. 3200, July 14, 2009, http://frwebgate.access.gpo.gov/cgi-bin/getdoc.cgi?dbname=111_cong_bills&docid=f:h3200ih.txt.pdf; *RLS*, August 6, 2009, http://www.rushlimbaugh.com/home/daily/site_080609/content/01125111.guest.html.

10. *RLS*, August 6, 2009, http://www.rushlimbaugh.com/home/daily/site_080609/content/01125111.guest.html; as a headline on Limbaugh's Web site put it, "Will Obamacare Access Your Bank Account Via Direct Deposit?"

11. *RLS*, August 10, 2009, http://www.rushlimbaugh.com/home/daily/site_081009/content/01125114.guest.html.

12. "Media Echo Serial Misinformer McCaughey's False End-of-Life Counseling Claim," July 31, 2009, quoted by MMA, http://mediamatters.org/research/200907310051.

13. *RLS*, July 30, 2009, http://www.rushlimbaugh.com/home/daily/site_073009/content/01125111.guest.html.

14. *RLS,* August 10, 2009, http://www.rushlimbaugh.com/home/daily/site_081009/content/01125114.guest.html.

15. H.R. 3200, July 14, 2009, http://frwebgate.access.gpo.gov/cgi-bin/getdoc.cgi?dbname=111_cong_bills&docid=f:h3200ih.txt.pdf.

16. Ezra Klein, "Is the Government Going to Euthanize your Grandmother? An Interview With Sen. Johnny Isakson," WashingtonPost.com, August 10, 2009, http://voices.washingtonpost.com/ezra-klein/2009/08/is_the_government_going_to_eut.html#more.

17. *RLS,* August 11, 2009, http://www.rushlimbaugh.com/home/daily/site_081109/content/01125108.guest.html.

18. *RLS,* January 28, 2010, http://www.rushlimbaugh.com/home/daily/site_012810/content/01125112.guest.html.

19. *RLS,* July 24, 2009, http://www.rushlimbaugh.com/home/daily/site_072409/content/01125111.guest.html.

20. Ibid.

21. *RLS,* February 15, 2010, http://www.rushlimbaugh.com/home/daily/site_021510/content/01125108.guest.html.

22. *RLS,* September 10, 2009, http://www.rushlimbaugh.com/home/daily/site_091009/content/01125111.guest.html.

23. *RLS,* September 10, 2009, http://www.rushlimbaugh.com/home/daily/site_091009/content/01125106.guest.html.

24. *RLS,* July 28, 2009, http://www.rushlimbaugh.com/home/daily/site_072809/content/01125108.guest.html.

25. *RLS,* April 2, 2010, http://www.rushlimbaugh.com/home/daily/site_040210/content/01125109.guest.html.

26. *RLS,* April 13, 2010, http://www.rushlimbaugh.com/home/daily/site_041310/content/01125113.guest.html.

27. *RLS,* June 24, 2009, http://www.rushlimbaugh.com/home/daily/site_062409/content/01125110.guest.html.

28. *RLS,* June 24, 2009, http://www.rushlimbaugh.com/home/daily/site_062409/content/01125110.guest.html.

29. *RLS,* June 18, 2009, http://www.rushlimbaugh.com/home/daily/site_061809/content/01125106.guest.html.

30. *RLS,* August 27, 2009, http://www.rushlimbaugh.com/home/daily/site_082709/content/01125104.guest.html.

31. *RLS,* June 18, 2009, http://www.rushlimbaugh.com/home/daily/site_061809/content/01125106.guest.html.

32. *RLS,* March 17, 2010, http://www.rushlimbaugh.com/home/daily/site_031710/content/01125114.guest.html.

33. *RLS,* June 8, 2009, http://www.rushlimbaugh.com/home/daily/site_060809/content/01125108.guest.html.

34. "Rush Interviewed by Sean Hannity, Part Two," Fox News Channel, Recorded: June 3, 2009, http://www.rushlimbaugh.com/home/daily/site_060509/content/01125106.guest.html.

35. *RLS,* July 31, 2009, http://www.rushlimbaugh.com/home/daily/site_073109/content/01125113.guest.html.

36. *RLS,* June 10, 2009, http://www.rushlimbaugh.com/home/daily/site_061009/content/01125117.guest.html.

37. *RLS,* May 4, 2009.

38. *RLS,* December 22, 2009, http://www.rushlimbaugh.com/home/daily/site_122209/content/01125113.guest.html; Julie Steenhuysen, "Swine Flu Has Killed 10,000 Americans Since April," Reuters, December 10, 2009, http://www.reuters.com/article/idUSTRE5AO3Z420091210.

39. *RLS,* August 13, 2009, http://www.rushlimbaugh.com/home/daily/site_081309/content/01125107.guest.html.

40. *RLS,* August 17,, 2009, http://www.rushlimbaugh.com/home/daily/site_081709/content/01125109.guest.html.

41. *RLS,* July 31, 2009, http://www.rushlimbaugh.com/home/daily/site_073109/content/01125113.guest.html.

42. *RLS,* July 28, 2009, http://img.rushlimbaugh.com/home/daily/site_072809/content/01125111.guest.html.

43. *RLS,* August 7, 2009, http://www.rushlimbaugh.com/home/daily/site_080709/content/01125112.guest.html.

44. *RLS,* April 5, 2010, http://www.rushlimbaugh.com/home/daily/site_040510/content/01125104.guest.html.

45. *RLS,* July 31, 2009, http://www.rushlimbaugh.com/home/daily/site_073109/content/01125107.guest.html.

46. *RLS,* July 31, 2009, http://www.rushlimbaugh.com/home/daily/site_073109/content/01125113.guest.html.

47. *RLS,* August 7, 2009, http://www.rushlimbaugh.com/home/daily/site_080709/content/01125112.guest.html.

48. *RLS,* August 10, 2009, http://mediamatters.org/limbaughwire/2009/08/10#0041.

49. *RLS,* July 30, 2009, http://www.rushlimbaugh.com/home/daily/site_073009/content/01125111.guest.html.

50. *RLS,* July 30, 2009, http://www.rushlimbaugh.com/home/daily/site_073009/content/01125107.guest.html.

51. *RLS,* July 23, 2009, http://www.rushlimbaugh.com/home/daily/site_072309/content/01125106.guest.html.

52. Ibid.

53. *RLS,* August 13, 2009, http://www.rushlimbaugh.com/home/daily/site_081309/content/01125112.guest.html.

54. "The World Health Organization's Ranking of the World's Health Systems," geographic.org http://www.photius.com/rankings/healthranks.html.

55. *RLS,* August 20, 2009, http://www.rushlimbaugh.com/home/daily/site_082009/content/01125104.guest.html.

56. Central Intelligence Agency, "Life Expectancy at Birth," *The World Factbook,* https://www.cia.gov/library/publications/the-world-factbook/rankorder/2102rank.html.

57. Associated Press, "Study: U.S. Slipping Down Life Expectancy Rankings," FoxNews.com, August 12, 2007, http://www.foxnews.com/story/0,2933,293008,00.html.

58. Ellen Nolte and C. Martin McKee, "Measuring the Health of Nations: Updating an Earlier Analysis," Commonwealth Fund, January 8, 2008, http://www.commonwealthfund.org/Content/Publications/In-the-Literature/2008/Jan/Measuring-the-Health-of-Nations–Updating-an-Earlier-Analysis.aspx.

59. *RLS,* August 14, 2009, http://www.rushlimbaugh.com/home/daily/site_081409/content/01125116.guest.html.

60. "Education Spending (% of GDP) (Most Recent) by Country," NationMaster.com, http://www.nationmaster.com/graph/edu_edu_spe-education-spending-of-gdp.

61. "The Welfare State and Social Expenditure > % of GDP (Most Recent) by Country," NationMaster.com, http://www.nationmaster.com/graph/eco_wel_sta_the_wel_sta_and_soc_exp_of_gdp-welfare-state-social-expenditure-gdp.

62. "Health Statistics > Total Expenditure as % of GDP (Most Recent) by Country," NationMaster.com, http://www.nationmaster.com/graph/hea_tot_exp_as_of_gdp-health-total-expenditure-gdp.

63. *RLS,* June 25, 2009, http://www.rushlimbaugh.com/home/daily/site_062509/content/01125112.guest.html.

64. *RLS,* August 14, 2009, http://www.rushlimbaugh.com/home/daily/site_081409/content/01125111.guest.html.

65. *RLS,* July 16, 2009, http://www.rushlimbaugh.com/home/daily/site_071609/content/01125110.guest.html.

66. *RLS,* July 20, 2009, http://www.rushlimbaugh.com/home/daily/site_072009/content/01125106.guest.html.

67. *RLS,* July 16, 2009, http://www.rushlimbaugh.com/home/daily/site_071609/content/01125106.guest.html.

68. *RLS,* July 20, 2009, http://www.rushlimbaugh.com/home/daily/site_072009/content/01125106.guest.html.

69. Ibid.

70. "Rush Limbaugh Press Conference in Hawaii," January 1, 2010, http://www.rushlimbaugh.com/home/daily/site_123109/content/01125119.guest.html.

71. Jessica Kutch, "Hell Freezes Over: Rush Limbaugh Loves Union Hospitals and Socialized Medicine," SEIU Blog, January 4, 2010, http://www.seiu.org/2010/01/hell-freezes-over-rush-limbaugh-loves-union-hospitals-and-socialized-medicine.php.

72. *RLS,* January 7, 2010, http://www.rushlimbaugh.com/home/daily/site_010710/content/01125111.guest.html.

73. Heidi Przybyla and Eric Sabo, "Limbaugh Embraces Costa Rica Socialized Medicine," Bloomberg News, March 16, 2010, http://www.bloomberg.com/apps/news?pid=20601103&sid=aL4mr0DkTNvw.

74. *RLS,* August 13, 2009, http://www.rushlimbaugh.com/home/daily/site_081309/content/01125109.guest.html.

75. Ibid.

76. Newt Gingrich, August 12, 2009, http://twitter.com/newtgingrich.

CHAPTER 9: THE KING OF TALK RADIO: LIMBAUGH'S MEDIA EMPIRE

1. Karl Rove, "Exclusive: Rush Remade American Politics," *Human Events,* July 28, 2008.

2. Arian Campo-Flores and Evan Thomas, "Rehabbing Rush," *Newsweek,* May 8, 2006.

3. Nigel Farndale, "The Man Who's Always Right," *Sunday Telegraph* (London), November 2, 2008.

4. *RLS,* August 26, 2009, http://www.rushlimbaugh.com/home/daily/site_082609/content/01125116.guest.html.

5. Michael Dolny, "Right Ebbs, Left Gains as Media 'Experts,'" Extra!, FAIR, September 3, 2009, http://www.fair.org/index.php?page=3857.

6. John Halpin, James Heidbreder, Mark Lloyd, Paul Woodhull, Ben Scott, Josh

Silver, and S. Derek Turner, "The Structural Imbalance of Political Talk Radio," *Center for American Progress,* June 20, 2007, http://www.americanprogress. org/issues/2007/06/talk_radio.html.

7. *RLS,* November 10, 2009, http://www.rushlimbaugh.com/home/daily/site_ 111009/content/01125110.guest.html.

8. Ibid.

9. *RLS,* August 28, 2009, http://www.rushlimbaugh.com/home/daily/site_082809/ content/01125106.guest.html.

10. *RLS,* July 13, 2004, quoted by MMA, http://mediamatters.org/research/ 200407150010.

11. *RLS,* June 18, 2009, http://www.rushlimbaugh.com/home/daily/site_061809/ content/01125110.guest.html.

12. Jim Rutenberg, "Conservatives Tailor Tone to Fit Course of the War," *New York Times,* March 28, 2003, http://www.nytimes.com/2003/03/28/international/ worldspecial/28PUND.html.

13. *RLS,* October 27, 2006, http://www.rushlimbaugh.com/home/eibessential3/ mjf0/recap.guest.html.

14. Maureen Balleza and Kate Zernike, "Memos on Bush Are Fake but Accurate, Typist Says," *New York Times,* September 15, 2004, http://www.nytimes.com/ 2004/09/15/politics/campaign/15guard.html?_r=2&ei=5006&en= 3f67b230dff29e57&ex=1095912000&oref=slogin&partner=ALTAVISTA1& pagewanted=print&position=.

15. *RLS,* July 20, 2009, http://www.rushlimbaugh.com/home/daily/site_072009/ content/01125106.guest.html.

16. *RLS,* July 20, 2009, http://www.rushlimbaugh.com/home/daily/site_072009/ content/01125106.guest.html.

17. "Qualified Nominators," Nobel Prize.org, http://nobelprize.org/nomination/ peace/nominators.html.

18. Rush Limbaugh, interview, *Sean Hannity Show,* Fox News Channel, January 19, 2009, http://www.rushlimbaugh.com/home/daily/site_012209/content/ 01125106.guest.html.

19. *RLS,* August 26, 2009, http://www.rushlimbaugh.com/home/daily/site_082609/ content/01125116.guest.html.

20. *RLS,* June 3, 2009, http://www.rushlimbaugh.com/home/daily/site_060309/ content/01125108.guest.html.

21. *RLS,* June 1, 2009, htt://www.rushlimbaugh.com/home/daily/site_060109/con tent/01125106.guest.html.

22. *RLS,* June 18, 2009, http://www.rushlimbaugh.com/home/daily/site_061809/content/01125110.guest.html.

23. *RLS,* June 5, 2009, http://www.rushlimbaugh.com/home/daily/site_060509/content/01125109.guest.html.

24. Letter to David Westin, ABC News, June 23, 2009, http://a.abcnews.go.com/images/Politics/Hon-Lamar-S-Smith.pdf.

25. Rush Limbaugh, interview with Greta van Susteren, *On the Record with Greta van Susteren,* Fox News Channel, July 23, 2009, http://www.rushlimbaugh.com/home/daily/site_072409/content/01125106.guest.html.

26. Ibid.

27. Lynn Sweet, "The Story Behind My Obama Question," *Chicago Sun-Times,* July 23, 2009, http://www.suntimes.com/news/sweet/1682926,CST-NWS-sweet24.article.

28. *RLS,* July 21, 2008.

29. *RLS,* November 7, 2008, http://www.rushlimbaugh.com/home/daily/site_110708/content/01125109.guest.html.

30. Rush Limbaugh, interview with Sean Hannity, January 19, 2009.

31. *RLS,* September 14, 2009, http://www.rushlimbaugh.com/home/daily/site_091409/content/01125106.guest.html.

32. Russell Goldman, "Tea Party Protesters March on Washington," ABCNews.com, September 12, 2009, http://abcnews.go.com/Politics/tea-party-protesters-march-washington/story?id=8557120.

33. Michael Ruane, "D.C.'s Inauguration Head Count: 1.8 Million," *Washington Post,* January 20, 2009, http://www.washingtonpost.com/wp-dyn/content/article/2009/01/21/AR2009012103884.html.

34. *RLS,* September 14, 2009, http://www.rushlimbaugh.com/home/daily/site_091409/content/01125110.guest.html.

35. FAIR, *The Way Things Aren't,* 58.

36. "Poll: News Media's Credibility Plunges," CBSNews.com, September 14, 2009, http://www.cbsnews.com/stories/2009/09/14/business/main5309240.shtml.

37. *RLS,* August 7, 2009, http://www.rushlimbaugh.com/home/daily/site_080709/content/01125107.guest.html.

38. David Stout, "Ex-Rep. Jefferson Convicted in Bribery Scheme," *New York Times,* August 5, 2009, http://www.nytimes.com/2009/08/06/us/06jefferson.html?_r=1&scp=2&sq=william%20jefferson&st=cse.

39. *RLS,* August 12, 2009, http://www.rushlimbaugh.com/home/daily/site_081209/content/01125109.guest.html.

40. *RLS*, August 11, 2009, http://www.rushlimbaugh.com/home/daily/site_081109/content/01125103.guest.html.

41. Rush Limbaugh TV show, April 6, 1995; http://www.fair.org/index.php?page=1305.

42. "Yet More Limbecile Statements," *Extra!* Update, June 1995, FAIR, http://www.fair.org/index.php?page=1305.

43. *RLS*, November 4, 2002; http://www.fair.org/index.php?page=1861.

44. "Limbaugh's Liberal Media Proof: Too Good To Be True," November 7, 2002, http://www.fair.org/index.php?page=1861.

45. *RLS*, June 27, 2006, quoted by MMA, http://mediamatters.org/research/200606270010.

46. *RLS*, June 1, 2005, quoted by MMA, http://mediamatters.org/research/200506020003.

47. "Limbaugh Falsely Claimed Media Didn't Mention 'Deep Throat' Mark Felt's Conviction, Pardon," June 2, 2005, http://mediamatters.org/research/200506020003.

48. Rush Limbaugh TV show, June 6, 1994; FAIR, *The Way Things Aren't*, 92.

49. Nadine Brozan, "Chronicle," *The New York Times*, May 30, 1994, http://www.nytimes.com/1994/05/30/nyregion/chronicle-248584.html.

50. Zev Chafets, "Late Period Limbaugh," *The New York Times Magazine*, July 6, 2008, http://www.nytimes.com/2008/07/06/magazine/06Limbaugh-t.html?_r=1&hp=&pagewanted=print.

51. See http://townhall.com/columnists/ZevChafets.

52. Eric Boehlert, "The NY Times Sends a Dittohead to Interview Rush Limbaugh," July 8, 2008, http://mediamatters.org/columns/200807080001.

53. "Talking a Red Streak," On the Media, July 4, 2008, http://onthemedia.org/transcripts/2008/07/04/05.

54. "Rush Limbaugh and '*New York Times*' Strange Bedfellows," CNN Moneyline, October 19, 1994.

55. "Talking a Red Streak," On the Media.

56. Ibid.

57. Zev Chafets, "The GOP's Real Go-To Guy," *Los Angeles Times*, September 29, 2008, http://www.latimes.com/news/opinion/commentary/la-oe-chafets29-2008sep29,0,4135839.story.

58. Liz Cox Barrett, "NYT's MTV Cribs-Like Limbaugh Profile," *Columbia Journalism Review*, July 2, 2008, http://www.cjr.org/the_kicker/nyts_mtv_cribslike_limbaugh_pr.php.

59. Chafets, "Late Period Limbaugh."

60. "Sentinel," description of imprint of Penguin Books, http://us.penguingroup
    .com/static/pages/publishers/adult/sentinel.html.

61. *RLS,* August 27, 2009, http://www.rushlimbaugh.com/home/daily/site_082709/
    content/01125109.guest.html.

62. *RLS,* August 14, 2009, http://www.rushlimbaugh.com/home/daily/site_081409/
    content/01125106.guest.html.

63. Ibid.

64. Brian Ross and Molly Dean, "'Washed-up Terrorist' Ayers Stays Mum on Ties
    to Obama," ABC News, October 27, 2008, http://abcnews.go.com/Blotter/
    Vote2008/story?id=6120141&page=1.

65. Brian Ross and Rehab El-Buri, "Obama's Pastor: God Damn America, U.S. to
    Blame for 9/11," ABC News, March 13, 2008, http://abcnews.go.com/Blotter/
    DemocraticDebate/story?id=4443788&page=1.

66. "ABC's Ross Reported Wright's 9-11 Remarks—but Not That Obama Dis-
    avowed Them," MMA, March 13, 2008, http://mediamatters.org/research/
    200803130008.

67. *RLS,* August 14, 2009, http://www.rushlimbaugh.com/home/daily/site_081409/
    content/01125106.guest.html.

68. Anne Kornblut and Katharine Seelye, "Papers Knew of Foley E-Mail but Did
    Not Publish Stories," *The New York Times,* October 3, 2006, http://www
    .nytimes.com/2006/10/03/washington/03media.html?_r=1&oref=slogin.

69. Reliable Sources, "Coverage of the Foley Scandal; Coverage of Bob Wood-
    ward's New Book," CNN, October 8, 2006, http://transcripts.cnn.com/
    TRANSCRIPTS/0610/08/rs.01.html.

70. *RLS,* August 14, 2009, http://www.rushlimbaugh.com/home/daily/site_081409/
    content/01125113.guest.html.

71. FAIR, "Exploding ABC's Unabomber Hoax," Extra! Update, June 1996, http://
    www.fair.org/index.php?page=1360.

72. FAIR, "SoundBites," *Extra!,* May/June 2006, http://www.fair.org/index.php?
    page=3508.

73. Bernard Goldberg, *A Slobbering Love Affair: The True (and Pathetic) Story of
    the Torrid Romance Between Barack Obama and the Mainstream Media* (New
    York: Regnery, 2009) 55.

74. *RLS,* May 14, 2009.

75. *RLS,* June 30, 2009, http://www.rushlimbaugh.com/home/daily/site_063009/
    content/01125111.guest.html.

76. *RLS,* June 1, 2009.

77. "Rush Interviewed by Sean Hannity, Part Two," *Sean Hannity Show,* Fox News Channel, June 3, 2009, http://www.rushlimbaugh.com/home/daily/site_060509/content/01125106.guest.html.

78. Rush Limbaugh, "Mr. President, Keep the Airwaves Free," *Wall Street Journal,* February 20, 2009, http://online.wsj.com/article/SB123508978035028163.html.

79. 395 U.S. 367 (1969).

80. Jeff Cohen, "The 'Hush Rush' Hoax: Limbaugh on the Fairness Doctrine," *Extra!,* FAIR, November/December 1994, http://www.fair.org/index.php?page=1256.

81. Ibid.

82. Limbaugh Letter, October 1993.

83. Steve Almond, "Who's Afraid of the Big, Bad Fairness Doctrine?" *Boston Globe,* November 9, 2009, http://www.boston.com/bostonglobe/editorial_opinion/oped/articles/2009/11/09/whos_afraid_of_the_big_bad_fairness_doctrine?mode=PF.

84. Ibid.

85. David Folkenflik, "CPB Memos Indicate Level of Monitoring," NPR, June 30, 2005, http://www.npr.org/templates/story/story.php?storyId=4724317.

86. Jeremy Egner, "The Probe: Unilateral Actions Exceeded Chair's Authority," *Current,* November 21, 2005, http://www.current.org/cpb/cpb0521ig.shtml.

87. *Bill Moyers Journal,* July 24, 2009, http://www.pbs.org/moyers/journal/07242009/transcript2.html.

88. *RLS,* August 3, 2009, http://www.rushlimbaugh.com/home/daily/site_080309/content/01125111.guest.html.

89. *RLS,* August 27, 2009, http://www.rushlimbaugh.com/home/daily/site_082709/content/01125110.guest.html.

90. *RLS,* August 26, 2009, http://www.rushlimbaugh.com/home/daily/site_082609/content/01125116.guest.html.

91. *RLS,* August 26, 2009, http://www.rushlimbaugh.com/home/daily/site_082609/content/01125113.guest.html.

92. *RLS,* April 11, 2005, quoted by MMA, http://mediamatters.org/mmtv/200508120005.

93. Deepak Chopra, "Why Rush Limbaugh Is the Icon of Right-Wing Outrage," AlterNet, March 9, 2009, http://www.alternet.org/mediaculture/130912/why_rush_limbaugh_is_the_icon_of_right-wing_outrage/.

94. *RLS,* September 30, 2009, http://www.rushlimbaugh.com/home/daily/site_093009/content/01125112.guest.html.

95. Valerie Richardson, "'After the Rush' Title Draws Fire," *Washington Times,* August 28, 1994.

96. Michael Levenson, "Limbaugh's Praise for Romney's Run Heard Loud and Clear—Host Talking Up Candidate, Rapping Rivals on the Air," *Boston Globe,* January 18, 2008.

97. Steve Rendall and Daniel Butterworth, "How Public Is Public Radio?" *Extra!,* FAIR, May/June 2004, http://www.fair.org/index.php?page=1180.

98. "Roper Public Opinion Poll on PBS—Highlights for 2009," http://www.scribd.com/doc/11799061/Roper-Public-Opinion-Poll-on-PBS-Highlights-for-2009.

99. "News Audiences Increasingly Politicized," Pew Research Center for the People & the Press, June 8, 2004, http://people-press.org/report/215/news-audiences-increasingly-politicized.

100. Rush Limbaugh, *See, I Told You So* (New York: Pocket Books, 1993) 372–373.

101. Paul Farhi, "A Record Audience for NPR's News Programs," *Washington Post,* March 24, 2009.

102. Michael Massing, "Katie and Diane: The Wrong Questions," *Columbia Journalism Review,* September 23, 2009, http://www.cjr.org/behind_the_news/katie_and_diane_the_wrong_ques.php.

103. Kellyn Brown, "Missoula Liberal Talk Radio Goes Conservative," *Flathead Beacon,* November 9, 2009, http://www.flatheadbeacon.com/articles/article/missoula_liberal_talk_radio_goes_conservative/14064.

104. "What's Up With the Evil Conservative Media Takeover?" November 5, 2009, http://4and20blackbirds.wordpress.com/2009/11/05/whats-up-with-the-evil-conservative-media-takeover.

105. *Talkers Magazine* award, June 6, 2009, http://www.rushlimbaugh.com/home/daily/site_060909/content/01125106.guest.html.

106. FAIR, *The Way Things Aren't,* 114.

107. *Hannity and Colmes,* Fox News Channel, October 18, 2005.

108. Rush Limbaugh, *The Way Things Ought to Be* (New York: Pocket Books, 1992) 271.

109. Paul Colford, *The Rush Limbaugh Story: Talent on Loan from God* (New York: St. Martin's Press, 1993) 132–133.

110. *RLS,* November 10, 2009, http://www.rushlimbaugh.com/home/daily/site_111009/content/01125111.guest.html.

111. Ibid.

112. Colford, *Rush Limbaugh Story,* 64.

113. Ibid., 67.

114. Ibid., 68.

115. Katy Bachman, "Radio's Head Rush," *Mediaweek,* August 11, 2003.

116. Ibid.

117. Colford, *Rush Limbaugh Story,* 215.

118. Brian Stelter, "Host Loses Some Sponsors After an Obama Remark," *New York Times,* August 13, 2009, http://www.nytimes.com/2009/08/14/business/media/14adco.html.

119. William Spain, "Advertisers Rushing Away from Limbaugh Show?" *CBS MarketWatch,* January 30, 2003.

120. Katy Bachman, "Radio's Head Rush."

121. "Friends Salute Rush Limbaugh," Human Events Online, August 13, 2008.

122. Matthew Flamm, "The Mouth that Roared," *Crain's New York Business,* March 9, 2009.

123. *RLS,* August 26, 2009.

124. Federal Trade Commission, "Information on LifeLock Settlement," http://ftc.gov/lifelock.

125. *RLS,* July 1, 2009, http://www.rushlimbaugh.com/home/daily/site_070109/content/01125111.guest.html.

126. *RLS,* June 16, 2009, http://www.rushlimbaugh.com/home/daily/site_061609/content/01125104.guest.html. See http://www.fda.gov/Newsevents/Newsroom/PressAnnouncements/ucm167065.htm. As a result of the FDA's action, the maker of Zicam recalled two of its products.

127. *All Things Considered,* NPR, January 25, 2007.

128. Chafets, "Late Period Limbaugh."

129. *RLS,* May 22, 2009.

130. *RLS,* April 2, 2009, http://www.rushlimbaugh.com/home/daily/site_040209/content/01125104.guest.html.

131. *RLS,* April 3, 2009.

132. *RLS,* September 28, 2009, http://www.rushlimbaugh.com/home/daily/site_092809/content/01125104.guest.html.

133. Howard Kurtz, "GATT Got Their Tongue? Limbaugh's Shows Say No to Pact Opponents' Ads," *The Washington Post,* November 19, 1994.

134. *RLS,* June 2, 2009, http://www.rushlimbaugh.com/home/daily/site_060209/content/01125110.guest.html.

135. *RLS,* June 5, 2009.

136. *RLS,* Limbaugh ad for GM, June 5, 2009.

137. *RLS,* June 10, 2009, http://www.rushlimbaugh.com/home/daily/site_061009/content/01125115.guest.html.

138. Ibid.

139. *RLS,* June 5, 2009, http://www.rushlimbaugh.com/home/daily/site_060509/content/01125108.guest.html.

140. *RLS,* August 13, 2009, http://www.rushlimbaugh.com/home/daily/site_081309/content/01125115.guest.html.

141. *RLS,* April 21, 2010, http://www.rushlimbaugh.com/home/daily/site_042110/content/01125111.guest.html.

142. *RLS,* April 28, 2009, http://www.rushlimbaugh.com/home/daily/site_042809/content/01125108.guest.html.

143. David Hinckley, "Rush's Star: Advertising," *New York Daily News,* April 8, 2008.

144. Rick Ellis, "The Surrender Of MSNBC," AllYourTV.com, February 25, 2003, http://www.allyourtv.com/index.php?option=com_content&view=article&id=259:surrendermsnbc&catid=78:featurescoveringmedia.

145. Associated Press, "MSNBC Fires Michael Savage after Anti-Gay Comments," *USA Today,* July 7, 2007, http://www.usatoday.com/news/nation/2003-07-07-talk-host-fired_x.htm.

146. *RLS,* September 28, 2007, http://www.rushlimbaugh.com/home/daily/site_092807/content/01125106.guest.html.

147. *RLS,* April 2, 2009.

148. Ibid.

149. Al Franken, *Rush Limbaugh Is a Big, Fat Idiot and Other Observations* (New York: Delacorte Press, 1996), 21.

150. *RLS,* March 11, 2009, quoted by MMA, http://mediamatters.org/print/research/200903120020.

151. Karl-Thomas Musselman, "Rush Limbaugh's Support of Rep. Mike McCaul Coming in Loud and Clear," *Burnt Orange Report,* May 27, 2009, http://www.burntorangereport.com/diary/8691/rush-limbaughs-support-of-rep-mccaul-coming-in-loud-and-clear.

152. Nigel Farndale, "The Man Who's Always Right," *Sunday Telegraph* (London), November 2, 2008.

153. *RLS,* November 13, 2009, http://www.rushlimbaugh.com/home/daily/site_111309/content/01125106.guest.html.

154. *RLS,* November 12, 2009, http://www.rushlimbaugh.com/home/daily/site_111209/content/01125107.guest.html.

155. *RLS,* August 3, 2009, http://www.rushlimbaugh.com/home/daily/site_080309/content/01125107.guest.html.

156. *Hardball with Chris Matthews,* MSNBC, October 9, 2000.

157. *RLS,* February 15, 2010, http://www.rushlimbaugh.com/home/daily/site_021510/content/01125112.guest.html.

158. *RLS,* November 1, 2004, quoted by MMA, http://mediamatters.org/research/200411020010.

159. Ibid.

160. *Tim Russert,* CNBC, November 28, 1998.

161. *RLS,* June 10, 2004, quoted by MMA, http://mediamatters.org/research/200406140006.

162. *Tim Russert,* CNBC, October 25, 1997.

163. Brian Williams, December 26, 2004, C-SPAN interview, quoted by MMA, http://mediamatters.org/research/200501240007.

164. Ibid.

165. Glenn Beck, "Rush Limbaugh," *Time 100,* April 30, 2009, http://www.time.com/time/specials/packages/article/0,28804,1894410_1893836_1894425,00.html.

166. *RLS,* December 4, 2008.

167. Limbaugh, *The Way Things Ought to Be,* 92.

168. Colford, *Rush Limbaugh Story,* 122.

169. David Brock, *Blinded by the Right: The Conscience of an Ex-Conservative* (New York: Crown, 2002), 258.

170. Peter J. Boyer, "Bull Rush," *Vanity Fair,* May 1992.

171. Terry Eastland, "Rush Limbaugh: Talking Back," *American Spectator,* September 1992.

172. Colford, *Rush Limbaugh Story,* 135.

173. Ibid.

174. "CBS considers adding Rush Limbaugh as newsmagazine commentator," *Montreal Gazette,* January 8, 1994.

175. *RLS,* September 5, 2006.

176. *RLS,* June 16, 2009, http://www.rushlimbaugh.com/home/daily/site_061609/content/01125107.guest.html.

177. Jim Rutenberg, "Seeking Sizzle at CNN," *The New York Times,* August 15, 2001, http://www.nytimes.com/2001/08/15/arts/tv-notes-seeking-sizzle-at-cnn.html.

178. *RLS,* November 21, 2002.

179. E.J. Dionne Jr., "The Rightward Press," *Washington Post,* December 6, 2002, http://www.washingtonpost.com/ac2/wp-dyn/A16431-2002Dec5?language= printer.

180. Clarence Page, *Reliable Sources,* CNN, May 24, 2009.

181. *RLS,* March 2, 2010, http://www.rushlimbaugh.com/home/daily/site_030210/ content/01125109.guest.html.

182. Eric Boehlert, "Playing Nice with Rush Limbaugh," Media Matters for America, October 31, 2006, http://mediamatters.org/columns/200610310013

183. Ibid.

184. Andrew Breitbart, "Rush to Judgment: A Media Hopelessly Divided," *Washington Times,* March 2, 2009.

185. Andrew Klavan, "The Limbaugh Challenge," April 2, 2009, http://andrewkla van.com/words/index.php?blog=5&title=the_limbaugh_challenge&more=1 &c=1&tb=1&pb=1.

186. *RLS,* February 21, 2008, http://www.rushlimbaugh.com/home/daily/site_ 022108/content/01125108.guest.html.

187. Michael Wolff, "The Man Who Ate the G.O.P.," *Vanity Fair,* May 2009, http:// www.vanityfair.com/politics/features/2009/05/rush-limbaugh200905.

188. *RLS,* October 15, 2007, http://www.rushlimbaugh.com/home/daily/site_101507/ content/01125113.guest.html.

189. Ibid.

CHAPTER 10: LIMBAUGH'S WAR ON INTELLECTUALS, LIBERALS, AND BLUE BLOODS

1. Rush Limbaugh, *See, I Told You So* (New York: Pocket Books, 1993), 34.

2. *RLS,* June 10, 2009, http://www.rushlimbaugh.com/home/daily/site_061009/ content/01125113.guest.html; *RLS,* http://www.rushlimbaugh.com/home/daily/ site_100509/content/01125109.guest.html; *RLS,* June 2, 2008, http://www .rushlimbaugh.com/home/daily/site_060208/content/01125115.guest.html; *RLS,* June 17, 2008, http://www.rushlimbaugh.com/home/daily/site_061708/ content/01125108.guest.html; *RLS,* August 4, 2008, http://www.rushlimbaugh .com/home/daily/site_080408/content/01125106.guest.html; *RLS,* April 20, 2009, http://www.rushlimbaugh.com/home/daily/site_042009/content/ 01125100.guest.html.

3. *RLS,* May 5, 2009; *RLS,* Sept. 4, 2008, www.rushlimbaugh.com/home/ daily/site_090408/content/01125108.guest.html; *RLS,* February 10, 2009,

www.rushlimbaugh.com/home/daily/site_021009/content/01125110.guest
.html; *RLS*, October 6, 2009, http://www.rushlimbaugh.com/home/daily/
site_100609/content/01125104.guest.html; *RLS*, July 16, 2009, http://www
.rushlimbaugh.com/home/daily/site_071609/content/01125112.guest.html;
RLS, Dec. 11, 2008, www.rushlimbaugh.com/home/daily/site_121108/content/
01125104.guest.html; *RLS*, June 17, 2008, www.rushlimbaugh.com/home/daily/
site_061708/content/01125106.guest.html.

4. *RLS*, April 22, 2009; *RLS*, April 22, 2009, http://www.rushlimbaugh.com/home/
daily/site_042209/content/01125107.guest.html; *RLS*, June 29, 2009, http://www
.rushlimbaugh.com/home/daily/site_062909/content/01125113.guest.html; *RLS*,
September 22, 2009, http://www.rushlimbaugh.com/home/daily/site_092209/
content/01125111.guest.html; *RLS*, November 30, 2009, http://www.rushlim
baugh.com/home/daily/site_113009/content/01125112.guest.html. More examples of Limbaugh's insults: He condemned Baltimore Sun columnist Thomas
Schaller as "this idiot" (*RLS*, October 16, 2007, http://www.rushlimbaugh
.com/home/daily/site_101607/content/01125107.guest.html), and the "blub-
bering, blathering, increasingly idiotic Chris Matthews" (*RLS*, October 27, 2009,
http://www.rushlimbaugh.com/home/daily/site_102709/content/01125106
.guest.html). He said Maureen Dowd "sounded like a complete idiot" (*RLS*,
November 12, 2008, http://www.rushlimbaugh.com/home/daily/site_111208/
content/01125114.guest.html).

5. *RLS*, August 12, 2009, http://www.rushlimbaugh.com/home/daily/site_081209/
content/01125107.guest.html.

6. *RLS*, August 21, 2009, http://www.rushlimbaugh.com/home/daily/site_082109/
content/01125112.guest.html.

7. *RLS*, July 24, 2009, http://www.rushlimbaugh.com/home/daily/site_072409/
content/01125114 .guest.html.

8. *RLS*, July 20, 2009, http://www.rushlimbaugh.com/home/daily/site_072009/
content/01125106.guest.html; *RLS*, June 30, 2009, http://www.rushlimbaugh
.com/home/daily/site_063009/content/01125115.guest.html; *RLS*, August 7,
2009, http://www.rushlimbaugh.com/home/daily/site_080709/content/01125112
.guest.html; *RLS*, July 1, 2009, http://www.rushlimbaugh.com/home/daily/site_
070109/content/01125109.guest.html; *RLS*, July 15, 2009, http://www.rush
limbaugh.com/home/daily/site_071509/content/01125108.guest.html; *The Ed
Show*, MSNBC, July 15, 2009, http://www.huffingtonpost.com/2009/07/15/ed-
schultz-challenges-rus_n_234594.html.

9. *RLS*, February 3, 2010, http://www.rushlimbaugh.com/home/daily/site_020310/
content/01125111.guest.html.

10. *RLS*, February 8, 2010, http://www.rushlimbaugh.com/home/daily/site_020810/
content/01125110.guest.html.

11. *Reliable Sources,* CNN, November 30, 2002.

12. Christopher Buckley, "My Brush with Rush," *The Daily Beast,* October 27, 2008, http://thedailybeast.com/blogs-and-stories/2008-10-27/my-brush-with-rush.

13. Molly Ivins, "Lyin' Bully," *Mother Jones,* May 1995, http://www.motherjones .com/politics/1995/05/lyin-bully.

14. *RLS,* August 5, 2004, http://www.rushlimbaugh.com/home/eibessential2/ germans_worried_about_iran_nukes.guest.html.

15. *RLS,* October 30, 2008, http://www.rushlimbaugh.com/home/daily/site_103008/ content/01125106.guest.html.

16. *RLS,* October 1, 2009, http://www.rushlimbaugh.com/home/daily/site_100109/ content/01125109.guest.html.

17. *RLS,* April 21, 2009, http://www.rushlimbaugh.com/home/daily/site_042109/ content/01125109.guest.html.

18. *RLS,* Sept. 22, 2009, http://www.rushlimbaugh.com/home/daily/site_092209/ content/01125111.guest.html.

19. *RLS,* February 26, 2010, http://www.rushlimbaugh.com/home/daily/site_022610/ content/01125104.guest.html.

20. *RLS,* April 25, 2007, quoted by MMA, http://mediamatters.org/research/ 200704270003.

21. *RLS,* July 29, 2009, quoted by MMA, http://mediamatters.org/research/ 200907290026.

22. *RLS,* March 29, 2007, http://www.rushlimbaugh.com/home/estack_12_13_06/ BarackSection/Obama_and_Sharpton_Have_Little_Dispute_.guest.html.

23. *RLS,* January 5, 2009, http://www.rushlimbaugh.com/home/daily/site_010509/ content/01125107.guest.html.

24. *RLS,* May 26, 2009, http://www.rushlimbaugh.com/home/daily/site_052609/ content/01125104.guest.html.

25. *RLS,* June 11, 2009, http://www.rushlimbaugh.com/home/daily/site_061109/ content/01125115.guest.html.

26. *RLS,* August 12, 2008, http://www.rushlimbaugh.com/home/daily/site_081208/ content/01125109.guest.html.

27. Carla Williams, "Childhood Obesity Linked to Future Heart Disease," ABC News, December 5, 2007, http://abcnews.go.com/Health/CardiacHealth/story? id=3958995&page=1&page=1.

28. *RLS,* August 29, 2006, quoted by MMA, http://mediamatters.org/research/ 200608290013.

29. *RLS,* September 25, 2009, http://www.rushlimbaugh.com/home/daily/site_ 092509/content/01125108.guest.html.

30. *RLS,* October 28, 2009, http://www.rushlimbaugh.com/home/daily/site_102809/content/01125104.guest.html.

31. *RLS,* December 11, 2009, http://www.rushlimbaugh.com/home/daily/site_121109/content/01125114.guest.html.

32. Limbaugh, *The Way Things Ought to Be,* 79.

33. Ibid., 118.

34. Joshua Hammer, "Welcome to Rush's World," *Newsweek,* September 28, 1992.

35. "Rush Limbaugh: Playboy Interview," *Playboy,* December 1993, http://www.playboy.com/articles/rush-limbaugh-interview/index.html.

36. *RLS,* July 23, 2009, http://www.rushlimbaugh.com/home/daily/site_072309/content/01125106.guest.html.

37. *RLS,* May 11, 2009, http://www.rushlimbaugh.com/home/daily/site_051109/content/01125107.guest.html.

38. *RLS,* June 12, 2009, http://www.rushlimbaugh.com/home/daily/site_061209/content/01125113.guest.html.

39. *RLS,* July 3, 2009, http://www.rushlimbaugh.com/home/daily/site_070309/content/01125116.guest.html.

40. *RLS,* September 15, 2009, http://www.rushlimbaugh.com/home/daily/site_091509/content/01125106.guest.html.

41. Limbaugh, *The Way Things Ought to Be,* 27.

42. *RLS,* March 16, 2004, quoted by MMA, http://mediamatters.org/research/200405020008.

43. Rush Limbaugh, Conservative Political Action Conference Speech, Washington, DC, February 28, 2009, http://www.rushlimbaugh.com/home/daily/site_030209/content/01125106.guest.html.

44. *RLS,* November 30, 2009, http://www.rushlimbaugh.com/home/daily/site_113009/content/01125110.guest.html.

45. *RLS,* June 3, 2004, quoted by MMA, http://mediamatters.org/research/200406070004.

46. *RLS,* April 23, 2008, http://www.rushlimbaugh.com/home/daily/site_042308/content/01125112.guest.html.

47. *RLS,* November 23, 2009, http://www.rushlimbaugh.com/home/daily/site_112309/content/01125106.guest.html.

48. *RLS,* August 13, 2009, http://www.rushlimbaugh.com/home/daily/site_081309/content/01125112.guest.html.

49. *RLS,* December 1, 2009, http://www.rushlimbaugh.com/home/daily/site_120109/content/01125110.guest.html.

50. *RLS,* November 13, 2009, http://www.rushlimbaugh.com/home/daily/site_111309/content/01125111.guest.html.

51. Rush Limbaugh, Conservative Political Action Conference Speech, Washington, DC, February 28, 2009, http://www.rushlimbaugh.com/home/daily/site_030209/content/01125106.guest.html.

52. *RLS,* March 22, 2010, http://www.rushlimbaugh.com/home/daily/site_032210/content/01125106.guest.html.

53. *Sean Hannity Show,* Fox News Channel, June 2, 2009, http://www.rushlimbaugh.com/home/daily/site_060409/content/01125106.guest.html.

54. *RLS,* April 19, 2007.

55. *RLS,* April 25, 2007, quoted by MMA, http://mediamatters.org/mobile/research/200704270003.

56. *Paula Zahn,* Fox News Channel, September 27, 1999.

57. *RLS,* April 9, 2009, quoted by MMA, http://mediamatters.org/limbaughwire/2009/04/09.

58. *RLS,* April 15, 2004, quoted by MMA, http://mediamatters.org/research/200405020008.

59. *RLS,* August 23, 2005, quoted by MMA, http://mediamatters.org/mmtv/200508240011.

60. *RLS,* March 24, 2010, http://www.rushlimbaugh.com/home/daily/site_032410/content/01125111.guest.html.

61. *RLS,* March 16, 2004, quoted by MMA, http://mediamatters.org/research/200405020008.

62. *RLS,* April 5, 2004, quoted by MMA, http://mediamatters.org/research/200405020008.

63. *RLS,* March 18, 2004, quoted by MMA, http://mediamatters.org/research/200405020008.

64. *RLS,* December 9, 2004, quoted by MMA, http://mediamatters.org/research/200412100007.

65. *RLS,* March 23, 2006, quoted by MMA, http://mediamatters.org/research/200603240010.

66. *RLS,* June 29, 2004, quoted by MMA, http://mediamatters.org/research/200407020004.

67. *RLS,* May 11, 2009, http://www.rushlimbaugh.com/home/daily/site_051109/content/01125107.guest.html.

68. *RLS,* February 14, 2005, quoted by MMA, http://mediamatters.org/research/200502180001.

69. Limbaugh, *The Way Things Ought to Be,* 118.

70. Limbaugh, *See I Told You So,* 87.

71. Ibid., 41.

72. *RLS,* November 4, 2009, http://www.rushlimbaugh.com/home/daily/site_ 110409/content/01125112.guest.html.

73. Rush Limbaugh TV show, November 18, 1993; FAIR, *The Way Things Aren't,* 102.

74. *RLS,* July 3, 2009, http://www.rushlimbaugh.com/home/daily/site_070309/ content/01125112.guest.html.

75. *RLS,* October 29, 2009, http://www.rushlimbaugh.com/home/daily/site_102909/ content/01125114.guest.html.

76. *RLS,* September 15, 2009, http://www.rushlimbaugh.com/home/daily/site_ 091509/content/01125111.guest.html.

77. *RLS,* July 27, 2009, http://www.rushlimbaugh.com/home/daily/site_072709/ content/01125108.guest.html.

78. Zev Chafets, "Late Period Limbaugh," *New York Times,* July 6, 2008, http:// www.nytimes.com/2008/07/06/magazine/06Limbaugh-t.html?_r=1.

79. "Rush Limbaugh: Playboy Interview," *Playboy,* December 1993, http://www .playboy.com/articles/rush-limbaugh-interview/index.html.

80. *RLS,* March 16, 2009, http://www.rushlimbaugh.com/home/daily/site_031609/ content/01125110.guest.html.

81. *RLS,* December 20, 2006, http://www.rushlimbaugh.com/home/daily/site_122006/ content/rush_is_right.guest.html.

82. "Rush Limbaugh: Playboy Interview."

83. *RLS,* August 3, 1993; FAIR, *The Way Things Aren't,* 102.

84. *RLS,* July 16, 2009, http://www.rushlimbaugh.com/home/daily/site_071609/ content/01125106.guest.html.

85. *Rush Limbaugh Morning Update,* February 17, 2009, http://therogersinstitute .blogspot.com/2009/02/rush-limbaughs-morning-update-flying.html.

86. Zev Chafets, "Late Period Limbaugh."

87. Rush Limbaugh, interview with Greta van Susteren, Fox News Channel, July 24, 2009, http://www.rushlimbaugh.com/home/daily/site_072409/content/01125121 .guest.html.

88. *RLS,* May 22, 2009.

89. *RLS,* August 26, 2009, http://www.rushlimbaugh.com/home/daily/site_082609/ content/01125104.guest.html.

90. *RLS,* September 22, 2009, http://www.rushlimbaugh.com/home/daily/site_092209/content/01125111.guest.html.

91. *RLS,* May 22, 2009.

92. Chris Baldwin, "Golf-loving Radio King Rush Limbaugh Hits It Right on Clooney, Clinton and Wie," BadGolfer.com, March 22, 2006, http://www.bad golfer.com/departments/features/rush-limbaugh-radio-king-golf-2124.htm.

93. *RLS,* June 26, 2009, http://www.rushlimbaugh.com/home/daily/site_062609/content/01125107.guest.html.

94. *RLS,* August 24, 2009, http://www.rushlimbaugh.com/home/daily/site_082409/content/01125106.guest.html.

95. *RLS,* September 18, 2009, http://www.rushlimbaugh.com/home/daily/site_091809/content/01125106.guest.html.

96. *RLS,* August 5, 2009, http://www.rushlimbaugh.com/home/daily/site_080509/content/01125110.guest.html.

97. "Rush Limbaugh: Playboy Interview."

98. Rush Limbaugh, interview with Barbara Walters, *20/20,* ABC, August 16, 1994.

99. *Talkers Magazine* award, June 6, 2009, http://www.rushlimbaugh.com/home/daily/site_060909/content/01125106.member.html.

100. Kathleen Parker, "Frayed Thread in a Free Society," *The Washington Post,* March 15, 2009, http://www.washingtonpost.com/wp-dyn/content/article/2009/03/13/AR2009031302273.html.

101. *On the Record with Greta Van Susteren,* Fox News Channel, May 20, 2009, http://www.rushlimbaugh.com/home/daily/site_052109/content/01125106.guest.html.

102. *RLS,* May 27, 2009, http://www.rushlimbaugh.com/home/daily/site_052709/content/01125109.guest.html.

103. Rush Limbaugh, interview, *Sean Hannity Show,* Fox News Channel, January 19, 2009, http://www.rushlimbaugh.com/home/daily/site_012209/content/01125106.guest.html.

104. *RLS,* May 19, 2009.

105. *RLS,* November 11, 2005, http://www.rushlimbaugh.com/home/eibessential/judicial_activism/moderate_rinos_undermine_the_gop.LogIn.html.

106. *RLS,* April 29, 2009.

107. Fareed Zakaria GPS, CNN, December 14, 2008.

108. *Larry King Live,* CNN, July 28, 2009, http://www.huffingtonpost.com/2009/07/28/colin-powell-suggests-rep_n_246662.html.

109. *RLS*, May 26, 2009.

110. Colin Powell, *Face the Nation*, May 24, 2009, http://www.cbsnews.com/video/watch/?id=5036892n.

111. *RLS*, November 16, 2009, http://www.rushlimbaugh.com/home/daily/site_111609/content/01125107.guest.html.

112. *RLS*, September 11, 2009, http://www.rushlimbaugh.com/home/daily/site_091109/content/01125104.guest.html.

113. *RLS*, November 23, 2009, http://www.rushlimbaugh.com/home/daily/site_112309/content/01125106.guest.html.

114. David Brock, *Blinded by the Right: The Conscience of an Ex-Conservative* (New York: Crown, 2002), 62.

115. *RLS*, July 15, 2009, http://www.rushlimbaugh.com/home/daily/site_071509/content/01125108.guest.html.

116. Chavets, "Late-Period Limbaugh."

117. *RLS*, November 10, 2009, http://www.rushlimbaugh.com/home/daily/site_111009/content/01125111.guest.html.

118. *All Things Considered*, NPR, January 25, 2007.

119. *RLS*, October 18, 2005, quoted by MMA, http://mediamatters.org/research/200510190010.

120. Nigel Farndale, "The Man Who's Always Right," *Sunday Telegraph* (London), November 2, 2008.

121. Colford, *Rush Limbaugh Story*, 61.

122. *RLS*, May 26, 2009, http://www.rushlimbaugh.com/home/daily/site_052609/content/01125107.guest.html.

123. *RLS*, November 13, 2009, http://www.rushlimbaugh.com/home/daily/site_111309/content/01125107.guest.html.

124. *RLS*, May 29, 2009, http://www.rushlimbaugh.com/home/daily/site_052909/content/01125109.guest.html.

125. Rush Limbaugh, Conservative Political Action Conference Speech.

126. *RLS*, May 21, 2009, quoted by FreeRepublic.com, http://www.freerepublic.com/focus/f-news/2255887/posts.

127. *RLS*, May 18, 2009, quoted by FreeRepublic.com, http://www.freerepublic.com/focus/f-news/2253526/posts.

128. Limbaugh, *The Way Things Ought to Be*, 302.

129. *RLS*, April 2, 2009, quoted by MMA, http://mediamatters.org/limbaughwire/2009/04/02.

130. *RLS*, April 2, 2009, quoted by MMA, http://mediamatters.org/limbaughwire/2009/04/02#0023.

131. Jim Derych, *Confessions of a Former Dittohead* (New York: Ig Publishing, 2006), 51.

132. "Rush Limbaugh Most Influential on Talk Radio: Mag," *New York Post*, February 23, 2010, http://www.nypost.com/p/news/national/rush_limbaugh_most_influential_on_i48ozFBE0gO3HVmgNrvOwO.

133. Kathleen Hall Jamieson and Joseph N. Cappella, *Echo Chamber: Rush Limbaugh and the Conservative Media Establishment* (New York: Oxford University Press, 2008), 232.

134. Ibid., 131.

135. Ibid., 132.

136. Ibid., xiii.

137. David Barker, *Rushed to Judgment: Talk Radio, Persuasion and American Political Behavior* (New York: Columbia University Press, 2002).

138. John Leland, "Why the Right Rules the Radio Waves," *New York Times*, December 8, 2002, http://www.nytimes.com/2002/12/08/weekinreview/why-the-right-rules-the-radio-waves.html.

139. Arthur Lupia and Mathew Daniel McCubbins, *The Democratic Dilemma: Can Citizens Learn What They Need to Know?* (New York: Cambridge University Press, 1998), 192.

140. *RLS*, January 21, 2010, http://www.rushlimbaugh.com/home/daily/site_012110/content/01125106.guest.html.

CHAPTER 11: THE LEADER OF THE REPUBLICANS: HOW LIMBAUGH IS DESTROYING CONSERVATISM

1. Barack Obama, White House Correspondents Association dinner, May 9, 2009.

2. Rush Limbaugh, interview with Sean Hannity, Fox News Channel, January 19, 2009, http://www.rushlimbaugh.com/home/daily/site_012209/content/01125106.guest.html.

3. Steve Forbes, "Empowerer of the Modern Conservative Movement," Human Events Online, July 31, 2008.

4. *Larry King Live*, CNN, October 6, 2009, http://thinkprogress.org/2009/10/06/bachmann-beck-limbaugh.

5. Zev Chafets, "Late Period Limbaugh," *New York Times Magazine*, July 6, 2008, http://www.nytimes.com/2008/07/06/magazine/06Limbaugh-t.html?_r=1&hp=&pagewanted=print.

6. "Nobles and Knaves," *Washington Times,* March 8, 2009.

7. Steve Forbes, "Empowerer of the Modern Conservative Movement," Human Events Online, July 31, 2008.

8. Mark Levin, "Rush: The Engine of Conservatism," Human Events Online, July 25, 2008.

9. Douglas Martin, "William F. Buckley Jr. Is Dead at 82," *New York Times,* February 27, 2008, http://www.nytimes.com/2008/02/27/business/media/27cnd-buckley.html?_r=2&ei=5088&en=c3500b8c6124758b&ex=1361854800&adxnnl=1&oref=slogin&partner=rssnyt&emc=rss&pagewanted=all&adxnnlx=1249906098-9W2leOJkDDEgTIfxaQYj2w; Harry Kloman, "Political Analysis," http://www.pitt.edu/~kloman/debates.html.

10. Paul Colford, *The Rush Limbaugh Story: Talent on Loan from God* (New York. St. Martin's Press, 1993), 180.

11. "Rush Interview," Human Events Online, July 25, 2008.

12. John Derbyshire, "How Radio Wrecks the Right," *The American Conservative,* February 23, 2009, http://www.amconmag.com/article/2009/feb/23/00006.

13. Kenneth Tomlinson, "Talk Radio Static," *Washington Times,* February 23, 2008.

14. Zev Chafets, "The GOP's Real Go-To Guy," *Los Angeles Times,* September 29, 2008, http://www.latimes.com/news/opinion/commentary/la-oe-chafets29-2008sep29,0,4135839.story.

15. Jeff Woods, "Zach Wamp Refuses to Apologize to El Rushbo," *Nashville Scene,* April 7, 2009, http://blogs.nashvillescene.com/pitw/2009/04/zach_wamp_refuses_to_apologize.php.

16. Michael Clancy, "Shadegg Optimistic for Economic Revival," *Arizona Republic,* April 21, 2009, http://www.azcentral.com/news/articles/2009/04/21/20090421phx-shadegg0422.html.

17. Ibid.

18. hipyphishy, "Congressman Jack Kingston Says No to Rush Limbaugh w/ Video," DailyKos.com, April 15, 2009, http://www.dailykos.com/story/2009/4/15/720540/-Congressman-Jack-Kingston-says-no-to-Rush-Limbaugh-w-video.

19. *RLS,* May 29, 2009, quoted by MMA, http://mediamatters.org/mmtv/200905290019.

20. Special Report with Bret Baier, Fox News Channel, August 10, 2009, http://www.rushlimbaugh.com/home/daily/site_081109/content/01125109.guest.html.

21. David Plouffe, "Minority Leader Limbaugh," *Washington Post,* March 4, 2009.

22. Tom Grace, "Tedisco: I'm Focused on Local Interests," TheDailyStar.com, March 20, 2009, http://www.thedailystar.com/local/local_story_079041516.html.

23. Andrew C. White, "NY-20: 'Rush Limbaugh Is Meaningless to Me'— UPDATED," DailyKos.com, March 20, 2009, http://www.dailykos.com/story/ 2009/3/20/711032/-NY-20:-Rush-Limbaugh-is-meaningless-to-me.

24. Jonathan Martin, "House GOP Member to Rush: Back Off," *Politico*, January 27, 2009, http://www.politico.com/news/stories/0109/18049.html.

25. *RLS*, January 28, 2009, http://www.rushlimbaugh.com/home/daily/site_ 012809/content/01125107.guest.html.

26. Yael T. Abouhalkah, "Limbaugh's 'Just an Entertainer,' Says GOP Congressman," *Kansas City Star*, April 15, 2009, http://voices.kansascity.com/node/4270; http://blogs.kansas.com/weblog/2009/04/tiahrt-limbaugh-is-an-entertainer.

27. Mike Memoli, "Q & A with Governor Mark Sanford," RealClearPolitics.com, February 25, 2009, http://www.realclearpolitics.com/articles/2009/02/q_a_with_ governor_mark_sanford.html.

28. Ryan Powers, "Limbaugh Responds To Sanford: The 'Hell We Don't' Want Obama To Fail! Just Need 'The Guts' To Say So," ThinkProgress.org, February 26, 2009, http://thinkprogress.org/2009/02/26/rush-sanford-idiot.

29. *RLS*, March 2, 2009, http://www.rushlimbaugh.com/home/daily/site_030209/ content/01125111.guest.html.

30. Ibid.

31. Mike Allen, "Steele to Rush: I'm sorry," Politico.com, March 2, 2009, http:// www.politico.com/news/stories/0309/19517.html.

32. Ibid.

33. Ibid.

34. "GOP Chairman Steele Backs Off Limbaugh Criticism," CNN.com, March 3, 2009, http://edition.cnn.com/2009/POLITICS/03/02/gop.steele.limbaugh.

35. *Face the Nation*, CBS, March 1, 2009.

36. Robert Mentzer, "Rush Limbaugh Critic Kevin Stevenson Ousted as Marathon County Republican Party Spokesman," *Wausau Daily Herald*, June 2, 2009, http:// www.wausaudailyherald.com/article/20090602/WDH0101/906020543/1981.

37. Ibid.

38. Faye Fiore and Mark Z. Barabak, "Who Elected Rush? He Did," *Los Angeles Times*, February 8, 2009.

39. *Larry King Live*, CNN, March 20, 2009, http://edition.cnn.com/2009/ POLITICS/03/20/lkl.mitt.romney.

40. *American Morning,* CNN, March 5, 2009, http://transcripts.cnn.com/TRAN
    SCRIPTS/0903/05/ltm.02.html.

41. Charlie Cook, "How Limbaugh Helps The GOP," *National Journal,* March 3,
    2009, http://www.nationaljournal.com/njonline/ot_20090303_6773.php.

42. Limbaugh, *The Way Things Ought to Be,* 292.

43. Pat Buchanan, Republican National Convention, Houston, Texas, August 17,
    1992, http://www.skepticfiles.org/conspire/patbuch.htm.

44. Limbaugh, *The Way Things Ought to Be,* 293.

45. Colford, *Rush Limbaugh Story,* 164.

46. Ibid.

47. Ibid., 167.

48. Ibid.

49. Ibid., 170.

50. Henry Allen, "Media to the Left! Media to the Right! Rush Limbaugh, On the
    Republicans' Wavelength," *Washington Post,* August 20, 1992.

51. Colford, *Rush Limbaugh Story,* 205–206.

52. FAIR, "The Way Things Aren't: Rush Limbaugh Debates Reality," Extra! July/
    August 1994, http://www.fair.org/index.php?page=1895.

53. "Rush Limbaugh: Playboy Interview," *Playboy,* December 1993, http://www
    .playboy.com/articles/rush-limbaugh-interview/index.html.

54. David Remnick, "Day of the Dittohead," *Washington Post,* February 20, 1994.

55. Colford, *Rush Limbaugh Story,* 208–210.

56. Ibid., 220.

57. Faye Fiore and Mark Z. Barabak, "Rush Limbaugh Has His grip on the GOP
    Microphone," *Los Angeles Times,* February 8, 2009, http://articles.latimes.com/
    2009/feb/08/nation/na-rush8.

58. Dianna Heitz, "Who Leads the GOP?" Politico.com, March 18, 2009.

59. "Countdown with Keith Olbermann," MSNBC, March 4, 2009.

60. "Just 11% of Republicans Say Limbaugh Is Their Party's Leader," Rasmussen
    Poll, March 4, 2009, http://www.rasmussenreports.com/public_content/politics/
    general_politics/march_2009/just_11_of_republicans_say_limbaugh_is_their_
    party_s_leader.

61. *RLS,* October 30, 2009, http://www.rushlimbaugh.com/home/daily/site_103009/
    content/01125109.guest.html

62. http://www.washingtonpost.com/wp-dyn/articles/A36733-2005Feb18.html.

63. Eric Boehlert, "Fake News, Fake Reporter," Salon.com, February 10, 2005.

64. Ibid.

65. Maureen Dowd, "Dick at the Heart of Darkness," *New York Times,* October 26, 2005, http://select.nytimes.com/2005/10/26/opinion/26dowd.html?hp.

66. Jamieson and Cappella, *Echo Chamber,* 47.

67. *RLS,* October 29, 2004, quoted by MMA, http://mediamatters.org/research/ 200410290010.

68. Interview with Dick Cheney, *Rush Limbaugh Show,* January 30, 2008, http:// georgewbush_whitehouse.archives,gov/news/releases/2008/01/20080130-9. html.

69. *RLS,* March 15, 2009.

70. Katharine Seelye, "On Talk Radio, Bob Dole Just Took Off the Gloves," October 18, 1996, *New York Times,* http://www.nytimes.com/1996/10/18/us/on-talk-radio-bob-dole-just-took-off-the-gloves.html.

71. *RLS,* October 3, 2006.

72. *RLS,* April 17, 2006, http://www.defenselink.mil/transcripts/transcript.aspx ?transcriptid=3448.

73. *RLS,* April 17, 2006; Tim Grieve, "Rumsfeld and Limbaugh, Playing Defense," Salon.com, April 18, 2006.

74. Ibid.

75. Ibid.

76. *RLS,* October 14, 2008 http://www.rushlimbaugh.com/home/daily/site_101408/ content/01125106.guest.html.

77. *RLS,* August 31, 2004, quoted by MMA, http://mediamatters.org/research/ 200409010003.

78. *RLS,* December 17, 2004, quoted by MMA, http://mediamatters.org/columns/ 200412230008.

79. *RLS,* June 6, 2008, quoted by DailyKos.com, http://www.dailykos.com/story/ 2008/6/6/531174/-Rush-boasts-of-insider-knowledge-of-pending-Iran-attack.

80. *RLS,* September 28, 2009, http://www.rushlimbaugh.com/home/daily/site_ 092809/content/01125104.guest.html.

81. *RLS,* September 25, 2009, http://www.rushlimbaugh.com/home/daily/site_ 092509/content/01125108.guest.html.

82. *RLS,* November 11, 2009, http://www.rushlimbaugh.com/home/daily/site_ 111109/content/01125122.guest.html.

83. *RLS,* May 11, 2009, http://www.rushlimbaugh.com/home/daily/site_051109/ content/01125107.guest.html.

84. Rush Limbaugh, Conservative Political Action Conference Speech, Washington, DC, February 28, 2009, http://www.rushlimbaugh.com/home/daily/site_030209/content/01125106.guest.html.

85. Limbaugh, *The Way Things Ought to Be*, 72.

86. *RLS*, June 18, 2004; Eric Boehlert, "Making American Forces Radio Fair and Balanced," *Salon*, June 24, 2004, quoted by MMA, http://mediamatters.org/research/200406210009.

87. *RLS*, July 8, 2004, quoted by MMA, http://mediamatters.org/research/200407090009.

88. *RLS*, April 7, 2009, http://www.rushlimbaugh.com/home/daily/site_040709/content/01125104.guest.html.

89. *RLS*, July 30, 2008, http://www.rushlimbaugh.com/home/daily/site_073008/content/01125104.guest.html.

90. *RLS*, August 29, 2008, http://www.rushlimbaugh.com/home/daily/site_082908/content/01125107.guest.html.

91. Matthew Mosk, "Palin Was a Director of Embattled Sen. Stevens's 527 Group," *Washington Post*, September 1, 2008, http://voices.washingtonpost.com/44/2008/09/01/palin_was_a_director_of_embatt.html.

92. *RLS*, April 7, 2009, http://www.rushlimbaugh.com/home/daily/site_040709/content/01125104.guest.html.

93. Stephen Talbot, "Wizard of Ooze," *Mother Jones*, May/June 1995, 75, http://motherjones.com/politics/1995/05/wizard-ooze.

94. David Brock, *Blinded by the Right: The Conscience of an Ex-Conservative* (New York: Crown, 2002), 281.

95. *RLS*, November 8, 2006, http://www.rushlimbaugh.com/home/estack_12_13_06/I_Feel_Liberated.guest.html.

96. C-SPAN, October 25, 2009, http://thinkprogress.org/2009/10/26/gingrich-beck-limbaugh.

97. *RLS*, March 9, 2009, http://www.rushlimbaugh.com/home/daily/site_030909/content/01125112.guest.html.

98. Ibid.

99. FAIR, *The Way Things Aren't*, 43.

100. Ibid.

101. Laurie Kellman, "Rush Rallies Freshmen to Fight On," *Washington Times*, December 11, 1994.

102. Ibid.

103. *RLS*, May 20, 2009.

104. FAIR, *The Way Things Aren't*, 42.

105. Ibid.

106. Ibid.

107. Jim Rutenberg, "Despite Other Voices, Limbaugh's Is Still Strong," *The New York Times*, April 24, 2000, http://www.nytimes.com/2000/04/24/business/despite-other-voices-limbaugh-s-is-still-strong.html.

108. David Barker, *Rushed to Judgement*: Brock, *Blinded by the Right*, 281.

109. "Calculate the Results," *The New York Times*, http://www.nytimes.com/images/2001/11/12/politics/recount/results/preset-v4.html.

110. *RLS*, February 4, 2008, in Jamieson and Cappella, *Echo Chamber*, 121.

111. Jamieson and Cappella, *Echo Chamber*, 115.

112. *The Tonight Show with Jay Leno*, NBC, May 13, 2009.

113. *RLS*, January 2, 2008, in Jamieson and Cappella, *Echo Chamber*, 121.

114. "Rush Limbaugh Succeeded in Defining John McCain's Credentials, New National Annenberg Election Survey Finds," Annenberg Public Policy Center, February 8, 2008, http://www.annenbergpublicpolicycenter.org/Downloads/Releases/NAES%202008/NAES2008rushreleaseFINAL.pdf, 4.

115. Ibid.

116. *RLS*, February 5, 2008, http://www.rushlimbaugh.com/home/daily/site_020508/content/01125110.guest.html.

117. *RLS*, January 21, 2008, http://www.rushlimbaugh.com/home/daily/site_012108/content/01125112.guest.html.

118. *RLS*, August 19, 2008, http://www.rushlimbaugh.com/home/daily/site_081908/content/01125108.guest.html.

119. Rich Lowry, "John McCain, Un-Unleashed," *National Review*, January 28, 2008, http://article.nationalreview.com/345653/john-mccain-un-unleashed/rich-lowry.

120. Elisabeth Bumiller and Michael Cooper, "Conservative Ire Pushed McCain From Lieberman," *The New York Times*, August 31, 2008, http://www.nytimes.com/2008/08/31/us/politics/31reconstruct.html?_r=2&oref=slogin.

121. Michael Cooper and Dalia Sussman, "Growing Doubts on Palin Take a Toll, Poll Finds," *The New York Times*, October 31, 2008, http://www.nytimes.com/2008/10/31/us/politics/31poll.html.

122. *RLS*, June 11, 2009, http://www.rushlimbaugh.com/home/daily/site_061109/content/01125110.guest.html.

123. *RLS*, July 15, 2009, http://www.rushlimbaugh.com/home/daily/site_071509/content/01125108.guest.html.

124. *RLS,* July 3, 2009, http://www.rushlimbaugh.com/home/daily/site_070309/content/01125108.guest.html.

125. *RLS,* February 28, 2006; March 14, 2006, http://mediamatters.org/research/200603150013.

126. *RLS,* June 6, 2006, quoted by MMA, http://mediamatters.org/research/200606080004.

127. "Bill Clinton Presidential Job Approval," Gallup Poll, http://www.gallup.com/poll/116584/presidential-approval-ratings-bill-clinton.aspx.

128. *RLS,* March 8, 2010, http://www.rushlimbaugh.com/home/daily/site_030810/content/01125106.guest.html.

129. "Direction of the Country," http://www.pollingreport.com/right.htm.

130. *RLS,* March 18, 2009, quoted by MMA, http://mediamatters.org/research/200903180032?f=h_top.

131. Ibid.

132. *RLS,* February 12, 2004, quoted by MMA, http://mediamatters.org/research/200407190002.

133. *RLS,* February 16, 2004, quoted by MMA, http://mediamatters.org/research/200407190002.

134. Reliable Sources, CNN, February 22, 2004, http://mediamatters.org/research/200407190002.

135. *RLS,* July 15, 2004, quoted by MMA, http://mediamatters.org/research/200407190002.

136. *RLS,* February 21, 2008, http://www.rushlimbaugh.com/home/daily/site_022108/content/01125108.guest.html.

137. Ben Dimiero, "Limbaugh Adopts Another 'Insane Conspiracy Theory' from the Conservative Blogosphere," MMA, April 14, 2010, http://mediamatters.org/blog/201004140040.

138. Jake Tapper, Twitter.com, April 14, 2010, http://twitter.com/jaketapper/status/12171089490.

139. *RLS,* October 20, 2009, http://www.rushlimbaugh.com/home/daily/site_102009/content/01125108.guest.html.

140. Jeffrey M. Jones, "GOP Losses Span Nearly All Demographic Groups," Gallup Poll, May 18, 2009, http://www.gallup.com/poll/118528/GOP-Losses-Span-Nearly-Demographic-Groups.aspx.

141. Brian Montopoli, "Limbaugh's Favorable Rating: 19 Percent," CBSNews.com, March 17, 2009, http://www.cbsnews.com/sections/politics/politicalhotsheet/main503544.shtml?start=100&keyword=poll.

142. Paul Steinhauser, "CNN Poll: Powell vs. Cheney and Limbaugh," CNN, May 25, 2009, http://politicalticker.blogs.cnn.com/2009/05/25/cnn-poll-powell-vs-cheney-and-limbaugh.

143. *RLS,* May 26, 2009, http://www.rushlimbaugh.com/home/daily/site_052609/content/01125104.guest.html.

144. Public Policy Polling, "Obama Not Faring Well in Arkansas," August 25, 2009, http://www.publicpolicypolling.com/pdf/surveys/2009_Archives/PPP_Release_AR_825.pdf.

145. *NBC News/Wall Street Journal* survey, June 12–15, 2009, http://msnbcmedia.msn.com/i/msnbc/sections/news/090617_NBC-WSJ_poll_Full.pdf.

146. *RLS,* July 27, 2009, http://www.rushlimbaugh.com/home/daily/site_072709/content/01125108.guest.html.

147. Paul Steinhauser, "CNN Poll: GOP Favorable Rating Lowest in a Decade," Political Ticker, October 23, 2009, http://politicalticker.blogs.cnn.com/2009/10/23/cnn-poll-gop-favorable-rating-lowest-in-25-years.

148. *RLS,* October 23, 2009, http://www.rushlimbaugh.com/home/daily/site_102309/content/01125111.guest.html.

149. David Brooks, "The Wizard of Beck," *The New York Times,* October 2, 2009, http://www.nytimes.com/2009/10/02/opinion/02brooks.html?bl.

150. Michael Calderone, "Rush Limbaugh on David Brooks: 'JEALOUS,'" Politico.com, October 2, 2009, http://www.politico.com/news/stories/1009/27844.html.

151. Michael Medved, "Will Talk Radio Get Wake-up Call? Appealing to the Right-Wing Fringe Is No Way to Build a Political Movement," *USA Today,* December 4, 2008, http://blogs.usatoday.com/oped/2008/12/will-talk-radio.html.

152. Reihan Salam, "Sugar Rush," Forbes.com, March 2, 2009, http://www.forbes.com/2009/03/01/rush-limbaugh-republicans-opinions-columnists_conservatives_obama.html.

153. Jay Cost, "How Much Does Rush Limbaugh Matter?" RealClearPolitics, March 2, 2009, http://www.realclearpolitics.com/horseraceblog/2009/03/how_much_does_rush_limbaugh_ma.html.

154. David Frum, "Why Rush Is Wrong," *Newsweek,* March 16, 2009, http://www.newsweek.com/id/188279.

155. Ibid.

156. John Derbyshire, "How Radio Wrecks the Right," *American Conservative,* February 2009, http://www.amconmag.com/print.html?Id=AmConservative-2009feb23-00006.

157. Ibid.

158. Ibid.

159. Richard Posner, "Is the Conservative Movement Losing Steam?" May 10, 2009, http://www.becker-posner-blog.com/archives/2009/05/is_the_conserva.html.

160. Email to author from Laura Bishop, chief research assistant to Richard Posner, May 14, 2009.

161. David Frum, "Why Rush Is Wrong."

162. Mark Helprin, "McCain and the Talk-Show Hosts," *Wall Street Journal*, February 12, 2008, http://online.wsj.com/article/SB120277844588960675.html.

163. Derbyshire, "How Radio Wrecks the Right."

164. John Mark Reynolds, "Rush Gave a Bad Speech," *The Scriptorium*, March 2, 2009, http://www.scriptoriumdaily.com/2009/03/02/rush-gave-a-bad-speech.

165. *Hardball with Chris Mathews*, MSNBC, June 8, 2009, http://www.rushlimbaugh.com/home/daily/site_060909/content/01125112.guest.html.

166. *Morning Joe*, MSNBC, October 5, 2009, http://mediamatters.org/mmtv/200910050011.

167. *RLS*, October 8, 2009, http://www.rushlimbaugh.com/home/daily/site_100809/content/01125109.guest.html.

168. *Morning Joe*, MSNBC, October 9, 2009, quoted at RLS, http://rushlimbaugh.com/home/daily/sit_100908/content/01125108.guest.html.

169. *All Things Considered*, NPR, January 25, 2007.

CONCLUSION

1. *RLS*, August 17, 2009, http://www.rushlimbaugh.com/home/daily/site_081709/content/01125108.guest.html.

2. *RLS*, March 9, 2009, http://www.rushlimbaugh.com/home/daily/site_030909/content/01125112.guest.html.

3. Clarence Page, "Do Rush Fans Get the Joke?" *Buffalo News*, May 18, 2009, http://www.buffalonews.com/248/story/674788.html.

4. Colford, *Rush Limbaugh Story*, 135.

5. Nigel Farndale, "The Man Who's Always Right," *Sunday Telegraph* (London), November 2, 2008.

6. *Reliable Sources*, CNN, May 28, 2006, http://transcripts.cnn.com/TRANSCRIPTS/0605/28/rs.01.html.

7. *RLS,* May 21, 2009, quoted by MMA, http://mediamatters.org/research/200905210020.

8. *RLS,* August 21, 2009, http://www.rushlimbaugh.com/home/daily/site_082109/content/01125107.guest.html.

9. *Today* show, NBC, October 9, 2009, http://www.msnbc.msn.com/id/33244211/.

10. Steve Cameron, "My Friend, Rush Limbaugh," *Merced Sun Star,* November 4, 2009, http://www.mercedsunstar.com/536/story/1151327.html.

11. *RLS,* July 28, 2009, http://www.rushlimbaugh.com/home/daily/site_072809/content/01125108.guest.html.

12. *RLS,* September 14, 2009, http://www.rushlimbaugh.com/home/daily/site_091409/content/01125111.guest.html.

13. Maureen Dowd, "Who Are You Calling a Narcissist, Rush?" *The New York Times,* November 4, 2009, http://www.nytimes.com/2009/11/04/opinion/04dowd.html?em.

14. Zev Chafets, "Late Period Limbaugh," *The New York Times Magazine,* July 6, 2008, http://www.nytimes.com/2008/07/06/magazine/06Limbaugh-t.html?_r=1&hp=&pagewanted=print.

15. Tom Shales, "TV Preview; Rush Limbaugh, Beneath The Bluster," *Washington Post,* February 28, 1995.

16. *RLS,* May 27, 2009, http://www.rushlimbaugh.com/home/daily/site_010710/content/01125114.guest.html.

17. *RLS,* June 10, 2009, http://www.rushlimbaugh.com/home/daily/site_061009/content/01125113.guest.html.

18. *RLS,* October 2, 2009, http://www.rushlimbaugh.com/home/daily/site_100209/content/01125107.guest.html.

19. Mark R. Levin, *Rescuing Sprite* (New York: Pocket Books, 2007), 105.

20. *RLS,* January 22, 2010, http://www.rushlimbaugh.com/home/daily/site_012210/content/01125108.guest.html.

INDEX

DATE DUE

MAR 26 2011	
APR 08 2011